Adaptive Physiology to Stressful Environments

Editors

Shlomo Samueloff, M.D.
Professor
Department of Physiology
The Hebrew University
Hadassah Medical School
Jerusalem, Israel

Mohamed K. Yousef, Ph.D.
Professor and Director
Desert Biology Research Center
Department of Biological Sciences
University of Nevada
Las Vegas, Nevada

CRC Press, Inc.
Boca Raton, Florida

Library of Congress Cataloging-in-Publication Data
Adaptive physiology to stressful environments.

Includes bibliographies and index.
1. Stress (Physiology) 2. Adaptation (Physiology)
3. Homeostasis. I. Samueloff, S. II. Yousef,
Mohamed K. [DNLM: 1. Adaptation, Physiological.
2. Environment. 3. Stress. QT 162.S8 A221]
QP82.2.S8A33 1987 612 87-18408
ISBN 0-8493-6458-2

Direct all inquiries to CRC Press, Inc., 2000 Corporate Blvd., N.W., Boca Raton, Florida, 33431.

International Standard Book Number 0-8493-6458-2

Library of Congress Card Number 87-18408
Printed in the United States

PREFACE

The Environmental Physiology Commission (EPC) of the International Union of Physiological Sciences (IUPS) organized part of the IUPS regional meeting held in August, 1984 in Jerusalem. The theme of the EPC Symposium was centered on physiological responses to various environmental stresses. In its general format it included sessions with individually invited lecturers and sessions with short communications and posters. This book is an outgrowth of the EPC Symposium containing the submitted manuscripts of the invited lectures. The subjects of the lectures in the majority of cases were assigned by the organizers of the Symposium to eminent authorities in the appropriate field, who summarized their own findings with recent data in the area of their expertise.

This book contains the invited lectures pertinent to the central theme of the EPC Symposium. The first two chapters ask what is adaptive physiology and what is a stressful environment? The following eleven chapters are concerned specifically with the adaptive responses of man to the stress of heat, cold, and underwater environments. The remainder of the book discusses mechanisms of adaptations as revealed using various animal models including some animals of great economic value. The authors of all chapters presented an up-to-date overview of his/her area of expertise. Each chapter has an extensive bibliography which can further aid the reader in keeping abreast of rapid developments in this field.

The intended audience of this book includes students, teachers, and researchers interested in various aspects of environmental physiology, biometeorology, comparative physiology, general physiology, ecology, agriculture, and zoology. It is hoped that this book will aid and help stimulate scientists who are motivated to resolve the many mysteries of adaptive physiology thus improving mans' well-being and physical performance in various stressful environments.

S. Samueloff, Jerusalem
M. K. Yousef, Las Vegas

ACKNOWLEDGMENTS

The editors acknowledge with great pleasure the help and cooperation of the contributors and members of the Environmental Physiology Commission of the International Union of Physiological Sciences. We are indebted to many people who aided in preparation and organization of the Symposium, especially the International Organization Committee; its chairman, S. Samueloff, and co-chairman, A. Shkolnik, and its members: Y. Shapiro, Y. Cassuto, M. Horowitz, P. Dejours, E. Nadel, J. Rutenfranz, and C.R. Taylor.

Several individuals have aided in preparation of the manuscripts and the international coordination between us. We especially wish to thank the superb efforts of Mrs. Dorothy Adashefski of the Department of Biological Sciences, University of Nevada, Las Vegas and Mrs. A. Cohen of the Department of Physiology, The Hebrew University, Jerusalem. We are grateful to Mrs. Annetta Yousef for editing and proofreading the manuscripts. Last and not the least, the staff at CRC deserve special recognition for their patience and excellence in preparation of this book. During the editing of this book, one of us (M.K.Y.) was on a sabbatical leave at the Department of Applied Physiology, University of Occupational and Environmental Health, 807 Kitakyushu, Japan. He was supported by a Fellowship Award from the Japan Society for Promotion of Science.

DEDICATION

This book is dedicated to Dr. Otto G. Edholm who inspired us by example and served as the first Chairman of the Environmental Physiology Commission of the International Union of Physiological Sciences.

THE EDITORS

Shlomo L. Samueloff, M.D., is a Professor of Physiology at the Hebrew University Hadassah (H.U.H.) Medical School and Head of the Division of Physiology at the H.U.H. School of Dental Medicine founded by the Alpha Omega Fraternity. He received his M.D. degree from the H.U.H. Medical School and his postdoctoral training in physiology with the late Professors Samson Wright (at the Middlesex Medical School, London) and Otto G. Edholm (at the Division of Human Physiology, Medical Research Council, London). In the early 1960s he established the Environmental Physiology Unit at the Negev Institute for Arid Zone Research in Beer Sheva and acted as its first Director. In the late 1960s he served as a Research Associate at the Department of Physiology, Mayo Clinic, Rochester, Minnesota. From 1967 till 1972 Dr. Samueloff acted as a Coordinator of a collaborative U.K.-Israel Population Study Research Project which was carried out in the framework of the International Biological Program. In 1973, he was elected as Member and since 1980, as Chairman of the Commission on Environmental Physiology of the International Union of Physiological Sciences. During the years 1976—79, he served as Visiting Scientist and leader of the Clinical Objective-Testing Team, and participated in the comprehensive state-wide survey on Vibration White Finger Syndrome carried out by the U.S. National Institute for Occupational Safety and Health. In recognition of his achievements in this study, he was awarded, in 1979, the NIOSH Commendation Certificate. During the last decade, as academic advisor in the H.U. Howard Caselle Centre of physical education, he has contributed to the advancement of teaching and research in exercise physiology in his alma mater. In 1986 he was elected as President of Israel Physiological and Pharmacological Society.

Dr. Samueloff is an author of a long list of publications on the physiology of adaptation of man and other animals to hot environments. His major research interest at present is in exercise physiology concerning the interrelationship between physical activity and mineral and water balance during exposure to heat.

Mohamed K. Yousef, Ph.D., is Professor of Biology and Director of the Desert Biology Research Center at the University of Nevada, Las Vegas. He received his training at Ein-Shams University in Cairo, Egypt, receiving the B.S. degree (honors) in 1959 and the M.S. and Ph.D. degrees in 1963 and 1966 from the University of Missouri at Columbia. From 1965 to 1967, he held a postdoctoral fellowship at the University of Missouri. He served as Assistant Professor at the Institute of Arctic Biology at the University of Alaska from 1967 to 1968, as Assistant Professor in the Department of Biological Sciences, University of Nevada, Las Vegas, and as Research Associate at the Desert Research Institute of the University of Nevada System from 1968 to 1971. Since 1971, he has been an Associate Professor and then Professor in the Department of Biological Sciences, University of Nevada, at Las Vegas. In 1978, he became the Director of the Desert Biology Research Center. Dr. Yousef is a member of various scientific and honorary societies including the American Physiological Society, the International Biometeorology Society, The Endocrine Society, and the Society for Experimental Biology and Medicine. He has served on several committees of professional societies and is currently a member of the Commission on Environmental Physiology of the International Union of Physiological Sciences. He has received the William F. Peterson Gold Medal Award for Animal Biometeorology (W.F. Peterson Foundation, The Netherlands), the Barrick Distinguished Scholar Award and the Outstanding Faculty Award (University of Nevada, Las Vegas), Senior Fulbright Lectureship Award to Sudan for 2 years, and the Senior Fellowship Award from Japan Society for Promotion of Science.

He has been the recipient of many research grants and contracts from the Environmental Protection Agency, U.S. Air Force, National Science Foundation, and the National Institutes of Health. Dr. Yousef is the editor or co-editor of 8 other books and has published more than 140 scientific publications. His major research interest is in comparative mechanisms of physiological adaptations to deserts.

CONTRIBUTORS

Jonathan H. Adler, Ph.D., V.M.D.
Professor
Department of Physiology
The Hebrew University
Hadassah Medical School
Jerusalem, Israel

Zeev Arad, Ph.D.
Senior Lecturer
Department of Biology
Technion
Haifa, Israel

Amichai Arieli, Ph.D.
Lecturer
Department of Animal Sciences
Faculty of Agriculture
Hebrew University of Jerusalem
Rehovot, Jerusalem

A. Berman, Ph.D.
Professor
Department of Animal Sciences
Faculty of Agriculture
Hebrew University of Jerusalem
Rehovot, Israel

Marvin H. Bernstein, Ph.D.
Professor
Department of Biology
New Mexico State University
Las Cruces, New Mexico

Thomas P. Davis, Ph.D.
Associate Professor
Department of Pharmacology
University of Arizona
Tucson, Arizona

Pierre Dejours, M.D.
Research Director and Professor
Laboratoire d'Etude des Regulations Physiologiques
Centre National de la Recherche Scientifique
Strasbourg, France

Zipora Etzion, Ph.D.
Scientist
Department of Physiology
Faculty of Health Sciences
Ben Gurion University of the Negev
Beer Sheva, Israel

Suzanne M. Fortney, Ph.D.
Assistant Professor
Department of Environmental Health Sciences
John Hopkins University
Baltimore, Maryland

Ralph Francesconi, Ph.D.
Research Chemist
Heat Research Division
U.S. Army Research Institute of Environmental Medicine
Natick, Massachusetts

Michal Horowitz, Ph.D.
Associate Professor
Department of Physiology
The Hebrew University
Hadassah Medical School
Jerusalem, Israel

A. J. Kielblock, Ph.D.
Director
Industrial Hygiene Laboratory
Chamber of Mines of South Africa
Johannesburg, South Africa

C. Lundgren, Ph.D.
Professor
Department of Physiology
State University of New York at Buffalo
Buffalo, New York

Dalia Mazor, Ph.D.
Corob Research Center
Unit of Physiology
Ben Gurion University of the Negev
Beer Sheva, Israel

Naomi Meyerstein, M.D., Ph.D.
Associate Professor
Faculty of Health Sciences
Ben-Gurion University of the Negev
Beer Sheva, Israel

Albert J. Olszowka, M.D.
Professor
Department of Physiology
State University of New York at Buffalo
Buffalo, New York

Kent B. Pandolf, Ph.D., M.P.H.
Director
Military Ergonomics Division
U.S. Army Research Institute of Environmental Medicine
Natick, Massachusetts

Berry Pinshow, Ph.D.
Senior Lecturer
Department of Biology
Ben-Gurion University of the Negev
Beer Sheba, Israel

Klaus Pleschka, M.D.
Professor
Max Planck Institut für Physiologische und Klinische Forschung
W. G. Kerckhoff Institut
Bad Nauheim, West Germany

Hermann Rahn, Ph.D.
Distinguished Professor
Department of Physiology
State University of New York at Buffalo
Buffalo, New York

Shlomo Samueloff, M.D.
Professor
Department of Physiology
The Hebrew University
Hadassah Medical School
Jerusalem, Israel

Michael N. Sawka, Ph.D.
Chief, Physiology Branch
Military Ergonomics Division
U.S. Army Research Institute of Environmental Medicine
Natick, Massachusetts

P. C. Schutte, Ph.D.
Chamber of Mines of South Africa
Johannesburg, South Africa

Yair Shapiro, Ph.D.
Professor
Department of Physiology
Ben-Gurion University Medical School
Soroka Medical Center
Beer Sheva, Israel

Roy J. Shephard, M.D., Ph.D.
Professor and Director
School of Physical and Health Education
University of Toronto
Toronto, Ontario, Canada

Arsenio Veicsteinas, M.D.
Professor
Department of Biomedical Sciences
University of Brescia
Brescia, Italy

Jürgen Werner, Ph.D.
Professor
Ruhr-Universität Bochum
Institut für Physiologie
AG Elektrophysiologie
Bochum, West Germany

David Wolfenson, Ph.D.
Lecturer
Department of Animal Sciences
Faculty of Agriculture
Hebrew University of Jerusalem
Rehovot, Israel

Reuven Yagil, D.V.M.
Associate Professor
Faculty of Health Sciences
Ben-Gurion University of the Negev
Beer Sheva, Israel

Mohamed K. Yousef, Ph.D.
Professor and Director
Desert Biology Reasearch Center
Department of Biological Sciences
University of Nevada
Las Vegas, Nevada

TABLE OF CONTENTS

PART A. ADAPTIVE PHYSIOLOGY OF MAN

Chapter 1
Adaptive Physiology: Introductory Remarks and Glossary ... 3
M. K. Yousef and S. Samueloff

Chapter 2
What is a Stressful Environment? An Introduction ... 11
P. Dejours

Chapter 3
Thermoregulatory Mechanisms: Adaptations to Thermal Loads ... 17
J. Werner

Chapter 4
Population Studies on Human Adaptability ... 27
Shlomo Samueloff

Chapter 5
Metabolic Consequence of Exercise in the Cold ... 35
Roy J. Shephard

Chapter 6
Shallow Water and Ascent Blackout During Breath-Hold Diving ... 43
H. Rahn, A. Olszowka, and C. Lundgren

Chapter 7
Changes of Muscle and Fat Insulation During Exercise in Water ... 51
Arsenio Veicsteinas

Chapter 8
Acclimatization and Acclimation to Heat — An Introduction ... 59
Yair Shapiro and Kent B. Pandolf

Chapter 9
The Evolution of Heat Acclimatization Practices and Procedures in the South African Gold Mining Industry with Special Reference to Fundamental Considerations ... 67
A. J. Kielblock and P. C. Schutte

Chapter 10
Thermoregulatory Adaptations to Inactivity ... 75
Suzanne M. Fortney

Chapter 11
Circulatory and Thermoregulatory Actions of Hydration During Exercise-Heat Stress ... 85
Michael N. Sawka, R. P. Francesconi, and Kent B. Pandolf

Chapter 12
Factors Which Alter Human Physiological Responses During Exercise-Heat Acclimation ... 91
Kent B. Pandolf, Michael N. Sawka, and Yair Shapiro

Chapter 13
Sweat Loss and Voluntary Dehydration During Work in Humid Heat 103
Thomas P. Davis and Mohamed K. Yousef

PART B. ADAPTIVE PHYSIOLOGY OF ANIMALS

Chapter 14
Hormonal Control of Heat Production and Homeothermy 113
M. K. Yousef

Chapter 15
Opioid Peptides and Adaptation to Environment 121
T. P. Davis and M. K. Yousef

Chapter 16
Adaptation to the Environment: The Role of Red Blood Cells 131
Naomi Meyerstein, Zipora Etzion, Dalia Mazor, and Reuven Yagil

Chapter 17
Interactions Between Circulation and Plasma Fluids During Heat Stress 139
Michal Horowitz and Shlomo Samueloff

Chapter 18
Blood Flow Partitioning in Respiratory Heat Dissipation: Its Relevance for
Whole Body and Brain Cooling 151
Klaus Pleschka

Chapter 19
The Effects of Temperature and PCO_2 on Avian Blood O_2 Affinity:
The Implications for Extrapulmonary O_2 Supply to the Brain and
for Life at High Altitude 159
Berry Pinshow, Marvin H. Bernstein, and Zeev Arad

Chapter 20
The Desert Camel — A Review 173
Reuven Yagil and Zipora Etzion

Chapter 21
An Exercise in the Evaluation of Body Fat Content as Illustrated by the Sand Rat
(*Psammomys obesus*) 181
Jonathan H. Adler

Chapter 22
Physiological Limitations to Dairy Production in the Subtropical Climate
of Israel 187
A. Berman and D. Wolfenson

Chapter 23
Displacement of Thermal Neutrality in the Artificial Acclimated and
Seasonal Acclimatized Domestic Fowl 197
Amichai Arieli

Index 205

Part A. Adaptive Physiology of Man

Chapter 1

ADAPTIVE PHYSIOLOGY: INTRODUCTORY REMARKS AND GLOSSARY

M. K. Yousef and S. Samueloff

TABLE OF CONTENTS

I. Introduction 4

II. Defining Adaptive Physiology 4

III. Glossary of Terms Used in Environmental Physiology 4

References 9

I. INTRODUCTION

How various animals are able to cope with stressful habitats has long fascinated environmental physiologists who find a stimulating challenge in discovering ways to improve man's well-being and adaptation to the many hostile environments which he encounters either in nature or in his workplace. The complex interrelating and environmentally interacting processes of man and other animals have been given many names: environmental physiology, ecophysiology, stress physiology, adaptive physiology, biometeorology, etc. The terminological problems arise and lead to confusion as many terms are used to describe the same or a similar phenomenon. Such a problem has not been created intentionally but as a result of the bias and particular emphasis of the scientists using them. In other words, this problem reflects no more than conflict of opinion between investigators. Yet, terminology has resulted in frustration for communication among specialists in the same field. This has prompted the International Union of Physiological Sciences (IUPS), through its Commissions on Thermal Physiology and Environmental Physiology, to provide a glossary of terms for improving precision of meaning and uniformity in their usage. This effort can simplify the integration of published data and enhance our understanding of adaptive physiology. However, it must be recognized that such a glossary, if complete, would be enormous, and a given list cannot be encyclopedic in its coverage. The Thermal Physiology Commission published its glossary in 1973;[1] members of the Environmental Physiology Commission have just completed their glossary which is included here. Also, the early and recent use of common terms describing responses of animals to adverse environments has been reviewed by Folk[2] and Yousef.[3]

II. DEFINING ADAPTIVE PHYSIOLOGY

Adaptive physiology deals with the study of various physiological, biochemical, and behavioral changes that an organism must induce and display to fit into a new stressful environment. Fitness in a hostile environment, i.e., desert, arctic, hypobaric, hyperbaric, etc., requires an integrative response of most, if not all, of the animal's organ systems. These responses or strategies have been under investigation at the subcellular, cellular, and the whole animal hierarchy levels to understand the efficiency of physiological adaptations, i.e., fitness, and thus the thriving of various animals in harmony with their adverse environmental conditions.

Defining a stressful environment is eloquently presented by Dejours[4] in Chapter 2 and the various physiological adjustments necessitated by the stresses of heat, cold, and underwater are summarized in the remaining chapters of this book. An examination of evidence for the survival of man and other mammals and birds under a wide range of environmental stresses points to our understanding of the importance of thermoregulatory principles and mechanisms. However, it becomes obvious that physiologists must agree on objective and acceptable indices for the various stresses. Moreover, the establishment of objective physiological criteria of the limits for various types of occupations where thermal stresses are encountered remains open to debate and further investigation. Additionally, good preventive measures to alleviate excessive thermal stress, especially in the workplace need to be established.

III. GLOSSARY OF TERMS USED IN ENVIRONMENTAL PHYSIOLOGY

The following glossary was prepared by the IUPS Commission on Environmental Physiology (1980-1986): S. Samueloff, Chairman, and members, J. Krog, E. R. Nadel, N. Tasaneva, R. J. Shephard, A. D. Slonim, and M. K. Yousef.

The idea for this glossary was promoted by the Council of the IUPS through its Board for Definition of Terms. The endeavor to prepare a glossary of terms in environmental physiology was undertaken by the IUPS Commission on Environmental Physiology under the leadership of its first chairman, the late Professor O. Edholm, who gave much effort, time, and initiative to promote the project. Many discussions, comments, and much hesitation were experienced in its preparation. The main concern of the Commission was the fact that it is difficult today to draw a line in an area as vast as that covered by environmental physiology. We are certain that much more can be added, edited, and discussed. However, our decision to publish the present version shows our conviction that we should stop somewhere, expose our work, and provide an opportunity to others for its extension and improvement.

Acceleration	Change of velocity with respect to time
Accommodation See also Acclimation, Acclimatization, Habituation in Thermal Physiology, Glossary — *J. Appl. Physiol.*, 35, 941, 1973	Short-term or immediate physiological change in sensitivity of a living organism or cell to alterations in the environment; when former conditions are restored the organism or cell reverts to previous state
Acculturation	Control of the microenvironment by using appropriate behavioral modification of the environment (clothing, heating, cooling, etc.)
Acrophase	The point in time during a diurnal cycle of physiological, psychological, or behavioral process when the magnitude of the process is maximum
Adiabatic process	A body is said to undergo an adiabatic change when its condition is altered without gain or loss of heat
Alarm reactions	The responses of an organism to unusual stimuli to which it is neither accustomed nor adapted
Allen's rule	In warm-blooded species there tends to be an increase of body surface area by an enlargement of the relative size of protruding body structures, such as ears, legs, and tail, with increasing temperature of the habitat, insofar as they play a role in temperature regulation
Ambient sound (vibration)	Measurable acoustic energy in the background; energy sources not clearly identifiable
Amplitude of sound	Magnitude of ambient sound above some reference level usually (0.002 μbars)
Anemometry	Measurement of the velocity of air flow by any suitable instrument that gives a signal related to rate of air movement
Attenuation	Reduction in signal strength
Audio frequency change	The part of the frequency spectrum that is audible; for man the maximum range is 20 to 20,000 Hz
Audiogram	A chart, table, or graph on which the threshold of hearing level for pure tones as a function of frequency recorded
Audiometry	The measurement of threshold of hearing for pure tones over a range of 200—8000 Hz
Autophasing	A phase-shifting of a biological clock-timed rhythm in organisms when all normal-operating phase-setting factors are held constant
Autoregulation	The autonomous regulation of physiological variables based on feedback mechanism

Autorhythmometry	The self-measurement of internal periodicities
Bends	A dull throbbing pain after release from a period of exposure to compressed air; the pain is usually localized to the extremities and it is removed by complete or partial recompression
Bergmann's rule	Within a polytypic warm-blooded species, or closely related species, the body-size of a subspecies usually increases as the temperature of its habitat decreases
Biological clocks	Mechanisms by which organisms provide the timing of their physiological and behavioral activity, which correlate with the environment or endogenous setting
Biological rhythms See also Circadian rhythm etc., in Thermal Physiology Glossary, *J. Appl. Physiol.*, 35, 941, 1973	Fluctuations of biological activity as a function of time
Biosphere	The region of the earth's surface, including air and water, in which life can exist
Biotope	A region that is uniform with respect to environmental and soil conditions and the population of plants and animals for which it is the habitat
Candela	S.I. unit of luminous intensity — 1 lm/sr
Chilblain	A mild form of cold injury characterized by red, swollen, tender extremities with itching or burning sensation
Chronobiology	The science of biological rhythms
Chronopathology	The study of biological rhythms in disease
Chronopharmacology	The study of relationship between drug action and biological rhythms
Chronotoxicology	The study of the relationship between toxic substances and biological rhythms
Cold-induced vasodilation	Cyclic dilatation of blood vessels in the skin during severe cooling mainly in extremities including tails and ears of many animals
Conductive hearing loss	Result of a deficiency in the sound-conducting mechanisms of the ear
Coriolis acceleration	The acceleration of an object moving above or on the earth; acceleration is toward the right in the northern hemisphere and toward the left in the southern; its magnitude is equal to the product of the angular velocity of the earth, the linear velocity of the subject, and the size of the angle between the earth and the direction of motion of the object
Coriolis force	The apparent force responsible for Coriolis acceleration
Decibel	One tenth of a bel; used in comparison of the magnitudes of pressures or powers; two powers, P_1 and P_2, are separated by n decibels where $n = 10 \log_{10} P_1/P_2$; two pressures, P_1 and P_2, are separated by m decibels where $m = 20 \log_{10} P_1/P_2$
Dehydration	Progressive loss of body water from an organism
Diapause	Physiological resting state in which a dormant organism is exceptionally resistant to environmental extremes; often a response to changing photoperiod

Doppler effect	The change in the observed frequency of a wave in a transmission medium caused by movement of the source of wave relative to the observer or by the change in distance between the source and point of observation
Dormancy	State of prolonged sleep, lasting several days or more, connected with special physiological changes under the influence of environment
Ecology	The branch of biology that deals with the complex network of mutual interactions between living organisms and their environment, both physical and biological, or the study of living organisms interacting among themselves and their environment
Endogenous rhythms	Rhythmical variations in an organism which may be (1) inherent, as of the heart; (2) linked with 24-hr cycles or lunar cycles; (3) linked with annual-seasonal cycles
Exogenous rhythms	The interrelationship between humans and their working environment
Ergonomics	The study of men and women in their working environment, or the study of work and working environments in relation to man
Free running rhythm	A bodily rhythm, correlated in nature with a geophysical period, that persists even when all natural phase-setting variables such as light and temperature are experimentally held constant or eliminated
Frostbite	Injury of varying degree of severity due to freezing of living tissue
Heat stress index	An index of environmental heat strain obtained by weighing the effect of its various components on man and animals (according to theoretical principles or experimental results)
Hyperbaric	Pertaining to pressure greater than 1 atm (ATA — atmosphere absolute)
Hypobaric	Pertaining to pressure smaller than 1 atm
Infrasound	Longitudinal pressure waves with a frequency below the audible range (16 Hz)
Ionizing radiation	Any electromagnetic or particulate radiation capable of producing ions in passing through matter
Lumen	S.I. unit of luminous flux used in describing the quantity of light emitted by a source or received by a surface; 1 candela (cd) emits a total of 4 lumens (lm) in all directions and 1 lm within unit solid angle (1 steradian, sr)
Lux	S.I. unit of illuminance, equal to 1 lm/m^2
Microclimate	(1) The immediate environment in the habitat of plants and animals; (2) the environment under clothing worn by man
Mountain sickness	A condition occurring on high mountains (1) with a fast ascent characterized by headache, loss of appetite, nausea, insomnia, and dyspnea on exertion, and (2) on prolonged stay characterized by cyanosis and polycythemia
Nystagmus	Involuntary rapid movements of the eyeball, either from side to side, up and down, in a circle, or in a combined motion, often with a slow component in one direction, followed by a fast movement in the opposite direction

Permanent threshold shift (PTS)	The component of threshold shift that shows no progressive reduction with the passage of time when the apparent cause has been removed
Photosensitivity	The capacity of an organ or organism or cell to react to light, including UV
Pitch	Quality of sound which depends primarily on the frequency of vibrations producing sound
Pollutant	An injurious substance in the environment, be this water, air, or soil
Presbyacusis	Decline in hearing acuity with age
Psychrometric chart	The standard chart from which dew points, relative humidity, vapor pressure, and water content of the air can be read from dry- and wet-bulb temperatures
Psychrometry	Use of wet and dry bulb thermometers to determine water vapor pressures
Pure tone	A tone in which the sound pressure varies sinusoidally with time
Random noise	Scattered sounds of variable and unpredictable frequency
Resistance (to cold, heat, etc.)	Morphophysiological (inherited or acquired) ability of the organism to tolerate cold, heat, hypoxia, hyperoxia, etc., connected with development of some defense response to such factors
Resonance	The tendency of a body to respond in concert with an externally generated vibration of constant magnitude which reaches a maximum at a particular frequency
Sound	The audible sensation produced by vibration when transmitted to the ear
Sound intensity	The mean rate of flow of sound energy per unit area normal to the direction of propagation
Sound power	The total sound energy radiated by a source in unit time (units: watts)
Sound pressure	Displacement of pressure from its mean value in a medium due to passage of sound waves (units: pascals)
Stress and strain	Strain represents the condition of the animal body exposed to stress, resulting in reversible or irreversible changes, measurable by performance or physiological or biochemical changes Stress refers to environmental conditions which can elicit strain, such as vibration, sound, high or low pressure, temperatures, etc.
Temporary threshold shift	The component of threshold shift (or hearing) that shows progressive reduction with the passage of time when the apparent cause has been removed
Tolerance	Ability to endure more than minimal displacement of normal physiological levels
Ultraviolet light	Band of electromagnetic radiation with wavelengths shorter than those of visible light
Vertigo	A condition in which a person wrongly perceives the outer world as turning with respect to his body (objective vertigo) or of the observer himself turning with respect to the outer world (subjective vertigo); a symptom of stimulation or dysfunction on the vestibular apparatus

Vibration (whole body and segmental)	Variable changes in position in space of man or animals applied through one or more primary supporting surfaces of the body or extremities

REFERENCES

1. **Bligh, J. and Johnson, K. G.,** Glossary of terms for thermal physiology, *J. Appl. Physiol.*, 35, 941, 1973.
2. **Folk, G. E., Jr.,** *Textbook of Environmental Physiology*, Lea & Febiger, Philadelphia, 1974.
3. **Yousef, M. K., Ed.,** *Stress Physiology in Livestock*, Vol. 1, CRC Press, Boca Raton, Fla., 1985.
4. **Dejours, P.,** What is a stressful environment? An introduction, in *Adaptive Physiology to Stressful Environments*, Samueloff, S. and Yousef, M. K., Eds., CRC Press, Boca Raton, Fla., 1987, chap. 2.

Chapter 2

WHAT IS A STRESSFUL ENVIRONMENT? AN INTRODUCTION

P. Dejours

TABLE OF CONTENTS

Abstract 12

I. Introduction 12

II. Ambient Factors 12

III. The Physicochemical Environment 12

IV. Stress 13

V. Organism-Environment Interactions 14

VI. Conclusions 14

References 15

ABSTRACT

Life arose in very particular physicochemical conditions. Ambient factors vary in the hydrosphere, the atmosphere, or the lithosphere, and may also vary in time, but for any given species, the range of variations is quite narrow. Approaching the upper or lower limits of any of these conditions is stressful; life becomes barely tolerable, and where the limits are passed, the strained organism is permanently damaged, or dies. The organism often adapts to overcome the stress. In nature, it can acclimatize during its lifetime to minimize strain, a phenotypic change, but genetic mutations favoring a successful reaction to stress may be expressed if the organism can reproduce.

I. INTRODUCTION

The physicochemical conditions of the environment prevailing on our planet have permitted the genesis of life. The probability of life having arisen is small as far as we can guess, since even one factor, e.g., too high or too low a temperature, would have hindered its development, or just stopped it forever.

II. AMBIENT FACTORS

The left column of Figure 1 lists various ambient factors. The list is incomplete; for example, one could add the characteristics for heat dissipation (capacity, conductivity); the pollutants; the unicellular organisms, plants, and animals, of a given ecosystem. These factors have to be considered in various milieus: water, soil, air.[1] Actually there are a great number of milieus.

The reality covered by the word hydrosphere is very complex.[2] Whereas open ocean water is a relatively stable physicochemical system whose characteristics are given in some remarkable books of oceanography, fresh waters are extremely variable. In fact, no two fresh waters are alike; for each, one needs to know its complete chemical composition in order to understand the respiratory and ionic exchanges of the living inhabitants. Of course, estuarine waters display a progressive change of properties between the physicochemical characteristics of open sea water and a given fresh water.

The atmosphere is, with some exceptions, relatively simple,[2] in the sense that one needs to know only its temperature, pressure, and relative humidity in order to find, in a book of physical constants, or by simple calculation, its viscosity, density, gas partial pressures, and heat dissipative properties.

The situation is quite complex for soil, the lithosphere, because its characteristics vary with its chemical nature, texture, and porosity.[1] If the soil is dry, and communication of the subsoil with air is free, the soil respiratory properties are close to those of air. Partially wet soil may be considered as a volume formed of a mineral matrix containing gas and water pockets. This soil, sometimes called porosphere, has properties intermediary between water and air for the living creatures who dwell in it.

III. THE PHYSICOCHEMICAL ENVIRONMENT

The physicochemical properties of the environments vary in time and space.[1] The chronological variations follow different cycles: tidal, circadian, lunar, circannual. The environmental factors, modified by their temporal and spatial traits, define a livable environment, a life-supporting space (Figure 1, right column). They constitute a complex geometrical space in a number (n) of dimensions in which life evolved throughout millions of years. The space boundaries are by no means well defined, because the factors which constitute

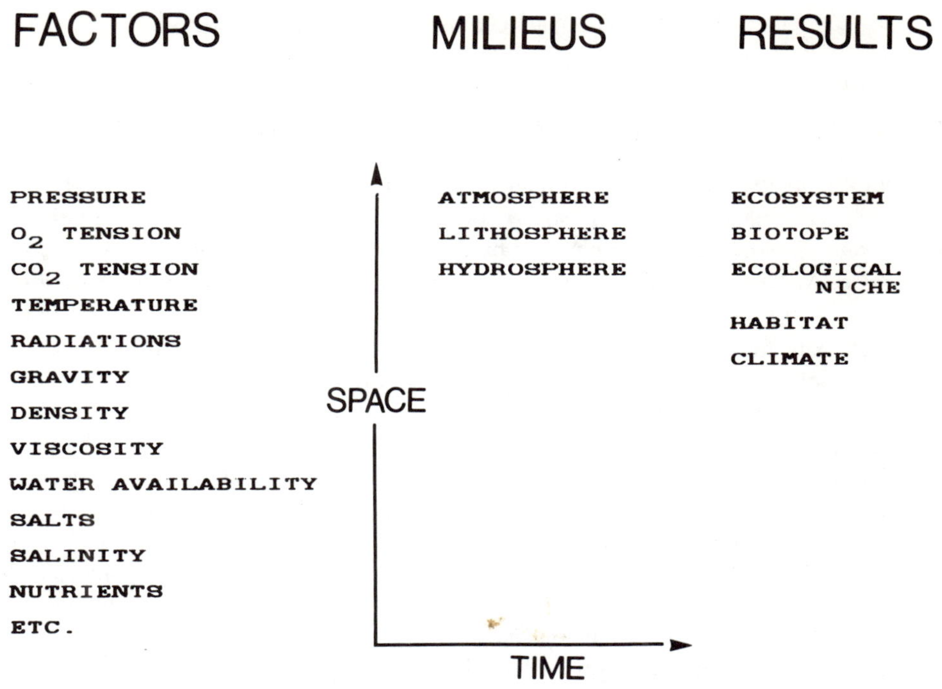

FIGURE 1. Surrounding factors which change in space and time in the various milieus, water, soil, and air, to result into a given environment.

the envelope of this environment are species-specific, and are not independent. Thus, the upper limit of heat stress is lowered if plenty of water is available, and the resistance to prolonged cold exposure is decreased if food energy is scarce. Within the n-dimensional livable space, the physicochemical properties are tolerable, and there are optimal zones where living beings can prosper, develop, and evolve relatively easily. The boundaries are limits beyond which life is impossible; just inside, the conditions are tolerable for a longer or shorter time, but they constitute a stressful environment.

IV. STRESS

When the word "stress" is applied to biology, we encounter a semantic problem: the environment may be stressful, its constitutive factors may be stressful and are often called "stressors". How shall we describe the organism exposed to stressful factors? Is it "strained" or is it "stressed"? A force applied to a spring elongates or compresses it. This force is a stress and the resulting relative change of the spring length is a strain. It is called a stress/strain relationship, the slope relating the two variables being a kind of sensitivity of the material to the stressing factor.

If the stressing force is too strong, the spring can be lengthened or compressed too much, and when the force ceases, the spring does not return to its original length. There, the force has overpassed the boundaries of the spring's reversible deformation, its elastic tolerance. It has been overstrained and is permanently deformed. In the case of living beings, this means permanent damage or death.

The words stress and strain are readily defined in the field of physics. For living beings, one should say that stressful conditions are those which tend to disrupt the biological equilibrium to a point which may endanger life. However, it is common, since Hans Selye's[3] writings speak of organismic stress. According to Selye's semantics, you are stressed by my prose, but according to linguists and physicists, you are strained by my stressful words.

V. ORGANISM-ENVIRONMENT INTERACTIONS

Obviously, the interrelationships between living creatures and the physical world, of this fitness of organisms, are amazing, and most of us probably think that living beings are adapted to their particular environment. Presumably the progressive changes of the environment throughout the history of our planet have obliged living beings to adapt and evolve. This is the basic idea of transformism, a concept enunciated by Lamarck in 1809 in his *"Philosophie Zoologique"* and developed by Darwin in 1859 in *"On the Origins of Species by Means of Natural Selection or the Preservation of Favoured Races in the Struggle for Life"*.

After Darwin, the problem of the mechanism of genetic evolution was raised, and it has not been completely solved. Thus, we are genetically adapted to a sort of mean environment, by processes which result in certain structural designs and functional behavior. However, if living beings are submitted repeatedly or permanently to stressful conditions, structural and functional adaptations take place, for example, respiratory adaptation in subjects who repeatedly trek at high altitude or go to live at high altitude. This adaptation is not genetically determined; it is an epigenetic phenomenon, an adaptation acquired during life and requiring conditioning. When the stress is removed, the structures and functions return more or less rapidly to a status corresponding to the ordinary regular activity imposed on the body.

This is the way, I think, to understand how organisms are fitted to the environment. However, some have considered fitness the other way around. L. J. Henderson (1913) wrote *"The Fitness of the Environment"* with a subtitle "An inquiry into the biological significance of the properties of matter". This book is provocative; I do not know if there are many modern biologists who accept the position of Henderson.

To conclude this section it is appropriate to recall the definitions of adaptation, acclimation, and acclimatization. They are inspired by the glossary for thermal physiology prepared by Bligh and Johnson.[4]

Adaptation consists in a change minimizing the physiological strain which results from a stressful environment. Acclimation and acclimatization correspond to two aspects of adaptation. Acclimation is a physiological change which occurs in the lifetime of an organism and minimizes the strain caused by experimentally induced stressful changes of particular ambient factors. Acclimatization designates the physiological change which occurs in the lifetime of an organism and which minimizes the strain caused by stressful changes in the natural environment. Acclimation is by definition phenotypic. Acclimatization, as it is defined above, is phenotypic, but it may also be genotypic. One will note that in the above definitions the difference between stress and strain is clear cut.

VI. CONCLUSIONS

In conclusion, we have seen that life evolves within an n dimensional space, the boundaries of which vary with the combination of various stressful factors, and the genetic and epigenetic adaptations. Is it possible to represent all these factors graphically? At present no, but some very practical diagrams do exist, in particular in thermophysiology and respiratory physiology. For example, the famous O_2-CO_2 diagram developed by Fenn et al.[5] allows one to visualize the tolerable zone vis à vis too much N_2, too much or too little O_2 and CO_2, and the interactions between these factors. This diagram has been considerably developed and has become a remarkable tool for respiratory physiologists.[6] It may also be used for aquatic animals.[7,8]

REFERENCES

1. **Odum, E. P.,** *Fundamentals of Ecology*, W. B. Saunders, Philadelphia, 1971, 574.
2. **Dejours, P.,** *Principles of Comparative Respiratory Physiology*, 2nd ed., Elsevier/North-Holland, Amsterdam, 1981, 265.
3. **Selye, H.,** *Stress*, Acta Medical Publ., Montreal, 1950, 1025.
4. **Bligh, J. and Johnson, K. G.,** Glossary of terms for thermal physiology, *J. Appl. Physiol.*, 35, 941, 1973.
5. **Fenn, W. O., Rahn, H., and Otis, A. B.,** A theoretical study of the composition of the alveolar air at altitude, *Am. J. Physiol.*, 146, 637, 1946.
6. **Rahn, H. and Fenn, W. O.,** *A Graphical Analysis of the Respiratory Gas Exchange. The O_2-CO_2 Diagram*, American Physiological Soc., Washington, D.C., 1955, 38.
7. **Willmer, E. N.,** Some observations on the respiration of certain tropical fresh-water fishes, *Br. J. Exp. Biol.*, 11, 283, 1934.
8. **Rahn, H.,** Aquatic gas exchange: theory, *Resp. Physiol.*, 1, 1, 1966.

Chapter 3

THERMOREGULATORY MECHANISMS: ADAPTATIONS TO THERMAL LOADS

J. Werner

TABLE OF CONTENTS

Abstract 18

I. Introduction 18

II. System-Theoretical Background 18

III. Experimental Evidence 20
A. Peripheral Adaptive Modifications 20
B. Central Thermoadaptive Modifications 21
C. Threshold Deviations for Effector Mechanisms 21

IV. Conclusions 24

References 25

ABSTRACT

This chapter discusses experimental evidence of adaptive mechanisms on the basis of system-theoretical considerations. It is shown that modifications of the passive system and of the characteristics of sensors, central processing, and effectors are involved.

I. INTRODUCTION

This topic is very extensive, so I chose one special aspect: to show the common system-theoretical background of some experimentally observed types of adaptive mechanisms. I confined myself to some experimental examples, chosen more or less arbitrarily.

Figure 1 presents a scheme of the system we are dealing with emphasizing four subsystems. One is the passive system, which has to be actively controlled. This is achieved by three controller-components: the receptors, which seem to be heterogeneously distributed all over the body, the central information processing and the effector mechanisms. As to the autonomous effector functions, in man these are mainly vasomotor action, metabolism, and sweat production. By this we dispose of a closed control-loop which is able to compensate environmental influences, i.e., temperature, humidity, air velocity, and work. Here, we are discussing a further, higher level of thermoregulation, namely a variety of long-term adaptive modifications which enable the organism to cope with environmental stress in a more efficient way. These are on the one hand (Figure 1) morphological adaptations, which in our terminology modify primarily the passive system, and on the other hand functional adaptations which may be present on the receptor, the controller, and/or the effector level.

Well-known examples for morphological changes are[1,2] changes of body size and shape, brown adipose tissue, fur, and fat. Morphological changes of capillarization and sweat glands modify the effector capacity. This mechanism is supported by functional changes within the neuronal and humoral mechanisms. The experimentally verified correlate of these functional changes is a change of gain and, more importantly, a threshold deviation as to the onset of effector activity.

II. SYSTEM-THEORETICAL BACKGROUND

In order to outline the system-theoretical background of adaptation, I want to recall my view of the steady-state mechanism of thermoregulation.[3,4] Each of the four subsystems (receptors, controller, effectors, passive systems as seen in Figure 1) may be represented by a resultant input/output open-loop characteristic; in the case of strong cold load three of them with a positive, one with a negative slope (Figure 2A), this being the necessary condition for negative feedback. In Figure 2B these four characteristics are drawn within a common coordinate system. The dotted line shows that arbitrary values of temperature, afferent and efferent frequencies, and metabolic rate do not yield a steady-state, because there is only one quadruple of values, represented by the unbroken rectangular line, which guarantees stable conditions at a fixed environmental temperature, T_{A1}.

If environmental temperature changes from T_{A1} to T_{A2} ($T_{A2} < T_{A1}$, broken line), a new steady-state has to be established with higher metabolic rate, but also with lower body temperature. The deviation ΔT, however, is smaller than the deviation ϵ which would have been achieved without a change of metabolic rate, i.e., without feedback control.

The type of the system's response to morphological changes of the passive system is essentially the same. For example, a better isolation can be represented in Figure 1 by a transition from the broken to the unbroken characteristic of the passive system. This evokes a lower metabolic rate and a higher body temperature. This is shown explicitly in Figure 3 by the transition from the unbroken to the broken lines. Now, if we add a functional change,

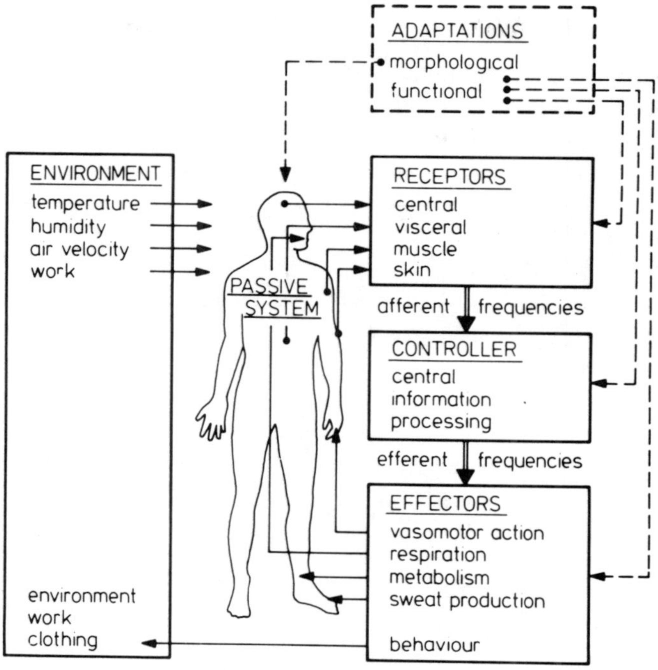

FIGURE 1. Scheme of the thermoregulatory system and its adaptive modifications.

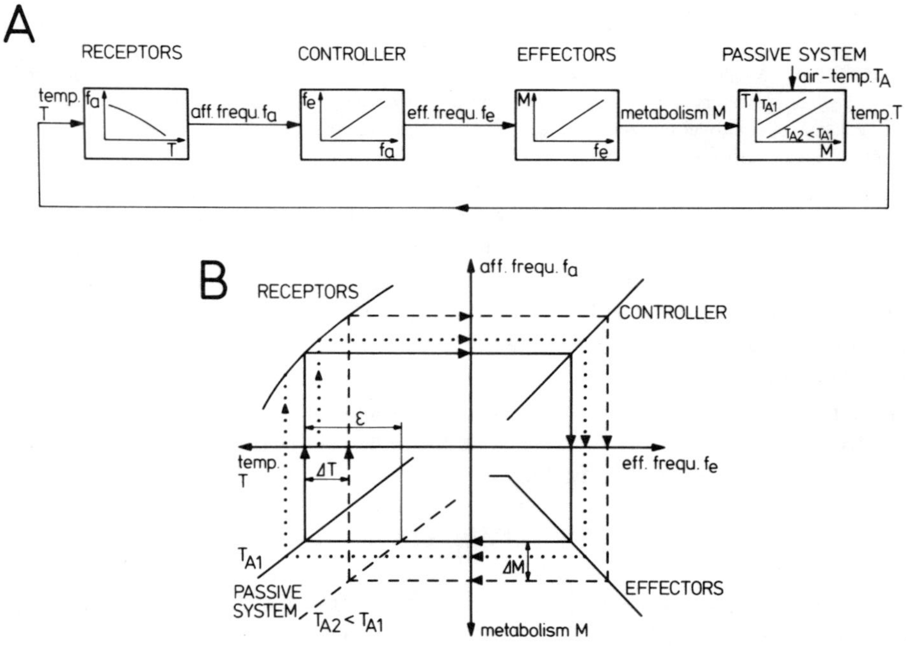

FIGURE 2. (A) Resultant steady-state open-loop characteristics of the four subsystems for strong cold load. (B) Mechanism of change of steady-state after strong cold load (transition from unbroken to broken lines). Dotted line: no steady-state.

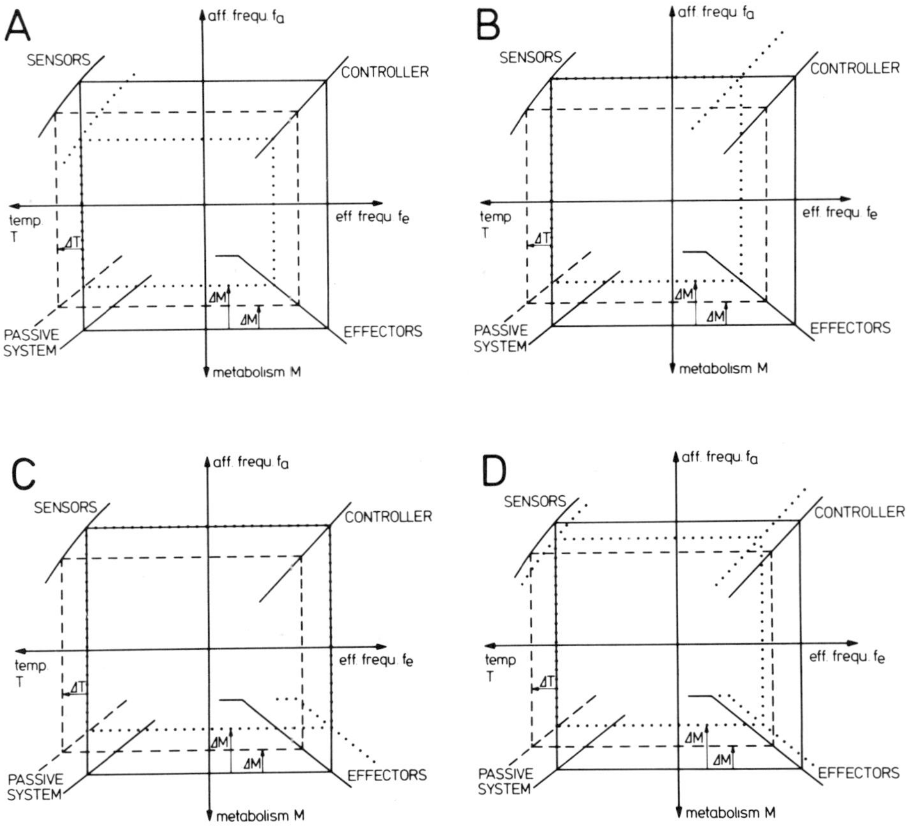

FIGURE 3. Mechanisms of change of steady-state after better isolation (transition from unbroken to broken lines) and functional changes (transition to dotted lines). (A) Change of sensor characteristic, (B) change of controller characteristic, (C) change of effector characteristic, and (D) change of sensor, controller, and effector characteristic.

e.g., of the sensor characteristic (Figure 3A: transition from the unbroken to the dotted lines), it is possible to get, by way of further lowering metabolic rate, constancy of body temperature. This can be equally achieved by a change of the central controller characteristic (Figure 3B), by a change of effector threshold (Figure 3C), or, of course, by modifications of all three subsystems together (Figure 3D). All four examples show the same decrease in metabolic rate ΔM, and no deviation in body temperature as compared to the original state (unbroken lines). So far the system-theoretical background, in my opinion, elucidates that generally, simultaneous adaptations in more than one subsystem may cooperate together in order to achieve a good performance.

III. EXPERIMENTAL EVIDENCE

Here I discuss experimental evidence of long-term adaptive changes within the subsystems due to persistent thermal loads. I skip the morphological modifications within the passive system, which were investigated very early and are rather well known.[1,2]

A. Peripheral Adaptive Modifications

There is some evidence for peripheral adaptive modifications which presumably are due to changes of the characteristics of peripheral sensors or afferents as shown by Hensel and Schäfer.[5,6] Two groups of cats were reared at 30 and 5°C for about 4 years. The average static frequencies recorded from the afferents from cutaneous thermoreceptors were somewhat lower in the cold-adapted group between 17 and 40°C ambient temperature. The average dynamic maxima were considerably lower in the cold-adapted group throughout the whole temperature range ($p = 0.1\%$). In addition, the maxima of the static and dynamic curves were shifted from 30 to 25°C in the cold-adapted group; however, it cannot be definitely decided whether these long-term changes are due to alterations of the cold receptors or of the thermal properties of the skin.

It was found, congruent with our theoretical considerations, that the weight of fur was higher (≈35%; better isolation within the passive system) and that metabolic rate was lower (≈20%) in the cold environment. It seems unlikely that these adaptive changes were maintained by a permanent decrease of core temperature, because rectal temperatures in the cold were about the same in both groups. This also corresponds with our theoretical introduction.

For shorter periods of cold adaptation, however, rectal temperature may decrease in the beginning of cold exposure by more than 2°C. Hensel[6] concluded that the thermal drives for the long-term adaptive modifications of the fur and effector mechanism originate mainly in the periphery.

B. Central Thermoadaptive Modifications

Central correlates of thermoadaptive modifications might be the consequence of changes in the afferents. In the rat, for example, the majority of neurons recorded within the pathways of the thermoafferent system are characterized by the properties shown in Figure 4A.[7] Up to a certain threshold for the peripheral stimulation temperature (of the scrotal, abdominal, or back skin), the neurons exhibit a relatively low firing rate, which is considerably increased above threshold; within a narrow threshold zone the neurons tend to oscillate between the two stable states, low or high, which should be due to even minor temperature influences from various body areas, because it has been shown that these neurons integrate information from all over the body.[8]

If we determine the percentage of neurons in the high state at a given stimulation temperature, we get a more or less S-shaped curve (Figure 4B—D). This empirical distribution function is significantly different for rats reared for 5 weeks at 3° and 23°C environmental temperature. For the cold-adapted rats the percentage of neurons with firing rates above the basal rate is higher than in the nonadapted rats. This holds for separate studies of thalamic,[9] midbrain,[9] and preoptic neurons.[10] It is concluded that after cold-adaptation the increase of firing rate starts on the average at a lower temperature. These threshold changes should be seen in the context of effector threshold changes (to be discussed later). It should be expected that after cold-adaptation the threshold for heat defense is decreased.

Before discussing the effectors, we should look at central correlates of adaptation which became evident by intrahypothalamic injection of noradrenaline (NA) and phentolamine.[11,12] Micro-injections of NA into an area caudally to the preoptic area under thermoneutral conditions increased shivering or nonshivering thermogenesis or both in guinea pigs. These metabolic reactions can be suppressed by increasing skin and/or internal body temperature. It has been concluded that the threshold for the thermogenetic reactions is shifted to a higher level by intrahypothalamic injection of NA. Phentolamine, an adrenergic α-blocking agent, has the reverse effect when given intrahypothalamically: the shivering threshold is decreased to values normally found in cold-adapted and in newborn guinea pigs. The shift in threshold is combined with a change of gain of the thermogenetic response as a function of temperature.

C. Threshold Deviations for Effector Mechanisms

First, I should recall the classical experiments of Brück and Wünnenberg,[13,14] demonstrating a downward shift of shivering threshold in guinea pigs which had been exposed to +5°C for 4 to 6 weeks. The threshold is given by a hyperbola as function of peripheral and central temperature.

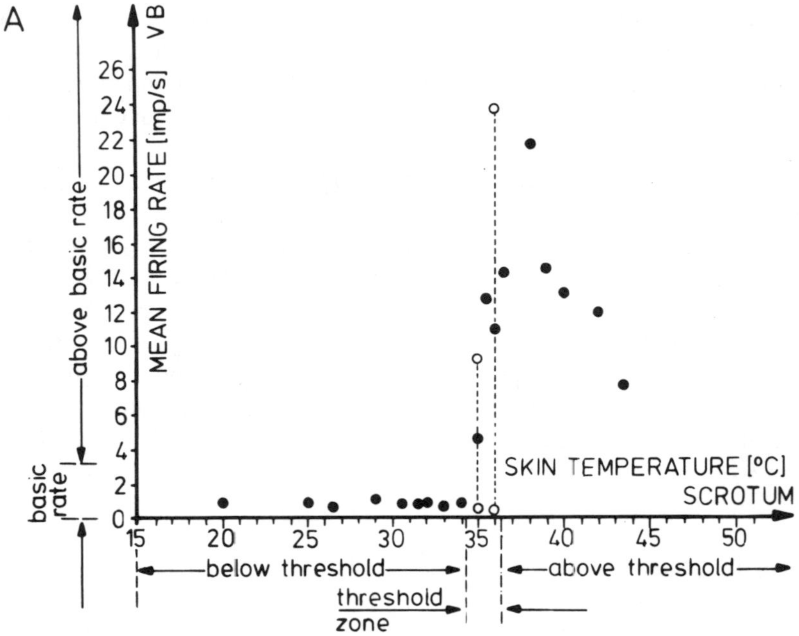

FIGURE 4A. Typical "switching neuron" within the thermoafferent pathway of the rat responding to peripheral thermal stimulation. Ventrobasal complex of thalamus (VB). (Filled circles) mean values over the last 60 sec of a constant temperature value, (open circles) minimum and maximum firing rate within the threshold zone.

The biological significance of this shift may be seen in the fact that it facilitates the suppression of shivering, which is brought about through the transport of heat from the brown adipose tissue to the cervical spinal cord area. This is thought to control shivering. From the energetic point of view it is advantageous to maintain body temperature at a somewhat lower level.

The cold-adaptive shift from shivering to nonshivering thermogenesis, accompanied by a marked increase in weight of brown adipose tissue and a development of metabolically active cells as shown by Heldmaier,[15] is combined with an increase in the metabolic response to a standard cold stress. This, of course, implies a waste of energy, which, when cold exposure continues, is replaced by more economical modifications such as growth of fur.

Figure 5 shows a survey from Brück[2] on the possible deviations of the thresholds for thermoregulatory metabolic and sweating responses in man. The scheme indicates the neutral zone of weighted body temperature T_b between onset of shivering and sweating. After cold exposure (four to seven times for 2 weeks between +5 and −5°C, 1 hr) the shivering threshold was shifted to a lower T_b, whereas the sweating threshold remained unchanged. By this, temperature regulation is not improved; on the contrary, the precision of control is reduced, but it allows the subject to tolerate cooler environments without metabolic waste.

A downward shift in both shivering and sweating threshold was found in long distance runners and swimmers.[16,17] This cross-adaptation may be advantageous, as it prolongs the time until a limiting high body temperature is reached.

In contrast to intermittent cold exposure, intermittent heat exposure of humans[18-23] leads to a lowering of the sweating threshold and thus to a narrowing of the interthreshold zone. By this, body temperature is more effectively defended against an upward deviation. No change of gain was seen, which increased during endurance training. Recent studies demonstrate a downward shift of the shivering threshold after strong heat adaptation (T_{es} >

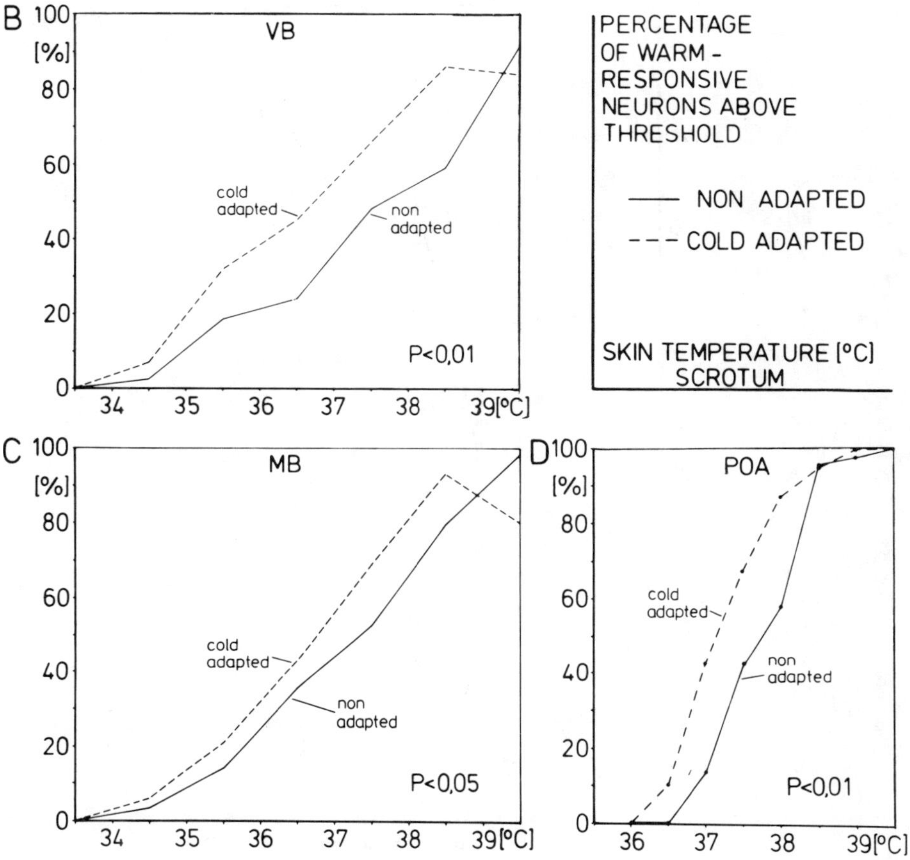

FIGURE 4B—D. Percentage of warm-responsive neurons above threshold in nonadapted and cold-adapted rats; (B) ventrobasal complex of thalamus (VB), (C) Raphe nuclei of midbrain (MB), and (D) preoptic area of hypothalamus (POA).

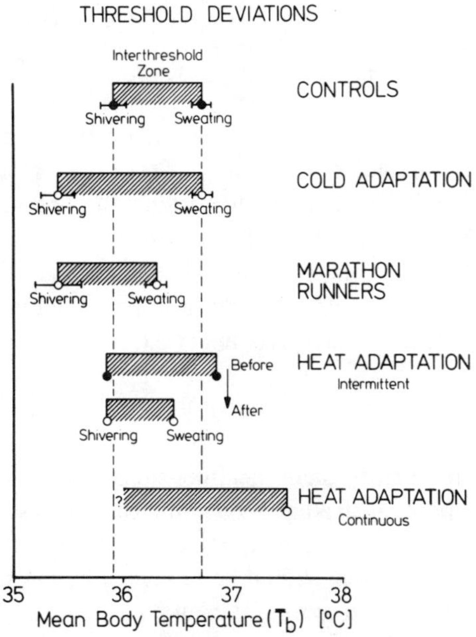

FIGURE 5. Survey on observed deviations in shivering and sweating thresholds in man. (From Brück, K., *Adv. Physiol. Sci.*, 23, 263, 1980.)

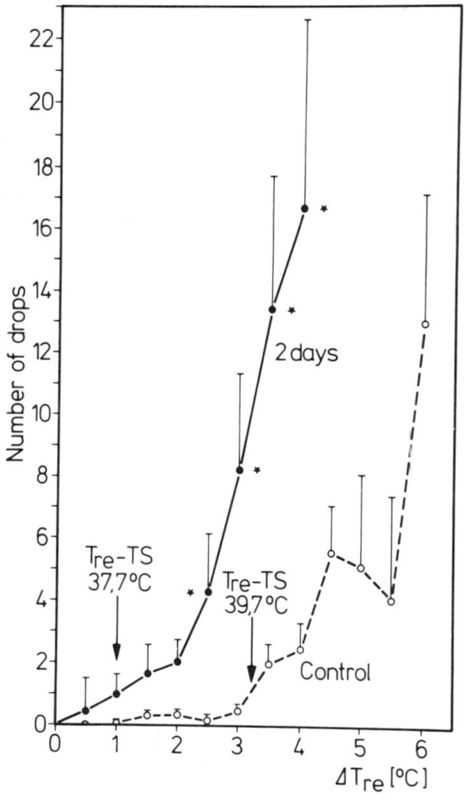

FIGURE 6. Saliva flow rates per each degree rise in rectal temperature in rats at the onset of salivation in controls and 2 days acclimated rats under exposure to heat stress (40°C). Arrows denote mean T_{re}-salivation threshold (T_{re}-TS): vertical lines denote SE of the mean; asterisk denotes significant difference (p <0.01; p <0.05) from the control group. (From Horowitz, M., et al., *Comp. Biochem. Physiol.*, 74A(No. 4), 945, 1983. With permission.)

38°C).[24] Long-term heat exposure develops tolerance adaptation against heat, i.e., T_b is higher after adaptations without inducing sweating.[25]

One example of threshold deviation that should be added is one published by Horowitz et al.[26] During heat stress (40°C) acclimated rats showed a decrease in threshold for salivation, in salivary flow rate, and in hyperthermic plateau. These studies are illustrated by Figure 6 which shows saliva flow per rate per each degree rise in rectal temperature at the onset of salivation in controls and 2 days acclimated rats under exposure to heat stress (40°C).

IV. CONCLUSIONS

Let us look again at the introductory theoretical considerations. Hensel's results should be due to a combination of morphological adaptation of the passive system and a modification of sensor characteristics, as he recorded no body temperature deviations (Figure 3A). Our findings within the thermoafferent system should be produced by the same mechanisms. As to the adaptation observed by effector recording, it cannot be decided whether they are based on the same effects observed within the afferent neuronal pathways (Figure 3A) or exclusively by central modifications (Figure 3B), effector-modification (Figure 3C), or by all three

(Figure 3D). All of these possibilities might evoke the same ΔM, because all experiments show the effector activity to be dependent on temperature without recording corresponding neuronal frequencies. One might speculate that generally all possibilities are involved simultaneously.

REFERENCES

1. **Hensel, H., Brück, K., and Rath, P.,** Homeothermic organisms, in *Temperature and Life,* Precht, H., Christophersen, J., Hensel, H., Larcher, W., Eds., Springer Verlag, Berlin, 1973, 505.
2. **Brück, K.,** Basic mechanisms in longtime thermal adaptation, in *Advances in Physiological Sciences,* Vol. 23, Szelényi, Z. and Székely, M., Eds., Pergamon Press, Oxford, 1981, 263.
3. **Werner, J.,** The concept of regulation for human body temperature, *J. Therm. Biol.,* 5, 75, 1980.
4. **Werner, J.,** *Regelung der Menschlichen Körpertemperatur,* de Gruyter, Berlin, 1984.
5. **Hensel, H. and Schäfer, K.,** Activity of cold receptors in cats after long-therm adaptation to various temperatures, *Pflugers Arch.,* 309, R56, 1979.
6. **Hensel, H.,** *Thermoreception and Temperature Regulation,* Academic Press, London, 1981.
7. **Schingnitz, G. and Werner, J.,** Responses of thalamic neurons to thermal stimulation of the limbs, scrotum and tongue in the rat, *J. Therm. Biol.,* 5, 53, 1980.
8. **Schingnitz, G. and Werner, J.,** Thalamic neurons in the rat responding to thermal and nocuous stimulation at various sites, *J. Therm. Biol.,* 8, 23, 1983.
9. **Werner, J., Schingnitz, G., and Hensel, H.,** Influence of cold adaptation on the activity of thermoresponsive neurons in thalamus and midbrain of the rat, *Pflugers Arch.,* 391, 327, 1981.
10. **Werner, J., Mathei, J., Schingnitz, G., and Hensel, H.,** Central neuronal correlates of thermal adaptation, in *Proc. of the 29th Int. Union Physiol. Sci.,* Davey, D. F., Ed., Sydney, 1983, 187.08.
11. **Zeisberger, E. and Brück, K.,** Alteration of shivering threshold in cold- and warm-adapted guinea pigs following intrahypothalamic injection of noradrenaline and of an adrenergic alpha-blocking agent, *Pflugers Arch.,* 362, 113, 1976.
12. **Zeisberger, E.,** Role of a central catecholaminergic system in the thermoregulatory threshold deviation, in *New Trends in Thermal Physiology,* Houdas, Y. and Guieu, J. D., Eds., Masson, Paris, 1978, 22.
13. **Brück, K. and Wünnenberg, W.,** Eine kälteadaptive Modifikation: Senkung der Schwellentemperaturen für Kältezittern, *Pflugers Arch.,* 293, 226, 1967.
14. **Brück, K. and Wünnenberg, W.,** Meshed control of two effector systems: nonshivering and shivering thermogenesis, in *Physiology and Behavior Temperature Regulation,* Hardy, J. D., Gagge, A. P., and Stolwijk, J. A. J., Eds., Charles C Thomas, Springfield, Ill., 1970, 562.
15. **Heldmaier, G.,** Temperature adaptation and brown adipose tissue in hairless and albino mice, *J. Comp. Physiol.,* 92, 281, 1974.
16. **Baum, E., Brück, K., and Schwennicke, H. P.,** Adaptive modifications in the thermoregulatory system of long-distance runners, *J. Appl. Physiol.,* 40, 404, 1976.
17. **Dressendorfer, R. H., Smith, R. M., Baker, D. G., and Hong, S. K.,** Cold tolerance of long-distance runners and swimmers in Hawaii, *Int. J. Biometeorol.,* 21, 51, 1977.
18. **Henane, R. and Valatx, J. L.,** Thermoregulatory changes induced during heat acclimatization by controlled hyperthermia in man, *J. Physiol. (London),* 230, 255, 1973.
19. **Gonzalez, R. R., Pandolf, K. B., and Gagge, A. P.,** Heat acclimation and decline in sweating during humidity transients, *J. Appl. Physiol.,* 36, 419, 1974.
20. **Schwennicke, H. P. and Brück, K.,** Thermoregulatory modifications in the course of repeated moderate heat-exposures in man, *Pflugers Arch.,* 365, R27, 1976.
21. **Henane, R., Flandrois, R., and Charbonnier, J. P.,** Increase in sweating sensitivity by endurance conditioning in man, *J. Appl. Physiol.,* 43, 822, 1977.
22. **Roberts, M. F., Wenger, C. B., Stolwijk, J. A. J., and Nadel, E. R.,** Skin blood flow and sweating changes following exercise training and heat acclimation, *J. Appl. Physiol.,* 43, 133, 1977.
23. **Brück, K.,** Ontogenetic and adaptive adjustments in the thermoregulatory system, in *New Trends in Thermal Physiology,* Houdas, Y. and Guieu, J. D., Eds., Masson, Paris, 1978, 65.
24. **Brück, K.,** Möglichkeiten und Grenzen der thermischen Adaptation, *Z. Phys. Med. Baln. Med. Klin.,* 14, 21, 1985.
25. **Raynaud, J., Martineaud, J. P., Bhatnagar, O. P., Viellefond, H., and Durand, J.,** Body temperatures during rest and exercise in residents and sojourners in hot climate, *Int. J. Biometeorol.,* 20, 309, 1976.
26. **Horowitz, M., Argov, D., and Mizrahi, R.,** Interrelationships between heat acclimation and salivary cooling mechanism in conscious rats, *Comp. Biochem. Physiol.,* 74A (No. 4), 945, 1983.

Chapter 4

POPULATION STUDIES ON HUMAN ADAPTABILITY

Shlomo Samueloff

TABLE OF CONTENTS

I. Introduction 28

II. Materials and Methods 29

III. Results 30

IV. Discussion 31

References 34

I. INTRODUCTION

The degree of physiological changes occurring in the process of acclimatization to various ambient conditions has usually been investigated in laboratory or field experiments on normal, healthy individuals. However, when such studies refer to physiological parameters of adaptability in populations exposed for generations to environmental stress, some problems should be taken into consideration, which are not relevant to the usual requirements of the ordinary experimental protocol.

Population studies indicate that cultural inheritance is more important for adjustment of man to his environment than changes in physiological characteristics. Although efficiency of physiological functions can be improved in the frame of phenotypic flexibility, the survival of populations in wide ranges of climatic conditions has been mediated by culturally acquired traits, behavior, social structure, type of clothing, home design, etc. The physiological changes which take place in the human organism after long-term exposure to severe climate can only alleviate existence but not determine it. The Australian aborigine, who can sleep naked through a moderately cold night without recourse to raise his body metabolism, exhibits a fall in body temperature to about 35°C.[1] However, although his endurance during exposure to cold with minimum protection is improved, this physiological characteristic is most probably a racial peculiarity rather than a determinant for his survival. The Antarctic Eskimo cannot tolerate a fall in his body temperature when exposed naked to cold. However, he exemplifies a greater metabolic heat production and maintains normal body temperature in extreme cold environment by protection with proper clothing and shelter.

Many investigations provide interesting information about physiological features of subjects belonging to different population groups. These features have usually been regarded as adaptive physiological changes induced by climate. However, the interpretation of these features is quite complicated, because they are results of multifunctional influences, and so far it has not been possible to evaluate the effect of climate in combination with other factors. For example, little is known about the influence of genetic constituents, nutritional status, pattern of daily activity, general state of health, and other factors on physiological changes induced by prolonged exposure to climatic conditions. There are obvious difficulties in experimental manipulation of these factors. An alternative approach for their evaluation is to seek situations where genetically contrasting population groups inhabit similar geographical areas and are exposed to the same climatic conditions, while engaged in similar occupations and while living at reasonably similar socioeconomic standards of life. In this respect, Israel provides attractive research opportunities to biologists.

Although a country of small size, Israel comprises four distinctly different climatic zones: (1) the coastal strip area with a mild Mediterranean type of climate, (2) the highland areas around Jerusalem and Galilee, (3) the subtropical regions of the Jordan Valley and the Dead Sea, and (4) the arid and semidesert areas of the Southern part of the country (the Negev), which extends into the Sinai peninsula.

Since the State of Israel was established in 1948, the large immigration has brought to the country Jewish people from different communities and habitats of the world. At present, one can find in the various climatic areas of the country villages inhabited by people of different ethnic origin. In many cases considerable genetic differences have been disclosed and reconfirmed between the subjects of different ethnic groups. Such a bio-demographic situation offers an attractive opportunity for investigation of the relative significance of genetic and environmental influences on physiological features which alleviate the strain of environment on man.[2]

The object of this presentation is to bring results which we have accumulated during the past decade regarding resting metabolic rate and peripheral circulation of subjects of contrasting ethnic origin living in two climatically different areas of the country — the host

South and the highland area around Jerusalem. All examinees were tested under controlled laboratory conditions during the summer, and tests were repeated during the winter. Resting metabolism and peripheral circulation are the basic physiological mechanisms involved in body heat production and dissipation by which body thermoregulation is achieved. Thus, the objective of these studies can be reworded as to assess inherited and acquired features of thermoregulatory adaptation of man.

II. MATERIALS AND METHODS

Both studies were carried out on healthy young subjects, aged 20 to 30, in a temperature controlled room at 24°C and 40% relative humidity, during the summer and repeated on the same subjects during the winter. The seasonal timing of the examination was such that one could assume that the examinees at the time of testing were naturally acclimatized to the prevalent climatic conditions of the season. The subjects were tested at least 6 hr postprandial, after a $\frac{1}{2}$ hr rest in a supine position. The examinees belonged to separate communities located either in the southern semiarid Negev and desert areas of Sinai or in the Judean hills around Jerusalem. The populations studied were Bedouin Arabs, Jews of Yemenite origin, Jews of Kurdish origin, and Central European Jews of Ashkenazi origin. Later in this chapter the participating subjects are referred to as Bedouins, Yemenites, Kurds and Ashkenazim.

While the genetic and demographic background of the Ashkenazim is thought to be heterogeneous, historic evidence regarding the Yemenites and Kurds indicate that in their loci of origin, before immigrating to Israel in the early 1960s, they had lived for a very long time in virtual isolation from other Jewish and non-Jewish communities, and they can be regarded as genetic isolates. This supposition has been supported by genetic studies which have revealed differences in blood heredity factors.[3] The Yemenites show close resemblance to the Yemenite Arabs, while the Kurds disclose greater similarity to the indigenous Kurds of Iran. However, the examined Kurds differ markedly from the examined Yemenites by having a higher incidence of six phosphate dehydrogenase deficiency and β-thalassemia trait in their blood cells. The Bedouin participants in this study came from primitive nomad tribes scattered in the Negev and Sinai. They were shepherds, farmers, or manual workers by occupation. By their social organization and available demographic information they can be classified as a distinctly closed population group.

Resting metabolism was examined in 135 subjects (95 men and 40 women). In the Negev 24 Yemenites (18 men and 6 women), 10 Bedouin men, 20 Kurds (15 men and 5 women), and 35 Ashkenazim (22 men and 13 women) were tested. From the Jerusalem area, the examinees consisted of 20 Yemenites (9 men and 11 women), 16 Kurds (11 men and 5 women), and 10 Ashkenazi men. Metabolism was determined by measuring respiratory gas exchange in an open circuit system and expiratory air collection for 5 min. The subject breathed through a low-resistance Otis McKerrow valve during a period allowing him to become familiar and used to the technique. The expired air was collected in a 300 ℓ Tissot spirometer, the dead space of which was repeatedly washed out prior to gas collection. After recording the volume of the gas collected during 5 min, samples for gas analysis were taken in nondiffusable vinyl plastic bags. Oxygen and carbon dioxide concentrations were estimated by Haldane apparatus and Beckman oxygen analyzer and standardized to STPD. Oxygen consumption (mℓ O_2/m^2 BSA/min and mℓ O_2kg BW/min) was calculated according to the procedure outlined by Consolazio et al.[4] Heart rates (beats per minute) were monitored with an ECG apparatus. Height and weight measurements were taken on a scale.

Forearm blood flow measurements were performed on 114 young men. Each individual was tested twice on two consecutive days in summer and winter. Prior to the test the subjects were medically examined and accustomed to the experimental procedures. After resting supine for about 1 hr, seven to eight consecutive measurements of forearm blood flow were performed. A second series of measurements were taken after 10 min rest. In each series of measurements the results were closed together and their mean values were calculated.

The measurement of forearm blood flow was carried out by venous occlusion plethysmography, using the mercury-in rubber strain gauge of Whitney. The hand blood flow was excluded by inflation of an occlusion cuff on the wrist to 250 to 300 mmHg.

The residency of the examined subjects and their ethnic origin was as follows: 42 Ashkenazim men, half of them residents of Jerusalem, the other half residents of Beer Sheva, which is located in the Negev. The second population group was made up of 21 Yemenites, all residents of the Negev. The subjects of both groups were either farmers or manual workers. The third population group was comprised of 51 Bedouins from three climatic areas: one third of them belonged to the tribes located around Bethlehem (near Jerusalem), one third came from the Arad-Negev arid zone, and one third from the A-Tour oasis in the Sinai desert.

In order to evaluate the relative significance of natural acclimatization to heat on the seasonal variations in forearm blood flow, ten Yemenite residents of the Negev were tested before and after artificial acclimatization to heat in the winter. The forearm blood flow procedure was as described before. Artificial acclimatization to heat was obtained by 3 hr daily exposure for 9 days in a climatic chamber at 40°C and 40% relative humidity.

During the heat exposure the subjects exercised and rested during consecutive half-hour periods. The exercise was carried out at two different levels: stepping on a 13 or a 20 cm high bench. The state of heat acclimatization was ascertained by the changes in heart rate, body temperature, and amount of collected forearm sweat during the exercise period on each day of the acclimatization procedure.

III. RESULTS

The data relevant to the study of resting metabolism are summarized in Tables 1 and 2. Table 1 refers to the body weight and heart rate data while the results of the measurements of oxygen consumption are presented in Table 2.

The Ashkenazim were found to be heavier than the Yemenites and the Kurds, both in the Negev and Jerusalem areas. The Negev Yemenites and Kurds had similar body weight in both sexes. In the Jerusalem area the Kurdish men and women were heavier than the Yemenites. During the winter all subjects exemplified a slight gain in body weight, which was not found to be statistically significant. In an attempt to confirm the accepted view about existence of linear relationship between metabolic and heart rate, ECG records were taken from all subjects during gas collection.

Significant differences in heart rates were found neither between the summer and winter data, nor between the data collected from subjects of the various ethnic groups.

The Negev Ashkenazim exhibit a lower resting metabolism than the Yemenites and Kurds of the same area, both men and women. The Negev Bedouins, Yemenites, and Kurds had similar metabolic rates during the winter. However, when the results of winter measurements of the Kurds, Yemenites, and Ashkenazim from both climatic areas were compared with those of the summer examinations, a seasonal variation in resting metabolism was obtained. The summer oxygen consumption data of all examinees (except the Jerusalem Kurdish women) were found to be lower than the winter data. This finding was reproduced when oxygen consumption was calculated per kilogram body weight, indicating that the observed trend of summer lowering of metabolic rate is not affected even by the observed slight gain in body weight during the winter.

The forearm blood flow data of the examined subjects of all population groups are presented in Table 3. Forearm blood flow is expressed as milliliters per minute per 100 mℓ tissue and mean values have been calculated from the seven to eight measurements obtained on two consecutive trials.

Table 1
SEASONAL VARIATIONS IN WEIGHT (kg) AND RESTING HEART RATE (BEATS/MIN) IN SUBJECTS OF DIFFERENT ETHNIC ORIGIN

	Weight (kg ± S.E.)					
	Men			Women		
Subjects' origin	n	Summer	Winter	n	Summer	Winter
Negev area						
Central Europe	22	68.8 ± 0.6	70.3 ± 3.1	13	56.1 ± 2.0	58.0 ± 2.1
Yemen	18	64.2 ± 2.3	64.8 ± 2.3	6	49.4 ± 5.2	51.6 ± 4.6
Kurdistan	15	63.9 ± 1.3	64.3 ± 1.5	5	56.3 ± 5.8	57.9 ± 5.5
Bedouins	10	—	63.7 ± 1.8	—	—	—
Jerusalem area						
Central Europe	10	—	72.7 ± 2.8	—	—	—
Yemen	9	53.8 ± 1.6	55.4 ± 1.6	11	50.4 ± 2.9	50.7 ± 3.0
Kurdistan	11	69.8 ± 3.1	70.3 ± 3.2	5	61.0 ± 4.8	61.5 ± 4.8
	Heart rate (beats/min)					
Negev area						
Central Europe	22	66 ± 3	69 ± 3	13	64 ± 2	73 ± 3
Yemen	18	69 ± 2	70 ± 2	6	83 ± 6	74.7 ± 4
Kurdistan	15	66 ± 2	66 ± 3	5	74 ± 2	85.6 ± 4
Bedouins	10	—	64 ± 3	—	—	—
Jerusalem area						
Central Europe	10	—	72 ± 3	—	—	—
Yemen	9	61 ± 2	62 ± 2	11	73 ± 1	71 ± 3
Kudristan	11	60 ± 3	62 ± 2	5	74 ± 2	74 ± 5

The Ashkenazim of the Negev and Jerusalem areas had similar forearm blood flows both in winter and summer. When the data of the Negev Ashkenazim and Yemenites are compared, the genetically different Yemenites exhibit significantly higher forearm blood flow, both in winter and in summer. Comparison of the data obtained from the Bedouin residents of three climatically different areas among themselves and with the other ethnic groups revealed similar forearm blood flow values to those of the Yemenites, and higher values than those of the Ashkenazim. The Bethlehem Bedouins had relatively lower forearm blood flow than their Negev and Sinai counterparts.

Wherever subjects were examined during one season and examinations repeated during the following season the summer values of forearm blood flow measurements were found to be lower than those of the winter. This seasonally determined change in peripheral circulation led us to the experiments in which subjects were artificially acclimated to heat during the winter at two levels of exercise. The data of resting forearm blood flow before and after heat acclimation are presented in Table 4. In both instances the testing was carried out at the standard comfortable ambient conditions. Acclimation to heat lowered the forearm blood flow of the examined subject. This change was more pronounced in the examinees which were exposed to a harder work program during the heat acclimation procedure.

IV. DISCUSSION

The examination of resting metabolism of subjects of four population groups during the winter and summer at thermoneutural controlled conditions revealed similar metabolic rates

Table 2
SEASONAL VARIATIONS IN RESTING METABOLISM OF SUBJECTS OF DIFFERENT ETHNIC ORIGIN

	O_2 cons. (mℓ/m² BSA/min ± S.E.)			
	Men		Women	
Subject's origin	Summer	Winter	Summer	Winter
Negev area				
Central Europe	148.0 ± 4.4	166.0 ± 5.2	129.6 ± 4.5	145.5 ± 5.0
Yemen	174.6 ± 4.4	184.0 ± 5.4	156.1 ± 5.8	164.8 ± 6.5
Kurdistan	166.5 ± 5.6	176.6 ± 4.1	152.8 ± 5.1	154.7 ± 5.1
Bedouin	—	172.1 ± 8.1	—	—
Jerusalem area				
Central Europe	—	164.8 ± 6.2	—	—
Yemen	134.7 ± 8.9	160.7 ± 5.7	148.6 ± 5.3	149.6 ± 3.6
Kurdistan	153.2 ± 6.6	160.2 ± 5.8	145.8 ± 8.0	141.0 ± 8.0

	O_2 cons. (mℓ/kg B.W./min ± S.E.)			
	Men		Women	
Subject's origin	Summer	Winter	Summer	Winter
Negev area				
Central Europe	3.9 ± 0.1	4.3 ± 0.2	3.6 ± 0.2	4.1 ± 0.1
Yemen	4.6 ± 0.1	4.9 ± 0.2	4.6 ± 0.3	4.8 ± 0.2
Kurdistan	4.5 ± 0.1	4.8 ± 0.3	4.2 ± 0.3	4.2 ± 0.1
Bedouin	—	4.8 ± 0.2	—	—
Jerusalem area				
Central Europe	—	4.2 ± 0.2	—	—
Yemen	4.0 ± 0.2	4.2 ± 0.2	3.9 ± 0.3	3.7 ± 0.3
Kurdistan	4.0 ± 0.2	4.2 ± 0.2	3.9 ± 0.3	3.7 ± 0.3

Table 3
FOREARM BLOOD FLOW (mℓ/min/100 mℓ TISSUE) OF MEN FROM DIFFERENT ETHNIC GROUPS

	Test A				Test B			
Subject's ethnic origin	n	Summer	n	Winter	n	Summer	n	Winter
Ashkenazim								
From Jerusalem	18	2.71 ± 0.2	18	2.87 ± 0.2	18	2.68 ± 0.2	18	3.02 ± 0.2
From Negev	46	2.66 ± 0.1	39	3.05 ± 0.2	46	2.77 ± 0.1	39	3.11 ± 0.2
Yemenites from Negev	42	3.53 ± 0.2	42	3.96 ± 0.2	42	3.72 ± 0.2	42	4.08 ± 0.2
Bedouins	20	3.15 ± 0.2	21	3.52 ± 0.3	20	3.12 ± 0.2	21	3.59 ± 0.3
From Bethlehem								
From Negev	—	—	10	4.09 ± 0.5	—	—	10	3.85 ± 0.4
From Sinai	40	3.73 ± 0.2	—	—	40	3.72 ± 0.2	—	—

in Yemenites, Kurds, and Bedouins and a lower one in Ashkenazim. In all examinees a seasonally determined change of resting metabolism occurred, the summer level being lower than the winter one.

The effect of environment on man's metabolism is an intricate physiological problem, whose solution has been tried in many studies. However, controversial conclusions can be

Table 4
THE EFFECT OF HEAT ACCLIMATION ON FOREARM BLOOD FLOW (mℓ/min/100 mℓ TISSUE)

Work load during acclimation	n	Test A		Test B	
		Before	After	Before	After
Light	10	4.14 ± 0.3	3.91 ± 0.4	4.23 ± 0.4	3.67 ± 0.5
Heavy	7	3.73 ± 0.3	2.27 ± 0.2	3.95 ± 0.3	2.24 ± 0.2

drawn out of the accumulated publications regarding the influence of environmental heat on the metabolism of inhabitants of hot areas.[5-11] In desert animals, low metabolism appears to be a property of adaptation to arid, hot ambient conditions and this feature is genetically transferred.[12] In humans, uncertainties still exist regarding the question as to the extent to which changes in energy metabolism are climatically or genetically determined. The lack of unanimous view can be related to the variability of experimental conditions at which the studies were performed, leading to different states of thermal equilibrium of the examinee at the time of testing. When heat balance in the human body becomes positive, resting metabolism increases and according to the Van't Hoff coefficient, the metabolic rate rises by about 13% for each degree centigrade above normal body temperature.[13] Thus, changes in body heat balance due to variability of outdoor climate during testing would affect the results and conclusions drawn from comparative studies. The experiments described in this study were standardized to a temperate ambient condition so that the influence of external heat or cold on body temperature has been prevented. Furthermore, all subjects were tested by the same examiners and with similar techniques. The subjects of each ethnic group came from closed communities and had similar demographic and genetic backgrounds. Their socioeconomic conditions were almost similar, with minimal variabilities in the state of health, nutrition, occupational activities, etc. Surprisingly, our results did not support the view of animal physiologists, that long-term exposure to hot environment induces an inherited lowering of metabolic rate. The results of this study revealed a lower resting metabolism in the Ashkenazim and not in the natural inhabitants of the desert, the Bedouins, who shared their metabolic level with the Kurds and Yemenites. It seems that in man, long-term exposure to hot climate does not affect the genetic markers of metabolic rate.

A seasonal variation in resting metabolism, however, was disclosed in all subjects, irrespective of their ethnic origin. It could be assumed that the low metabolic rate during the summer as compared to the winter is part of the state of natural acclimatization to seasonal climate. Exposure to summer heat lowers the endogenously produced metabolic heat, thus increasing heat capacity of the body and facilitating thermoregulation.

No seasonal changes in resting heart rate were observed in this study. This contradicts the general view that a straight relationship exists between cardiac activity and metabolic rate. However, in a separate study on Yemenites and Kurds, when long-term integrated heart rates were examined the values accumulated during the nights in summer were found to be lower than the integrated heart rates of the winter nights.[14]

The study of the peripheral circulation revealed a difference between the long-term (for generation) and seasonal effect of heat on the blood flow of the forearms of subjects from various ethnic origins. It has been demonstrated in the past that when people are exposed to heat in climatic chambers their forearm blood flow increases and the magnitude of this change diminishes progressively when the exposures are repeated on successive days.[15] Only a few observations exist in the literature regarding peripheral circulation of indigenous inhabitants of hot areas. Whittow[16] has tested Asian subjects living in Singapore and his estimated rate of their forearm blood flow (2.70 mℓ/min/100 mℓ tissue) at about 28°C ambient temperature was of the same order as that reported for people in the U.K. and the U.S. (2.6 to 3.1 mℓ/min/100 mℓ tissue) examined at 18.5 to 20°C ambient temperature.

The data presented in this study indicate that indigenous people of hot areas have higher forearm blood flow than subjects originating from temperate countries, both subject groups tested at 24°C. Furthermore, subjects of similar ethnic origin, living in climatically different locations, do not exhibit differences in peripheral circulation. It seems that the level of forearm blood flow is an inherited physiological characteristic facilitating adaptation to the environment; however, seasonal changes in peripheral circulation do occur in the process of natural acclimatization to summer heat. The fall in summer forearm blood flow when tested at comfortable conditions is an acquired phenomenon induced by the circulatory stress during acclimatization.

Considering both studies together, the seasonally related changes show a similar trend. Both resting metabolism and forearm blood flow were lower during the summer than in winter. It is suggested that this finding obtained at 24°C reveals a widening of the range at which both parameters can change at exposure to a hot environment.

REFERENCES

1. **Hammel, H. T.,** Terrestrial animals in cold; recent studies of primitive man, *Handbook of Physiology — Adaptation to the Environment,* Sect. 4, Am. Physiol. Soc., Bethesda, Md., 1964, 413.
2. **Edholm, O. G. and Samueloff, S.,** Biological studies of Yemenite and Kurdish Jews in Israel — introduction, background and methods, *Phil. Trans. R. Soc. London Ser. B,* 266, 97, 1973.
3. **Godber, M. J., Kopec, A. C., Mourant, A. E., Tills, D., and Lehman, E. E.,** The hereditary blood factors of the Yemenite and Kurdish Jews, *Phil. Trans. R. Soc. London,* 266, 169, 1973.
4. **Consolazio, C. F., Johnson, R. E., and Pecora, L. J.,** *Physiological Measurements of Metabolic Functions in Man,* Sect. 1, McGraw-Hill, New York, 1963.
5. **Steggerda, M. and Benedict, F. G.,** Metabolism in Yucatan: a study of the Maya Indians, *Am. J. Physiol.,* 100, 274, 1932.
6. **Quenouille, M. H., Boyne, A. W., Fisher, W. B., and Leitch, J.,** Statistical Studies of Recorded Energy Expenditure of Man, Commonwealth Bureau of Animal Nutrition, Rowett Institute, Aberdeen, Scotland, 1951.
7. **Osiba, S.,** The seasonal variation of basal metabolism and activity of thyroid gland in man, *Jpn. J. Physiol.,* 7, 355, 1957.
8. **Banerjec, S. and Sen, R.,** Body composition of Indians and its relation to basal metabolic rate, *J. Appl. Physiol.,* 12, 29, 1958.
9. **Malhotra, M. S., Ramaswamy, S. S., and Ray, S. N.,** Effect of environmental temperature on work and resting metabolism, *J. Appl. Physiol.,* 15, 769, 1960.
10. **Yoshimura, M., Yukiyoshi, K., Yoshioka, T., and Takeda, H.,** Climatic adaptation of basal metabolism, *Fed. Proc.,* 25, 1169, 1966.
11. **Gold, A. J., Zornitzer, A., and Samueloff, S.,** Influence of season and heat on energy expenditure during rest and exercise, *J. Appl. Physiol.,* 27, 9, 1969.
12. **Ben-Porat, J., Adler, J. H., and Samueloff, S.,** On thermoregulation in *Psammomys obesus, Meriones crassus* and *Meriones tristrami, Isr. J. Med. Sci.,* 12, 897, 1976.
13. **Du Bois, E. F.,** *Basal Metabolism in Health and Disease,* 3rd ed., Lea & Febiger, Philadelphia, 1936.
14. **Edholm, O. G., Humphrey, S., Lourie, J. A., Tredre, B. E., and Brotherhood, J.,** Energy expenditure and climatic exposure of Yemenite and Kurdish Jews in Israel, *Phil. Trans. R. Soc. London Ser. B,* 266, 127, 1973.
15. **Wyndham, C. H.,** Effect of acclimatization on circulatory response to high environmental temperatures, *J. Appl. Physiol.,* 4, 383, 1951.
16. **Whittow, G. C.,** Flow of blood in the forearm of persons acclimatized to heat, *Nature (London),* 192, 759, 1961.

Chapter 5

METABOLIC CONSEQUENCE OF EXERCISE IN THE COLD

Roy J. Shephard

TABLE OF CONTENTS

I. Introduction 36

II. The Problem of Thermal Homeostasis 36

III. Voluntary Exercise 36

IV. Shivering and Exercise 36

V. Nonshivering Thermogenesis 37

VI. Tactics of Acclimatization 38

VII. Fat Loss with Exercise in Cold 39

VIII. Cold Therapy for Obesity 40

IX. Interactions Between Physical Condition and Cold Exposure 40

X. Conclusions 41

Acknowledgment 41

References 41

I. INTRODUCTION

Other contributors to this symposium have described the elegant physiological adaptations to extremes of climate that have evolved in various species colonizing the desert habitat. This chapter considers human responses to extreme cold, with particular reference to Canada, where the tactics adopted by the indigenous Inuit may be contrasted with the responses of more recent migrants who have had little opportunity to make genetic adaptations to cold.

II. THE PROBLEM OF THERMAL HOMEOSTASIS

Urban Canadians who dash from their heated cars to air-conditioned homes and shopping plazas seem largely hostages of their homeothermic condition. Hypothermic deaths are well-recognized even in large cities. Partly because of a slowing of all metabolic reactions, and partly because of a shift in the CO_2 dissociation curve, brain function begins to deteriorate at core temperatures below 35°C. Below 34°C, the shivering mechanism also fails, leading to a rapid and dangerous cooling of the body. Vasoconstriction also fails at 32°C, nerve block occurs at 10°C, and the tissues begin to freeze at −1°C.[24]

What quantity of heat can be safely lost by the body? Given a mass of 70 kg and a specific heat of 3.48 kJ/kg, the maximum safe loss is 70 × 2 × 3.48 kJ, or just under 500 kJ. Under severe winter conditions (still air at −40°C, but a much higher environmental temperature with a stiff wind or vigorous body movement) a person wearing standard sweat-free arctic clothing (insulation 4 CLO units) loses at least 2 kJ of heat per minute. Unless there is some form of compensation, this environment can thus be tolerated for only about 4 hr. The simplest tactic to restore homeostasis is "morphological" — to put on more clothes — but if this is not possible, an alternative is to increase metabolic activity. Options include (1) voluntary activity, (2) shivering, and (3) nonshivering thermogenesis.

III. VOLUNTARY EXERCISE

Deliberate exercise is superficially attractive as a method of keeping warm. A sedentary young man has a maximum energy expenditure of perhaps 60 kJ/min. However, it is difficult to sustain more than one third of the maximum energy expenditure during endurance activities. In documented incidents of hypothermia such as the disastrous "Four Inns" walk of 1964,[21] loss of insulation increased the heat needs of the body, while the energy output of the walkers dropped below the critical level needed for homeostasis because of a lack of fitness, hunger, or injury. Exercise may in itself lead to a dramatic increase of heat loss, partly because of changes in tissue insulation (see Chapter 7). Other factors in an active individual are (1) increased ventilation and thus respiratory heat loss, (2) increased air or water movement over the body surface, and (3) a pumping of air beneath protective clothing.[24] Figure 1 illustrates the energy expenditure needed for thermal equilibrium, using various clothing assemblies at various environmental temperatures. The "Four Inns" walkers had only about 1 CLO of insulation, due to wetting of their clothing, and they thus needed an energy expenditure of about 30 kJ/min even at 0°C. A well-equipped Canadian, with insulation of 4 CLO, would also need to generate 15 kJ/min rather than 2 kJ/min in order to reach equilibrium at −40°C.

IV. SHIVERING AND EXERCISE

Shivering is the main recourse of the person who cannot exercise vigorously enough to keep warm. Studies by Pugh[21] for a man cycling against a cold, wet wind, and Nadel et al.[17] for a person swimming in cold water have both demonstrated that when power output

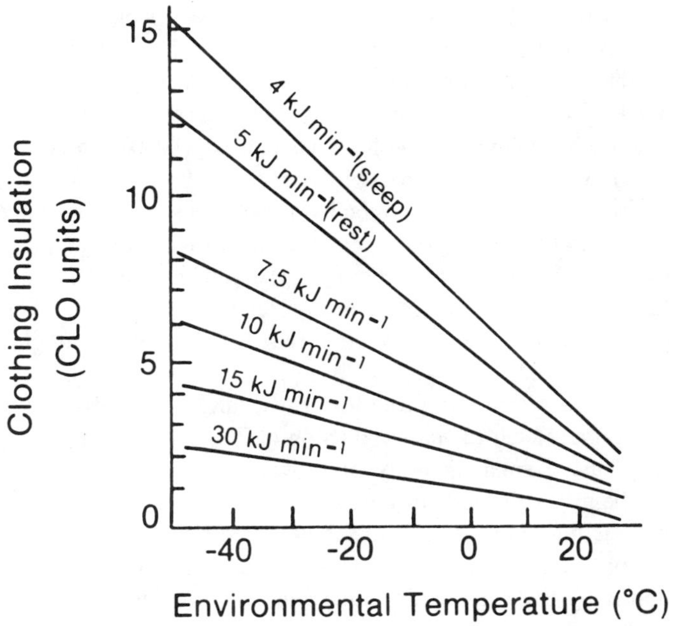

FIGURE 1. Energy expenditures needed to sustain thermal equilibrium in still air when wearing various clothing assemblies at specified environmental temperatures. (From Burton & Edholm, 1969, from the author's book *Physiology and Biochemistry of Exercise*, Praeger, New York, 1982. With permission.)

is insufficient to sustain body temperature, the oxygen cost of any given task is boosted by an increase of muscle tone plus bursts of shivering. The peak effect in humans is probably a fivefold rise of resting energy expenditure, providing up to 21 kJ/min of body heating.

Shivering is a useful expedient in an emergency, but it makes any coordinated motor task difficult to perform. A climber may slip and sustain an injury, while a swimmer may inhale water because of difficulty in coordinating arm and breathing movements. Glycogen reserves are also depleted, hastening the onset of fatigue and hypothermial confusion, and causing an associated water loss. If cold exposure is continued, both glycogen and water reserves are replenished over the next 2 to 3 days.

Cold acclimatization is associated with a downward shift of the shivering threshold, i.e., a person becomes colder before shivering begins. Subjective feelings of coldness and discomfort are reduced, and in any given environment the core temperature is allowed to drop to a lower level. The process seems to be an example of negative conditioning of habituation, coordinated by the pre-frontal cortex;[4] the response disappears after pre-frontal leucotomy.[5]

The course of acclimatization is normally quite rapid (half-time 2 to 3 days), and adjustments continue even if subjects are exposed to a warm environment for a part of the day.[6] Studies of Labrador fishermen who have spent several months living under temperate conditions show a persistence of their habituation to cold.[15] Moreover, acclimatization develops more rapidly with second or third exposure to cold conditions.[4]

V. NONSHIVERING THERMOGENESIS

The third possible homeostatic tactic is nonshivering thermogenesis. LeBlanc[13] has questioned its existence in adults. He has argued that if the intensity of shivering is plotted against energy consumption, the intercept corresponding to zero shivering does not differ significantly from the basal rate of energy expenditure.

One major point of discussion in this controversy has been the presence of brown fat in the human adult. Substantial amounts of brown fat are found in small mammals, possibly because they face thermal problems from a large surface to mass ratio. Newborn children also carry 50 to 100 g of brown fat, and at this stage in life up to 95% of the thermal response to moderate cold is due to nonshivering thermogenesis.[9] In adults, brown fat is much less obvious. However, there is some evidence for its persistence and for its hypertrophy with outdoor exercise in winter.[10] Thermography has shown some intriguing "hot patches" between the scapulae immediately following injections of catecholamines or acute cold exposure. Rothwell and Stock[23] suggested that these patches were regions of brown fat, activated by cold exposure; however, needle biopsies of the "hot" regions did not demonstrate any brown fat,[1] and it was thus proposed that the patches might be a vascular reaction to adrenaline or cold.

This does not completely rule out a role for brown fat. The metabolic activity of brown adipose tissue is extremely high (a heat production of 70 J/g/min, compared with 3 J/g/min in active muscle. Thus, a small quantity of brown fat could contribute significantly to metabolism, while being overlooked in biopsies of 10 to 20 kg of normal adipose tissue. Brown fat may also help to mobilize and metabolize free fatty acids from white fat depots.

Current explanations of the extraordinary heat production in brown fat include a loosening of metabolic coupling by free fatty acids which penetrate mitochondrial membranes, membrane depolarization by noradrenaline, with increased energy usage by the sodium pump, a proton leak dependent on a 32 kdalton protein, and secretion of some unidentified hormone that stimulates metabolism in other tissues.[18]

Other possible sources of heat, stimulated by the secretion of noradrenaline, include a "futile" cycle of breakdown and resynthesis of neutral fat, together with the formation of cyclic AMP (cAMP) and the reformation of ATP. Energy is also spent in mobilization of glycogen and protein in muscle and liver, and in the repolarization of the muscle membrane after shivering. Finally, noradrenaline may alter the sensitivity of the muscle spindle receptors. The intent is to "fine tune" the shivering mechanism, but there are also major implications for both the energy cost and the performance of skilled physical activity.[7,25]

VI. TACTICS OF ACCLIMATIZATION

Human acclimatization to cold favors a hypothermic, insulative response, rather than a humorally mediated hypertrophy of brown fat with increased thermogenesis. This may reflect differences in the pattern of cold exposure between humans and small mammals.[14] The Canadian who rushes from a car to a heated shopping mall encounters brief bouts of severe cold, whereas animal experiments have examined responses to prolonged but more moderate cold. In the human situation, the hypothermic responses have some adaptive value, sparing glycogen reserves for external work, although it also has an adverse effect upon manual dexterity.

The cross-channel swimmer, the hillwalker, and the pearl diver who works a full union shift encounter more continuous cold, and there is now mounting evidence that in such situations there is an increase of metabolism that cannot be explained entirely by shivering.[8,11,12] Interestingly, the adaptations have disappeared in those divers who have made the morphological adaptation of buying themselves wet diving suits!

By analogy with animal experiments, humoral features of the response to continuous cold include a transitory secretion of adrenaline and cortisol, a more long-lasting increase of noradrenaline output, and an increased sensitivity to noradrenaline. In rats, cold resistance can also be increased by injections of noradrenaline, although the entire picture of cold acclimatization cannot be reproduced by this tactic.

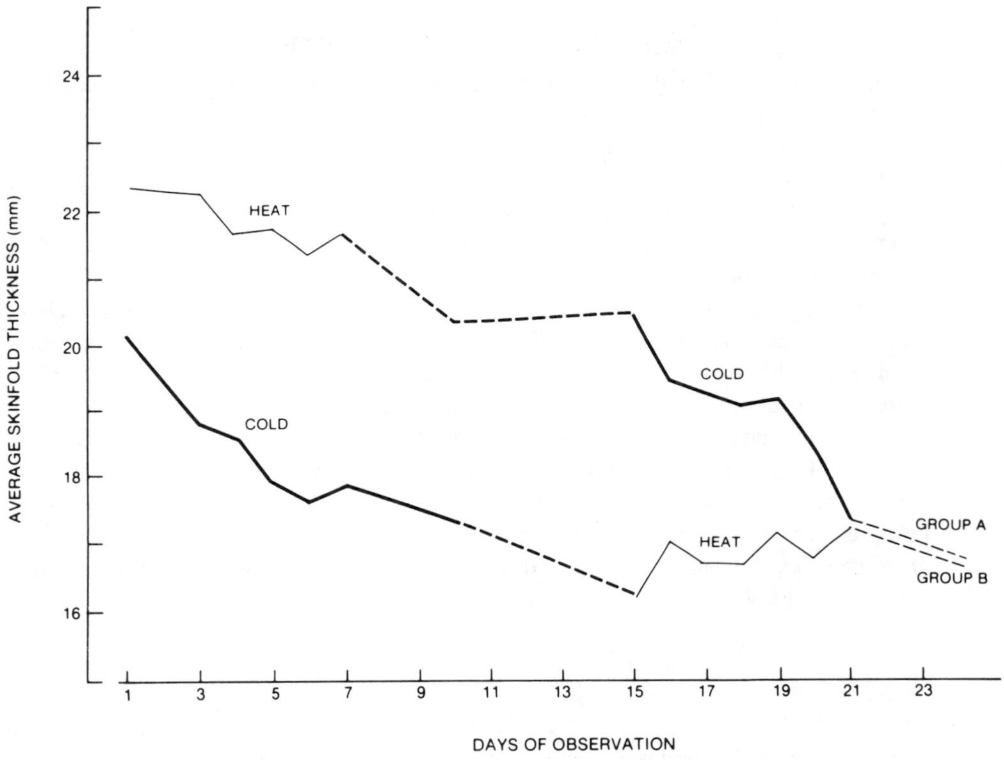

FIGURE 2. Cross-over trial illustrating the specificity of fat loss in the cold. Note that skinfold thicknesses decrease when exercise is performed in the cold environment, but not when the same exercise is performed under temperate conditions. (From O'Hara, W. J., et al., *J. Appl. Physiol. Resp. Environ. Exercise Physiol.*, 46, 872, 1979. With permission.)

VII. FAT LOSS WITH EXERCISE IN THE COLD

Our interest in fat metabolism was stimulated by the empirical observations that Canadian troops engaged in arctic field trips showed a substantial loss of subcutaneous fat over 1 to 2 weeks.[19] Interestingly, a thinner British contingent with less experience of Canadian climates did not show this response. Fat loss was greatest in the suprailiac, and least in the abdominal and triceps folds. There was also some decrease of body mass, this showing an oscillation in association with dehydration and rehydration.

Daytime temperatures encountered by the troops averaged −30°C, with a windspeed of 16 km/hr, while the overnight bivouac was a little below freezing. The apparent rigor of this environment was tempered by heavy arctic clothing (insulation 4 CLO units). Moderately strenuous physical work (energy cost 13 to 16 mJ/day) was balanced by standard arctic survival rations (15.2 mJ/day). Body mass declined by 1 kg, but skinfolds decreased by 38% over the 2 weeks, implying a 3.9 kg loss of body fat and some synthesis of lean tissue. Marked proteinuria and ketonuria were also observed. In essence, it seemed that exercise was potentiating a thermogenic reaction to cold.

Repetition of our experiments in a climatic chamber showed essentially similar findings, both in young men and in middle-aged, obese subjects. The specific nature of the cold stimulus was further confirmed by a cross-over trial (Figure 2). This demonstrated that skinfold readings declined in the cold, but not when the same amount of exercise was performed under temperate conditions.[20] The prime stimulus to fat mobilization seemed a local cooling of the skin surface, since there was a significant correlation between fat loss and the decrease of skin temperature.

Among possible factors contributing to the fat loss:

1. A small energy deficit (0.4 to 0.6 mJ/day in some trials); at most this would have caused a fat loss of 0.2 to 0.4 kg over 2 weeks.
2. The energy cost of synthesizing 2 to 3 kg of new lean tissue; assuming that this was mostly protein, with a water content of 74% and a 50% efficiency of synthesis, the energy cost (30 mJ) would have been equivalent to about 1 kg of fat.
3. Energy loss in ketosis; we saw a urinary excretion of only 1 to 2 g of ketone per day, but there may also have been some accumulation of ketones in blood, tissue water, and fat. An upper limit to energy losses from ketone shunting is set by a diabetic patient (ketone excretion of up to 200 g/day); this normally leads to a ketonic coma, but if it could be sustained for 2 weeks, it could account for a fat loss of about 2 kg.
4 Increased metabolism while sleeping; nocturnal restlessness and various futile cycles may have increased energy expenditures by 10% relative to the assumed resting metabolism. This would have burned 0.20 to 0.25 kg of fat over 2 weeks.
5. Cold dehydration may have caused the body muscles to contract less efficiently; however, in the climatic chamber experiments, the metabolic cost of the various exercise tasks was measured and did not differ materially from that observed under warm conditions.

VIII. COLD THERAPY FOR OBESITY

How practical is cold stress as a therapy for obesity? Potential clinical hazards include a worsening of systemic hypertension, angina, bronchospasm, and pulmonary hypertension. Moreover, some preliminary experiments[26] suggest that female subjects respond less readily than males. After 5 days of exercise in the cold chamber, our female subjects showed a slight reduction of subcutaneous fat, a decrease of respiratory quotient, and a rise of blood and urinary ketone levels, but no changes in hydrostatic estimates of body fat.

How can we explain the differing response of the women? They were relatively more fit than many of our previous subjects, and were not particularly obese. Moreover, the male subjects in the earlier experiments had been allowed to drink coffee with their meals. Finally, the observations on the women were limited to 5 days; this may have been long enough to cause some translocation of fat from white to brown tissue, reducing skinfolds but leaving total body fat relatively unchanged. If this hypothesis is correct, a longer experiment might reveal a similar fat loss to that seen in the men. However, it is also possible that the female has a greater preference for the hypothermic tactic, partly because this is made practicable by the greater body fat, and partly because there is adaptive advantage in conserving energy stores for pregnancy and lactation.

IX. INTERACTIONS BETWEEN PHYSICAL CONDITION AND COLD EXPOSURE

The impact of physical conditioning upon metabolic responses to cold remains a matter of debate.[2,14,16] In brief, there have been reports of cross-adaptation between cold and fitness. Some authors have observed an increase and others a decrease of heat production when cold exposure has been repeated after training, while some authors have merely found a decrease of interindividual variability.

There is likewise remarkably little information on how cold exposure affects physical fitness. Acute cold exposure increases the tone of the peripheral veins, and (by an increase of central blood volume) increases physical working capacity.[3] Because chronic cold exposure stimulates vigorous activity and fat loss, some improvement of aerobic power might be anticipated, but in practice, cold weather has its main impact on fitness through the added energy cost of walking over rough snow and ice.[22]

X. CONCLUSIONS

Humans have only a limited potential to increase body temperature by either voluntary exercise or shivering. The main recourse in a cold climate is thus applied morphology — the choosing of clothing appropriate to the activity that must be undertaken. Nevertheless, repeated cold exposure leads to some acclimatization over the course of about 10 days. The main change is a decrease of discomfort, with a lowering of the shivering threshold; however, sustained exposure to moderate cold may also induce nonshivering thermogenesis. The associated mobilization of body fat suggests a potential to exploit this phenomenon in the treatment of obesity, but more information is still needed on the optimal environmental conditions for stimulating this process. Moreover, possible gender-related differences in the cold response must be clarified.

ACKNOWLEDGMENT

Our investigations of fat loss in the cold have been supported in part by research grants from the Defence and Civil Institute of Environmental Medicine, Toronto.

REFERENCES

1. **Åstrup, A., Bulow, J., Christensen, N. J., and Madsen, J.,** Ephedrine-induced thermogenesis in man: no role for interscapular brown adipose tissue, *Clin. Sci.*, 66, 179, 1984.
2. **Bruck, K.,** Cold adaptation in man, in *Regulation of Depressed Metabolism and Thermogenesis,* Jansky, L. and Musacchia, X. J., Eds., Charles C Thomas, Springfield, Ill., 1976, 42.
3. **Bryan, C.,** Commentary. Proceedings of International Symposium on Physical Activity and Cardiovascular Health, *Can. Med. Assoc. J.*, 96, 804, 1967.
4. **Glaser, E. M.,** *The Physiological Basis of Habituation,* Oxford University Press, London, 1966, 1.
5. **Glaser, E. M. and Griffin, J. P.,** Influence of the cerebral cortex on habituation, *J. Physiol. (London),* 160, 429, 1962.
6. **Glaser, E. M. and Shephard, R. J.,** Simultaneous experimental acclimatization to heat and cold in man, *J. Physiol. (London),* 169, 592, 1963.
7. **Goodenough, R. D., Royle, G. T., Nadel, E. R., Wolfe, M. H., and Wolfe, R. R.,** Leucine and urea metabolism in acute human cold exposure, *J. Appl. Physiol. Resp. Environ. Exercise Physiol.*, 53, 367, 1982.
8. **Hong, S. K.,** Pattern of cold adaption in women divers of Korea (ama), *Fed. Proc.*, 32, 1614, 1973.
9. **Hull, D. and Smales, O. R. C.,** Heat production in the newborn, in *Temperature Regulation and Energy Metabolism in the Newborn,* Sinclair, J. C., Ed., Grune & Stratton, New York, 1978, 129.
10. **Huttunen, P., Hirvonen, J., and Kinnula, V.,** The occurrence of brown adipose tissue in outdoor workers, *Eur. J. Appl. Physiol.*, 46, 339, 1981.
11. **Itoh, S.,** *Physiology of Cold-Adapted Man,* Hokkaido University School of Medicine, Sapporo, 1974.
12. **Jessen, K.,** An assessment of human regulatory thermogenesis, *Acta Anaesth. Scand.*, 24, 138, 1980.
13. **LeBlanc, J.,** *Man in the Cold,* Charles C Thomas, Springfield, Ill., 1975.
14. **LeBlanc, J.,** Adaptation of man to cold, in *Strategies in Cold,* Wang, L. C. H. and Hudson, J. W., Eds., Academic Press, New York, 1978, 695.
15. **LeBlanc, J. and Pouliot, M.,** Importance of noradrenaline in cold adaptation, *Am. J. Physiol.*, 207, 853, 1964.
16. **Moriyama, K.,** Cross-adaptation mechanisms between exercise training and cold adaptation; assessment of free fatty acids metabolism in norepinephrine induced heat production and finger temperature responses to local cooling, in *Proceedings of 6th International Symposium on Circumpolar Health,* Fortuine, R., Ed., University of Washington Press, Seattle, 1985.

17. **Nadel, E. F., Holmer, I., Bergh, U., Åstrand, P. O., and Stolwijk, J. A. J.,** Energy exchanges of swimming man, *J. Appl. Physiol.*, 36, 465, 1974.
18. **Nicholls, D. G. and Locke, R. M.,** Thermogenic mechanisms in brown fat, *Physiol. Rev.*, 64, 1, 1984.
19. **O'Hara, W. and Allen, C.,** Changes in Body Composition During an Arctic Winter Exercise, Rep. 74-R-1061, Defence and Civil Institute of Environmental Medicine, Toronto, 1974.
20. **O'Hara, W. J., Allen, C., Shephard, R. J., and Allen, G.,** Fat losses in the cold — a controlled study, *J. Appl. Physiol. Resp. Environ. Exercise Physiol.*, 46, 872, 1979.
21. **Pugh, L. G. C. E.,** Accidental hypothermia among hill-walkers and climbers in Britain, in *Environmental Effects on Work Performance*, Cumming, G. R., Snidal, D., and Taylor, A. W., Eds., Canadian Association of Sports Sciences, Ottawa, 1972.
22. **Rode, A. and Shephard, R. J.,** Cardiorespiratory fitness of an Inuit community, *J. Appl. Physiol.*, 31, 519, 1971.
23. **Rothwell, N. J. and Stock, M. J.,** A role for brown adipose tissue in diet-induced thermogenesis, *Nature (London)*, 281, 31, 1979.
24. **Shephard, R. J.,** *Physiology and Biochemistry of Exercise*, Praeger Press, New York, 1982.
25. **Webster, A. J. F.,** Physiological effects of cold exposure, in *Environmental Physiology*, Robertshaw, D., Ed., University Park Press, Baltimore, 1974.
26. **Murray, B., et al.,** in preparation.

Chapter 6

SHALLOW WATER AND ASCENT BLACKOUT DURING BREATH-HOLD DIVING

H. Rahn, A. Olszowka, and C. Lundgren

TABLE OF CONTENTS

I. Introduction 44

II. Shallow Water Dives 44

III. Deep Dives 45

IV. 100 m Dives and Ascent Blackout 45

V. Summary 49

References 49

I. INTRODUCTION

The margin between normal performance and unconsciousness during breath-hold diving can be a matter of seconds. There are no prior warnings to the diver, and this accounts for the many reported drowning accidents among sports divers, most often the top performers among their peers. On the other hand, when one observes the Ama of Japan and Korea during their daily working dives there is no hint of diving hazard as they routinely descend to 5 to 7 m, or the assisted Ama to 20 m, and repeat dive after dive like clockwork for 1 to 2 hr. There are about 30,000 women and men in this food harvesting profession with traditions that can be traced back for nearly 2000 years.[1-3] Drowning accidents rarely occur. These divers do not compete in the same sense as sports divers trying for underwater distance or time records,[4] spear fishers for larger trophies,[22] or Tuamotu pearl divers when they discover a new pearl shell bed.[5] Under these competitive conditions accident rates are high and can be related to gradual hypoxia leading to shallow-water blackout, or acute hypoxia during ascent blackout when returning from depths below 20 m. Table 1 provides an overview of various types of breath-hold dives, which are discussed below.

II. SHALLOW WATER DIVES

Craig[4] followed up 58 reported cases of loss of consciousness during breath-hold diving, usually occurring in swimming pools where young people (average age 18 years) had competed for distance records. Those that survived (35 cases) reported that they had "learned the value of hyperventilation in extending distance or time under water and had hyperventilated before the accident". As Craig[6] pointed out, hyperventilation before breath-holding delays the onset of the urge to breathe. Before the CO_2 tension increases enough to initiate the "breaking point" the O_2 tension fell sufficiently to produce unconsciousness. There are no signs of warning similar to those experienced for a few seconds when loss of consciousness is induced by acute hypotension.

It is of interest to examine the changes in alveolar O_2 and CO_2 tension during breath-holding on the O_2-CO_2 diagram as originally presented by Craig[7] and Craig and Harley.[8] Figure 1 represents a simplified interpretation of his diagram. Based on a large number of different types of performance tests under various degrees of hypoxia[9] and hypocapnia[10] one can describe an area of useful performance shown in the center of the diagram bordered by regions of hypocapnia, hypoxia, and hypercarbia where performance becomes severely impaired. The arrow at the right shows the changes in alveolar composition with apnea after hyperventilation on pure oxygen, starting with a PCO_2 of 20 torr and breaking at a PCO_2 of approximately 60 torr.[11] In this case the high CO_2 tension is primarily responsible for the breaking point. The left shows the apneic alveolar pathway after hyperventilation on air, where the breaking point stimulus is largely due to hypoxia. After a full inspiration of air, both low O_2 and high CO_2 contribute to the breaking point.

Figure 2 shows the levels of CO_2 stores in the tissues and blood and how they are affected by various degrees of hyperventilation (modeled after Farhi and Rahn[12,13]). The faucet on the right depicts the metabolic CO_2 production which is added to the blood-tissue stores, but in the resting state is balanced by an equal CO_2 loss from the lung (the steady-state). The normal resting alveolar Co_2 level is pictured at 40 torr and an RQ of 0.8 as well as the apneic alveolar pathway ending at the breaking point. One can now postulate that in prolonged hyperventilation prior to apnea the CO_2 stores are reduced to such a low level that during the breath-hold dive they are not sufficiently replenished to raise the alveolar-arterial PCO_2 level above 40 torr. Under these circumstances the breaking point depends only on low PO_2, which is not a stimulus sufficient to force the diver to terminate the dive, and eventually unconsciousness ensues. It is this interpretation that one can describe as one type of "shallow water blackout" occurring during breath-hold diving.

Table 1
TYPES OF BREATH-HOLD DIVES

Type	Depth (m)	Objective	Location	Ref.
Shallow	1—2	Distance record	Swimming pools	4
Intermediate	5—20	Food	Korea, Japan	1
	5—15	Spear fishing	South Africa	22
Deep	30—40	Pearl shells	Tuamotu Archipelago	5
	105	Depth record	Mediterranean Sea	16

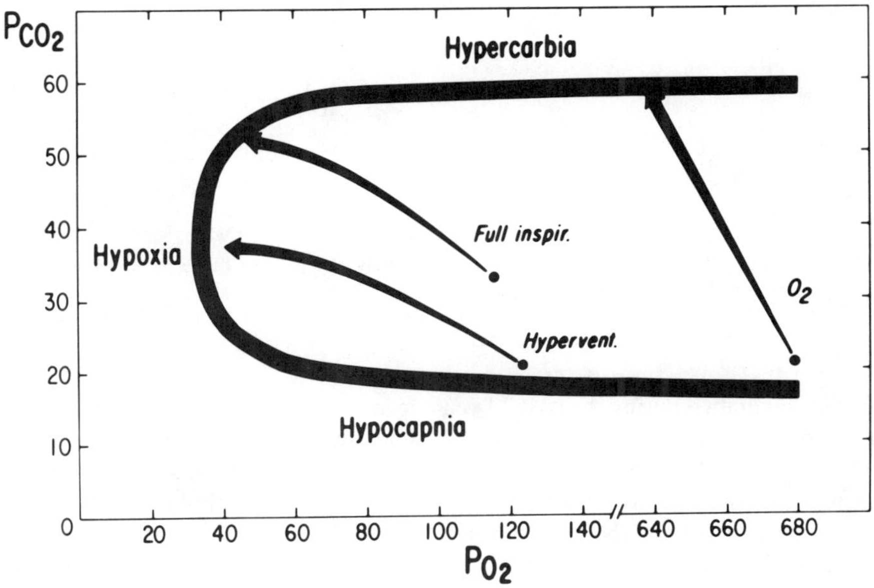

FIGURE 1. The O_2-CO_2 diagram depicting the range of normal performance inside the heavy line.[9,10] The arrows indicate apneic alveolar pathways leading to the breaking point after a full inspiration of air, hyperventilation on air, and hyperventilation on O_2.[7]

III. DEEP DIVES

Among the spear fishing breath-hold groups in South Africa there is much competition in quest of special trophies. Landsberg[22] reports 13 deaths since 1968, usually among the best divers. An unusual situation is described by Cross[5] during the pearling season in the Tuamotu Archipelago when several hundred Polynesians dive in a lagoon to depths of 30 to 40 m. He reported that during a single day, among 235 divers, 47 experienced problems; most of them (34 cases) suffered vertigo, nausea, and mental anguish, 6 experienced partial paralysis; 3, temporary unconsciousness, 2 became mentally affected, and 2 died. The paralysis usually recedes in days or weeks, suggesting spinal hits by bubbles released during decompression, while cases of vertigo and nausea suggest severe acute exposure to hypoxia. That decompression sickness can occur after repeated dives to 15 to 20 m was described by Paulev.[14] The occurrence of acute exposure to severe hypoxia during ascent from 30 to 40 m is discussed later.

IV. 100 m DIVES AND ASCENT BLACKOUT

Records for maximal depth reached during a breath-hold dive competition in the Medi-

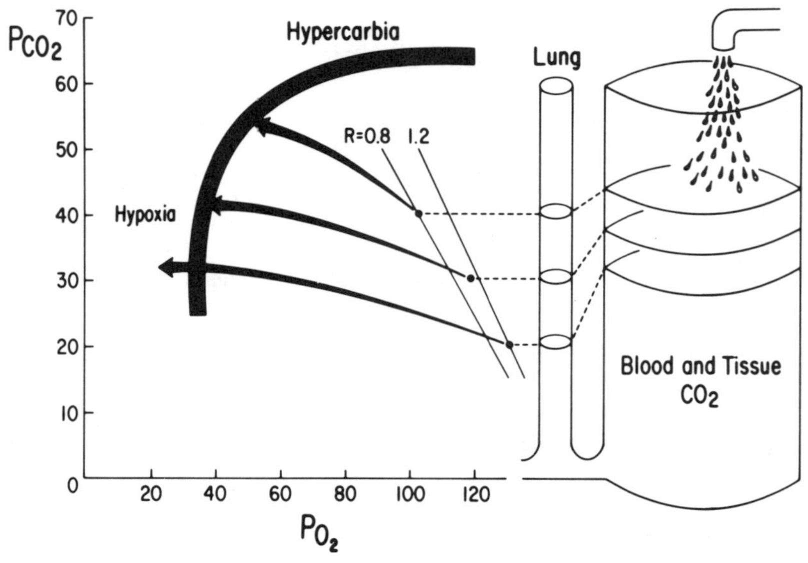

FIGURE 2. The O_2-CO_2 diagram showing apneic alveolar pathways after breathing air at rest and after hyperventilation. (Right) Blood and tissue stores modeled after Farhi and Rahn.[8,9] Flow from the faucet emptying into the reservoir represents the metabolic CO_2 production. For details see text.

terranean have climbed during the past 30 years from 35 to 105 m,[15,16] although a seemingly reliable report of an 83 m depth was reached by a Greek sponge diver as early as 1913.[17] To explore the alveolar gas concentrations during such a dive a computer model was developed which allows one to simulate the consequences of breath-holding on the O_2, CO_2, and N_2 changes occurring in the lung, the arterial and mixed venous blood, and the tissues.[16] Figure 3 describes the O_2 tensions of the alveolar gas during a 100 m dive based on the lung volume and diving time of Maiorca[23] who in a 1984 dive reached a depth of 94 m. Three curves are shown, assuming a continuous oxygen consumption of 240, 300, and 360 mℓ/min. These values can be compared with those reported by Hong et al.[18] for nine subjects holding their breaths at 1 ATA for 4 min after a full inspiration but without prior hyperventilation. Their oxygen consumption averaged 247 mℓ/min. Every 30 sec they expired into a small bag to obtain an alveolar gas sample and then reinspired, which probably accounted for their long apnea.

Returning to the simulated descent at a rate of 0.91 m/sec the 100 m depth (11 atmospheres absolute, ATA) was reached in 110 sec, with alveolar PO_2 exceeding 1 ATA. Upon ascent the O_2 falls rapidly due to recompression of lung gases and during the last seconds falls below the values of the 1 ATA breath-hold curve.

Figure 4 examines in more detail the last 60 sec of ascent based upon the model described by Olszowka and Rahn.[16] In this case the alveolar PO_2 falls from 95 torr at 160 sec to 25 torr at the end of the dive. Also shown is the mixed venous blood PO_2 which falls from 57 torr at 160 sec to 40 torr at the end of the dive. The unusually high mixed venous PO_2 at 160 sec is due to the high alveolar-arterial O_2 throughout most of the dive, transferring O_2 stores from the lung to the blood.[16] At 173 sec the alveolar PO_2 is 55 torr and equal to the mixed venous blood PO_2, the crossover point marked by the arrow, and the ambient pressure is near 5 ATA as shown on the top abscissa. If no further O_2 were removed from the lung beyond this point, the alveolar PO_2 of 55 torr would fall to 11 torr since the lung volume expands fivefold by the time the surface is reached. The hypothetical course of the alveolar O_2 in such a case is shown by the broken line. However, the alveolar O_2 actually continues

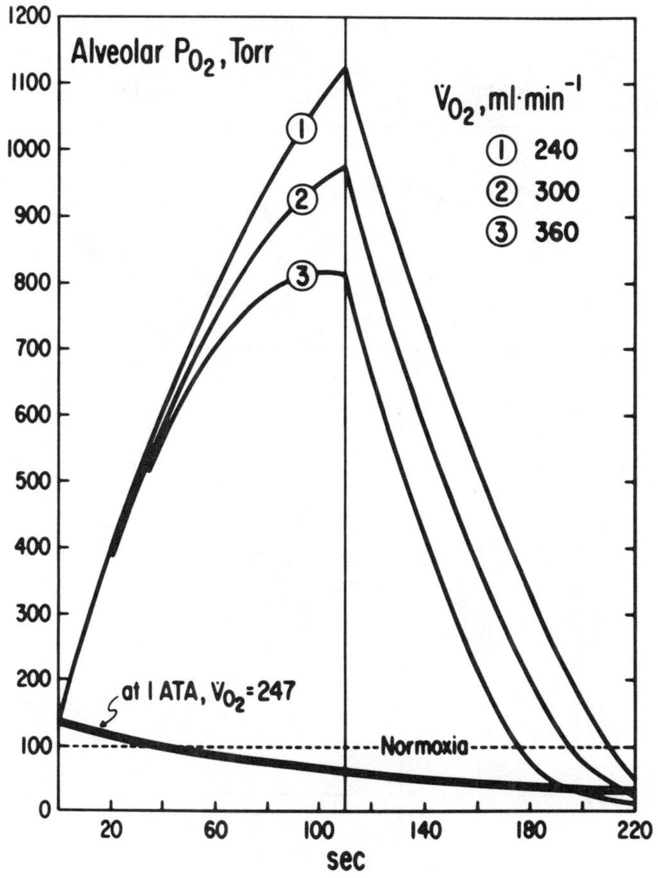

FIGURE 3. Alveolar PO_2 as a function of breath-hold time. Bottom curve represents the values reported by Hong et al.[18] for 9 subjects breathholding at sea level. The 3 upper curves show the values at 3 different rates of O_2 consumption during a dive to 100 m based upon a computer model described by Olszowka and Rahn.[16]

along a much higher level because O_2 is now transferred from the mixed venous blood to the lung, the reversal of O_2 flux. The total amount of O_2 that is transferred in this case is 58 mℓ STPD, and at the end of the dive the alveolar O_2 is 25 instead of 11 torr.

As pointed out by Olszowka and Rahn[16] the actual time during ascent when the crossover point occurs depends upon the initial O_2 stores in the lung and the metabolic rate during a dive. Thus, for example, with a working dive to 30 m (4 ATA) where the O_2 uptake is 600 mℓ/min and the alveolar PO_2 has been reduced before ascent to 80 torr, the alveolar and consequently the arterial PO_2, would fall to 20 torr by the time the surface is reached if no oxygen were taken up during ascent. Thus, ascent blackout would be anticipated[8,19] and would explain some of the observations reported by Cross[5] for the Tuamotu pearl divers, and in breath-hold chamber dives by Lanphier and Rahn.[19] There are probably two mechanisms providing a margin of safety for the diver. One is that after the crossover point is reached, the arterial PO_2 is supported by oxygen from the mixed venous blood preventing alveolar PO_2 from falling as rapidly as otherwise dictated by the drop in total alveolar gas pressure. This support is indicated by the dotted area in Figure 4. The other aspect is that the crucial activity of swimming toward the surface, like other automated motor functions, probably is less sensitive to hypoxia than higher mental functions.

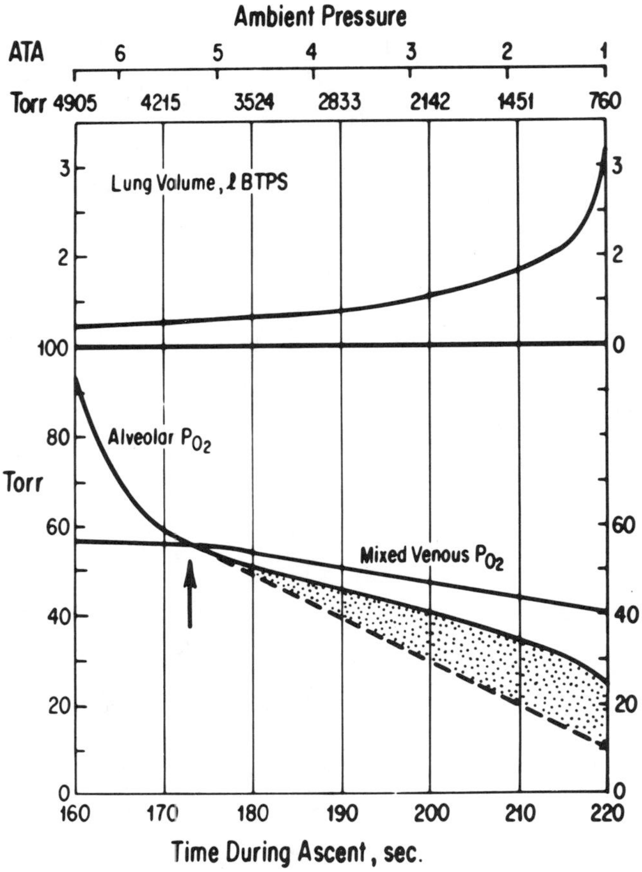

FIGURE 4. (Lower graph) Changes in alveolar PO_2 and mixed venous PO_2 during the last 60 sec of a 100 m dive. For explanation see text. (Upper graph) Changes in lung volume and ambient pressure during the last 60 sec of the 100 m dive. In this example the initial lung volume was 5350 mℓ (BTPS), 1996 mℓ were removed during the dive (45% by transfer of O_2 and 55% by transfer of N_2 to blood and tissues; CO_2 change was negligible), leaving the final lung volume at 3354 mℓ (BTPS).

What is the evidence that O_2 reversal from the mixed venous blood to the alveoli occurs during ascent from breath-hold divers? If one assumes that during breath-hold dives mixed venous PO_2 levels are maintained above 30 to 35 torr, then alveolar levels below this value found with the first exhalation upon ascent from a dive would suggest that oxygen flux reversal had taken place. The upper part of Table 2 shows the alveolar O_2 and CO_2 levels with the first exhalation following ascent from working dives. These averaged values are rather similar in spite of diving time or depth. The data from Teruoka[20] are from assisted dives in Japan, the data from Hong et al.[21] are from unassisted dives in Korea, and those from Lanphier and Rahn[19] are from a chamber dive while working on a bicycle (VO_2 = 580 mℓ/min). In the lower part of the table we have selected individual dives where unusually low alveolar O_2 values were reported. There is little question that at least two subjects in the chamber experiments showed markedly impaired performance at the end of their simulated dives.[19] These observations of unusually low alveolar O_2 tensions at the end of the dives would support the concept of oxygen flow reversal due to rapid lung expansion during the last 10 to 20 m of ascent, a phenomenon that may cause what we have described as ascent blackout.

Table 2
AVERAGE ALVEOLAR O_2 AND CO_2 VALUES OF THE FIRST EXHALATION UPON RETURN FROM WORKING DIVES TO VARIOUS DEPTHS AND VARIOUS DIVING TIMES

	Depth (m)	Time (sec)	P_{AO_2} (torr)	P_{ACO_2} (torr)	No. subj.	No. dives	
Teruoka[20]	18	63	47	43	2	19	Ama — assisted dives
Hong et al.[21]	11	45	41	42	2	6	Ama — free dives
Lanphier & Rahn[19]	10	60	45	43	4	8	Chamber dive ($\dot{V}_{O2}$ = 580 mℓ/min)
Teruoka	21	65	30	39	1	1	
	13	95	26	39	1	1	
	14	87	24	40	1	1	
Hong et al.	13	50	28	48	1	1	
Lanphier & Rahn	10	80	27	41	3	2	
	10	80	24	42	1	2	

Note: In lower part 6 dives have been selected, none of which showed alveolar O_2 values above 30 torr.

V. SUMMARY

In both types of blackout or loss of consciousness the cause can be sought in severe hypoxia. In shallow water blackout the hypoxia develops gradually as shown by the 1 ATA breath-hold curve in Figure 3 assisted by hyperventilation which lowers the PCO_2 below the breaking point threshold. During deep dives the alveolar O_2 can be maintained for some time at normal or above normal levels throughout most of the dive but falls rapidly upon ascent due to lung expansion; it can easily fall below the mixed venous level, causing a reversal of O_2 flux and blackout.

REFERENCES

1. **Hong, S. K.,** Hae-Nyo, the diving women of Korea, in *Physiology of Breath-Hold Diving and the Ama of Japan,* Rahn, H. and Yokoyama, T., Eds., National Academy of Sciences, Washington, D. C., 1965, 99.
2. **Hong, S. K. and Rahn, H.,** The diving women of Korea and Japan, *Sci. Am.,* 216, 34, 1967.
3. **Rahn, H. and Yokoyama, T.,** Physiological problems of breath-hold diving, past and future, in *Hyperbaric Medicine and Underwater Physiology,* Shiraki, K and Matsuoka, S., Eds., Univ. Occup. Environ. Health, Kitakyushu, Japan, 1983, 3.
4. **Craig, A. B., Jr.,** Summary of 58 cases of loss of consciousness during underwater swimming and diving, *Med. Sci. Sports,* 8, 171, 1967.
5. **Cross, E.,** Taravana: diving syndrome in the Tuamoto diver, in *Physiology of Breath-Hold Diving and the Ama of Japan,* Rahn, H. and Yokoyama, T., Eds., National Academy of Sciences, Washington, D.C., 1965, 207.
6. **Craig, A. B., Jr.,** Underwater swimming and loss of consciousness, *JAMA,* 176, 255, 1961.
7. **Craig, A. B., Jr.,** Causes of loss of consciousness during underwater swimming, *J. Appl. Physiol.,* 16, 1961, 586.
8. **Craig, A. B., Jr. and Harley, A. D.,** Alveolar gas exchanges during breath-hold dives, *J. Appl. Physiol.,* 24, 182, 1968.
9. **Otis, A. B., Rahn, H., Epstein, M. A., and Fenn, W. O.,** Performance as related to composition of alveolar air, *Am. J. Physiol.,* 146, 207, 1946.
10. **Rahn, H., Otis, A. B., Hodge, M., Epstein, M. A., Hunter, S. W., and Fenn, W. O.,** The effects of hypocapnia on performance, *J. Aviat. Med.,* 17, 164, 1946.

11. **Klocke, F. J. and Rahn, H.,** Breath holding after breathing of oxygen, *J. Appl. Physiol.*, 14, 689, 1959.
12. **Farhi, L. E. and Rahn, H.,** Gas stores of the body and the unsteady state, *J. Appl. Physiol.*, 7, 472, 1955.
13. **Farhi, L. E. and Rahn, H.,** Dynamics of changes in carbon dioxide stores, *Anesthesiology*, 21, 604, 1960.
14. **Paulev, P.,** Decompression sickness following repeated breath-hold dives, in *Physiology of Breath-Hold Diving and the Ama of Japan*, Rahn, H. and Yokoyama, T., Eds., National Academy of Sciences, Washington, D.C., 1965, 221.
15. **Craig, A. B., Jr.,** Depth limits of breath-hold diving, *Resp. Physiol.*, 5, 14, 1968.
16. **Olszowka, A. J. and Rahn, H.,** Breath-hold diving, in *Hypoxia and Cold*, Sutton, J. R., Houston, C. S., and Coates, G., Eds., Praeger Scientific, New York, in press, 1987.
17. **Musenga, G.,** Un pescatore di spunge (sommozzatore) che senza apparecchio si tuffa fino a 60 metri, *Ann. Med. Nav. Coloniale Unk.*, 163, 1915.
18. **Hong, S. K., Lin, Y. C., Lally, D. A., Yim, B. J. M., Kominami, N., Hong, P. W., and Moore, T. O.,** Alveolar gas exchanges and cardiovascular functions during breath holding with air, *J. Appl. Physiol.*, 30, 540, 1971.
19. **Lanphier, E. H. and Rahn, H.,** Alveolar gas exchange during breath-hold diving, *J. Appl. Physiol.*, 18, 471, 1963.
20. **Teruoka, G.,** Die Ama und ihre Arbeit, *Arbeitsphysiologie*, 5, 23, 1932.
21. **Hong, S. K., Rahn, H., Kang, D. H., Song, S. H., and Kang, B. S.,** Diving pattern, lung volumes, and alveolar gas of the Korean diving women (Ama), *J. Appl. Physiol.*, 18, 457, 1963.
22. **Landsberg, P. G.,** personal communication.
23. **Maiorca, E.,** personal communication.

Chapter 7

CHANGES OF MUSCLE AND FAT INSULATION DURING EXERCISE IN WATER

Arsenio Veicsteinas

TABLE OF CONTENTS

I. Introduction 52

II. Measurement of Tissue Insulation 52
- A. Total Body Insulation 52
- B. Skin and Fat Insulation 52

III. Insulation at Rest 54

IV. Insulation During Exercise 55

V. Conclusion 56

References 57

I. INTRODUCTION

As a very simple and classic model, the body immersed in cool water can be compared to a core (body interior with relatively homogeneous temperature) surrounded by a shell composed of the skin, subcutaneous fat, and muscle layers.[1-4]

At rest, the heat is produced essentially in the core. The shell acts as a resistance to core cooling. The blood flow is virtually zero, and therefore the shell provides maximal insulation. During exercise, heat is produced mainly in the muscle. Muscle perfusion decreases its insulation, and only skin and fat remain as a barrier to core cooling.

Based on the core-shell model, it is the purpose of this chapter to provide quantitative data on the insulation of muscle, subcutaneous fat, and skin at rest and during exercise in cool water immersion of man.

II. MEASUREMENT OF TISSUE INSULATION

The insulation of a tissue has been classically measured by a formula analogous to Ohm's law for electrical circuits.[3]

The insulation, I, is equal to

$$I = (T_2 - T_1)/\dot{H} \qquad (1)$$

where $T_2 - T_1$ is the thermal gradient (corresponding to voltage of Ohm's law) and H is heat flow (corresponding to current). When a tissue is composed of several layers in series, the total insulation is due to the sum of the separate insulations provided by each layer.

A. Total Body Insulation

By applying the above equation the total body insulation, I_T, during immersion in water has been determined as:[5,6]

$$I_T = (T_c - T_{sk})/\dot{H}_s \qquad (2)$$

where T_c is rectal or esophageal temperature, T_{sk} is skin temperature measured by thermocouples or assumed to be equal to water temperature (T_w), and $\dot{H}_s$ is skin heat loss, calculated from metabolic rate (oxygen consumption) corrected for respiratory heat loss and changes of body heat content or by heat flow transducers.

The application of this method to determine I_T in air has been severely criticized;[7] however, particularly during long-lasting immersion, reliable and consistent results have been obtained.[8-13]

B. Skin and Fat Insulation

Following Equation 1, Veicsteinas et al.[12] have recently determined separately the insulation of skin and subcutaneous fat layers, using thermocouple needles inserted at different depths below skin surfaces and heat flow discs glued to the skin.

Figure 1 shows the changes of subcutaneous fat temperature (T_{sf}) at a depth of 9 mm in the lateral side of the thigh, of skin temperature (T_{sk}), of regional heat flow ($\dot{H}_R$), and the corresponding insulation (I_R) of 2 mm of skin and of 7 mm of subcutaneous fat. These data refer to a resting subject immersed up to the neck for 4 hr in well-stirred water. When steady conditions for the different variables were reached, T_w was increased up to 38°C at definite steps. Continuous changes of T_{sf} and $\dot{H}_R$ were observed as a consequence of the T_w increases, however, only at a definite T_{sk} value does a decrease in I_R occur. These I_R values are

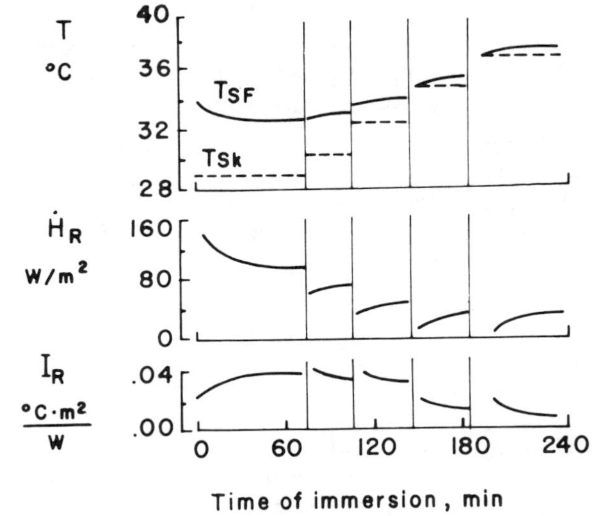

FIGURE 1. Insulation and related variables during water immersion at rest. From top to bottom: changes of subcutaneous fat temperature (T_{sf}, 9 mm below skin surface); skin temperature, T_{sk}; regional heat flow, $\dot{H}_R$; and skin plus fat insulation, I_R, as a function of time of immersion. After 75 min of immersion at CWT (29°C), water temperature was increased about 2°C at 40 min intervals until a T_w of 37°C was reached.[12]

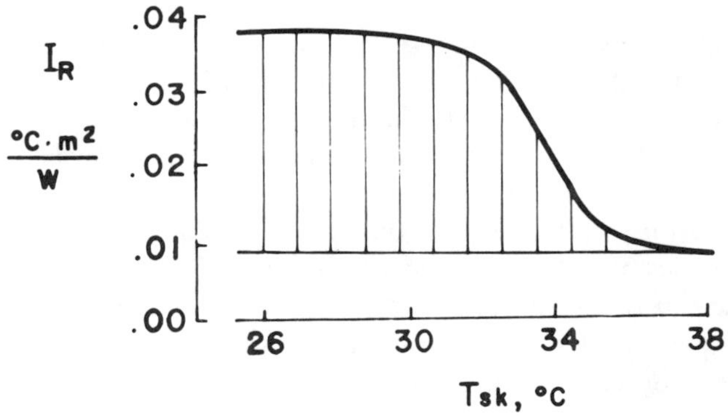

FIGURE 2. Effect of water temperature on skin and fat insulation. Skin plus fat insulation, I_R, of the lateral side of the thigh as a function of water temperature. The curve refers to 3 different experiments similar to that shown in Figure 1. The tissue thickness (2 mm skin + 7.5 mm subcutaneous fat) was maintained the same in all experiments. No change of insulation occurred until skin temperature (practically equal to T_w) of 32°C was reached. The hatched area indicates the maximal decrease of insulation of 9.5 mm of tissue.

emphasized in Figure 2, where the curve represents the average I_R values obtained in a number of experiments with constant tissue thickness. I_R remained steady until T_{sk} reached 32°C, then decreased sharply to a lower plateau at a T_{sk} of 35°C, where the I_R value is about one fourth that found in colder water.[12] This large decrease of I_R of skin and fat is the consequence of increased perfusion due to thermoregulatory mechanisms.[1]

To provide anatomical evidence that in addition to the skin,[1,3] the fat can also be highly perfused, a morphometric study was purposely conducted on slices of subcutaneous fat obtained on the occasion of an orthopedic surgery of the thigh.[14] It was found that the total length in micrometers of capillaries in 1 μm^3 of fat is independent of depth, and the length ranges between 3.5 and 4 $\mu m/\mu m$.[3] Though quantitative estimation of blood perfusion cannot be done, the high capillary density observed in fat supports the thesis of a large decrease of insulation found in warm water.

From I_R measured in one region, when fat thickness in various body areas is known and allowance of constant I_R values in the whole body is made, the insulation provided by skin and fat for the whole body can be calculated by applying the law of parallel resistors (parallel regional insulation):

$$\frac{1}{I_{sk+fat}} = \frac{1}{I_R^{arms}} + \frac{1}{I_R^{trunk}} + \frac{1}{I_R^{legs}} + \frac{1}{I_R^{hands+feet}} \tag{3}$$

when heat flow through a region is proportional to the regional body surface considered (arm, 0.16 of body surface area; trunk, 0.38; legs, 0.33; hands plus feet, 0.07) and inversely proportional to the correspondent mean skin plus fat thickness.[3,12]

III. INSULATION AT REST

When thermocouple needles were inserted at different depths (d) below the skin in several subjects immersed at a $T_w < 32°C$, it was found that the insulation of skin plus subcutaneous fat is linearly related to tissue thickness as[12]:

$$I_R(°C \cdot m^2/W) = 0.0048\ d\ (mm) - 0.052 \qquad (r = 0.95) \tag{4}$$

In the same subjects during similar experimental conditions, the insulation of skin itself was 0.0022°C · m²/W/mm and that for fat alone 0.0048°C · m²/W/mm. These values correspond to the insulation of in vivo unperfused skin[1] and in vitro fat values,[15,16] respectively. This suggests that below 32°C T_w skin and fat are unperfused, and hence their insulation is maximal.

With the core-shell model in mind, and on the basis of Equations 2 and 3, the total body fat and skin insulations have been determined separately in subjects of different adiposity. Following the method of Rennie et al.[6] to reach the maximal total body insulation, the experiments were performed at critical water temperature (CWT) defined as the coldest T_w at which no increase of metabolic rate (i.e., no shivering) is detected in resting subjects at the end of 3 hr of immersion. In well-stirred water, CWT is inversely proportional to T_w and ranges from 27 to 33°C for skin plus mean subcutaneous fat thickness of 12 to 3 mm,[12] respectively.

In Figure 3, the top line I_T indicates the total body insulation, which increases linearly with skin plus mean subcutaneous fat thickness, d. Values from different sources[5,6,8,10-13] with comparable experimental conditions are consistent with the relationship given. The middle line I_{sk+fat} is the insulation of skin and subcutaneous fat which depends on the thickness of these two unperfused layers. The bottom line represents the insulation of 2 mm of skin, which is obviously constant.

It is clear from this figure that the slope of I_T vs. d is much steeper than the slope of I_{sk+fat} vs. d. Thus, skin and fat tissues cannot account for the observed total body insulation at rest. In the core-shell model, considering muscle, subcutaneous fat, and skin as in series insulators, only muscle, as also previously noted,[2,6] can be responsible for such a large difference.

From Figure 3 it appears also that the insulation of muscle itself increases linearly with

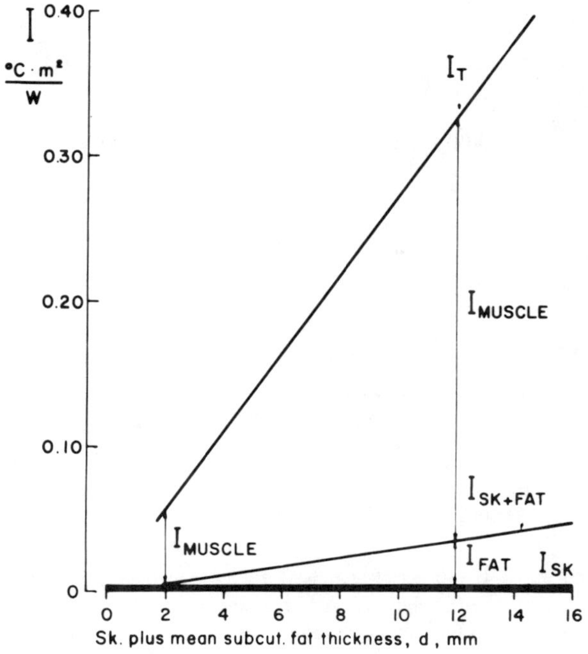

FIGURE 3. The different components of total body insulation at rest. Insulation, I, as a function of skin plus fat thickness at the end of 3 hr of immersion at CWT (32 to 27°C). I_T, total body insulation; I_{sk+fat}, skin plus fat insulation of the whole body; I_{sk}, insulation of 2 mm of skin. The difference between the total body and the skin plus fat insulation is the insulation provided by muscle, which increases with adiposity (i.e., is inversely proportional to T_w).[12]

adiposity. This effect is probably a consequence of the lower CWT of fat subjects. The lower T_w leads to the higher activity of cutaneous cold receptors and hence to a more severe muscle vasoconstriction.[8-13] This assumption has been recently demonstrated to be true by measuring blood flow in muscle by ^{133}Xe washout. In resting subjects immersed up to the neck, the colder the water temperature the lower the muscle perfusion.[17]

IV. INSULATION DURING EXERCISE

Subjects of different adiposity performed long-term arm and leg exercises (30 and 70% of the total load, respectively) in well-stirred water at CWT. The exercise levels were up to 8 MET[12,17,18] (1 MET, resting metabolic rate corresponds to an oxygen consumption of 300 mℓ/min). I_T and I_{sk+fat} were measured at rest. With increasing exercise intensity both slope and intercept of the regression lines of I_T vs. d were continuously decreasing in respect to the corresponding lines found at rest and shown in Figure 3. Evidently, muscular hyperemia reduces the total body insulation as also previously predicted by different authors[1-3] and observed by Nadel et al.[9] during swimming at high speed. On the contrary, in the same subjects and experimental conditions, in spite of the extra heat produced by working muscles, the insulation of skin plus fat was unchanged until an exercise intensity of 3 MET was reached. Then, at a metabolic rate of 8 MET I_{sk+fat} decreased to about 50% of the resting value.

The different pattern of the insulation of muscle in comparison to skin and fat suggests that the shell of the core shell model should be separated into two functional components,

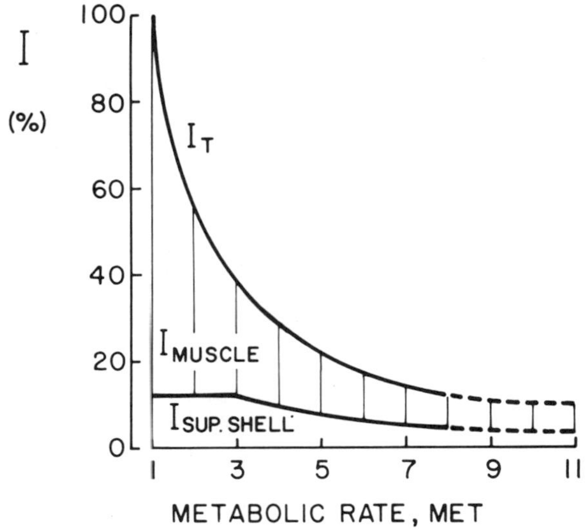

FIGURE 4. Effect of exercise on muscle and superficial shell insulation. Total body, I_T, and superficial shell (skin plus fat) insulation as a function of exercise intensity (1 MET = 300 mℓ of oxygen consumed/min) during immersion at CWT (30°C). With mild exercise muscle insulation decreases substantially, while the superficial shell insulation remains unchanged. At heavier work loads even the insulation of the superficial shell decreases. Subjects mean fat plus skin thickness = 6 mm. Plotted according to data from References 12, 17, and 18.

the outer layers most, skin plus subcutaneous fat, labeled as superficial shell on one side, and the muscle layer on the other. Figure 4 illustrates the relative contribution of the insulation provided by the muscle and by the superficial shell to the total body insulation, set equal to 100% at rest. At rest, about 85% of the I_T is insulation provided by muscle and 15% by the superficial shell. During exercise a dramatic decrease of muscle takes place, even during mild exercise; however, up to a metabolic rate of 3 MET the superficial shell insulation still remains at its maximal level, as at rest. At heavier exercise levels, coupled to a very low muscle insulation, a decrease of the insulative properties of the superficial shell begins to occur. Evidently, the vasodilation threshold is surpassed and the perfusion on the superficial shell is evoked by a thermoregulatory mechanism to dissipate heat. At exercise levels higher than about 5 MET the total body insulation is only a negligible fraction of that at rest. Of this fraction about 30 to 50% are provided by the superficial shell.

Figure 4 refers to a specific subject (mean fat thickness 4 mm, CWT 30°C) for the experimental condition given. The curves shown in the figure would change, though not to a great extent, if water temperature and adiposity were different. This is also true when arms rather than legs are mainly involved in the exercise. In fact, Toner et al.[19] found a greater conductive and convective heat loss during arm than during leg exercise with similar metabolic rate.

V. CONCLUSION

The shell of the core-shell model can be divided into two functional components, muscle and superficial shell. Each of these provides a distinct fraction of insulation during immersion in cool water in resting and exercising man.

At rest, before shivering, 85 to 90% of the total body insulation is provided by muscle, whose perfusion is lower, the lower the water temperature. The insulation of the superficial shell (10 to 15%) is independent from water temperature and similar to thermal resistivity of unperfused fat in vitro.

During mild exercise, muscle insulation is greatly reduced by exercise hyperemia. On the contrary, the superficial shell insulation remains unchanged and provides 30 to 40% of the total insulation, until moderate exercise is performed. In the latter condition, however, even the superficial shell is perfused and its insulation begins to decrease. At heavier work loads, the continuous decrease of muscle insulation is accompanied by a parallel decrease of the insulation of the superficial shell, which is about 50% of the total.

At rest the heat conservation system has priority in preventing core cooling in the investigated range of water temperatures. During exercise, on the other hand, the muscles' need for blood has priority over temperature regulation, and a fine tuning of the perfusion of the superficial shell occurs allowing for the most effective regulation of the core temperature.

REFERENCES

1. **Burton, A. C. and Edholm, O. G.,** *Man in a Cold Envrionment,* Edward Arnold, London, 1955.
2. **Bullard, R. W. and Rapp, G. M.,** Problems of body heat loss in water immersion, *Aerospace Med.,* 41(11), 1269, 1970.
3. **Newburg, L. H.,** *Physiology of Heat Regulation and the Science of Clothing,* Hafner, New York, 1968.
4. **Keatinge, W. R.,** *Survival in Cold Water,* Blackwell Scientific, Oxford, 1969.
5. **Carlson, L. D., Hsieh, A. C. L., Fullington, F., and Elsner, R. W.,** Immersion in cold water and body tissue insulation, *J. Aviat. Med.,* 29, 145, 1958.
6. **Rennie, D. W., Covino, B. G., Howell, B. J., Song, S. H., Kang, B. S., and Hong, S. K.,** Physical insultion of Korean diving women, *J. Appl. Physiol.,* 17, 961, 1962.
7. **Brengelmann, G. L.,** Control of sweating rate and skin blood flow during exercise, in *Problems with Temperature Regulation During Exercise,* Nadel, E. R., Ed., Academic Press, New York, 1977, 27.
8. **Hanna, J. M. and Hong, S. K.,** Critical water temperature and effective insulation in Scuba divers in Hawaii, *J. Appl. Physiol.,* 33, 770, 1972.
9. **Nadel, E. R., Holmér, I., Bergh, U., Åstrand, P. O., and Stolwijk, J. A. J.,** Energy exchanges of swimming man, *J. Appl. Physiol.,* 36, 465, 1974.
10. **Kollias, J., Barlett, L., Bergsteinova, V., Skinner, J. S., Buskirk, E. R., and Nicholas, W. C.,** Metabolic and thermal responses of women during cooling in water, *J. Appl. Physiol.,* 36, 577, 1974.
11. **Veicsteinas, A. and Rennie, D. W.,** Thermal insulation and shivering threshold in Greek sponge divers, *J. Appl. Physiol. Resp. Environ. Exercise Physiol.,* 52, 845, 1982.
12. **Veicsteinas, A., Ferretti, G., and Rennie, D. W.,** Superficial shell insulation in resting and exercising man in cold water, *J. Appl. Physiol. Resp. Environ. Exercise Physiol.,* 54, 1708, 1983.
13. **Park, Y. S., Rennie, D. W., Lee, I. S., Park. Y. D., Paik, K. S., Kang, D. H., Suh, D. J., Lee, S. H., Hong, S. Y., and Hong, S. K.,** Time course of deacclimatization to cold water immersion in Korean women divers, *J. Appl. Physiol. Resp. Environ. Exercise Physiol.,* 54, 1708, 1983.
14. **Ferrario, V. F., Vizzotto, L., Molinari Tosatti, M. P., and Borsellino, G.,** Valutazioni morfoquantitative del letto vascolare nel sottocute dell'uomo, Trieste, 1983.
15. **Hardy, J. D. and Soderstorm, G. F.,** Heat loss from the nude body and peripheral blood flood at temperatures of 22°C to 35°C, *J. Nutr.,* 16, 494, 1938.
16. **Hatfield, H. S. and Pugh, L. G. C. E.,** Thermal conductivity of human fat and muscle, *Nature (London),* 168, 918, 1951.
17. **Rennie, D. W., Park, Y., Veicsteinas, A., and Pendergast, D.,** Metabolic and circulatory adaptation to cold water stress, in *Exercise Bioenergetics and Gas Exchange,* Cerretelli, P. and Whipp, B. J., Eds., Elsevier/North Holland, Amsterdam, 1980.
18. **Veicsteinas, A., Ferretti, G., Perini, R., and Rennie, D. W.,** Superficial shell insulation in cold water during severe exercise: role of core and skin temperature, *Physiologist,* 26, A-98, 1983.
19. **Toner, M. M., Sawka, M. N., and Pandolf, K. B.,** Thermal responses during arm and leg and combined arm-leg exercise in water, *J. Appl. Physiol. Resp. Environ. Exercise Physiol.,* 56, 1355, 1984.

Chapter 8

ACCLIMATIZATION AND ACCLIMATION TO HEAT — AN INTRODUCTION

Yair Shapiro and Kent B. Pandolf

TABLE OF CONTENTS

I. Introduction 60

II. Changes Consequent to Acclimatization 60

References 65

I. INTRODUCTION

Adaptation to heat may be described as the series of physiological adjustments that occur when a person who is accustomed to living in a cool environment is transferred to a hot climate.

More than 200 years ago, in 1768, Lind[1] in "An Essay on Diseases Incidental to Europeans in Hot Climate" pointed out that habituation to hot climates reduced the danger to health.

II. CHANGES CONSEQUENT TO ACCLIMATIZATION

The classical physiological changes of acclimatization are heightened sweating response, lowered heart rate, and lowered skin and rectal temperatures during exercise in heat (Figure 1), and these therefore reduce the risk of heat injury.[2,3]

Robinson et al.[4] suggested that skin temperature decreases during acclimatization by a greater amount than did rectal temperature, and therefore the gradient between core and periphery increases, a phenomenon which helps to shift the metabolic heat from the central organs to the skin.

A full acclimatization occurs after 10 to 14 days of exposure to heat, but two thirds or even 75% of the adaptation can be achieved over 5 days.[2,3]

In 1963, Lind and Bass[2] showed that the most economical procedures are to expose the subjects once a day for 100 min; that method was found to be more effective than once a day for 50 min, twice a day 50 min each, and even two daily exposures of 100 min each (Figure 2). On the other hand, Avellini et al.[5] pointed out in 1980 that daily exposure of 100 min exercise in heat is sufficient to acclimate subjects for 2 hr of exposure, but it is not sufficient for 4 hr of exposure.

Decreased body temperature after acclimatization is a result of reduced heat storage, since the latter is the difference between heat production and heat dissipation. The body has to react through one of two components: metabolism or evaporative heat loss in order to achieve lower body temperatures. Recently, Sawka et al.[6] showed a reduction of about 5% in metabolic rate during acclimation. This observation might explain one part of the mechanism — decreased heat production; an increase in evaporative heat loss can be activated by an increase in sweat rate, reduction in the threshold of onset of sweating, and an increase in sweat sensitivity.

Hernane and Valaty[7] showed that after acclimatization the sweat sensitivity is higher and the threshold of onset of sweating is lower. Those who do not change their sweat sensitivity or the onset of sweating remain intolerant to heat.

Roberts et al.[8] found that the full shift in sweat threshold happens only after a course of exercises in heat; exercise alone was not sufficient to reduce the threshold in full range (Figure 3).

Pandolf et al.[9] proved the relationship between maximal aerobic power ($\dot{V}O_2$ max) and acclimation (Figure 4).

The participation of the endocrine system in the acclimatization mechanism can be demonstrated by the sodium conservation mechanism[10] During acclimatization sweat becomes progressively more diluted with regard to sodium and chloride. This led to the concept that the acclimatization process was, in part, directed toward salt conservation. This in turn aided in maintaining the volume and composition of the body fluids. Salt conservation is most probably based on the pituitary-adrenal axis function.

Heat exposure challenges the cardiovascular system, since a significant portion of cardiac output is needed to convect heat from core to skin, especially in the first stage when the sweat sensitivity is still low, and heat vasodilation is evident. High heart rate is a temporary compensatory mechanism of the cardiovascular system to the increase of the vascular bed.

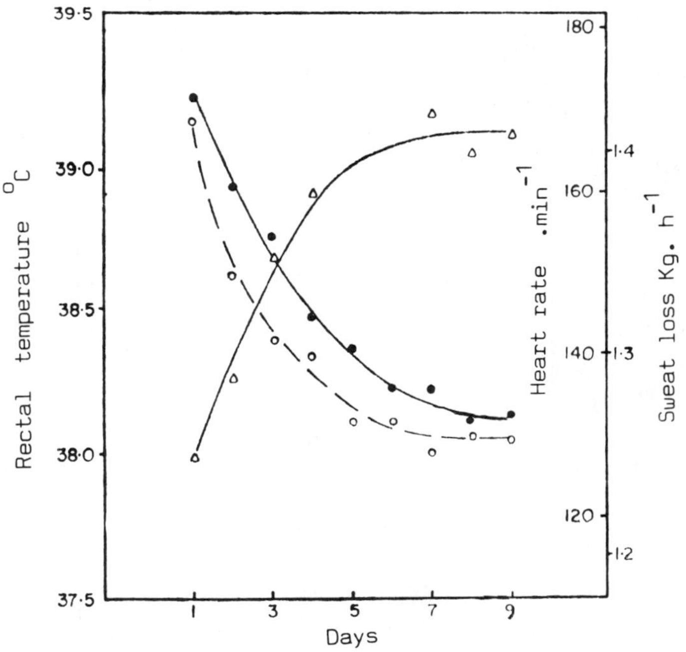

FIGURE 1. Typical average rectal temperatures (●), heart rates (○), and sweat losses (△) of a group of men during the development of acclimatization to heat. The men worked for 100 min at an energy expenditure of 300 kcal/hr in dry-bulb temperature at 49°C and wet-bulb at 27°C. (From Lind, A. R. and Bass, D. E., *Fed. Proc.*, 22, 704, 1963. With permission.)

A new balance between the blood volume and the vascular bed volume is achieved by expansion of both plasma and extracellular fluid volumes. The increase in the extracellular fluid can be explained partially by the salt conservation mechanism. This mechanism is not sufficient to explain the magnitude of the plasma volume expansion. The latter is related by Senay et al.[11] to influx of protein to the intravascular volume.

The connection between plasma volume expansion and the adjustment of the cardiovascular system was demonstrated by Senay et al.[11] The heart rate dropped more when higher plasma volume expansion was observed, while it remained unchanged when the change in plasma volume was minimal (Figure 5).

Natural acclimatization is defined as a physiological change, occurring within the lifetime of an organism, which reduced the strain caused by stressful changes in the natural climate, while artificial acclimation is defined as a physiological change occurring within the lifetime of an organism, which reduces the strain caused by experimentally induced stressful changes in particular climatic factors.[12] The difference between the two definitions is whether the changes are induced by natural or artificial climatic stimuli.

Shapiro et al.[13] emphasized the differences between these two. It was found that natural acclimatization affects rectal temperature more than the artificial one, i.e., natural acclimatization reduces the thermoregulatory set point more intensively than artificial acclimation (Figure 6).

Despite 10 days of acclimation, the winter thermoregulatory set point remained higher than in the summer. The latter, together with lower sweat rates after acclimation in the winter, seemed to represent the lower sweating sensitivity of the acclimated humans in the winter season than in the summer. In the same study it was shown that plasma volume expansion is more enhanced during summer, but winter acclimation causes more cellular compartments expansion (Figure 7). In other words, during winter acclimation the blood

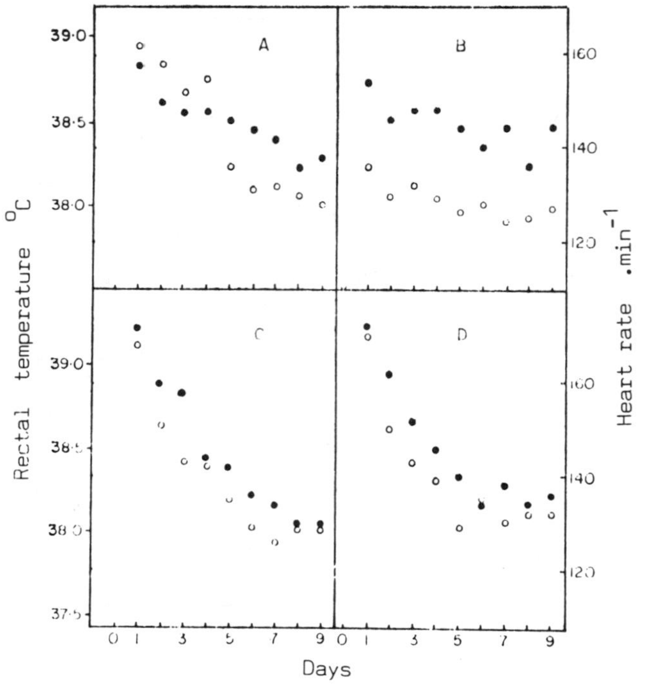

FIGURE 2. The average rectal temperatures (●) and pulse rates (○) of 4 teams during exposure for 9 successive days to a climate with dry- and wet-bulb temperatures of 49 and 27°C; all men worked at an energy expenditure of 300 kcal/hr. The daily exposure for each team was (A) 50 min each morning, (B) 50 min each morning and each afternoon (i.e., a total of 100 min/day), (C) 100 min each morning, and (D) 100 min each morning and each afternoon (200 min/day). Of the different regimens examined, the most economical for the full development of acclimatization as quickly as possible was a single daily exposure of 100 min (C). (From Lind, A. R. and Bass, D. E., *Fed. Proc.*, 22, 704, 1963. With permission.)

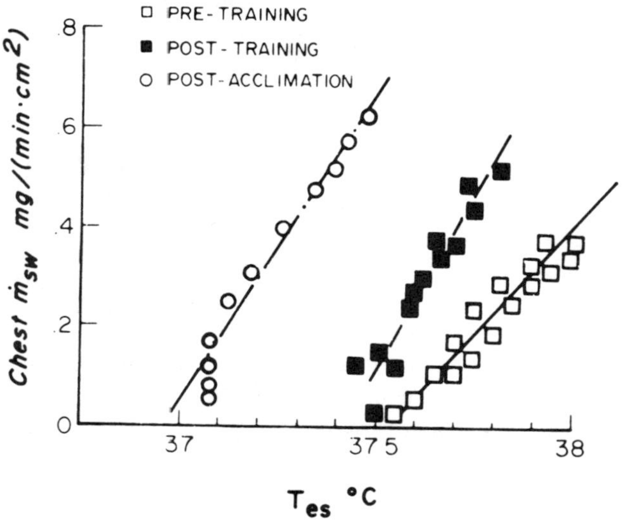

FIGURE 3. Chest sweat rate plotted vs. esophageal temperature for one subject exercising at an ambient temperature of 25°C. (□) Pre-exercise training data, (■) post-exercise training data (○) post-heat-acclimation data. (From Roberts, M. F. et al., *J. Appl. Physiol.*, 43, 133, 1977. With permission.)

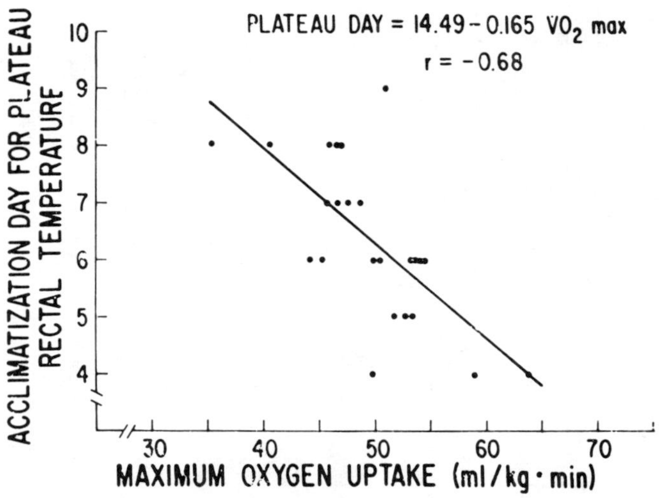

FIGURE 4. The relationship between the acclimatization day for a plateau rectal temperature (°C) and the maximal oxygen uptake (mℓ/kg/min). (From Pandolf, K. B. et al., *Ergonomics*, 20, 399, 1977. With permission.)

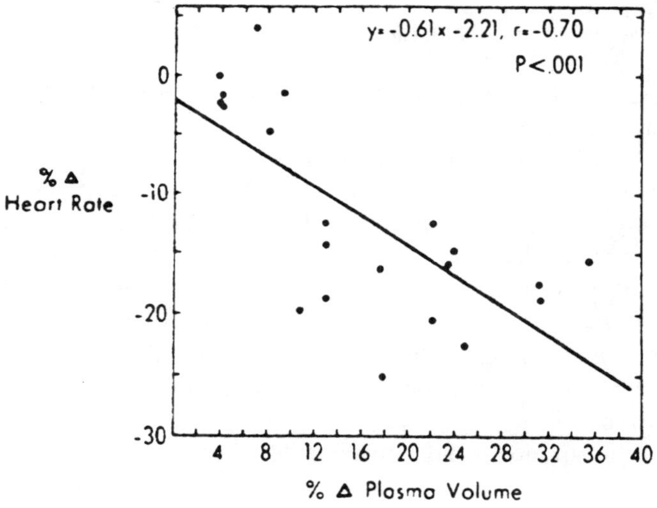

FIGURE 5. Percent changes in 4th hour heart rates expressed as a function of percent changes in plasma volume; 1st day heat exposure values were taken as control values. (From Senay, L. C. et al., *J. Appl. Physiol.*, 40, 786, 1976. With permission.)

volume expansion was due to expansion both in the plasma and cellular compartments, whereas in the summer the acclimation resulted in only plasma volume expansion.

The main changes of the acclimatization process can be summarized as follows:

1. Heat acclimatization is an improved effectiveness of heat dissipating, represented by:
   A. Decreased rectal and skin temperature
   B. Decreased heat storage
   C. Increased sweat rate, sweat sensitivity, and decreased onset of sweating

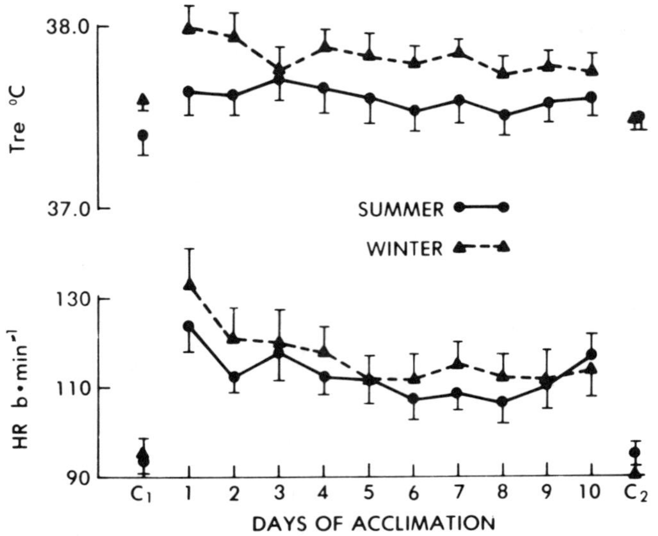

FIGURE 6. Final rectal temperature (T_{re}), and heart rate (HR) values during each day of summer (——) and winter (-----) exposures are displayed. C_1 and C_2 are two control days, and 1 through 10 are acclimation days. (From Shapiro, Y. et al., *J. Appl. Physiol. Resp. Environ. Exercise Physiol.*, 50, 792, 1981. With permission.)

2. Cardiovascular adjustment, represented by lower heart rate depends on extracellular fluids and plasma volume expansion
   A. Protein influx to the intravascular volume
   B. Sodium conservation
3. The metabolic rate (heat production) of the acclimatized man is lower in comparison to the nonacclimatized
4. A full acclimatization takes 10 to 14 days, 75% of it is achieved after 5 days
5. Daily exposure of 100 min is an effective procedure of acclimatization
6 Effective acclimatization demands both heat and exercise
7 There is a negative correlation between physical fitness and the time needed for acclimatization
8. Natural acclimatization is more effective than artificial acclimation

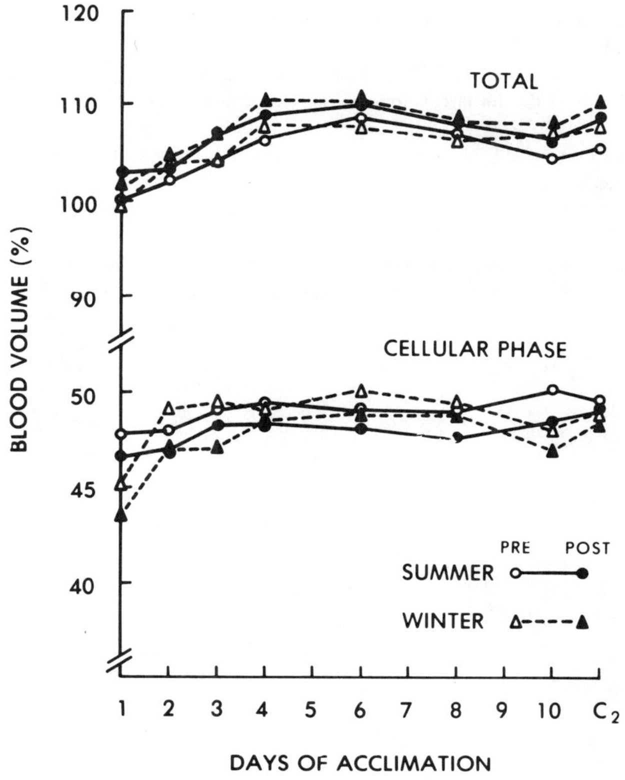

FIGURE 7. Changes in blood volume (whole blood and cellular compartment of blood) during summer (——) and winter (-----) exposures are given. Pre- (○△) and postexposure values (●▲) for last control day (C_2) and 10 acclimation days (1 through 10) are shown. Preexposure values for the 1st acclimation day of each season are defined as 100% for whole blood. Cellular compartment values are whole blood values multiplied by hematocrit. (From Shapiro, Y. et al., *J. Appl. Physiol. Resp. Environ. Exercise Physiol.*, 50, 792, 1981. With permission.)

REFERENCES

1. **Lind, J.,** An Essay on Diseases Incidental to Europeans in Hot Climates, T. Becket, London, 1768.
2. **Lind, A. R. and Bass, D. E.,** The optimal exposure time for the development of acclimatization to heat, *Fed. Proc.*, 22, 704, 1963.
3. **Bass, D. E., Kleeman, C. R., Quinn, M., Henschel, A., and Hegnauer, A. H.,** Mechanisms of acclimatization to heat in man, *Medicine (Baltimore)*, 34, 323, 1955.
4. **Robinson, S., Meyer, F. R., Newton, J. L., Ts'ao, C. H., and Holgersen, L. O.,** Relations between sweating, cutaneous blood flow and body temperature in work, *J. Appl. Physiol.*, 20, 575, 1965.
5. **Avellini, B. A., Shapiro, Y., Pandolf, K. B., Pimental. N. A., and Goldman, R. F.,** Physiological responses of men and women to prolonged dry heat exposure, *Aviat. Space. Environ. Med.*, 51, 1081, 1980.
6. **Sawka, M. N., Pandolf, K. B., Avellini, B. A., and Shapiro, Y.,** Does heat acclimation lower the rate of metabolism elicited by muscular exercise?, *Aviat. Space Environ. Med.*, 54, 27, 1983.
7. **Henane, R. and Valaty, J. L.,** Thermoregulatory changes induced during heat acclimatization by controlled hyperthermia in man, *J. Physiol. (London)*, 230, 255, 1973.
8. **Roberts, M. F., Wenger, C. B., Stolwijk, J. A. J., and Nadel, E. R.,** Skin blood flow and sweating changes following exercise training and heat acclimation, *J. Appl. Physiol.*, 43, 133, 1977.

9. **Pandolf, K. B., Burse, R. L., and Goldman, R. F.,** Role of physical fitness in heat acclimatization, decay and reinduction, *Ergonomics,* 20, 399, 1977.
10. **Wyndham, C. H., Benade, A. J. H., Williams, C. G., Strydom, M. B., Goldin, A., and Heyns, A. J. A.,** Changes in control circulation and body fluid spaces during acclimatization to heat, *J. Appl. Physiol.,* 25, 586, 1968.
11. **Senay, L. C., Mitchell, D., and Wyndham, C. H.,** Acclimatization in a hot, humid environment: body fluid adjustments, *J. Appl. Physiol.,* 40, 786, 1976.
12. **Bligh, J. and Johnson, K. G.,** Glossary of terms for thermal physiology, *J. Appl. Physiol.,* 35, 941, 1973.
13. **Shapiro, Y., Hubbard, R. W., Kimbrough, C. M., and Pandolf, K. B.,** Physiological and hematological responses to summer and winter dry-heat acclimation, *J. Appl. Physiol. Resp. Environ. Exercise Physiol.,* 50, 792, 1981.

Chapter 9

THE EVOLUTION OF HEAT ACCLIMATIZATION PRACTICES AND PROCEDURES IN THE SOUTH AFRICAN GOLD MINING INDUSTRY WITH SPECIAL REFERENCE TO FUNDAMENTAL CONSIDERATIONS

A. J. Kielblock and P. C. Schutte

TABLE OF CONTENTS

Abstract 68

I. Historical Background 68

II. Current Practices and Procedures 69

III. Fundamental Considerations 69
  A. Risk Assessment 70
  B. Heat Acclimatization 70
  C. Wet-Bulb Temperature 71
  D. Heat Tolerance Testing 71

IV. Future Directions 73

References 74

ABSTRACT

With virgin rock temperatures approaching 60°C, and allaying dust by means of water sprays, environmental conditions in South African gold mines are typically hot and humid. The level of mechanization is low (as a result of the geology of the gold bearing reefs) and, consequently, many tasks are physically demanding. Obviously, such conditions constitute a considerable physiological stress which ultimately may impair functional efficiency and even threaten the health and safety of workers.

I. HISTORICAL BACKGROUND

In 1930, soon after gold mines started to exceed depths of 1000 m, 26 heat stroke fatalities were recorded, which, when extrapolated to the total underground population, amounted to 93 deaths per 100,000 workers. With hindsight, the roots of modern heat acclimatization practices and procedures can be traced back to this disaster,[1] but it was not until some 20 years later that a comprehensive scientific approach to the problem was launched.

The first formal heat acclimatization program was introduced in 1953. It involved two stages of 6 days each during which men were first allocated to relatively cold work areas and subsequently to relatively hot areas. However, in practice it soon became evident that the two-stage method was not sufficiently reliable to accommodate the uncontrolled fluctuations in environmental temperatures and work rates associated with actual mining operations. The consequences of such fluctuations were suboptimal levels of heat acclimatization and, invariably, heat exhaustion (or even heat stroke). For these reasons, surface climatic chambers were introduced in the mid-1960s; underground conditions could be simulated and controlled to within about 0.5°C, while a progressive increase in work rate was achieved by a simple, yet effective block-stepping procedure. Also, supervision was facilitated and medical treatment, when indicated, could be instituted within minutes.[2]

The benefit of surface climatic chambers was first apparent in terms of a reduction in the heat stroke mortality by a factor of about 50%. Secondly, it was apparent in terms of a 33% reduction in the number of shifts required to achieve a satisfactory level of heat acclimatization. Figure 1 shows the decline in heat stroke mortality over the past 50 years in relation to the growing underground labor force despite a general and gradual increase in the underground temperature.

The obvious differences in individual responses to a formal, standardized heat acclimatization program are manifestations of inherent differences in heat tolerance. The logical sequel was the development of a heat tolerance test (HTT) to select individuals with a degree of natural heat tolerance sufficiently high to obviate conventional heat acclimatization. This test was introduced in 1977 and, although it did not gain wide acceptance initially, the impact has been considerable. More recently, the HTT has also been used for reallocation of workers from relatively cool to relatively hot areas as well as a screening procedure following absence from work.

Despite decided health and safety benefits, conventional climatic chamber heat acclimatization features a number of disadvantages, e.g., the onerous nature of the process, the sheer boredom thereof, and from mine management's point of view, the number of unproductive shifts. Thus, research was challenged with the development of a method of heat acclimatization without its attendant negative features. These constraints stimulated an investigation into the use of microclimate cooling, and subsequent research demonstrated that with coolant in contact with about one third of the body surface area, the rise in body temperature during work in heat is controlled to the extent that heat acclimation occurs in a normal way. A rise in body temperature, a prerequisite to heat acclimation, is not prevented; it is only prevented from rising excessively.[3] A large-scale field trial was undertaken and

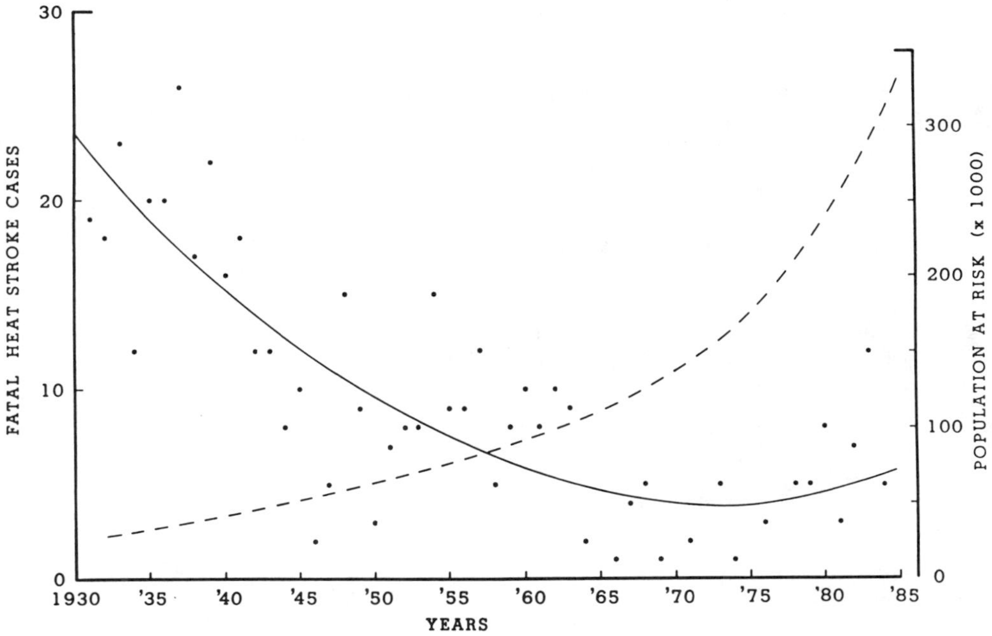

FIGURE 1. The general decline in heat stroke fatalities in the South African gold mining industry (unbroken graph) related to the mining population at risk (broken graph). The dots represent the heat stroke fatalities recorded for each year.

the results of this study confirmed that heat acclimatization can be achieved through microclimate cooling and that its application is not restricted to carefully controlled laboratory experiments, but that it has a significant and practicable industrial application.[4]

A cool microclimate is achieved by means of the sublimation of dry-ice contained in a specially designed jacket.[1] The dry-ice blocks are manufactured from liquid carbon dioxide using a "snow-maker" and press system. Eligibility for selection is based on individual responses to the HTT.[4,5]

Microclimate acclimatization was first implemented in 1982, and is currently used as a standard method of heat acclimatization at nine gold mines in South Africa. Its major advantages are related to a saving in unproductive shifts and improved morale.

II. CURRENT PRACTICES AND PROCEDURES

The sequence of events currently in practice to prepare men for work in heat is outlined by way of a flow-diagram (Figure 2). The procedures cater for (1) hyper-heat-tolerant men who do not require further heat acclimatization, i.e., productive from the outset, (2) the selection of men who qualify for microclimate acclimatization (MCA) and are likewise immediately available for production, and (3) the selection of men who would only achieve full acclimatization through conventional means. The approximate proportion, which exhibits considerable variation, is 30:60:10.

III. FUNDAMENTAL CONSIDERATIONS

The ultimate objective of the innovations described here is in terms of productivity/profitability through health and safety. It should therefore be appreciated that the research philosophy adopted has been determined largely by pragmatism.

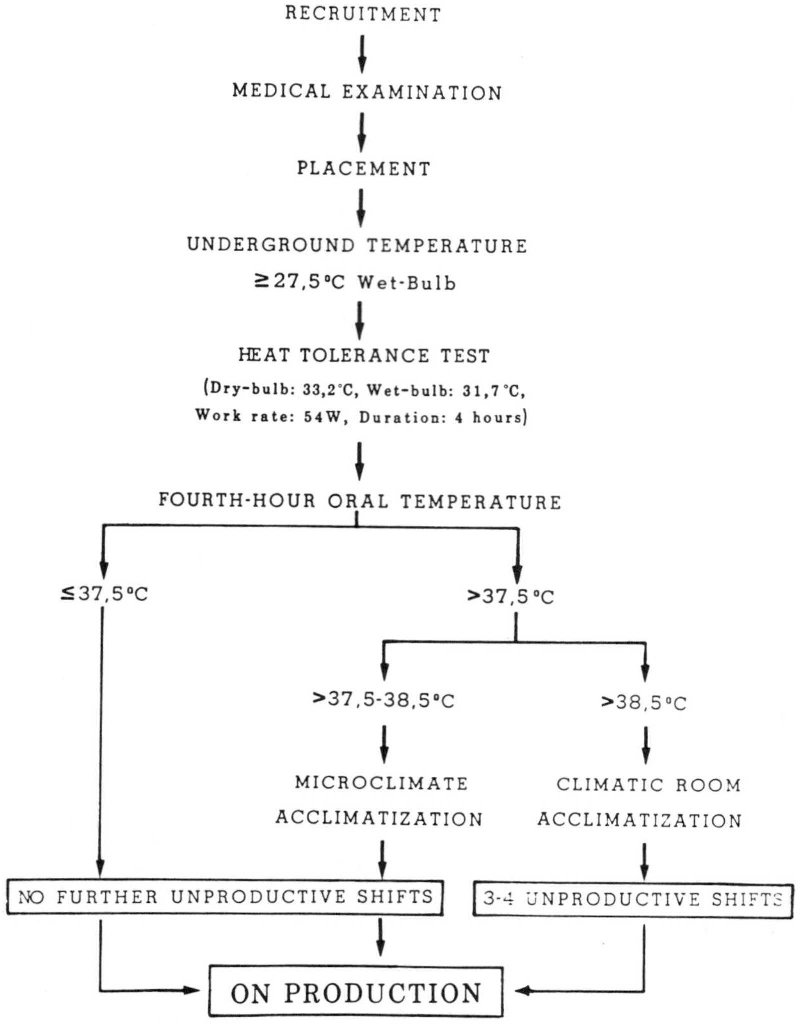

FIGURE 2. Sequence of events to select or acclimatize men for work in heat in the South African gold mines.

A. Risk Assessment

Fundamentally related to the development of newer methods is risk assessment. The risk of developing hyperthermia is regarded as unacceptable when the chances of rectal temperature exceeding 40°C exceed 10^{-6}, i.e., 99.9999% confidence limits are applied. Although instances of heat stroke have been reported with rectal temperatures of below 40°C on admission, an analysis of the literature, both experimental[6] and clinical,[7,8] suggests that heat stroke fatalities are unlikely to occur at core temperatures of less than 40°C.

In this regard, the approach here differs significantly from that of the more conservative wet-bulb globe temperature (WBGT) index. This difference is ascribed primarily to the respective populations at risk: where the WBGT has to cater for unscreened, seasonally-acclimatized workers of variable age, sex, health, and occupation, gold mining is done by a thoroughly screened, predominantly youthful (mean: 26 years), male population.

B. Heat Acclimatization

Although an oversimplification, heat acclimatization is achieved by shifting the burden of thermoregulation from the cardiovascular system onto the sweat mechanism. In designing

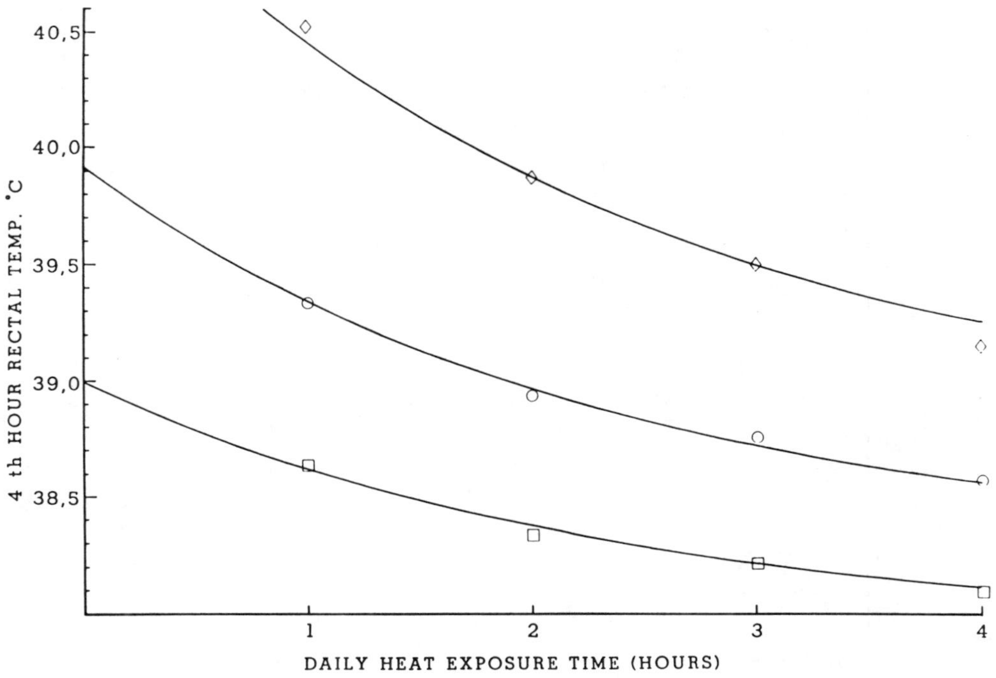

FIGURE 3. Heat tolerance, in terms of rectal temperature, depicted as a function of daily exposure to work (54 W) in heat (dry-bulb: 33.2°C; wet-bulb: 31.7°C, air movement: 0.5 m/sec) during a standard 4-hr heat tolerance test. The graphs show the mean response (○) and 95% confidence limits (◇/□). Each exposure was repeated on 5 consecutive days and the heat tolerance test was conducted on the 6th day.

a heat acclimatization program it is essential to appreciate that the degree of acclimatization achieved is, within physiological limits, a function of the level of hyperthermia achieved during exposure and the duration thereof. Figure 3 clearly reveals the progression of heat acclimatization as a function of exposure time for given environmental conditions and work rate. However, in view of the specificity of the process, considerable unnecessary controversy exists in the literature with regard to the role of physical conditioning as a method to achieve heat acclimatization.

A corollary to the specificity of heat acclimatization is that overacclimatization serves no useful purpose; in fact, it is counterproductive in terms of wasted time and morale (Figure 4).

C. Wet-Bulb Temperature

The introduction of heat acclimatization in the South African mining industry was prompted by the occurrence of heat stroke. Since heat stroke is fundamentally related to the hot, humid conditions typical of the gold mining environment, an analysis of heat stroke incidents was carried out to pinpoint the critical wet-bulb temperature, irrespective of work rate, air movement, etc. (From a practical point of view, wet-bulb temperature adequately describes the environmental heat load in mines, which in terms of the WBGT index, averages about 30°C.) Data in Figure 5 suggest that this value is about 27°C wet-bulb.

D. Heat Tolerance Testing

By definition in this context, heat tolerance refers to natural tolerance to heat as opposed to heat tolerance acquired by artificial means. Thus, in the development of a heat tolerance test the physiological requirement specified is that the degree of natural heat tolerance would be such that formal heat acclimatization would not confer any added physiological benefit.

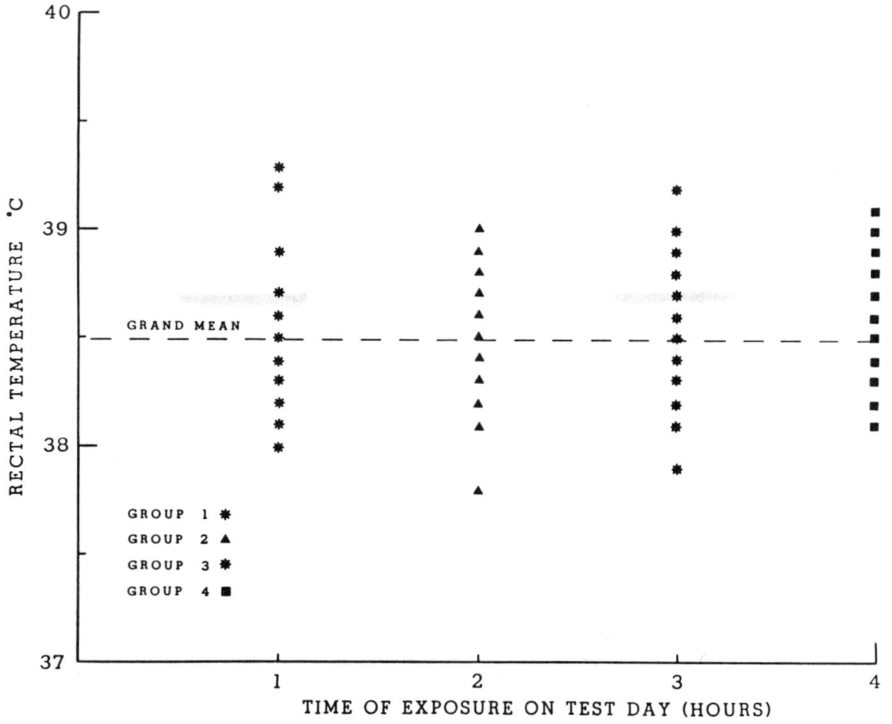

FIGURE 4. Rectal temperature distributions during a heat tolerance test after periods corresponding to the daily exposure time during the preceding 5-day acclimatization regimen (see caption for Figure 3 for detail). Group 1 was exposed for 1 hr on each day of acclimatization, group 2 for 2 hr, etc. Group 1 is as well acclimatized for 1 hr work in heat as group 4 is for 4 hr work in heat.

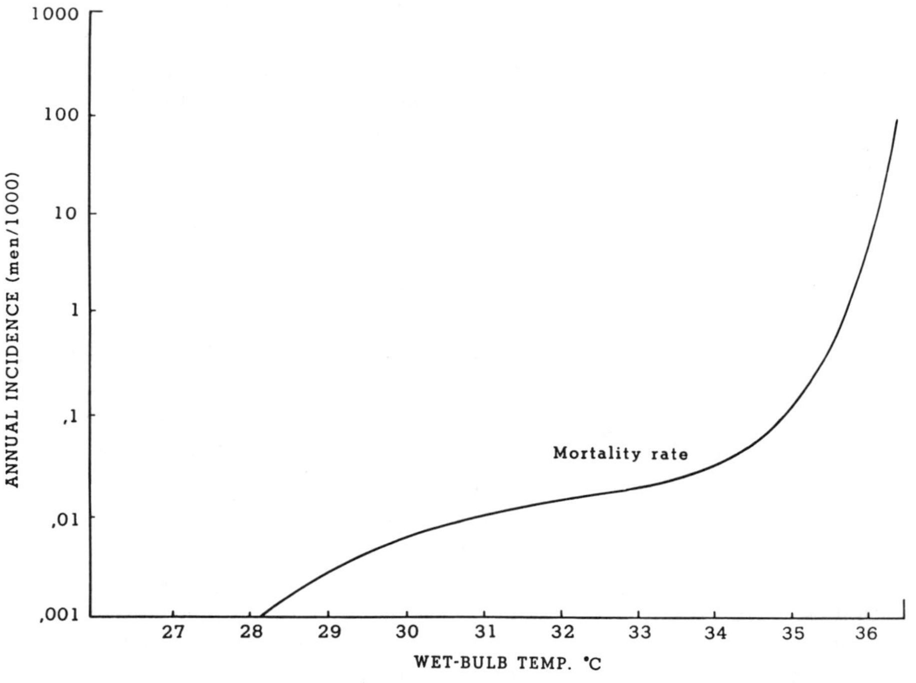

FIGURE 5. The predicted annual incidence of heat stroke fatalities as a function of wet-bulb temperature in South African gold mines. It should be stressed that a high wet-bulb temperature per se can only be identified in certain instances. The graph, therefore, refers to all incidents irrespective of the exact causal factor(s).

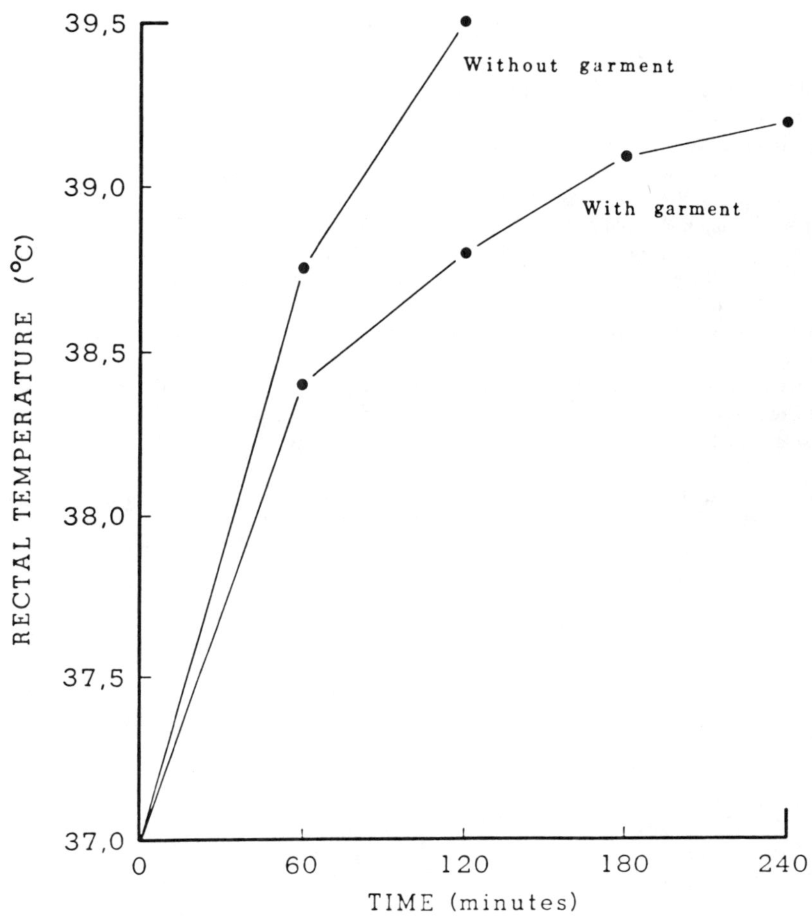

FIGURE 6. Protection afforded by body cooling jackets containing dry-ice (total mass: 4 kg, excluding the jacket). Experimental conditions comprised a dry-bulb of 35.5°C, a wet-bulb of 34.0°C, an air movement of 0.5 m/sec and an external work rate of 70 W. Subjects had previously been acclimatized by a standard method currently in practice in the South African mining industry.[1]

While the precise mechanism through which natural heat tolerance is conferred is not well understood, it seems to bear some relationship to a more sensitive sweat response. This is in agreement with the observation that heat acclimatized individuals exhibit a more profuse sweat rate pattern than unacclimatized men.[5]

IV. FUTURE DIRECTIONS

Present indications are that prolonged, strenuous physical labor, even as far as highly acclimatized men are concerned, cannot be performed at wet-bulb temperatures in excess of 32.5°C without undue risk of contracting heat stroke. Future directions will therefore be determined largely by the success of cost-effective mine cooling procedures. However, if mines become hotter, it is obvious that physiological limitations may be exceeded to the extent that a protection strategy, in contrast to one of selection and acclimatization, would have to be adopted. Rescue brigadesmen, especially are likely to benefit from the protection afforded of one such innovation, i.e., body cooling garments. Although still in an experimental stage, prototypes are capable of providing the necessary cooling power and they are sufficiently robust to withstand the rugged underground terrain. Preliminary results are promising (Figure 6), and it is therefore not unrealistic to envisage a new era of challenging the heat hazard in the South African mining industry.

REFERENCES

1. **Kielblock, A. J., Schutte, P. C., and Strydom, N. B.,** Heat acclimatization: perspectives and trends, *J. Mine Vent. Soc. S. Afr.,* 35, 53, 1982.
2. **Wyndham, C. H.,** The physiological and psychological effects of heat, in *The Ventilation of South African Gold Mines,* Burrows, J. H. J., Ed., Cape and Transvaal Printers, Cape Town, 1974, 93.
3. **Schutte, P. C., Rogers, G. G., Van Graan, C. H., and Strydom, N. B.,** Heat acclimatization by a method utilizing microclimate cooling, *Aviat. Space Environ. Med.,* 49, 710, 1978.
4. **Kielblock, A. J., Schutte, P. C., and Van der Walt, W. H.,** Development of microclimate acclimation in the South African gold mining industry, *Thermal Physiology,* Hales, J. R. S., Ed., Raven Press, New York, 1984, 483.
5. **Strydom, N. B., Van der Walt, W. H., and Kielblock, A. J.,** The evaluation of heat tolerance, *Physiologist,* 24, 13, 1981.
6. **Hubbard, R. W., Bowers, W. D., Matthew, W. T., Curtis, F. C., Criss, R. E. L., Sheldon, G. M., and Ratteree, J. W.,** Rat model of acute heatstroke mortality, *J. Appl. Physiol.,* 42, 809, 1977.
7. **Shibolet, S., Lancaster, M. C., and Dannon, Y.,** Heatstroke: a review, *Aviat. Space Environ. Med.,* 47, 280, 1976.
8. **Stewart, J. M.,** Practical aspects of human heat stress, in *Environmental Engineering in South African Gold Mines,* Burrows, J. H. J., Ed., Cape and Transvaal Printers, Cape Town, 1982, 535.

Chapter 10

THERMOREGULATORY ADAPTATIONS TO INACTIVITY

Suzanne M. Fortney

TABLE OF CONTENTS

Abstract 76

I. Introduction 76

II. Experimental Methods and Results 77

III. Discussion 81

IV. Conclusions 82

Acknowledgments 82

References 83

ABSTRACT

Exercise conditioning is usually accompanied by increases in blood volume and improvements in heat tolerance. Deconditioning, on the other hand, especially when produced by extended periods of bedrest, is accompanied by a decrease of blood volume. In this study, the effects of bedrest deconditioning on exercise thermoregulatory responses were studied, both with and without an accompanying reduction in plasma volume. Two groups of women underwent identical 12-day bedrest protocols. Group 1 (n = 12) was administered no hormonal treatment, and their plasma volumes were significantly reduced (19.9%) at the end of the bedrest. Group 2 (n = 7) received daily estrogen supplementation (1.25 mg premarin) during bedrest, and they did not suffer a significant reduction in plasma volume during the last days of bedrest. Both groups, however, had impaired thermoregulatory responses after bedrest. Therefore deconditioning, even if unaccompanied by a reduction in plasma volume, results in an impairment of thermoregulatory function.

I. INTRODUCTION

Although many studies have examined the effect of increasing fitness level on heat tolerance,[1-5] very few[6] have looked at the effect of deconditioning. There are many reasons to suspect that heat tolerance would be impaired following periods of inactivity, especially if that inactivity involved physical confinement, for example, as often occurs in patients confined to bed for several days or weeks. Bedrest results not only in a reduction in fitness level, but also is known to result in pronounced reduction in body fluid compartments.[7,8] Hypovolemia both with and without electrolyte losses, has been shown to alter significantly both the vasodilatory and the sweating heat loss responses in exercising humans.[9-11]

The effect of increasing fitness level on local sweating and skin blood flow responses was studied by Roberts and co-workers.[12] The local sweat response was measured with sweat capsules placed on the chest and connected to a resistance hygrometry sweat system. The local sweat rate was plotted as a function of the internal body temperature, which was measured with a thermocouple placed in the esophagus at heart level. A plot of the chest sweat rate (SR) as a function of the rise in deep body temperature (T_{es}) characterized the effect of increased fitness. An increase in the slope of this SR/T_{es} relationship indicated that the sensitivity of the sweating response increased during the training program, which produced an 11% increase in the maximum oxygen uptake (VO_2max) in these subjects. The T_{es} threshold at which sweating began was reduced significantly. The skin blood flow (SkBF) response was measured by electrocapacitance plethysmography. Again, this thermoregulatory response was characterized by plotting the skin blood flow values as a function of the rise in T_{es}. The slope of the SkBF/T_{es} relationship was only slightly altered following training, however, the T_{es} threshold at which vasodilation occurred was significantly reduced during the training program.

Thus, changes in fitness level may be expected to alter both the sweating and the skin blood flow responses. We would hypothesize further that after deconditioning, the internal temperature during an exercise challenge would be elevated to a greater extent than before deconditioning. The higher core temperature would be due to a reduction in the slope of the sweating response, and an elevation in the thresholds of the sweating and skin blood flow responses. Deconditioning as a result of bed confinement would be expected to result in even further impairment of heat tolerance. The combined effects of hypovolemia and deconditioning during bedrest would be predicted to act in an additive manner to impair thermal exercise responses.

Table 1
PHYSICAL CHARACTERISTICS OF THE SUBJECTS

	Group 1 (n = 12)	Group 2 (n = 7)
Mean weight (kg)	60.5	62.7
± SD	8.0	9.8
Mean age (years)	27	26
± SD	6	4
Pre-bedrest VO_2max (mℓ/kg/min)	37.5	37.2
± SD	5.7	7.7

II. EXPERIMENTAL METHODS AND RESULTS

To test our hypothesis that thermoregulatory responses would be impaired following deconditioning, we studied the exercise responses of 12 young healthy women before and after 12-day programs of horizontal bedrest. Then to further test the contribution of hypovolemia on the impairment of exercise thermal responses, a second group of seven women performed an identical 12-day bedrest protocol, except they were given a daily estrogen supplement (premarin) several days before and during the bedrest. The estrogen supplement resulted in an attenuation of the loss of body fluids during bedrest so that deconditioning responses might be separated from hypovolemic effects.

Table 1 illustrates the physical characteristics of the two groups of women. All the women in this study reported a normal menstrual cycle history, with a total cycle length consistently between 25 and 32 days. Group 1 was composed of 12 women who did not regularly take medication of any kind, including oral contraceptives. They were between 21 and 39 years of age, with a group mean age of 27. They were of average fitness as determined by VO_2max testing. Group 2 had similar physical characteristics, but had at some point in their lives used an estrogen-containing oral contraceptive without suffering significant side effects. These women were instructed to ingest one tablet (1.25 mg) of premarin each morning starting on the third cycle day (where day 1 is the first day of bleeding) immediately before the bedrest, and to continue this treatment until 2 days after the bedrest.

The bedrest procedure consisted of 12 days of horizontal bedrest. Each woman maintained a horizontal position during all but 18 min in each 24 hr interval. These 18 min were spent in the sitting position and this was the total accumulative time in which the subjects traveled by wheelchair to and from the bathroom. At no time did a subject support her weight by standing or walking. At the same time each morning during the bedrest, a blood sample was drawn without stasis to determine the hematocrit and hemoglobin concentrations. These values were used to calculate[13] the relative changes in plasma volume between the first and and each succeeding day of the bedrest.

The absolute red cell volume and plasma volume of each woman was determined by radioisotope dilution.[14] ^{99m}Technetium pertechnetate was used to label a sample of each subject's red blood cells to determine absolute red cell volume, and ^{99m}technetium-labeled human serum albumin was used to determine absolute plasma volume. Absolute red cell and plasma volume determinations were performed 1 day before and within 48 hr after each bedrest.

Although significant reductions in red cell volume have been reported during longer bedrest procedures,[15] in this study there was a tendency to reduce red cell volume during bedrest, but these differences were not significant (p <0.05 from t-test determinations). Red cell volume averaged 1474 ± 44 and 1326 ± 95 before bedrest for groups 1 and 2, respectively.

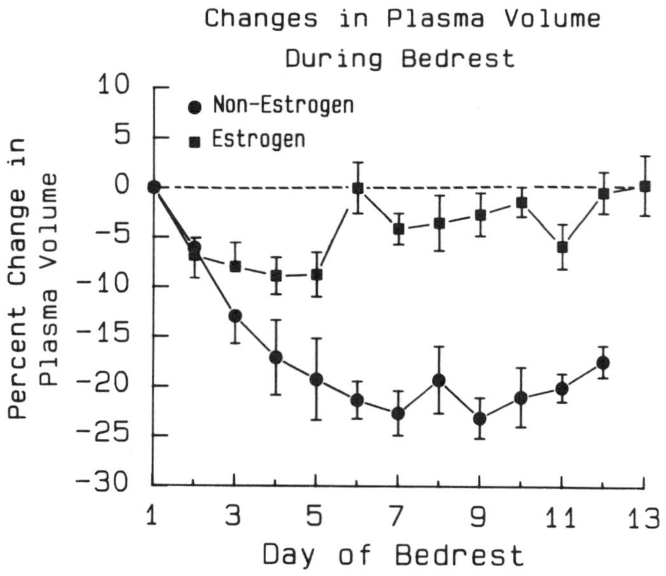

FIGURE 1. The percent changes in plasma volume (changes from day 1) during bedrest. Shown are the mean ± standard error of the mean for the women (n = 12) who did not take estrogens, and the women (n = 7) who took estrogen supplements.

The red cell volumes for the two groups averaged 1389 ± 42 and 1240 ± 90 mℓ after bedrest.

Figure 1 illustrates the changes in plasma volume during the two bedrest procedures. Plasma volume decreased significantly during the first 4 to 5 days of bedrest in the women who did not receive estrogen supplement (group 1). A markedly different pattern however was seen in group 2. Plasma volume decreased significantly during the first 2 days of bedrest. Then the decrease in plasma volume was attenuated and even reversed, such that the plasma volume in the group of women who received estrogen supplement was not significantly different ($p < 0.05$, Duncan Multiple Range comparisons) from their first day of bedrest during 7 of the last 8 days of the bedrest.

Submaximal exercise tests were performed in a warm (30° C, 50 to 60% relative humidity) temperature-controlled room, 1 day before and immediately after bedrest. The exercise intensity on the low-sit cycle ergometer was adjusted to 70% of each subject's pre-bedrest VO_2 max, which was determined previously and defined by a plateau in the oxygen consumption/exercise intensity relationship measured during progressive cycle exercise tests. The submaximal tests continued for 30 min, or until a subject's heart rate exceeded 95% of her pre-bedrest maximum heart rate value.

Submaximal exercise tolerance was reduced significantly in both groups of women following bedrest, despite the marked differences in plasma volume decrease during bedrest between groups 1 and 2. Whereas, before bedrest each woman was able to comfortably complete the 30-min exercise task, following bedrest, only one woman in group 1, and none of the women in group 2 could complete the 30 min of exercise without being instructed to stop because her heart rate had reached 95% of her maximal heart rate.

The heart rate responses during these submaximal tests are illustrated in Figure 2. The average plus or minus standard error values for the first group of women are shown in the top panel of this figure for both pre- and post-bedrest exercise. Since the submaximal exercise tests were performed immediately after bedrest, a postural stress was induced by the assumption of the sitting position in the low-sit cycle for 30 min before the start of exercise.

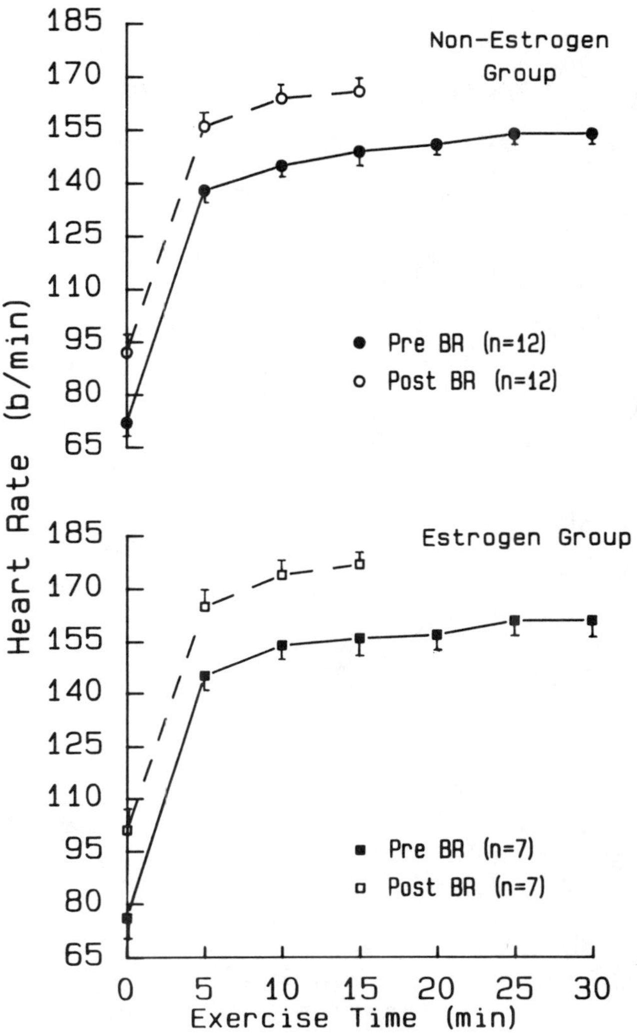

FIGURE 2. The absolute heart rates (beats/min) during the submaximal exercise tests which were performed before (solid lines) and after (dashed lines) bedrest. Each point represents the mean ± the standard error of the mean for the women who did not take estrogens during bedrest (top panel) and the women who took estrogen supplements (bottom panel).

Thus, even at rest, heart rates were significantly higher than pre-bedrest values in the post-bedrest tests. Initially, we attributed at least part of the increase in heart rate after bedrest to a hypovolemic effect. The average plasma volume at the start of exercise was 432 mℓ lower during the post-bedrest test than during the pre-bedrest test.

However, the results in the bottom half of Figure 2 illustrate the heart rate responses in the second group of women. The average difference in plasma volume at the start of exercise between the pre- and post-bedrest tests was only 130 mℓ (nonsignificant). Yet an examination of the heart rate responses following bedrest shows a similar pattern as seen in group 1 that is a similar increase in heart rate post-bedrest.

Continuous measurement of body core temperature was obtained during each exercise test from a thermocouple placed in the esophagus at the level of the heart and these results are illustrated in Figure 3. Again the responses from group 1 are shown in the top panel of this

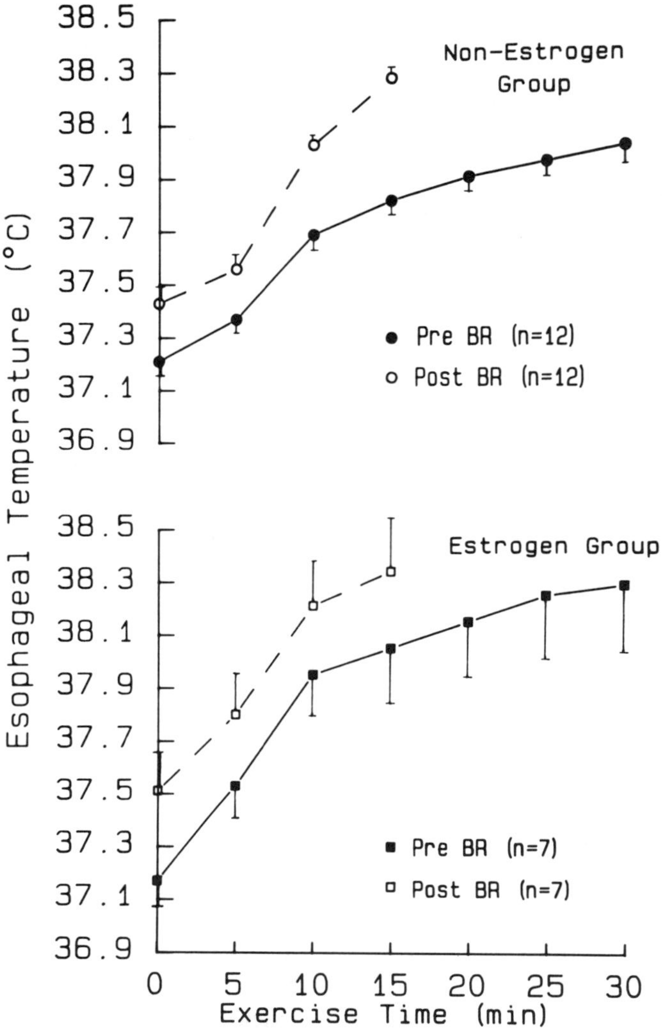

FIGURE 3. The esophageal temperature responses during submaximal exercise tests which were performed before (solid lines) or after (dashed lines) bedrest. Each point represents mean ± standard error of the mean for the group of women who did not take estrogens during bedrest (top panel), and the women who took estrogen supplements (bottom panel).

figure. Like the heart rate responses, the esophageal temperature (T_{es}) already was elevated significantly above pre-bedrest levels before the start of the post-bedrest test. T_{es} remained higher than pre-bedrest time-matched values throughout exercise following bedrest. A similar pattern of T_{es} response occurred in the pre- and post-bedrest tests in group 2 (bottom panel). However, the rise in T_{es} during post-bedrest exercise was significantly greater than before bedrest in group 1 ($p < 0.02$), but not in group 2 ($p < 0.67$).

The total sweat output was estimated in these exercise tests by accurately weighing each subject in dry cotton clothing before and after exercise. The changes in body weight are shown in Table 2.

The total change in body weight (g) was less in the post-bedrest tests, in part due to the shorter exercise period. When the sweat rate was expressed as a weight loss per minute of exercise (g/min), the total sweat rate was significantly higher in the post-bedrest tests for both groups 1 and 2. It appears that the sweating response was not inhibited by deconditioning

Table 2
TOTAL BODY SWEAT LOSSES DURING EXERCISE

	Group 1 (nonestrogen)		Group 2 (estrogen)	
	Pre-bedrest	Post-bedrest	Pre-bedrest	Post-bedrest
Change of body weight	512	436[a]	486	409
± S.E. (g)	20	19	33	47
Min of exercise	30	21[a]	30	16[a]
± S.E. (min)	0	2	0	2
Total sweat rate	17.31	22.19[a]	16.19	26.84[a]
± S.E. (g/min)	2.56	4.59	2.73	5.00
Increase in T_{es}	0.62	0.78[a]	0.89	0.83
± S.E. (°C)	0.06	0.07	0.16	0.09

[a] Post-bedrest value significantly different from pre-bedrest value ($p \leq 0.05$). Paired *t*-test comparison.

following bedrest, and that the higher post-bedrest sweat rate would be expected to accompany the higher T_{es} values. We had predicted an inhibition of sweating in the hypovolemic exercise condition (group 1, post-bedrest), as compared to the normovolemic post-bedrest conditions (group 2). Although there was a tendency for the sweat rates to be lower in group 1 than in group 2 following bedrest, these differences were barely significant ($p < 0.06$).

III. DISCUSSION

In these studies we have developed a model to examine the effects of bedrest, both with and without plasma volume reduction, on submaximal exercise responses. We predicted that exercise tolerance would be reduced following bedrest for two reasons. First, a certain degree of physical deconditioning would be expected following 2 days of bedrest; then, since the same absolute exercise intensity (70% of the pre-bedrest VO_2max was used in the pre- and post-bedrest tests, post-bedrest exercise was performed at a higher relative exercise intensity. Second, it has been reported in men during bedrest[15] that a spontaneous diuresis occurs in the first few days of a bedrest procedure. Presumably a Henry-Gauer type of reflex is elicited[16] by an increase in central blood volume caused by the cephalad movement of body fluids with the assumption of the horizontal position. Cardiopulmonary stretch receptors are then stimulated resulting in an increased urine output and a decrease in total body fluids. In this study the decrease in plasma volume averaged about 20% in group 1. In previous studies[10,11,17] in which plasma volume was reduced to a similar degree through the use of diuretics or by blood withdrawal before submaximal exercise, the thermoregulatory responses were impaired significantly. The surprising finding in this study was that exercise responses following bedrest were equally impaired in these subjects, whether the plasma volume was reduced (by about 20%), or restored to the pre-bedrest level before exercise testing. An attempt was made to measure the decrease in VO_2max within 48 hr after the end of the bedrest procedure. However, following bedrest, we were not able to consistently attain our criteria for determination of VO_2max, i.e., a plateau of the oxygen consumption/exercise intensity curve. Only peak oxygen uptake values could be obtained, because most subjects stopped the progressive exercise test due to leg fatigue rather than a cardiovascular limitation. The peak VO_2 value obtained following bedrest in group 1 averaged an 11.5% reduction from the pre-bedrest values. Group 2 showed a 21.5% average reduction. There was tremendous variation in the responses of the individual subjects in each group, and so the decrease in peak VO_2 seen following bedrest was not statistically different ($p < 0.05$) between groups 1 and 2. Thus, there is no reason to believe that the deconditioning effect was different between the two groups.

An alteration in thermoregulatory responses was evident after bedrest even before the start of exercise. The higher resting core temperature and heart rate in the post-bedrest tests occurred before the initiation of the sweating reflex. This fact, together with the lack of a significant reduction in the sweat rate following bedrest, argues against the idea that deconditioning may have inhibited the sweating response, and thus been responsible for the higher body temperatures after bedrest.

There are two other possible explanations for the impaired heat tolerance after bedrest. The first is that there was a change in the resting metabolic rate after bedrest, such that the total body heat production increased both at rest and during exercise. This explanation seems unlikely, as one would expect that if any change occurred in the resting oxygen consumption during bedrest, VO_2 would decrease, not increase.

The second more likely explanation is that there was an alteration in vasomotor tone following bedrest, producing a greater vasoconstriction which decreased heat exchange between the skin surface and the environment. Indirect evidence to support this hypothesis is the greater venoconstriction we reported in a group of women at rest and during exercise following bedrest.[18] At the time of this report, we suggested that following bedrest there was an increase in peripheral venoconstrictor tone which helped to compensate for the reduction in plasma volume, and which functioned to maintain central blood volume. Although in this previous study we measured an increase in forearm venous tone, we might also expect a greater cutaneous arteriolar tone, since both venous and arteriolar constrictor responses are produced by the increased sympathetic drive which occurs with the onset of exercise. Although the cutaneous vessels may show an increase in tone following bedrest, a decrease in the tone may occur in the deeper blood vessels of the lower extremities or of the splanchnic region. Thus, following bedrest when the subjects in this study sat upright just prior to the exercise tests, blood may have pooled in dependent body regions, eliciting a vasoconstrictor response and impairing cutaneous heat exchange. The potential for blood pooling following bedrest may be so great, that even when the plasma volume was restored during bedrest (group 2), blood still pooled in the lower extremities, producing a vasoconstrictor response and impairing heat loss. Thus, even an expansion of plasma volume following bedrest may not improve exercise tolerance, but may simply lead to greater blood pooling, and in extreme cases, may produce lower body edema.

IV. CONCLUSIONS

Bedrest in healthy young women resulted in impairment of thermoregulatory responses both at rest and during exercise in a warm environment. The higher body temperature following bedrest may have been due to effects caused by deconditioning or to effects caused by the hypovolemia which normally accompanies bedrest. In this study the sweating responses were not significantly altered following bedrest. It is most likely that the higher body temperatures were caused by a cutaneous vasoconstrictor response which functioned to oppose blood pooling in the lower extremities. Restoring blood volume to pre-bedrest values was ineffective in reversing the impairment of thermoregulatory responses.

ACKNOWLEDGMENTS

This work was supported by NASA Contract NAS9-16703. Thanks to Clarke Tankersley, Kirstin Levine, and Kay Chadwell for their help in the preparation of this manuscript.

REFERENCES

1. **Strydom, N. B., Wyndham, C. H., Williams, C. G., Morrison, J. F., Bredell, G. A. G., Benade, A. J. S., and Von Rahden, M.,** Acclimatization to humid heat and the role of physical conditioning, *J. Appl. Physiol.*, 21, 636, 1966.
2. **Piwonka, R. W., Robinson, S., Gay, V. L., and Manalis, R. S.,** Preacclimatization of men to heat by training, *J. Appl. Physiol.*, 20, 379, 1965.
3. **Pandolf, K. B.,** Effects of physical training and cardiorespiratory physical fitness on exercise-heat tolerance: recent observations, *Med. Sci. Sports,* 11, 60, 1979.
4. **Gisolfi, C. and Robinson, S.,** Relations between physical training, acclimatization, and heat tolerance, *J. Appl. Physiol.*, 26, 530, 1969.
5. **Henane, R., Flandrois, R. I., and Charbonnier, J. P.,** Increase in sweating sensitivity by endurance conditioning in man, *J. Appl. Physiol.*, 43, 822, 1977.
6. **Greenleaf, J. E. and Reese, R. D.,** Exercise thermoregulation after 14 days of bedrest, *J. Appl. Physiol.*, 48, 72, 1980.
7. **Taylor, H. L., Erickson, L., Henschell, A., and Kaye, A.,** The effect of bedrest on the blood volume of normal young men, *Am. J. Physiol.*, 144, 227, 1945.
8. **Hargens, A. R.,** Fluid shifts in vascular and extravascular spaces during and after simulated weightlessness, *Med. Sci. Sports,* 15, 421, 1983.
9. **Horstman, D. H. and Horvath, S. M.,** Cardiovascular and temperature regulatory changes during progressive dehydration and euhydration, *J. Appl. Physiol.*, 33, 446, 1972.
10. **Nadel, E. R., Fortney, S. M., and Wenger, C. B.,** Effect of hydration state on circulatory and thermal regulations, *J. Appl. Physiol.*, 49, 715, 1980.
11. **Fortney, S. M., Nadel, E. R., Wenger, C. B., and Bove, J. R.,** Effect of blood volume on sweating rate and body fluids in exercising humans, *J. Appl. Physiol.*, 51, 1594, 1981.
12. **Roberts, M. F., Wenger, C. B., Stolwijk, J. A. J., and Nadel, E. R.,** Skin blood flow and sweating changes following exercise training and heat acclimation, *J. Appl. Physiol.*, 43, 133, 1977.
13. **Dill, D. B., and Costill, D. L.,** Calculation of percentage changes in volumes of blood, plasma, and red cells in dehydration, *J. Appl. Physiol.*, 37, 247, 1974.
14. **Glass, H. I.,** Standard techniques for the measurement of red-cell and plasma volume, *Br. J. Haematol.*, 25, 801, 1973.
15. **Greenleaf, J. E.,** Physiological responses to prolonged bedrest and fluid immersion in humans, *J. Appl. Physiol.*, 57, 619, 1984.
16. **Gauer, O. H., Henry, J. P., and Sieker, H. H.,** Cardiac receptors and fluid volume control, *Prog. Cardiovasc. Dis.*, 4, 1, 1961.
17. **Fortney, S. M., Nadel, E. R., Wenger, C. B., and Bove, J. R.,** Effect of acute alterations of blood volume on circulatory performance in humans, *J. Appl. Physiol.*, 50, 292, 1981.
18. **Fortney, S. M., Beckett, W., Turner, C., Vroman, N. B., and Wilkinson, L.,** Alteration of venous responses during exercise following bedrest, *Fed. Proc.*, 42, 584, 1983.

Chapter 11

CIRCULATORY AND THERMOREGULATORY ACTIONS OF HYDRATION DURING EXERCISE-HEAT STRESS*

Michael N. Sawka, Ralph P. Francesconi, and Kent B. Pandolf

TABLE OF CONTENTS

Abstract 86

I. Introduction 86

II. Water Loss 86

III. Physiological Effects 87

References 90

* The views, opinions, and/or findings contained in this chapter are those of the authors and should not be construed as an official Department of the Army position, policy, or decision, unless so designated by other official documentation.

ABSTRACT

During exercise in the heat, sweat output often exceeds water intake and this results in hypohydration. Hypohydration during exercise causes greater heat storage and reduces endurance in comparison with euhydration levels. The greater heat storage is attributed to a decreased sweating rate as well as decreased cutaneous blood flow. These response decrements are attributed to both plasma hyperosmolality and plasma hypovolemia. In addition, plasma hypovolemia will result in a reduced cardiac output response, relative to euhydration, during exercise-heat stress. Hyperhydration, or body fluid excess, only provides the advantage of delaying the onset of hypohydration.

I. INTRODUCTION

Exercise performance in a hot environment has been shown to be primarily affected by state of heat acclimation,[1] aerobic fitness,[2] and hydration level.[3] Heat acclimated individuals who are aerobically fit and fully hydrated will have less body heat storage and may achieve optimal performance during exercise-heat stress. Hydration level is particularly important during exercise in the heat because the body fluid deficit will neutralize the thermoregulatory advantages conferred by aerobic fitness[4] and heat acclimation.[5,6]

II. WATER LOSS

In hot environments, body fluid is primarily lost via eccrine sweat gland secretion which enables evaporative cooling of the body. For a given individual, sweating rate is dependent upon the environmental conditions, clothing and physical activity level.[7] Hypohydration will occur if the volume of fluid ingested is less than sweat output. However, simple *ad libitum* water intake may not ensure maintenance of euhydration. Several studies[8,9] have reported that *ad libitum* water intake results in incomplete fluid replacement or ''voluntary'' dehydration during exercise in the heat. A person's state of heat acclimation may also influence the level of ''voluntary'' dehydration incurred during exercise in the heat.[8,9] Eichna et al.,[8] as well as Greenleaf et al.[9] reported that water deficits during exercise-heat stress were markedly reduced when subjects were heat acclimated. Therefore, heat acclimation may improve the relationship between thirst and body water needs.

If euhydration is not maintained, sweat loss will result in a reduction of total body water. Of particular importance for thermoregulation and exercise performance is the influence of hypohydration on the volume and composition of plasma fluid. Hypohydration has been consistently reported to reduce plasma volume below euhydration levels,[10-12] and the magnitude of this hypovolemia probably increases with the severity of hypohydration.[10,12] However, recent study indicates that plasma volume is defended and does not continue to decrease at severe levels (7% reduction in body weight) of hypohydration.[12]

Eccrine sweat is ordinarily hypotonic relative to plasma. Therefore, the plasma will become hyperosmotic when hypohydration is primarily mediated by sweat output. Plasma osmolality has been reported to increase from euhydrated levels of approximately 283 mOsm/kg to levels exceeding 300 mOsm/kg when hypohydration occurred by exercise-heat stress.[12] Later, it will be demonstrated that the plasma hypovolemia as well as plasma hyperosmolality contribute to the less efficient thermoregulatory responses when hypohydration occurs during exercise-heat stress. The plasma hypovolemia and hyperosmolality also appear to be the triggering mechanisms for adaptive hormonal responses to conserve body fluids during dehydration. For example, our research indicates that the renin-aldosterone responses during exercise-heat stress mirror the changes in plasma volume induced by hydration levels.[13-15]

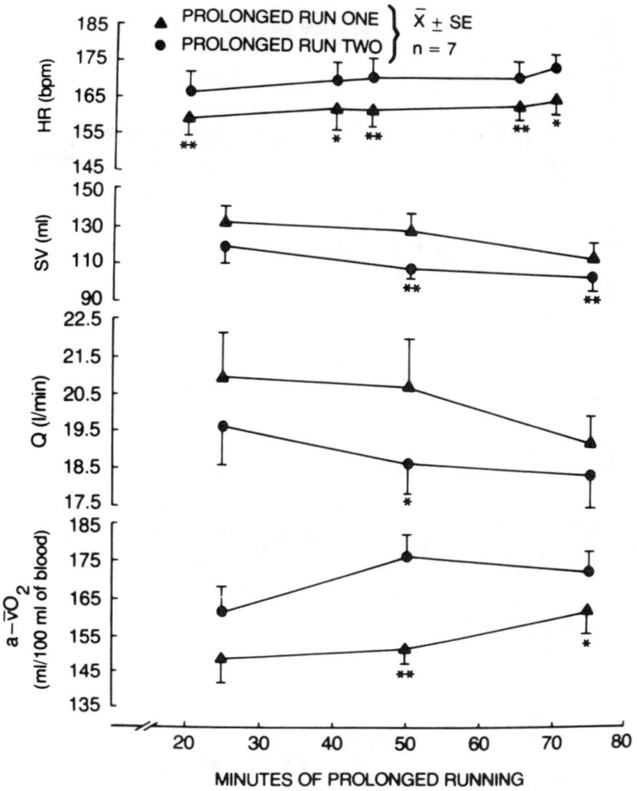

FIGURE 1. Heart rate, stroke volume, cardiac output, and arteriovenous oxygen difference responses of subjects during two prolonged runs spaced by a brief rest period. During these exercise bouts the subject experienced progressive dehydration and hyperthermia. $*p < 0.05$ and $**p < 0.01$.

III. PHYSIOLOGICAL EFFECTS

Hypohydration reduces maximal exercise performance[3,6,16] and this performance reduction increases with the magnitude of fluid deficit.[3,16] In addition, these maximal exercise performance decrements are potentiated by the presence of heat stress.[3] The mechanisms responsible for hypohydration and heat stress-mediated decrements in exercise performance probably reside in the cardiovascular system. The hypovolemia associated with hypohydration results in a decreased effective central blood volume and this reduces venous return and cardiac output during exercise.[17,18] Likewise, the presence of heat strain results in competition between central and peripheral circulation for the limited blood volume.[17,18] As body temperature increases during exercise, cutaneous vasodilation occurs, which decreases venous resistance and pressure. These cardiovascular adaptations to heat strain appear to be consistent with the potentiated exercise performance decrement mediated by hypohydration with heat stress. Figure 1 presents the cardiovascular responses of subjects performing two prolonged exercise (70% of $\dot{V}O_2$ max) bouts that were spaced by a brief rest period. During the exercise bouts, the subjects were gradually dehydrated (to a 4% reduction in body weight) and incurred rectal temperatures in excess in 40°C.[18] During these exercises bouts, heart rate increased but was unable to compensate for the falling stroke volume and therefore, cardiac output decreased.

Hypohydration during exercise causes a greater heat storage which elevates core temperature

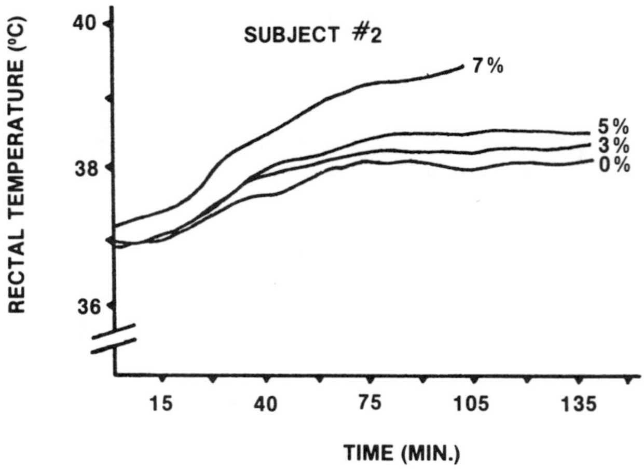

FIGURE 2. A representative subject's rectal temperature response to exercise-heat stress when euhydrated (0%) and hypohydrated by 3, 5, and 7% of his body weight.

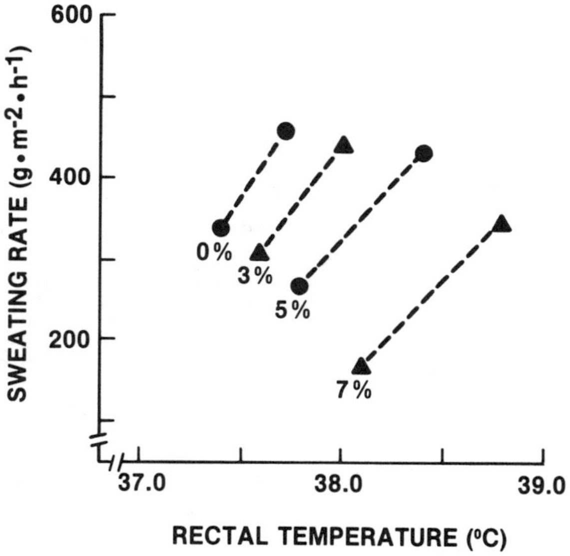

FIGURE 3. A plot of group mean sweating rate and rectal temperature responses to exercise-heat stress when euhydrated (0%) and hypohydrated by 3, 5, and 7% of their body weight.

above euhydration levels.[5,6,12,18,19] These elevated core temperature responses do not represent a "threshold" effect,[3] but increase linearly with hypohydration level.[12,19] The magnitude of the core temperature increment mediated by hypohydration is specific to the conditions of exercise intensity and to the environmental conditions.[20] Figure 2 provides data of a typical subject's rectal temperature response to four hydration levels during standardized regimens of exercise-heat stress. Since hypohydration does not influence metabolic rate,[12] the elevated core temperatures must be the result of decreased heat dissipation. The relative contribution of evaporative and dry heat exchange depends on the specific environmental condition, however, both avenues of heat dissipation are adversely affected by hypohydration.[3,12,17]

Figure 3 shows sweating rate responses plotted against rectal temperatures for individuals

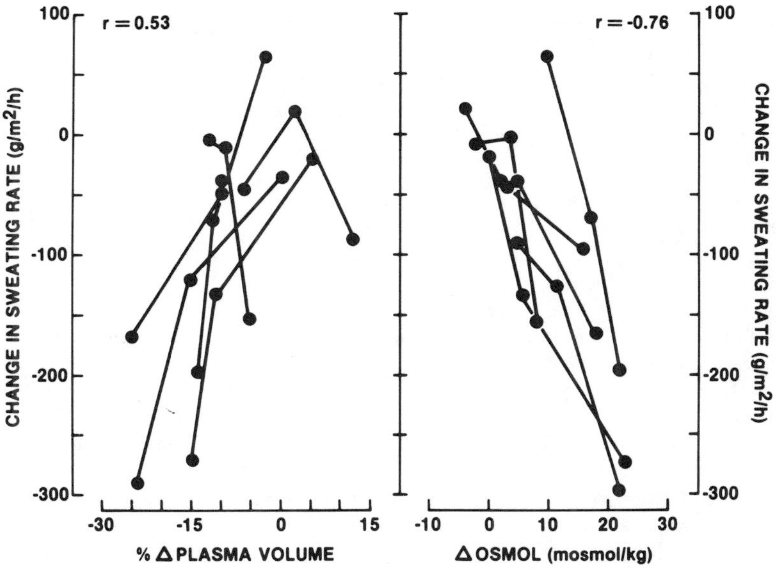

FIGURE 4. Individual relationships between the change in sweating rate from euhydration levels, with the change in plasma volume and change in osmolality from euhydration levels.

at four hydration levels during exercise-heat stress.[12] The sweating rate responses were systematically decreased at a given core temperature with increased severity of hypohydration. The singular and combined effects of plasma hypovolemia and hyperosmolality have been suggested as mediating the reduced sweating rate response when hypohydrated.[3] Figure 4 presents individual relationships of the change in sweating rate from euhydration levels during exercise to the plasma volume and osmolality changes from euhydration levels when hypohydrated.[12] Elevated plasma osmolality provided a strong and consistent relationship with reduced sweating rate responses. This finding is consistent with the data of Harrison et al.[21] who reported that plasma hyperosmolality will elevate core temperature response during exercise-heat stress despite the maintenance of euhydration. Hyperosmolality may have a direct CNS effect on the hypothalamic thermoregulatory centers or a peripheral effect on the eccrine sweat gland.[3]

Plasma volume loss provides a weaker and less consistent relationship (than hyperosmolality) with the reduced sweating rate responses. Fortney et al.[22] have provided evidence that an isosmotic hypovolemia (~15% plasma volume reduction) caused a reduced sweating rate during exercise in the heat. Their observation is in agreement with Figure 4, which suggests that plasma volume reductions of about 10 to 15% are necessary for consistent reductions of sweating rate. Fortney et al.[22] theorized that hypovolemia will unload atrial baroreceptors which may have afferent input to the hypothalamic thermoregulatory centers which control sweating rate. Similarly, Nadel et al.[17] reported that an isosmotic hypovolemia (~18% plasma volume reduction) will reduce cutaneous blood flow for a given core temperature and thus, the potential for dry heat exchange. These high levels of hypovolemia induced by diuretics[17,22] appear to be greater than those levels generally observed to be elicited by exercise-heat dehydration for moderate (up to 5% reduction in body weight) hypohydration levels.[6,10,12,18]

If hypohydration reduces performance, can excess body fluids improve performance beyond the levels achieved when euhydrated? If hyperhydration does improve performance during exercise-heat stress, these improvements would most likely be mediated by hypervolemia or expanded plasma volume.[3] Several recent studies on the effects of artificially expanded plasma volume have indicated no differences in core temperature,[17,23] sweating rate,[22,23] cardiac output,[17] arterial blood pressure,[23] or peripheral blood flow[17] during exercise-heat stress. These data indicate that hyperhydration does not provide a thermal advantage during exercise-heat stress, but will delay the development of hypohydration.

REFERENCES

1. **Nadel, E. R., Pandolf, K. B., Roberts, M. F., and Stolwijk, J. A. J.,** Mechanisms of thermal acclimation to exercise and heat, *J. Appl. Physiol.,* 37, 515, 1974.
2. **Pandolf, K. B.,** Effects of physical training and cardiorespiratory physical fitness on exercise-heat tolerance: recent observations, *Med. Sci. Sports Exercise,* 11, 155, 1979.
3. **Sawka, M. N., Francesconi, R. P., Young, A. J., and Pandolf, K. B.,** Influence of hydration level and body fluids on exercise performance in the heat, *JAMA,* 252, 1165, 1984.
4. **Cadarette, B. S., Sawka, M. N., Toner, M. M., and Pandolf, K. B.,** Aerobic fitness and the hypohydration response to exercise-heat stress, *Aviat. Space Environ. Med.,* 55, 507, 1984.
5. **Buskirk, E. R., Iampietro, P. F., and Bass, D. E.,** Work performance after dehydration: effects of physical conditioning and heat acclimatization, *J. Appl. Physiol.,* 12, 189, 1958.
6. **Sawka, M. N., Toner, M. M., Francesconi, R. P., and Pandolf, K. B.,** Hypohydration and exercise: effects of heat acclimation, gender and environment, *J. Appl. Physiol.,* 55, 1147, 1983.
7. **Shapiro, Y., Pandolf, K. B., and Goldman, R. F.,** Predicting sweat loss response to exercise, environment and clothing, *Eur. J. Appl. Physiol.,* 48, 83, 1982.
8. **Eichna, L. B., Bean, W. B., and Ashe, W. F.,** Performance in relation to environmental temperature, *Bull. Johns Hopkins Hosp.,* 76, 25, 1945.
9. **Greenleaf, J. E., Brock, P. J., Keil, L. C., and Morse, J. T.,** Drinking and water balance during exercise and heat acclimation, *J. Appl. Physiol.,* 54, 414, 1983.
10. **Costill, D. L., Cote, R., and Fink, W.,** Muscle water and electrolytes following varied levels of dehydration in man, *J. Appl. Physiol.,* 40, 6, 1976.
11. **Sawka, M. N., Francesconi, R. P., Pimental, N. A., and Pandolf, K. B.,** Hydration and vascular fluid shifts during exercise in heat, *J. Appl. Physiol.,* 56, 91, 1984.
12. **Sawka, M. N., Young, A. J., Francesconi, R. P., Muza, S. R., and Pandolf, K. B.,** Thermoregulatory and blood responses during exercise at graded hypohydration levels, *J. Appl. Physiol.,* 59, 1394, 1985.
13. **Francesconi, R. P., Sawka, M. N., Hubbard, R. W., and Mager, M.,** Acute albumin-induced plasma volume expansion and exercise in the heat: effects on hormonal responses in men, *Eur. J. Appl. Physiol.,* 51, 121, 1983.
14. **Francesconi, R. P., Sawka, M. N., and Pandolf, K. B.,** Hypohydration and heat acclimation: plasma renin and aldosterone during exercise, *J. Appl. Physiol.,* 55, 1790, 1983.
15. **Francesconi, R. P., Sawka, M. N., Pandolf, K. B., Hubbard, R. W., Young, A. J., and Muza, S.,** Plasma hormonal responses at graded hypohydration levels during exercise/heat stress, *J. Appl. Physiol.,* 59, 1855, 1985.
16. **Craig, F. N.,** Dehydration and muscular work, *J. Appl. Physiol.,* 21, 670, 1966.
17. **Nadel, E. R., Fortney, S. M., and Wenger, C. B.,** Effect of hydration state on circulatory and thermal regulation, *J. Appl. Physiol.,* 49, 715, 1980.
18. **Sawka, M. N., Knowlton, R. G., and Critz, J. B.,** Thermal and circulatory responses to repeated bouts of prolonged running, *Med. Sci. Sports,* 11, 177, 1979.
19. **Strydom, N. B. and Holdsworth, L. D.,** The effects of different levels of water deficit on physiological responses during heat stress, *Int. Z. Angew Physiol.,* 26, 95, 1968.
20. **Sawka, M. N. and Pandolf, K. B.,** Exercise-Heat Strain During Hypohydration: Interaction with Heat Acclimation and Aerobic Fitness, 14th Commonwealth Defence Conference US-4, Melbourne, Australia, 1985.
21. **Harrison, M. H., Edwards, R. J., and Fennessy, P. A.,** Intravascular volume and tonicity as factors in the regulation of body temperature, *J. Appl. Physiol.,* 44, 69, 1978.
22. **Fortney, S. M., Nadel, E. R., Wenger, C. B., and Bove, J. R.,** Effect of blood volume on sweating rate and body fluids in exercising humans, *J. Appl. Physiol.,* 51, 1594, 1981.
23. **Sawka, M. N., Hubbard, R. W., Francesconi, R. P., and Horstman, D. H.,** Effects of acute plasma volume expansion on altering exercise-heat performance, *Eur. J. Appl. Physiol.,* 51, 303, 1983.

Chapter 12

FACTORS WHICH ALTER HUMAN PHYSIOLOGICAL RESPONSES DURING EXERCISE-HEAT ACCLIMATION*

Kent B. Pandolf, Michael N. Sawka, and Yair Shapiro

TABLE OF CONTENTS

Abstract 92

I. Introduction 92

II. Physical Training and Aerobic Fitness 92
  A. Historical Perspective 92
  B. Recent Observations 94

III. Gender Considerations 96
  A. Historical Observations 96
  B. Recent Findings 96

IV. Effects of Aging 98

References 101

* The views, opinions, and/or findings contained in this report are those of the Department of the Army position, policy, or decision, unless so designated by other official documentation.

ABSTRACT

Researchers generally agree that high aerobic fitness achieved through physical training will reduce the physiological strain to exercise in the heat, but does not replace the benefits of an exercise-heat acclimation program. In addition, high aerobic fitness is hypothesized as a major factor in the small decay and rapid reacclimation of individuals after they ceased exercising in hot environments. However, recent work from our laboratory suggests that improved aerobic fitness by physical training must be associated with significant elevations in core temperature during the training process in order to improve exercise-heat tolerance. Thus, high levels of aerobic fitness, per se, cannot always be associated with improved exercise-heat tolerance. Despite the disadvantages to heat transfer of being smaller and having larger skinfold thicknesses as compared to men, women do not appear to be at a comparative disadvantage during the performance of exercise in the heat. Two recent studies comparing men and women with similar aerobic fitness indicate no major physiological differences between genders in both humid and dry heat for cardiovascular and thermoregulatory responses to these environments either before or after acclimation. Our laboratory has reported that after exercise-heat acclimation under wet conditions (mild or hot), females tolerate the heat in a more efficient fashion than males, while under hot-dry conditions males seem to be at some physiological advantage. Even fewer studies are reported which evaluate physiological differences in heat tolerance to exercise in relation to age. In general, exercise-heat tolerance is reduced in prepubertal children (boys and girls) and older adults (men and women) compared to young men and women. However, aerobically fit older adults seem to have far fewer decrements in the performance of exercise in the heat than less fit older adults.

I. INTRODUCTION

This chapter addresses three factors which are thought to alter human physiological responses during exercise-heat acclimation. These factors are (1) the influence of cardiorespiratory endurance training and aerobic fitness on the exercise-heat acclimation process, (2) the physiological comparison between genders during the performance of exercise in the heat, and (3) the physiological effects of aging on exercise-heat acclimation. Topics are discussed from a brief historical perspective followed by recent observations. All three of these factors should be of some interest to environmental and thermoregulatory physiologists, clinicians, and industrial and military scientists.

II. PHYSICAL TRAINING AND AEROBIC FITNESS

A. Historical Perspective

The importance of endurance training and/or aerobic fitness on the physiological adjustments to exercise in the heat and the process of heat acclimation has been a controversial subject for nearly two decades. However, two recent reviews[1,2] have evaluated this topic in detail from a historical perpective. Both reviews suggest possible methodological flaws in most of the early studies concerning this topic which make them difficult to evaluate.

Improved aerobic fitness from physical training has been suggested to increase the sensitivity of the sweating response (peripheral effect) without changing the threshold temperature for this response.[3] These same authors further suggested that exercise-heat acclimation lowered the threshold temperature without altering the sensitivity of the sweating response. Therefore, peripheral adaptations for heat dissipation appeared to be potentiated with improved aerobic fitness while central adaptations became involved during exercise-heat acclimation.

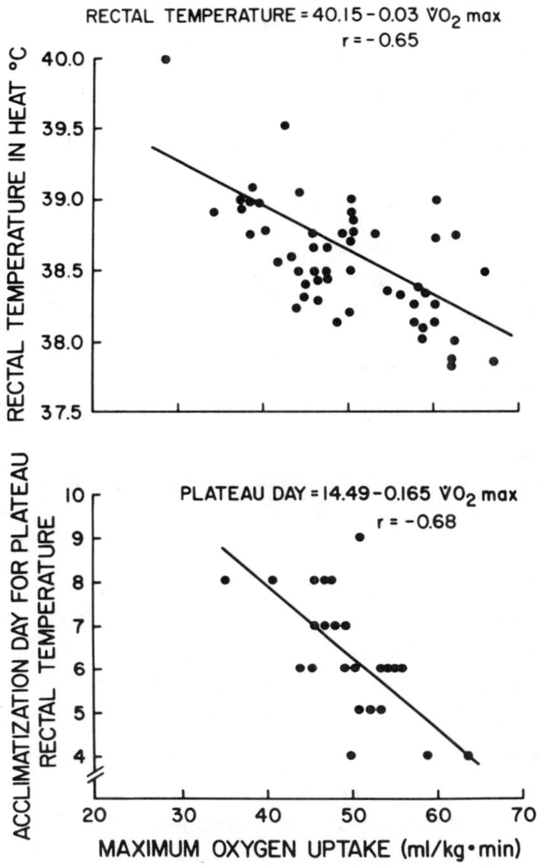

FIGURE 1. Maximal oxygen uptake (mℓ/kg/min) in relation to either the final rectal temperature in hot environments or the acclimatization day for a plateau in rectal temperature. (From Pandolf, K. B., *Med. Sci. Sports,* 11, 60, 1979. With permission.)

Another debatable issue is whether maximal aerobic power ($\dot{V}O_2$ max) is related to either improved exercise-heat tolerance or a more rapid rate of heat acclimation. As illustrated in Figure 1, two different authors[4,5] utilizing different climates (wet and dry) independently reported that an individual's $\dot{V}O_2$ max accounted for between 42 to 46% of the variability determining the core temperature after 3 hr of exercise in the heat,[5] or the heat acclimation day for a plateau in core temperature.[4] In contrast, other authors[6,7] have reported insignificant relationships between $\dot{V}O_2$ max and either exercise endurance or final core temperature in the heat. However, most of the studies which have shown a lack of relationship used relatively few subjects and/or homogeneously fit subjects.

Table 1 compares the percentage loss of heat acclimation during winter months observed by two different authors[4,8] for final rectal temperature (T_{re}) and heart rate (HR) responses. One author[8] showed significant losses for both physiological responses after the 1st, 2nd, and 3rd weeks in cool conditions with the entire acclimation gain for HR being lost by the 3rd week, and also nearly half of the T_{re} improvement being lost. The other author[4] showed nonsignificant losses for both responses at somewhat comparable time periods. While the earlier study[8] failed to quantify the aerobic fitness levels of their subjects, Pandolf et al.[4] hypothesized that the high aerobic fitness of their subjects was related to the small decay and rapid reinduction of acclimation.

Table 1
PERCENTAGE LOSS OF ACCLIMATION IN WINTER

Weeks	1st	2nd	3rd	Ref.
Rectal temperature	26	35	45	8
	13[a]	18[a]	4[a]	4
	(6 days)	(12 days)	(18 days)	
Heart rate	65	87	92	8
	23[a]	20[a]	29[a]	4

[a] Not significantly different from last (9th) day of acclimation.
From Pandolf, K. B., *Med. Sci. Sports*, 11, 60, 1979. With permission.

B. Recent Observations

Recently, Avellini et al.[9] studied the effects of physical training on exercise-heat tolerance. Three groups (n = 5, each) of male volunteers were matched initially for $\dot{V}O_2$ max and then physically trained on a cycle ergometer for 1 hr/day,[1] 5 days/week at 75% of their individual $\dot{V}O_2$ max for 4 weeks. One group trained on land and the other two groups trained while immersed to the neck in water of either 20° or 32°C. After 1 hr of training, T_{re} rose about 1.1°C for land training, 0.6°C for the warm water (32°C) group, but showed a steady decline in the cold water (20°C) group. After training, total body sweat rate averaged 600 $g/m^2/hr$ for the land group, 200 $g/m^2/hr$ for the warm water group with no measureable loss in cold water. After 4 weeks of training, the $\dot{V}O_2$ max increased significantly in all three groups. For the land training group, the $\dot{V}O_2$ max increased by 16% while the warm water group increased 13% and the cold water group increased 15%. There were no significant differences in $\dot{V}O_2$ max between groups after this month-long training period.

Figure 2 shows the mean values of final T_{re} and mean skin temperature (T_{sk}) for each of the three groups for pretraining (heat stress 1), post-training (heat stress 2), and postacclimation (heat stress 3). The post-training evaluation also served as the preacclimation session. All heat stress tests were identical 3-hr exposures at 49°C, 20% relative humidity while walking at about 30° $\dot{V}O_2$ max. Before physical training, no significant differences were observed between groups for T_{re}. After training, T_{re} decreased by about 0.5°C for the land and warm water groups but increased significantly for the cold water group. The cold water group differed significantly from the other two groups after training. After heat acclimation, final T_{re} was 38.1, 38.3, and 38.4°C for the land, warm water, and cold water groups, respectively. There were no significant differences between groups after acclimation; however, all groups displayed lower values compared to post-training (preacclimation). Similar trends can be seen for T_{sk} between groups for these same comparisons.

As seen in Figure 3, final HR responses were expectedly similar between the three groups prior to training. Final HR decreased significantly in all three groups following physical training. However, the greatest decline was seen for land training (29 beats/min) while the warm water group decreased 14 beats/min and the cold water group decreased by 18 beats/min after training. Heat acclimation served to further significantly reduce final HR to similar levels in all three groups.

These findings suggest that improved aerobic fitness by physical training must be associated with significant elevations in core temperature during the training process in order to improve the thermoregulatory component of exercise-heat tolerance. However, the cardiovascular component to exercise-heat tolerance can be enhanced somewhat through these different training regimens. Therefore, high levels of aerobic fitness, per se, cannot in all instances be associated with improved exercise-heat tolerance, particularly from a thermoregulatory standpoint.

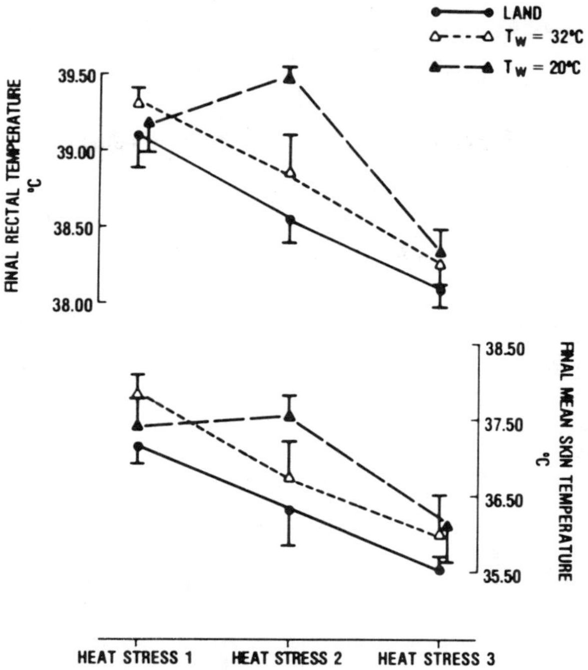

FIGURE 2. Final rectal and mean skin temperatures for the land, warm-water, and cold-water training groups as evaluated before physical training (heat stress 1), after physical training (heat stress 2), and after heat acclimation (heat stress 3). (From Avellini, B. A. et al., *J. Appl. Physiol. Resp. Environ. Exercise Physiol.*, 53, 1291, 1982. With permission.)

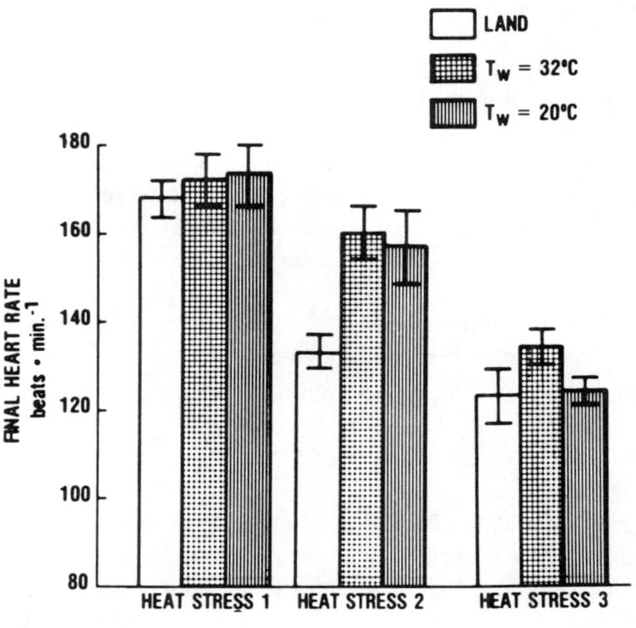

FIGURE 3. Final heart rate responses for the same three physical training groups and same periodic evaluations as in Figure 2. (From Avellini, B. A. et al., *J. Appl. Physiol. Resp. Environ. Exercise Physiol.*, 53, 1291, 1982. With permission.)

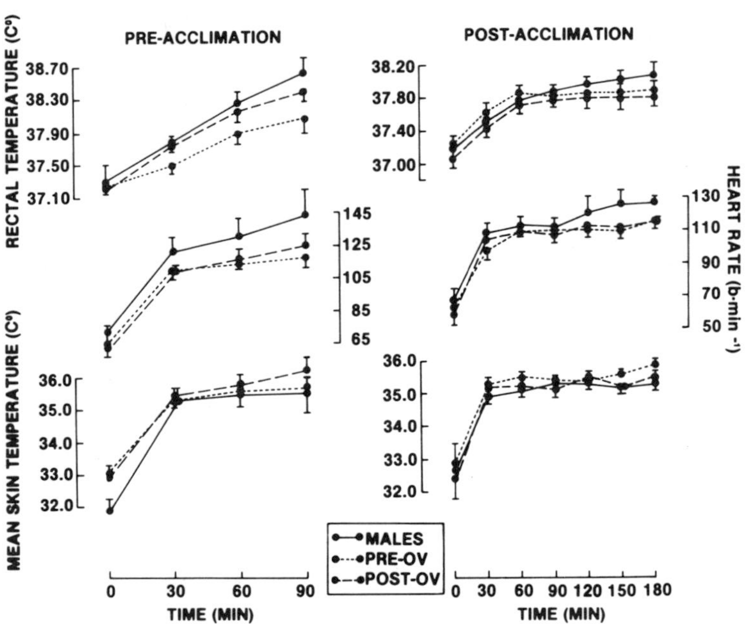

FIGURE 4. Rectal temperature, heart rate, and mean skin temperature over time comparing men and women both pre- and postacclimation. Men and women were matched for maximal aerobic power, surface area, and surface area to mass ratio.[16]

III. GENDER CONSIDERATIONS

A. Historical Observations

The responses of men to alterations in environmental temperature have provided the basis for our understanding of human exercise-heat tolerance and thermoregulation. There is less certainty about the thermoregulatory response patterns of women. Physiological responses to exercise-heat stress may be different between genders due to several factors, including the lower cardiorespiratory fitness, the higher percent body fat, the lower body weight, the lower skin surface area, and the higher surface area-to-mass ratio (A_D/wt) of women than men. In addition, hormonal fluctuations of estrogen and progesterone associated with the menstrual cycle may alter women's tolerance to exercise-heat stress.

Several investigators have shown that women thermoregulate less effectively than men when exposed to an acute heat stress.[10-12] Under the same thermal load, deep body temperatures and HRs were higher and sweating rates were lower in women.[12-14] Although heat acclimation eliminates many of these gender-related physiological differences, sweating rate still remained lower for women.[12,15] However, none of these studies matched the genders prior to evaluation in terms of $\dot{V}O_2$ max, physical, and/or any morphological considerations.

B. Recent Findings

Figure 4 depicts the findings of Avellini et al.[16] both before and after a 10-day heat acclimation program for four men and four women matched for aerobic power, surface area, and A_D/wt during an attempted 3-hr heat stress test in humid heat (T_{db} = 36°C, T_{wb} = 32°C) while walking at 1.56 m/sec (2% grade). Before acclimation, the final T_{re} for the men averaged 38.60°C while comparative values were lower at 38.04°C (preovulatory) and 38.40°C (postovulatory) for the women. In addition, the HR responses for the men were consistently 13 to 25 b/min higher than for the women throughout the preacclimation

Table 2
FINAL VALUES FOR RECTAL AND MEAN SKIN TEMPERATURES, HEART RATE, AND MEAN SWEAT RATE FOR MEN AND WOMEN BOTH PRE- AND POSTACCLIMATION TO DRY HEAT

		Variable			
State of acclimation	**Sex**	**T_{re} (°C)**	**T_{sk} (°C)**	**HR (beats/min)**	**Mean $\dot{M}_{sw}$ (W/m²)**
Preacclimation	Women	39.01 ± 0.19	38.37 ± 0.71	141.6 ± 9.6	289.6 ± 47.8
	Men	38.57 ± 0.40	37.90 ± 0.43	129.9 ± 12.1	390.4 ± 7.8
	Level of significance	NS	NS	NS	$p < 0.05$
Postacclimation	Women	38.12 ± 0.13	37.15* ± 0.40	120.6* ± 10.5	407.8* ± 24.2
	Men	37.96 ± 0.23	36.71* ± 0.28	106.3* ± 9.5	430.2* ± 29.7
	Level of significance	NS	NS	NS	NS

Note: Values are means ± SD. Asterisk indicates a significant ($p < 0.05$) change from pre- to postacclimation.

From Frye, A. J. and Kamon, E., *J. Appl. Physiol. Resp. Environ. Exercise Physiol.*, 50, 65, 1981. With permission.

exposure. Although the men began the preacclimation exposure with a 1°C lower T_{sk}, there were no differences between genders at other time comparisons.

After acclimation, the T_{re}, T_{sk}, and HR responses between genders were similar at 90 min. At 180 min the T_{re} and HR responses were higher for the men compared to the women; however, T_{sk} did not differ between genders at this time point. A trend was noted for the men to have higher sweat rates particularly in the preacclimation state in this study. These authors[16] concluded that "when fitness levels are similar, the previously reported sex-related differences in response to an acute heat exposure seem to disappear except for the higher sweat rate for men".

Table 2 summarizes the pre- and postacclimation observations of Frye and Kamon[17] who compared four men and four women matched for maximal aerobic power and A_D/wt during an attempted 3-hr exposure at 30% $\dot{V}O_2$ max to dry heat (T_{db} = 48°C, T_{wb} = 25°C). Prior to acclimation, the women had slightly but not significantly higher final values for T_{re}, T_{sk}, and HR; however, the final mean sweat rate ($\dot{M}_{sw}$) was significantly higher for the men. After acclimation, the same trends between genders were observed, although differences in final $\dot{M}_{sw}$ between genders were not significant. These authors[17] "concluded that sex alone does not determine responses to heat stress. Consideration should also be given to the relative cardiovascular strain, state of acclimation, and the ambient conditions."

Gender related trends in thermoregulatory responses to a variety of climates are summarized in Table 3.[18] In comfortable climatic conditions (20°C, 40% RH), men and women have similar physiological responses. Under wet conditions (mild or hot), women appeared to tolerate the heat slightly better than men. The women displayed lower deep body and skin temperatures, and therefore had less heat storage (ΔS), while showing reduced sweating rates and subsequently less dehydration than men. In contrast, under hot-dry conditions, the men appeared to be at a slight physiological advantage. Compared to the women, they had lower T_{re}, T_{sk}, HR, and ΔS, but similar sweating rates. A possible explanation for these differences could involve three considerations. The higher A_D/wt for women may be a morphological advantage in hot-wet climates, and a disadvantage in hot-dry climates. Women seemed to have better peripheral feedback from skin wettedness which suppressed nonefficient sweating in humid environments. Women also appeared to have a higher central

Table 3
SUMMARY OF GENDER-RELATED TRENDS IN THERMOREGULATORY RESPONSES TO VARIOUS CLIMATES

	Comfort	Mild-wet	Hot-wet	Hot-dry
T_{re}	=	−	−	+
HR	=	=	=	+
T_{sk}	=	−	−	+
ΔS	=	−	−	= or +
$\dot{M}_{sw}$	=	−	−	=
Dehydration	=	=	−	=
H_2O consumption	=	=	+	+

Note: =, no difference; −, females are lower than males; +, females are higher than males.

thermoregulatory set point than men, and therefore were more intolerant of hot-dry environments. However, significant differences were generally not found between the genders in subsequent experimentation for HR, core temperature, and sweat loss during additional hot-wet and hot-dry experiments.[19]

It was further concluded from the earlier experiments by our laboratory that prolonged exposure (4 hr) did not enhance any gender-related physiological differences in response to dry heat.[20] Women seemed to be able to maintain sufficiently high sweating rates over 4 hr to reach and maintain thermoequilibrium. Additionally, it was found that both genders acclimated to a hot-dry environment at the same rate.[21]

Most recently, our laboratory has studied the gender related physiological responses during exercise in three environmental conditions (comfortable, hot-dry, and hot-wet) when 5% hypohydrated.[19] In general, significant differences were not found between the genders for final exercise T_{re}, T_{sk}, or HR in these conditions when either eu- or hypohydrated. We also found that cell volume and vascular fluid shifts were not different between genders when either eu- or hypohydrated in a hot-dry environment.[22] The present data indicated that physiological differences between genders were not systematically altered by level of hydration. In conclusion, when genders are similar with regard to aerobic fitness level, A_D/wt, and percent body fat, they do not differ dramatically in exercise-heat tolerance, thermal strain, and rate of heat acclimation; these reactions are not altered between genders when hypohydrated.

IV. EFFECTS OF AGING

Few studies have reported the effect of age on the physiological responses to exercise-heat stress. As shown in Figure 5, Wagner et al.[23] compared preadolescent boys (11 to 14 years) to young men (25 to 30 years) before and after heat acclimation (8 consecutive days) while walking (1.56 m/sec) in dry heat (T_{db} = 49°C, T_{wb} = 26.6°C). Both before and after acclimation, these boys displayed higher T_{re}, T_{sk}, and HR responses, and lower evaporative cooling than the young men. Postadolescent boys (15 to 16 years) displayed better temperature regulation than preadolescent boys but did not perform as well as these same young men both pre- and postacclimation.[23] Similar trends in thermoregulatory responses were reported by Drinkwater and Horvath[24] but for young girls. These authors concluded that preadolescent children (boys and girls) appeared more exercise-heat intolerant due to the instability of an immature cardiovascular system[24] and/or a limited sweating capability.[23]

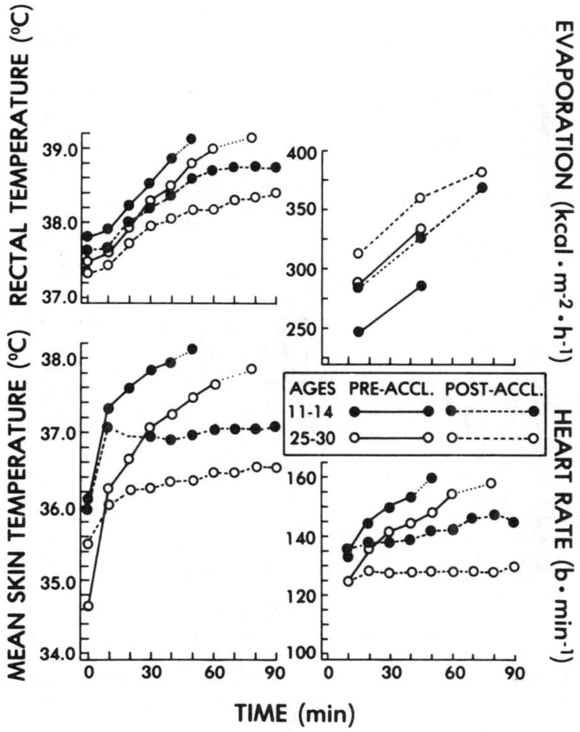

FIGURE 5. Rectal temperature, mean skin temperature, heart rate, and sweat evaporative rate over time comparing preadolescent boys and young men both pre- and postacclimation.[23]

In general, exercise-heat tolerance is believed to be reduced in older adults.[23,24] Older men (46 to 47 years) have been shown to have higher T_{re}, T_{sk}, and HR responses, and lower evaporation rates than younger men (20 to 29 years) during exercise (walking, 1.56 m/sec) in the heat (T_{db} = 49°C, T_{wb} = 26.6°C) both pre- and postacclimation[23] as illustrated in Figure 6. Thus, these older men showed the same trends in these selected physiological responses when compared to the younger men as did the younger boys both pre- and postacclimation.[23] These same patterns of reduced exercise-heat tolerance were reported by Drinkwater and Horvath[24] but for older women. It has also been reported that older adults started to sweat later and less during exercise in the heat than younger adults.[25,26] Some authors have concluded that older individuals are more exercise-heat intolerant because of a limited sensitivity and secretory capacity of their sweating response,[23] and/or the decrease in cardiovascular fitness common to most older individuals.[24]

The acclimation responses to exercising (walking, 1.56 m/sec at 4 to 5.6% grade) in the heat (T_{db} = 40°C, T_{wb} = 23.5°C) of men during 1942 and these same individuals 21 years later have been reported (Figure 7).[27] By some of the usual physiological criteria (T_{re}, T_{sk}, and HR), these older men acclimated to exercise in the heat in the same manner, and to the same extent as when they were younger. However, the initial cardiovascular strain seen prior to acclimation was greater for the older men in terms of relative cardiac cost given what is known about the reduction in maximum HR with increasing age. Nevertheless, these older men exhibited about the same degree of overall strain during exercise in the heat as they did 21 years earlier, and acclimated about as well;[27] however, these individuals may not be "typical" old men because of their habitually active lifestyles. More definitive research is needed to advance our understanding of exercise in the heat and its interaction with aging.

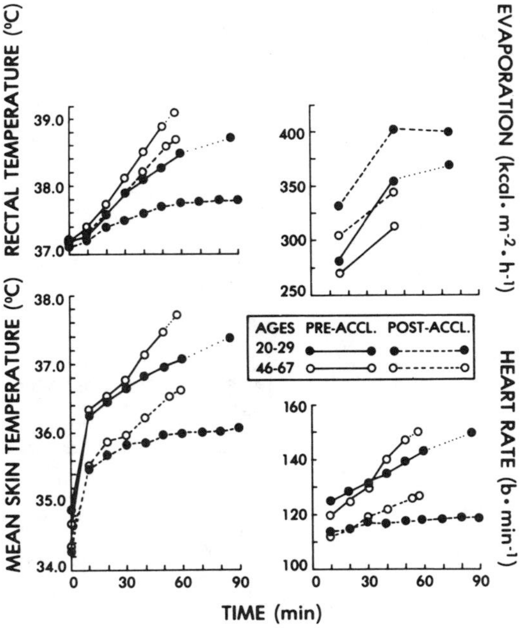

FIGURE 6. Rectal temperature, mean skin temperature, heart rate, and sweat evaporative rate over time comparing younger and older men both pre- and postacclimation.[23]

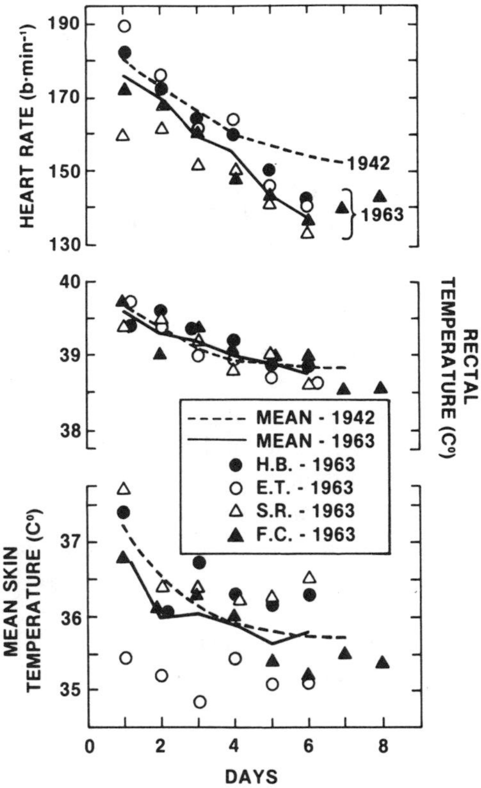

FIGURE 7. Rectal temperature, mean skin temperature, and heart rate responses of 4 men evaluated over 8 days of acclimation to heat in 1942 and these same men evaluated in 1963.[27]

In closing, we would hypothesize that if older and younger men were matched for maximal aerobic power and surface area to mass ratio, many of the reported differences in heat tolerance to exercise with aging would disappear.

REFERENCES

1. **Gisolfi, C. V. and Cohen, J. S.,** Relationships among training, heat acclimation, and heat tolerance in men and women: the controversy revisited, *Med. Sci. Sports,* 11, 56, 1979.
2. **Pandolf, K. B.,** Effects of physical training and cardiorespiratory physical fitness on exercise-heat tolerance: recent observations, *Med. Sci. Sports,* 11, 60, 1979.
3. **Nadel, E. R., Pandolf, K. B., Roberts, M. F., and Stolwijk, J. A. J.,** Mechanisms of thermal acclimation to exercise and heat, *J. Appl. Physiol.,* 37, 515, 1974.
4. **Pandolf, K. B., Burse, R. L., and Goldman, R. F.,** Role of physical fitness in heat acclimatisation, decay and reinduction, *Ergonomics,* 20, 399, 1977.
5. **Shvartz, E., Shapiro, Y., Magazanik, A., Meroz, A., Birnfeld, H., Mechtinger, A., and Shibolet, S.,** Heat acclimation, physical fitness, and responses to exercise in temperate and hot environments, *J. Appl. Physiol. Resp. Environ. Exercise Physiol.,* 43, 678, 1977.
6. **Drinkwater, B. L., Denton, J. E., Kupprat, I. C., Talag, T. S., and Horvath, S. M.,** Aerobic power as a factor in women's responses to work in hot environments, *J. Appl. Physiol.,* 41, 815, 1976.
7. **Greenleaf, J. E., Castle, B. L., and Ruff, W. K.,** Maximal oxygen uptake, sweating and tolerance to exercise in the heat, *Int. J. Biometeorol.,* 16, 375, 1972.
8. **Williams, C. G., Wyndham, C. H., and Morrison, J. F.,** Rate of loss of acclimation in summer and winter, *J. Appl. Physiol.,* 22, 21, 1967.
9. **Avellini, B. A., Shapiro, Y., Fortney, S. M., Wenger, C. B., and Pandolf, K. B.,** Effects on heat tolerance of physical training in water and on land, *J. Appl. Physiol. Resp. Environ. Exercise Physiol.,* 53, 1291, 1982.
10. **Dill, D. B., Yousef, M. K., and Nelson, J. D.,** Responses of men and women to two-hour walks in desert heat, *J. Appl. Physiol.,* 35, 231, 1973.
11. **Shoenfeld, Y., Udassin, R., Shapiro, Y., Ohri, A., and Sohar, E.,** Age and sex difference in response to short exposure to extreme dry heat, *J. Appl. Physiol. Resp. Environ. Exercise Physiol.,* 44, 1, 1978.
12. **Wyndham, C. H., Morrison, J. F., and Williams, C. G.,** Heat reactions of male and female Caucasians, *J. Appl. Physiol.,* 21, 357, 1965.
13. **Fox, R. H., Lofstedt, B. E., Woodward, P. M., Eriksson, E., and Werkstrom, B.,** Comparison of thermoregulatory function in men and women, *J. Appl. Physiol.,* 26, 444, 1969.
14. **Hertig, B. A., Belding, H. S., Kraning, K. K., Batterton, D. L., Smith, C. R., and Sargent, F., II,** Artificial acclimatization of women to heat, *J. Appl. Physiol.,* 18, 383, 1963.
15. **Weinman, K. P., Slabachova, Z., Bernauer, E. M., Morimoto, T., and Sargent, F., II,** Reactions of men and women to repeated exposure to humid heat, *J. Appl. Physiol.,* 22, 533, 1967.
16. **Avellini, B. A., Kamon, E., and Krajewski, J. T.,** Physiological responses of physically fit men and women to acclimation to humid heat, *J. Appl. Physiol. Resp. Environ. Exercise Physiol.,* 49, 254, 1980.
17. **Frye, A. J. and Kamon, E.,** Responses to dry heat of men and women with similar aerobic capacities, *J. Appl. Physiol. Resp. Environ. Exercise Physiol.,* 50, 65, 1981.
18. **Shapiro, Y., Pandolf, K. B., Avellini, B. A., Pimental, N. A., and Goldman, R. F.,** Physiological responses of men and women to humid and dry heat, *J. Appl. Physiol. Resp. Environ. Exercise Physiol.,* 49, 1, 1980.
19. **Sawka, M. N., Toner, M. M., Francesconi, R. P., and Pandolf, K. B.,** Hypohydration and exercise: effects of heat acclimation, gender and environment, *J. Appl. Physiol. Resp. Environ. Exercise Physiol.,* 55, 1147, 1983.
20. **Avellini, B. A., Shapiro, Y., Pandolf, K. B., Pimental, N. A., and Goldman, R. F.,** Physiological responses of men and women to prolonged dry heat exposure, *Aviat. Space Environ. Med.,* 51, 1081, 1980.
21. **Shapiro, Y., Pandolf, K. B., and Goldman, R. F.,** Sex differences in acclimation to a hot-dry environment, *Ergonomics,* 23, 635, 1980.
22. **Sawka, M. N., Francesconi, R. P., Pimental, N. A., and Pandolf, K. B.,** Hydration and vascular fluid shifts during exercise in the heat, *J. Appl. Physiol. Resp. Environ. Exercise Physiol.,* 56, 91, 1984.
23. **Wagner, J. A., Robinson, A. S., Tzankoff, S. P., and Marino, R. P.,** Heat tolerance and acclimatization to work in the heat in relation to age, *J. Appl. Physiol.,* 33, 616, 1972.

24. **Drinkwater, B. L. and Horvath, S. M.,** Heat tolerance and aging, *Med. Sci. Sports,* 11, 49, 1979.
25. **Hellon, R. F. and Lind, A. R.,** Observation on the activity of sweat glands with special reference to the influence of ageing, *J. Physiol. (London),* 133, 132, 1956.
26. **Lind, A. R., Humphreys, P. W., Collins, K. J., Foster, K., and Sweetland, K. F.,** Influence of age and daily duration of exposure on responses of men to work in heat, *J. Appl. Physiol.,* 28, 50, 1970.
27. **Robinson, S., Belding, H. S., Consolazio, F. C., Horvath, S. M., and Turrell, E. S.,** Acclimation of older men to work in heat, *J. Appl. Physiol.,* 20, 583, 1965.

Chapter 13

SWEAT LOSS AND VOLUNTARY DEHYDRATION DURING WORK IN HUMID HEAT

Thomas P. Davis and Mohamed K. Yousef

TABLE OF CONTENTS

I. Introduction 104

II. Materials and Methods 104
  A. Males 104
  B. Females 104

III. Results 105
  A. Males 105
  B. Females 106

IV. Conclusions 109

References 109

I. INTRODUCTION

The delay in complete rehydration following water loss either by sweating or by water deprivation is termed voluntary dehydration,[1] progressive dehydration,[2] hypohydration,[3] and since man does not reduce his rate of fluid intake ''voluntarily'', involuntary dehydration.[3] A controversy exists among environmental physiologists concerning the possibility of preventing involuntary dehydration or maintaining homeostasis of body fluids by replacing sweat losses by drinking either water or water fortified with various concentrations of salt.[1,4-8] Initially, water depletion was hypothesized to decrease sweat rate and predisposed one to heat stroke and death.[9] Water restriction was also reported to decrease performance of men during a prolonged march.[10]

Physiological responses of women to heat and/or exercise have been intensively investigated in the past decade.[11,12] There is considerable disagreement in the scientific literature regarding the existence of any fundamental differences between the sexes in the functioning of their thermoregulatory system.

The objectives of the present study were (1) to determine in both males and females if involuntary dehydration can be better reduced by drinking water or a sweetened, carbonated salt solution (i.e., 10-K^{tm}, Hansen's Natural Foods, Inc. Industry, Calif.), (2) to assess whether dehydration and rehydration influence sweat rate and sweat composition, and (3) to measure endurance time and associated thermoregulatory changes in response to different levels of water deficit during exercise in heat.

II. MATERIALS AND METHODS

A. Males

Voluntary informed consent was obtained from 18 healthy men ranging in age from 18 to 57 years (average age, 28.2 years). Each volunteer exercised in the upright position on a Monark^{tm} bicycle ergometer with an average work load of 2 kp (600 kg–meter/min) requiring about 40 to 50% of VO_2max (VO_2 of 24.6 mℓ/kg/min). All experiments were conducted in a climatic chamber with a dry (T_{db}) and wet (T_{wb}) bulb temperature of 40 and 30°C, respectively. Each volunteer exercised for as long as he could in three experiments: without drinking (D), with distilled water available *ad libitum* (W), and with drinking *ad libitum* a carbonated salt solution (10-K^{tm}) containing Na^+, Cl^-, and K^+ in concentrations of 23, 29, and 8 mEq/ℓ, respectively. Before and after each experiment body weight ($\pm$ 10 g), rectal temperature (T_{re}), and a blood sample (3 mℓ) were obtained. During exercise, heart rate (HR) and skin temperature (T_{sk}) on four different sites (forehead, arm, thigh, and neck), were measured once every 10 min. Sweat rate (SR) was calculated from the total body weight loss. Sweat samples were analyzed for electrolytes (Na^+, K^+, and Cl^-) and blood was analyzed for hematocrit (Hct) and hemoglobin (Hb). Total plasma proteins (Ps), Na^+, K^+, and Cl^- concentrations were measured.

B. Females

Voluntary informed consent was obtained from 20 healthy young women ranging in age from 19 to 45 years (average age, 26.7 years). Volunteers exercised in the upright position on a Monark^{tm} bicycle ergometer with a work load between 1 and 1.5 kp or 300 and 450 kg. The work load was adjusted for each volunteer to require either 25 or 40% of her VO_2max depending on level of physical fitness. All experiments were conducted in a climatic chamber with a T_{db} and T_{wb} bulb temperature of 40 and 30°C, respectively. Each volunteer exercised for as long as she could in three experiments: without drinking (D), with distilled water available *ad libitum* (W), and with drinking *ad libitum* a carbonated salt solution (10-K^{tm}) containing Na^+, Cl^-, and K^+ in concentrations of 23, 29, and 8 mEq/ℓ, respectively. Before

Table 1
AMOUNT OF BODY FLUID DEFICIT (% BFD) IN MALES DRINKING WATER OR SALT SOLUTION

	No. of subjects		
	Water	10-K[tm]	No water
No deficit	6	5	—
>50% BFD	6	10	—
<50% BFD	6	3	—
100% BFD	—	—	18
Duration of work (min)	61	73	86

Table 2
EFFECT OF DRINKING WATER (W) AND SALT SOLUTION (10-K[tm]) ON MALE SWEAT RATE (SR) EXPRESSED IN g/m²/min AND SWEAT ELECTROLYTES EXPRESSED IN mEq/ℓ

Experiment	SR ($g/m^2/min$)	Na^+ (mEq/ℓ)	Cl^- (mEq/ℓ)	K^+ (mEq/ℓ)
D	10.5 ± 2.8	60.4 ± 27.1	55.6 ± 26.2	12.1 ± 4.9
W	10.6 ± 2.9	55.9 ± 26.2	54.2 ± 27.3	11.1 ± 5.0
10-K[tm]	9.4 ± 2.4	53.9 ± 27.5	49.8 ± 24.3	11.2 ± 4.1

Note: D = no water; w = water; ± S.D.; N = 18.

and after each experiment body weight (± 10 g), rectal temperature (T_{re}, °C), and a blood sample (3 mℓ) were obtained. During exercise, heart rate (HR) and skin temperature (T_{sk}) on four different sites (forehead, arm, thigh, and neck) were measured once every 10 min. Sweat samples were collected using rubber hand gloves throughout the exercise period. Sweat rate (SR) was calculated from the total body weight loss. The percentage of body fluid deficit (% BFD) was calculated as:

$$= \frac{\text{sweat loss, g} - \text{fluid consumed}}{\text{sweat loss, g}} \times 100$$

Sweat samples were analyzed for electrolytes (Na^+, K^+, and Cl^-) and blood was analyzed for hematocrit (Hct) and hemoglobin (Hb). Total plasma proteins (Ps), Na^+, K^+, and Cl^- concentrations were measured.

III. RESULTS

A. Males

Drinking volumes of either water or the salt solution (10-K[tm]) varied among individuals tested. Only about one third of the male volunteers were able to prevent dehydration by drinking an adequate volume of fluid to replace their sweat loss (Table 1).

The average sweat rate and sweat chemical composition during the exercise is shown in Table 2. It is evident from this table that both sweat rate and sweat electrolytes are independent of drinking either water or 10-K[tm] in the male subjects. However, when one studies the

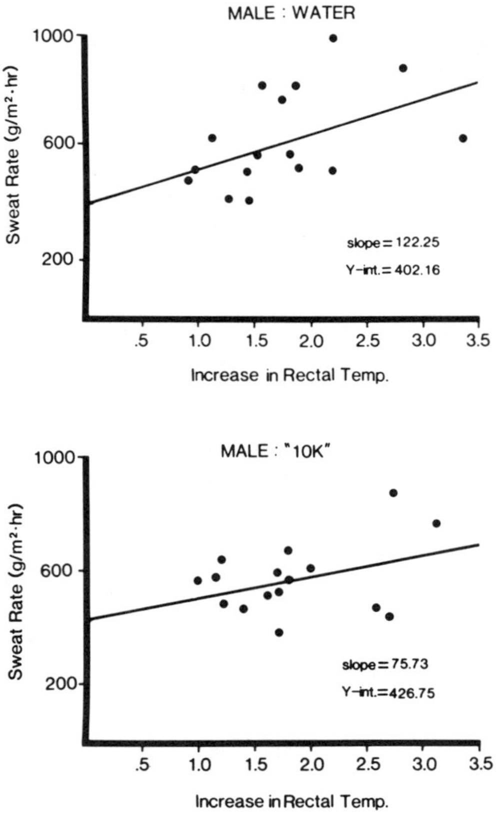

FIGURE 1. Effect of drinking water or salt solution (10-K^{tm}) on the increase in rectal temperature vs. sweat rate in males.

effect of water vs. 10-K^{tm} consumption on rectal temperature increase vs. sweat rate it should be noted there was a significant decrease in the slope of the best fit line when the subjects drank 10-K^{tm} as compared to water (Figure 1). Consuming 10-K^{tm} had a positive effect on rectal temperature (Figure 1).

When subjects were not given water or salt solution to drink during the exercise, the heat stress as documented by an increase in rectal temperature (T_{re}) and heart rate (HR) was significantly greater (Table 3).

Drinking water or 10-K^{tm} reduced the increase in rectal temperature and final heart rate while causing a much smaller increase in plasma volume (Table 3). With a relatively higher plasma volume resulting from drinking either water (PV = −6.9%) or 10-K^{tm} (PV = −5.1), the stress on the cardiovascular system was lessened as expressed by a lower final heart rate for subjects drinking water (HR = 150) or 10-K^{tm} (HR = 141).

B. Females

The exercise load used in these experiments (1 to 1.5 kp; 300 and 450 kg–meter/min) yielded a percent total body weight loss per hour ranging from 0.68 to 2.03% and averaged 1.21%. Nine of the female volunteers were unable to finish 1 hr of work. The work time for these nine individuals ranged from 26 to 53 min. Eleven of the female volunteers completed 1 hr or longer. One volunteer exercised 110 min. The average work time for the 11 women tested was 55.2 min for no drinking, 77.8 min for drinking water, and 84.1 min for drinking the salt solution (Table 4). In both men and women the work time was longest

Table 3
EFFECTS OF DRINKING WATER (W) AND SALT SOLUTION (10-K^{tm}) ON CHANGES IN MALE T_{re}, FINAL HR, HEMATOCRIT (Hct), HEMOGLOBIN (Hb), AND PLASMA VOLUME (PV)

Parameter	D	W	10-K^{tm}
ΔT_{re} C	1.86 ± 0.52	1.44 ± 0.66	1.23 ± 0.52
Final HR/min	169 ± 13	150 ± 11	141 ± 9
ΔHct%	1.6	1.0	0.7
ΔHb, g/100 mℓ	1.0	0.8	0.6
ΔPV, %	−9.2	−6.9	−5.1

Note: D = no water; W = water; ± S.D.; N = 18; Δ = rate of change.

Table 4
DURATION OF WORK AND LEVELS OF BODY FLUID DEFICIT (% BFD) IN WOMEN DRINKING WATER (W) OR SALT SOLUTION (10-K^{tm})

	No. of subjects		
	Water	10-K^{tm}	No Water
No deficit	11	14	—
>50% BFD	7	6	—
<50% BFD	2	—	—
100% BFD	—	—	20
Duration of work in (min)	79.8	84.1	55.2

when drinking 10-K^{tm}. Fourteen of 20 women had no body fluid deficit when drinking 10-K^{tm}, but only 11 when drinking water (Table 4).

Drinking water or the salt solution improved endurance time 44.6 and 52.4%, respectively. Only two female volunteers were unable to finish 1 hr of exercise when drinking was allowed. The shortest period of exercise when fluids were consumed was 41 min as compared to 26 min when drinking was not permitted.

Drinking water or 10-K^{tm} under the experimental conditions presented (i.e., average level of dehydration, 1.2%), resulted in complete replacement of lost body fluids in more than 50% of the female volunteers (55% for water and 70% for 10-K^{tm}) as shown in Table 4. The incomplete rehydration in 30 to 45% of the subjects is termed voluntary dehydration,[1] progressive dehydration,[2] or hypohydration.[3] Among the subjects who rehydrated by drinking back their loss in body weight, four to seven of them had a level of dehydration in 1 hr ranging from 0.82 to 0.99% total body weight loss. Female volunteers with sweat concentrations averaging 47.3 mEq/ℓ for sodium, 53.2 mEq/ℓ for chloride, and 16.1 mEq/ℓ for potassium were unable to rehydrate. The highest level of involuntary dehydration was observed in female volunteers with the greatest sweat salt concentrations and percent total body weight loss.

Table 5
EFFECTS OF DRINKING WATER (W) AND SALT SOLUTION (10-K^{tm}) ON FEMALE SWEAT RATE (SR) EXPRESSED IN g/m^2/min AND SWEAT ELECTROLYTES

Experiment	SR (g/m^2/min)	Na^+ (mEq/ℓ)	Cl^- (mEq/ℓ)	K^+ (mEq/ℓ)
D	7.02 ± 0.40	47.3 ± 20.4	46.2 ± 25.3	12.0 ± 6.0
W	6.95 ± 0.33	46.5 ± 17.6	41.6 ± 17.2	13.1 ± 6.6
10-K^{tm}	6.62 ± 0.33	44.8 ± 18.4	40.9 ± 18.4	12.4 ± 5.9

Note: D = no water, W = water, ± SD, N = 20.

Table 6
EFFECTS OF DRINKING WATER (W) AND SALT SOLUTION (10-K^{tm}) ON CHANGES IN FEMALE T_{re}, SERUM PROTEIN (Ps), FINAL HEART RATE (HR), HEMATOCRIT (Hct), HEMOGLOBIN (Hb), AND PLASMA VOLUME (PV)

Parameter	D	W	10-K^{tm}
ΔT_{re} C/hr	1.48	0.86	0.76
Final HR/min	169	164	158
ΔHct%	1.1	1.5	1.3
ΔHb, g/100 mℓ	0.5	0.5	0.6
ΔPs, g/100 mℓ	0.7	0.6	0.6
ΔdPV, %	−5.4	−6.2	−6.5

Note: D = no water; W = water; N = 20; Δ = rate of change.

The effect of drinking water or 10-K^{tm} on average sweat rate (SR) and sweat electrolyte composition is described in Table 5.

It is evident from these data that both sweat rate and sweat electrolyte concentrations are independent of drinking either water or 10-K^{tm}. The data did not reveal any trend toward decreased sweat rate with increased dehydration.

Drinking water or 10-K^{tm} reduced heat stress in all women as shown by the lower rise in rectal temperature (°C/hr) for water (0.86) or 10-K^{tm} (0.76) as compared to no water (1.48) (Table 6). The greater increase in rectal temperature in dehydrated subjects without a decrease in sweat rate suggests that the higher rise in rectal temperature does not appear to be due to a decrease in sweat rate. The degree of hemoconcentration as evidenced from the changes in hematocrit, hemoglobin, serum protein, and plasma volume was similar under all experimental conditions (Table 6) as compared to the male data (Table 3), where 10-K^{tm} consumption showed a significant advantage over water or no drinking. Therefore, the final heart rate was not significantly reduced when fluids were available for drinking in the female subjects but was in the male subjects. This difference in the female subjects is probably due to the relatively smaller level of dehydration when drinking was not permitted.

IV. CONCLUSIONS

In a 5-hr desert walk taken by five men, Dill et al.[6] concluded that the volume of water drawn from body reserves was closely related with the concentration of chloride in sweat. However, when studying the data from our study for the male volunteers there was no significant correlation between sweat electrolytes and the percent of body fluid deficit. The female volunteers with the greatest sweat salt concentrations and percent total body weight loss had the highest level of involuntary dehydration. Therefore, these individuals needed to consume fluids to maintain a constant osmolarity of extracellular fluids. The differences noted between our results on the male subjects and Dill's results[6] may be accounted for in the difference between our acute work regimen (1 to 2 hr) vs. Dill's 5-hr desert walks[6] and the possible fitness differences between the study subjects.

It was also evident from our study on both men and women that both sweat rate and sweat electrolytes are independent of drinking either water or a salt solution. Dill et al.[6] found that during the 5-hr desert walk, five men maintained their sweat rate even though they had a body water loss of between 600 to 1700 mℓ. Other workers have shown that drinking water or various sodium chloride fortified solutions during exercise in the heat produced no significant alteration in sweat electrolytes.[5,13,14]

The observed greater increase in rectal temperature in the dehydrated subjects without a decrease in sweat rate is similar to data reported by others.[2,15] Senay and Christensen[15] suggested that the higher rise in rectal temperature does not appear to be due to a decrease in sweat rate but rather to a lack of responsiveness of the sudomotor vasomotor systems to increases in body temperature.

In conclusion, based on the physiological responses observed in this study, it is obvious that most men and women did not or could not drink sufficient water or salt solution to prevent involuntary dehydration. Drinking did improve endurance time for performing the same work load and reduced the rate of rise in rectal temperature but had no significant effect on sweat rate and sweat composition. It should be noted that the improvement in work time and rectal temperature was more evident using the salt solution (10-K^{tm}) than by using water alone.

REFERENCES

1. **Adolph, E. F.,** *Physiology of Man in the Desert,* Interscience, New York, 1947.
2. **Hertzman, A. B. and Ferguson, I. D.,** Failure in temperature regulation during progressive dehydration, *U.S. Armed Forces Med. J.,* 11, 542, 1960.
3. **Greenleaf, J. E., Brock, P. J., Keil, L. C., and Morse, J. T.,** Drinking and water balance during exercise and heat acclimation, *J. Appl. Physiol.,* 54, 414, 1983.
4. **Dill, D. B., Bock, A. V., and Edwards, H. T.,** Mechanisms for dissipating heat in man and dog, *Am. J. Physiol.,* 104, 36, 1933.
5. **Dill, D. B., Yousef, M. K., and Nelson, J. D.,** Responses of men and women to two-hour walks in desert heat, *J. Appl. Physiol.,* 35, 231, 1973.
6. **Dill, D. B., Soholt, L. F., and Oddershede, I.,** Physiological adjustments of young men to five-hour desert walks, *J. Appl. Physiol.,* 40, 236, 1976.
7. **Greenleaf, J. E. and Sargent, F., II,** Voluntary dehydration, *J. Appl. Physiol.,* 20, 719, 1965.
8. **Baker, E. M., Plough, I. C., and Allen, T. J.,** Water requirements of men as related to salt intake, *Am. J. Clin. Nutr.,* 12, 394, 1963.
9. **Leithead, C. S. and Pallister, M. A.,** Observations on dehydration and sweating, *Lancet,* 2, 114, 1960.
10. **Strydom, N. B., Wyndham, C. H., van Graan, C. H., Holdsworth, L. D., and Morrison, J. F.,** The influence of water restriction on the performance of men during a prolonged march, *S. Afr. Med. J.,* 40, 539, 1966.

11. **Yousef, M. K.,** Responses of men and women to desert heat, *Int. J. Biometeorol.*, 24(Suppl.), 29, 1980.
12. **Yousef, M. K., Dill, D. B., Vitez, T. S., Hillyard, S. D., and Goldman, A. S.,** Thermoregulatory responses to desert heat: age, race and sex, *J. Gerontol.*, 39, 406, 1984.
13. **Cage, G. W., Wolfe, S. M., Thompson, R. J., and Gordon, R. S., Jr.,** Effects of water intake on composition of thermal sweat in normal human volunteers, *J. Appl. Physiol.*, 29, 687, 1970.
14. **Yousef, M. K. and Dill, D. B.,** Sweat rate and concentration of chloride in hand and body sweat in desert walks: male and female, *J. Appl. Physiol.*, 36, 82, 1974.
15. **Senay, L. C. and Christensen, M. I.,** Cutaneous circulation during dehydration and heat stress, *J. Appl. Physiol.*, 20, 278, 1965.

Part B. Adaptive Physiology of Animals

Chapter 14

HORMONAL CONTROL OF HEAT PRODUCTION AND HOMEOTHERMY

M. K. Yousef

TABLE OF CONTENTS

I. Introduction 114

II. Hormones and Heat Production 114

III. Is Metabolic Rate Adaptive? Hormonal Mechanisms 116
A. Small Mammals 116
B. Large Mammals 117

IV. Hormones and Adaptation to Thermal Stress 117
A. Adaptation to Cold 117
B. Adaptation to Heat 118

V. Conclusions 119

Acknowledgment 119

References 119

I. INTRODUCTION

Homeothermy is maintained as a result of a sensitive balance between heat production (HP) and heat loss. Thus, it is essential to understand the mechanisms of HP in order to fully comprehend the essence of thermoregulation. Measurement of HP provides a criterion for the sum of energy transformation taking place in an animal per unit of time. Overwhelming evidence indicates that both the nervous and endocrine systems are the primary components of the controlling mechanisms of HP. Although it is difficult to separate the influence of both systems on HP, in this chapter only the hormonal control is considered.

As a frame of reference for discussion of the hormonal control of HP, the interactions of the involved elements or components are illustrated in Figure 1. In simple terms, a response to a stressful stimuli depends on a well-rehearsed chain of events in which a sensor detects the stimuli, and in turn the controlling element releases a substance which activates or inhibits other cells until, finally, effector cells are evoked and the appropriate responses are initiated. More specifically, environmental stresses either via the cutaneous receptors and/or the internal receptors stimulate the central nervous system (CNS), the hypothalamic region in particular, providing alterations in secretion of the releasing factors or hormones to stimulate the hierarchy of the endocrine glands with resulting changes in blood calorigenic hormones, and in turn HP and body temperature. The output signals from the neuroendocrine system directly influence either the shivering or nonshivering mechanisms to change HP and other physiological responses to maintain homeothermy.

II. HORMONES AND HEAT PRODUCTION

The close association of calorigenic hormones, i.e., thyroxine (T4), triiodothyronine (T3), growth hormone (GH), glucocorticoids and catecholamines, and metabolic rate (MR) or HP has been documented by in vivo and in vitro studies. Notable among this work is the reexamination of the role of the pituitary and its target organs in calorigenesis by Evans et al.[1] They concluded that the thyroid hormone and adrenal steroids act jointly in control of MR, but can act as independent factors in determining the levels of calorigenesis. Administration of calorigenic hormones in small animals acclimated to the thermoneutral zone and to heat increased VO_2 in both groups (Figure 2). The decrease in VO_2 of animals acclimated to heat was diminished by the administration of the hormones, suggesting that hypometabolism of heat-acclimated animals results from hyposecretion of these hormones.

Several workers have confirmed the role of thyroid hormone on MR or VO_2 after a latent period of several hours in rats; in large animals (cattle) this period was 2 to 3 days at 18°C and 1 to 2 days at 34°C.[7] The shortening of the T4 latent period under hot conditions in cattle was confirmed in a recent study using the desert wood rat, *Neotoma lepida,* as shown in Figure 3. In this species, T4 significantly increased VO_2 at 12 and 24 hr postinjection at 28° and 36°C, respectively.

Scanty information is available on the duration of the latent period of other hormones. Following a single dose of hydrocortisone in cattle, the latent period was 3 to 4 and 2 to 3 hr at 18° and 35°C, respectively.[9] Also, using the same species, the latent period for GH was 10 to 24 at 18°C and 4 to 10 hr at 38°C.[8] Similar studies are needed using other species and other environmental stresses. The available data provide preliminary evidence that calorigenic hormones had a shorter latent period in heat-exposed animals. Also, duration of the latent period varied in small and large animals. The significance of the latent period and its controlling mechanisms is beyond the scope of this chapter; however, it is of interest to note that whatever the mechanisms are, exposure and/or acclimation to heat modify the regulatory mechanism controlling the latent period.

A single dose of some calorigenic hormones was found to have a carryover effect (bio-

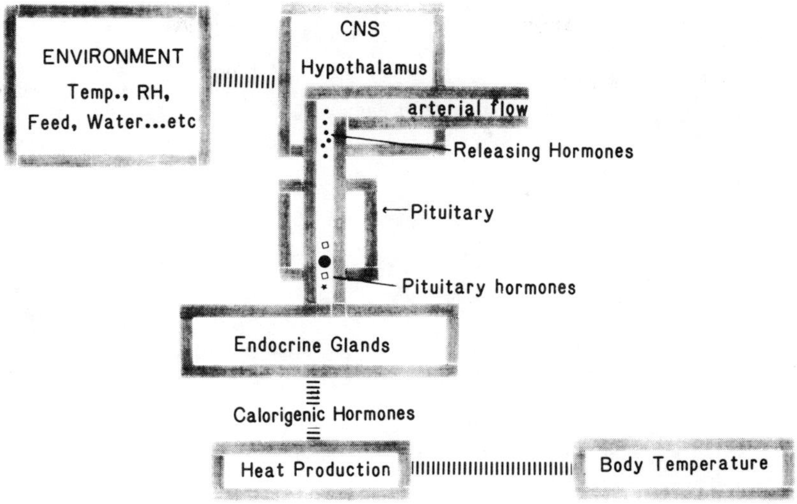

FIGURE 1. A schematic presentation of the interactions of the involved elements of the neuroendocrine system in controlling heat production and homeothermy.

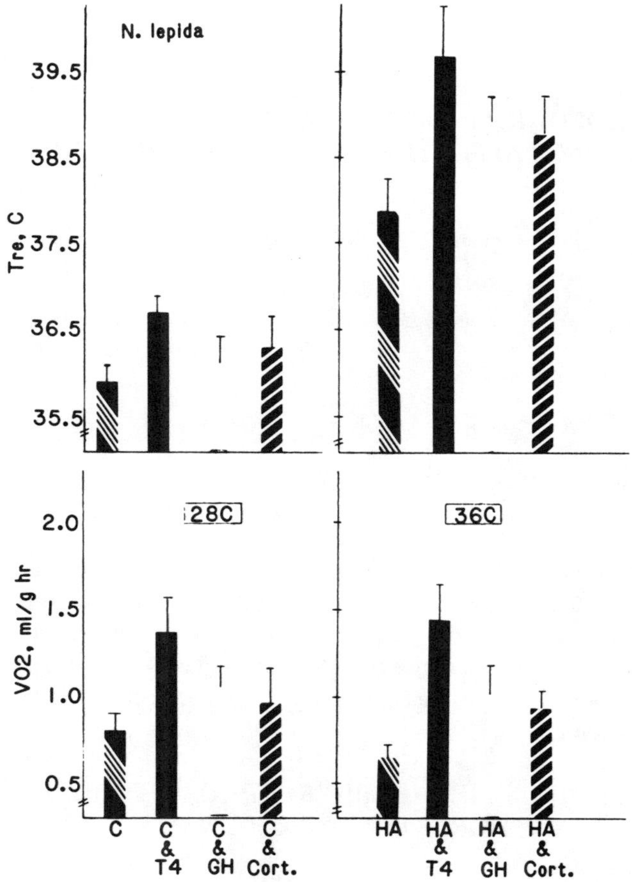

FIGURE 2. The effects of various hormones on rate of oxygen consumption (VO_2) in animals acclimated to heat and thermoneutral zone.

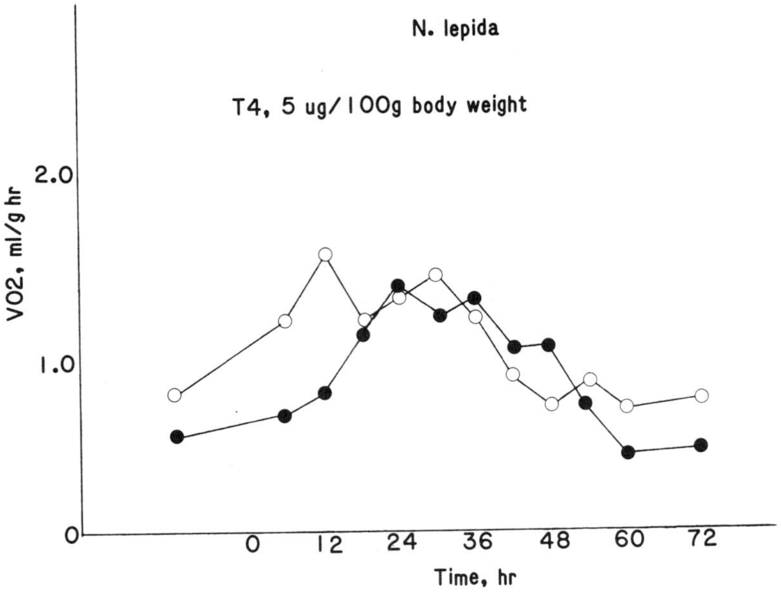

FIGURE 3. Changes in rate of oxygen consumption (VO_2) following a single injection of thyroxine.

Table 1
THE BIOLOGICAL EFFECTIVE TIME (BET) OF VARIOUS HORMONES AFFECTING VO_2 IN DIFFERENT ANIMALS

Hormone	Animals	BET	Environmental temp. (°C)	Ref.
T4	Rats	6 days or more	—	14
	Woodrats	30—36 hr	28	This chapter
		30 hr	35	This chapter
	Cattle	3—4 days	18	7
		5—6 days	34	7
GH	Cattle	40 hr	18	8
		50 hr	38	8
Hydrocortisone	Cattle	3 hr	18	9
		5 hr	35	9

logical effective time) on VO_2 for periods of time ranging from hours to days as shown in Table 1.[7-9,14] It is evident that T4 has the longest biological effective time of the hormones studied. At least in cattle, it seems that acclimation to heat increases the duration of the biological effective time. This finding conflicts with the data on wood rats, and the question of whether environmental stresses, species, dose, and age affect this duration remains open for further investigation.

III. IS METABOLIC RATE ADAPTIVE? HORMONAL MECHANISMS

A. Small Mammals

The generalization of Scholander et al.[16] that the basal metabolic rate of terrestrial mammals from the tropics to the arctic regions is determined by a size relation according to the formula cal/day = 70 Wkg 0.7 (i.e., the mouse-to-elephant curve) and is phylogenetically nonadaptive to external temperature conditions has been questioned. Recent reviews have documented that most small desert animals and some large ones possess MR that is lower than expected from the mouse-to-elephant equation.[3,17,18] Although large gaps remain to be bridged, some effort has been made to explain the phenomenon of hypometabolism in these desert animals. It has been suggested that the low MR of desert rodents is related to increased body fat content when kept under laboratory conditions with minimum activity and abundant food.[19] The different MR of two desert ground squirrels, i.e., round tail (*Spermophilus tereticaudus*) and antelope (*Ammospermophilus leucurus*) was found to correlate with the thyroidal iodine release rate of both species.[22] The role of thyroid activity as a mechanism for lowered VO_2 was strengthened by a study on thyroxine secretion rate (TSR) and MR of 12 species representing three families of desert rodents.[4] Rodent species inhabiting low desert areas have low MR and TSR, whereas species occupying the arid-woodland or montane forest habitats have high MR and TSR. This finding was confirmed by measurements of plasma T4 levels[5] and by the release rate technique on eight species of ground squirrels.[23] Maximal and minimal thyroidal release rates were found in the high altitude (high MR) species, i.e., *S. lateralis* and the desert (low MR) species, *S. townsendi,* respectively. The authors of this study[23] concluded that the low VO_2 in ground squirrels is due to a relatively inactive thyroid gland. Additionally, using woodchucks[24] it was found that the seasonal variations in T4 and T3 represent adaptations influencing MR.

The role of other calorigenic hormones has been given little or no attention. The possible role of glucocorticoids was examined in six species of desert rodents.[6] Corticosterone plasma levels appeared to be related to ecologic distribution and hypometabolism. Additional studies to examine secretion rates and biokinetics of corticosteroids and other calorigenic hormones will be of great value in enhancing our understanding of the possible mechanisms underlying the adaptive significance of MR in ecological distribution of various species.

B. Large Mammals

The question of whether resting MR of large mammals is adaptive requires further investigation. Only a few of the desert large mammalian species have been reported to have lower MR than is expected from the predicted values from the mouse-to-elephant equations.[17] Animals which were reported to have low MR include the camel, desert goats, and the small antelope, dik dik. An attempt to reveal the mechanism of the hypometabolic state in large animals with different resting MR was made.[10] The difference between the high MR (per unit metabolic body weight) of the donkey than that of the llama was found to be unrelated to thyroid function. However, a decrease in MR of both species during exposure to heat for 3 to 4 days was found to be associated with a decline in thryoid function. The inconsistency in the relationship of thyroid function and resting MR of small and large mammals remains a mystery. The possible role of calorigenic hormones in controlling MR should be tested in large mammals.

IV. HORMONES AND ADAPTATION TO THERMAL STRESS

For most mammals to survive thermal stress, their body temperatures must be maintained relatively constant as a result of balancing heat production and heat loss. The role of the endocrine system in controlling the adaptive changes in heat production has been an area of active research.[2-4,14,17,25-27]

A. Adaptation to Cold

In a cold environment, the increased MR in acclimated and acclimatized animals is found to be controlled by the neuroendocrine system.[17,25] The early studies of Dempsey and Astwood[28] showed that thyroxine secretion rate as measured by the replacement technique

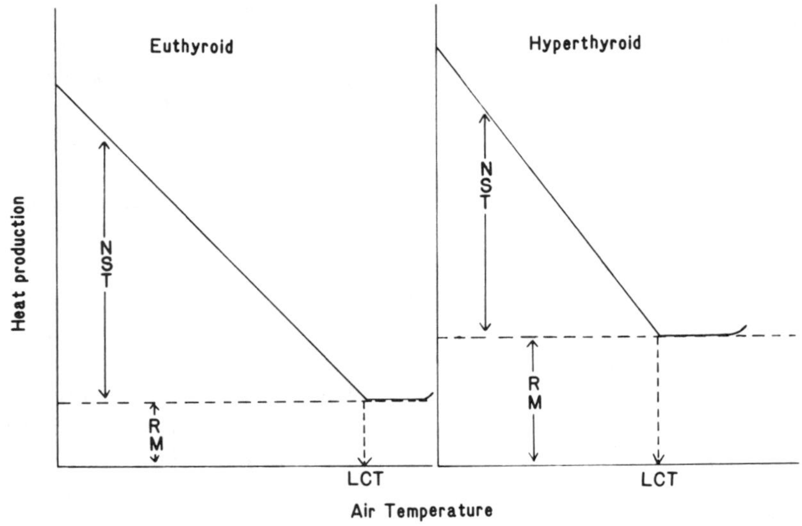

FIGURE 4. Effects of thyroxine on the LCT of hyperthyroid and euthyroid desert wood rats.

increased at a cold temperature (1°C). This finding was confirmed by numerous workers using different techniques.[25,29] In the absence of thyroid hormones, rats were unable to achieve the MR necessary to maintain thermoregulation.[30] In a recent study on *N. lepida,* daily administration of T3 for 3 weeks caused a significant rise in resting VO_2 and shifted the lower critical temperature (LCT) to the left, thus aiding the animals in better tolerating exposure to severe cold (− 10°C) as compared to the control group. The shift in the LCT of normal (euthyroid) and injected (hyperthyroid) groups is schematically presented in Figure 4.

Nonshivering mechanisms have been carefully examined, and there is an agreement that nonshivering shows a specificity for noradrenaline.[31,32] In addition to thyroid hormones and their synergistic effect with epinephrine, corticosteroids have been shown to play at the least a transient role during the process of cold adaptation. Relatively few studies have examined the role of other hormones such as insulin, GH, and prolactin.[32]

B. Adaptation to Heat

Animals acclimated or acclimatized to heat have reduced MR as a mechanism to aid their ability to thermoregulate and survive.[33] The useful adaptive mechanism of low VO_2 may be attributed to a consequently reduced need for food and water, which are at a premium in arid zones. The time course of changes in VO_2 following sudden exposure to heat (34°C) was studied in rats.[34] The VO_2 after 5 to 6 days of continuous exposure to heat decreased significantly. It was suggested that the decrease in VO_2 may be attributed to a decline in endocrine function since hypothyroidism was found to increase heat tolerance in rats.[35] This finding was confirmed by a study on the response pattern of rectal temperature (T_{re}) to acute heat (44°C) exposure after injections of T4, thyrotrophin releasing hormone (TRH), and a propylthiouracil (PTH) in different groups of desert kangaroo rats, *Dipodomys merriami* (34°C). The hypothyroid group (PTH) tolerated heat better than the control group. The increased heat tolerance may have been associated with an increase in the upper critical temperature due to low VO_2. On the contrary, the hyperthyroid groups (T4 and TRH) failed to attain a noticeable equilibrium in T_{re}, indicating lower heat tolerance than the control.

The low VO_2 in heat acclimated animals may be caused, at least in part, by the decrease in cellular binding of T4 to the nucleus and mitochondrial fractions.[34] Such shifts in binding of T4 may explain the chemical thermosuppression observed at the cellular level as evidenced by a decline in oxidative enzymatic activity and total body protein turnover.[25,34]

Studies on the role other hormones play in metabolic adaptions to heat are limited,[2,3,17] and firm conclusions at this time would be premature. Additional studies are needed to provide a better understanding of the hormonal contribution in mammalian adaptations to heat.

V. CONCLUSIONS

If homeothermy is to be maintained, heat production and heat loss must remain equal under adverse climatic conditions. A key element in controlling MR of various mammalian species is the alterations in the activity of the calorigenic hormones. Such alterations would require precise integration between the stimuli, i.e., environmental conditions, and the controlling system, i.e., the neuroendocrine system. The close association of the calorigenic hormones and MR has been established in many small and large mammals. However, the controlling mechanism(s) of this relationship remains open for debate and investigation.

Hormonal control of MR as related to thermoregulation has been established only in part. The role of the thyroid gland and the neuroendocrine axis in control of nonshivering thermogenesis has been an area of active research resulting in better understanding of the mechanisms of cold adaptation. Also the contribution of the hypothalamo-pituitary-thyroid axis to heat-induced chemical thermosuppression resulting in increasing heat tolerance has been demonstrated and accepted by some investigators. Further studies on the importance of other hormones on thermogenesis will be of great merit in revealing the hormonal control in physiological adaptations to thermal stresses.

ACKNOWLEDGMENT

Preparation of this paper was completed when the author was on a sabbatical leave at the Department of Applied Physiology, University of Occupational and Environmental Health, Kitakyushu, Japan and was supported by a Fellowship Award from the Japan Society for Promotion of Science.

REFERENCES

1. **Evans, E. S., Contopoulos, A. N., and Simpson, M. E.,** Hormonal factors influencing calorigenesis, *Endocrinology,* 60, 403, 1957.
2. **Yousef, M. K.,** Thyroid and adrenal function in desert animals: a view on metabolic adaptation, in *Environmental Physiology of Desert Organisms,* Hadley, N. F., Ed., Dowden, Hutchinson & Ross, Stroudsburg, Pa., 1975, 188.
3. **Yousef, M. K.,** Effect of heat on energy metabolism and related endocrine functions in rodents, in *Progress in Animal Biometeorology,* Johnson, H. D., Ed., Swets & Zeitlinger, Amsterdam, 1976, 195.
4. **Yousef, M. K. and Johnson, H. D.,** Thyroid activity in desert rodents: a mechanism for lowered metabolic rate, *Am. J. Physiol.,* 229, 427, 1975.
5. **Scott, I. M., Yousef, M. K., and Johnson, H. D.,** Plasma thyroxine levels of mammals: desert and mountain, *Life Sci.,* 19, 807, 1976.
6. **Vanjonack, W. J., Scott, I. M., Yousef, M. K., and Johnson, H. D.,** Corticosterone plasma levels in desert rodents, *Comp. Biochem. Physiol.,* 51A, 17, 1975.
7. **Yousef, M. K. and Johnson, H. D.,** Calorigenesis of dairy cattle as influenced by thyroxine and environmental temperature, *J. Anim. Sci.,* 25, 150, 1966.
8. **Yousef, M. K. and Johnson, H. D.,** Calorigenesis of cattle as influenced by growth hormone and environmental temperature, *J. Anim. Sci.,* 25, 1076, 1966.

9. **Yousef, M. K. and Johnson, H. D.,** Calorigenesis of cattle as influenced by hydrocortisone and environmental temperature, *J. Anim. Sci.*, 26, 1087, 1967.
10. **El-Nouty, F. D., Yousef, M. K., Magdub, A. B., and Johnson, H. D.,** Thyroid hormones and metabolic rate in burros, *Equus asinus,* and llamas, *Lama glama:* effects of environmental temperature, *Comp. Biochem. Physiol.*, 60A, 235, 1978.
11. **Denckla, W. D. and Marcum, E.,** Minimal O2 consumption as an index of thyroid status: standardization of method, *Endocrinology,* 93, 61, 1973.
12. **Cassuto, Y. and Amit, Y.,** Thyroxine and norepinephrine effects on the metabolic rates of heat-acclimated hamsters, *Endocrinology,* 82, 17, 1968.
13. **Cassuto, Y., Chayoth, R., and Rabi, T.,** Thyroid hormone in heat acclimated hamsters, *Am. J. Physiol.*, 218, 1287, 1970.
14. **Carlson, L. D.,** Some comments on low temperatures in the desert and at altitudes, in *Physiological Adaptations: Desert and Mountain,* Yousef, M. K., Horvath, S. M., and Bullard, R. W., Eds., Academic Press, New York, 1972, 65.
15. **Baker, S. B. and Klitgaard, H. M.,** Metabolism of tissues excised from thyroxine-injected rats, *Am. J. Physiol.*, 170, 81, 1952.
16. **Scholander, P. F., Hock, R., Walters, V., and Irving, L.,** Adaptation to cold in arctic and tropical mammals and birds in relation to body temperature, insulation, and basal metabolic rate, *Biol. Bull.*, 99, 259, 1950.
17. **Yousef, M. K.,** Adaptive responses of ungulates to environment, in *Biometeorological Survey,* Vol. 1, Tromp, S. W. and Bouma, J. J., Eds., Heyden & Son, London, 1979, 90.
18. **Bradley, W. G. and Yousef, M. K.,** Small mammals in the desert, in *Physiological Adaptations: Desert and Mountain,* Yousef, M. K., Horvath, S. M., and Bullard, R. W., Eds., Academic Press, New York, 1972, 127.
19. **Hayward, J. S.,** Metabolic rate and its temperature — adaptive significance in six geographic races of *Peromyscus, Can. J. Zool.*, 43, 132, 1965.
20. **McNab, B. K.,** The influence of fat deposits on the basal rate of metabolism in desert homeotherms, *Comp. Biochem. Physiol.*, 26, 337, 1968.
21. **Scott, I. M., Yousef, M. K., and Bradley, W. G.,** Body fat content and metabolic rate of rodents: desert and mountain, *Proc. Soc. Exp. Biol. Med.*, 141, 818, 1972.
22. **Hudson, J. W. and Wang, L. C.,** Thyroid function in desert ground squirrels, in *Physiological Systems in Semiarid Environments,* Hoff, C. C. and Riedesel, M. L., Eds., University of New Mexico Press, Albuquerque, 1967, 17.
23. **Hudson, J. W. and Deavers, D. R.,** Thyroid function and basal metabolism in the ground squirrels, *Ammos permophilus leucurus* and *Spermophilus* spp., *Physiol. Zool.*, 49, 425, 1976.
24. **Young, R. A., Danforth, E., Jr., Vagenakis, A. G., Krupp, P. P., Frink, R., and Sims, E. A. H.,** Seasonal variation and the influence of body temperature on plasma concentrations and binding of thyroxine and triiodothyronine in the woodchuck, *Endocrinology,* 104, 996, 1979.
25. **Chaffee, R. R. J. and Roberts, J. C.,** Temperature acclimation in birds and mammals, *Ann. Rev. Physiol.*, 33, 155, 1971.
26. **Yousef, M. K. and Johnson, H. D.,** Endocrine system and thermal environment, in *Stress Physiology in Livestock,* Vol. 1, Yousef, M. K., Ed., CRC Press, Boca Raton, 1985, 133.
27. **Collins, K. J. and Weiner, J. S.,** Endocrinological aspects of exposure to high envrionmental temperature, *Physiol. Rev.*, 48, 785, 1968.
28. **Dempsey, E. W. and Astwood, E. B.,** Determination of the rate of thyroid hormone secretion at various environmental temperatures, *Endocrinology,* 32, 509, 1943.
29. **Carlson, L. D.,** Nonshivering thermogenesis and its endocrine control, *Fed. Proc.*, 19, 25, 1960.
30. **Hsieh, A. C. L. and Carlson, L. D.,** Role of the thyroid in metabolic response to low temperature, *Am. J. Physiol.*, 188, 40, 1957.
31. **Smith, R. E. and Horwitz, B. A.,** Brown fat and thermogenesis, *Physiol. Rev.*, 46, 67, 1969.
32. **Thompson, G. E.,** Physiological effects of cold exposure, in *Environmental Physiology II,* Robertshaw, D., Ed., University Park Press, Baltimore, 1977, 29.
33. **Yousef, M. K.,** Responses of small animals to heat stress and exercise, in *Environmental Physiology: Aging, Heat and Altitude,* Horvath, S. M. and Yousef, M. K., Eds., Elsevier/North Holland, New York, 1981, 91.
34. **Yousef, M. K. and Johnson, H. D.,** Time course of oxygen consumption in rats during sudden exposure to high environmental temperature, *Life Sci.*, 6, 1221, 1967.
35. **Fregley, M. J., Cook, K. M., and Otis, A. B.,** Effect of hypothyroidism on tolerance of rats to heat, *Am. J. Physiol.*, 204, 1039, 1963.

Chapter 15

OPIOID PEPTIDES AND ADAPTATION TO ENVIRONMENT

T. P. Davis and M. K. Yousef

TABLE OF CONTENTS

I. Introduction 122

II. Opioid Peptides 122

III. Opioids and Thermoregulation 124
A. Morphine and Thermoregulation 124
B. Endogenous Opioids and Thermoregulation 124

IV. Central Processing and/or Metabolism of Endorphins in Temperature Acclimated Rodents 125
A. Studies at Thermoneutrality 125
B. Studies in Heat- and Cold-Acclimated Animals 125

V. Conclusions 128

References 128

I. INTRODUCTION

Many physiological mechanisms can be best understood in terms of animal responses to various environmental stresses. For example, numerous studies on animals inhabiting or evolved in stressful thermal environments, i.e., desert and arctic, have documented that mammalian body temperature ranges from strict homeothermic levels to well-regulated states of hypo- and hyperthermia. Bligh[1] has suggested that these variations to some extent are undoubtedly matters of genetic selection. The degree of strict homeothermy is not, however, necessarily a fixed property and may vary with the changes in environmental and physiological circumstances. These patterns of mammalian thermoregulation are a result of the integrative functions of all organ systems and the behavioral mechanisms which are controlled by the nervous and endocrine systems. Thermal lability is not a failure in the thermoregulatory mechanisms, but it represents one of the finest examples of the adaptive mechanisms displayed by some species to survive periods of thermal stress and absolute or relative water and caloric deprivations.[2]

Thermoregulation involves a sensitive balance between heat production and heat loss which can change quickly in accordance with the environmental thermal demand. The central nervous system (CNS) controls both heat production and heat loss. Bligh[1] has published an eloquent presentation of how the CNS equates thermal disturbances and corrective responses resulting in a regulated state of homeothermy. He also reviewed the various models of afferent and efferent systems accounting for regulation of body temperature. However, many answers to questions on the role of the CNS in adaptation to environment remain unproven. In recent years, the possible physiologic role of endogenous brain peptides on mammalian thermoregulation has been actively investigated.[3-5] In this paper, emphasis is given to the role of endorphins on thermoregulation. Endorphins are referred to as endogenous opioid peptides because they are naturally occurring morphine-like substances which bind directly to the opiate receptor and activate it. The physiological actions of endorphins are antagonized by the opiate antagonist naloxone, and endorphins are known to displace tritiated naloxone and morphine from brain membranes.

II. OPIOID PEPTIDES

The discovery of opioid peptides in 1975 presented new challenges for understanding the complex chemical control of brain functions. The biochemistry, metabolism, and characterization of various brain endogenous opioid peptides are beyond the scope of this chapter. However, for the sake of clarity, a brief description showing the relationship of precursor proteins to the biologically active opioid peptides to be discussed thereafter is shown diagrammatically in Figure 1.

In general, opioid peptides are known to be derived from three main precursor proteins proopiomelanocortin (POMC; 265 amino acids), proenkephalin A (263 amino acids), and proenkephalin B (256 amino acids).[6-10] The carboxyterminal 91 amino acids of proopiomelanocortin (POMC) contain the sequence of β-MSH and β-endorphin (βE βE(1-31)). Recent studies have shown βE to be proteolytically processed (metabolized) in vitro to various biologically active peptide fragments as shown in Figure 2.

These peptides have been shown to be present in vivo including α-endorphin (α-E; βE (1-16)) and γ-endorphin (γ-E; βE(1-17)).[6,11-15] Although these two peptide fragments differ by only a single amino acid they have quite different behavioral effects when administered to animals [6,10,15] The α-type endorphins have been shown by some investigators to exhibit amphetamine-like behavior whereas γ-type endorphins have been shown to exhibit neuroleptic-like activity in animal tests. Although the behavioral effects have not been reproduced in all laboratories, it is generally accepted that a single parent peptide may serve as a precursor

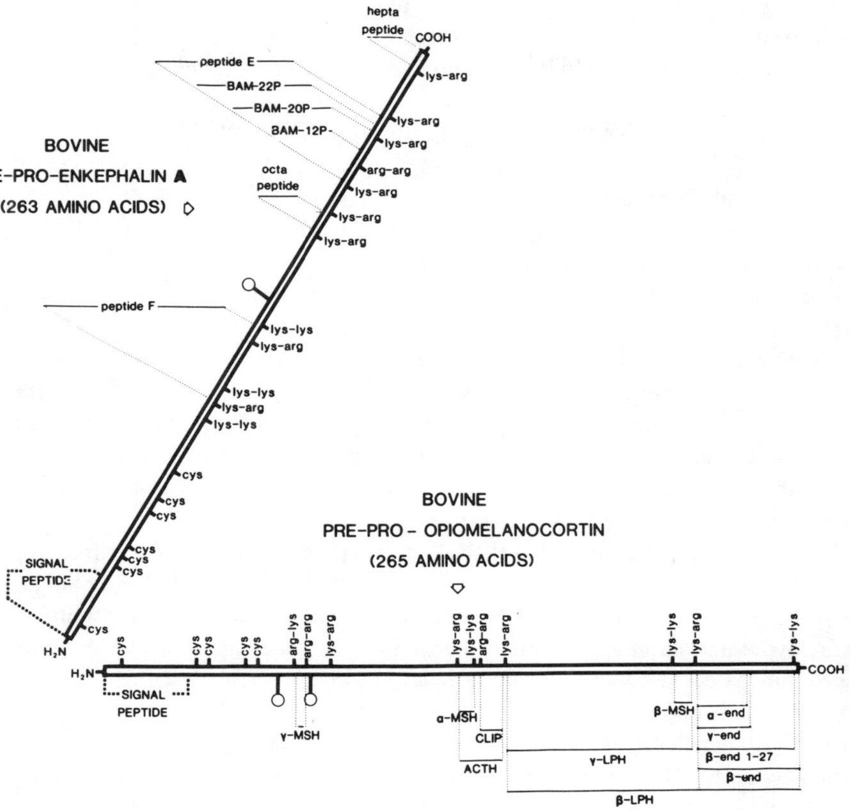

FIGURE 1. Precursor proteins as related to structure of various biologically active opioid peptides.[17]

β-LPH 61 62 66 76 77

β-ENDORPHIN H-Tyr-Gly-Gly-Phe-Met-Thr-Ser-Glu-Lys-Ser-Gln-Thr-Pro-Leu-Val-Thr-Leu-
1 2 3 4 5 6 7 8 9 10 11 12 13 14 15 16 17

Phe-Lys-Asn-Ala-Ile-Ile-Lys-Asn-Ala-Tyr-Lys-Lys-Gly-Glu-OH
18 19 20 21 22 23 24 25 26 27 28 29 30 31

γ-ENDORPHIN	1 —— 17
DTγE	2 —— 17
α-ENDORPHIN	1 —— 16
DTαE	2 —— 16
D-ENKEPHALIN-γ-ENDORPHIN	6 —— 17
D-γ-β-E	18 —— 31

FIGURE 2. Structures of some identified endorphins.

for peptide fragments which can have differing biological effects.[6,10,12,16,17] Additionally, administration of various peptide fragments associated with POMC has been shown to modify thermoregulatory responses of animals exposed to heat or cold environments.[14,18-21] It has also been shown that antagonism of β-endorphinergic transmission by administration of the opioid receptor antagonist naloxone results in a disorder in thermoregulation.[5,21] Based on these results, Brown[4] suggests that endogenous opioid peptides may be involved in adaptation to both extremes of thermal environment. However, characterization of the fate or metabolism of βE in the brain of thermally stressed animals has not been addressed until recently.[22]

III. OPIOIDS AND THERMOREGULATION

A. Morphine and Thermoregulation

The pioneering work of Krueger and co-workers[23] in 1941 has demonstrated that narcotics alter body temperature. This finding has been confirmed in various animal species.[24-26] Administration of morphine either peripherally or centrally evoked hypo- or hyperthermic responses in rodents and cats. Rats developed a biphasic response to administration of morphine in which hyperthermia was preceded by hypothermia.[24,25] Also, low morphine doses caused hyperthermia, but high doses resulted in hypothermia.[26-30] The hypothermic effect of morphine in rats was found to be dependent on ambient temperature (Ta), being greater at low Ta and lessened or reversed to hyperthermia at high Ta. It has been suggested that morphine effects on thermoregulation in rats may be driven via the alteration of the feedback signals from the peripheral thermosensors.[31]

Studies on cats have demonstrated that when morphine was injected peripherally or centrally it caused hyperthermia regardless of the Ta at which the animals were maintained.[32,33] The increase in body temperature in a cold Ta (4 to 6°C) was associated with shivering. However, hyperthermia in a hot Ta (33 to 36°C) was not accompanied by shivering but was associated with a decrease in the elevated respiratory frequency. Although the narcotic effects or alterations of mammalian body temperature were revealed as early as 1941, it is still too early to fully understand the involved mechanisms. The crucial question that must be addressed if we are to really understand the narcotic-thermoregulation interactions is by what central or peripheral processes does the CNS translate the disturbance signals received resulting from the administration of narcotics.

B. Endogenous Opioids and Thermoregulation

After the discovery of the endogenous opioid peptides, the role of these morphine-like substances in thermoregulation has been under active investigation.[4,5,16,18-21,34] Injections of the opiate receptor antagonist naloxone in acute and chronic heat-exposed rats resulted in behavioral and physiological signs related to hyperthermia (i.e., weight loss, escape attempts, salivation, and elevated colonic temperatures). Also, hypophysectomy attenuated or blocked the effects of naloxone in heat-exposed animals.[14,19,20] On the contrary, naloxone had no effect on cold-exposed rats.[35] The blockade of brain and pituitary endorphins by narcotic antagonists was found to cause an acute disturbance in the rat's ability to acclimatize to severe changes in Ta.[21] This finding suggests that endogenous peptides may have a physiological role in regulating body temperature of rats undergoing sudden exposure to thermal stress.

Administration of methionine-enkephalin, leucine enkephalin, and β-endorphin (βE) in rats, mice, and cats caused hyperthermia which was not diminished by naloxone.[35-37] Centrally injected βE in mice produced a dose-dependent and long-lasting hyperthermia.[37] This hyperthermic response was observed at the same magnitude in temperature acclimated (6°, 22, 32, and 37°C) and nonacclimated mice. Hyperthermia in the mice was developed by doses that had little or no effect on antinociception, suggesting that mice are more sensitive to the βE-induced hyperthermia than to analgesia or behavior effects.

The mechanism of action of βE was suggested to be mediated by: (1) an alteration in the brain thermoregulatory center, i.e., resetting of the brain's central thermostat and/or (2) mobilization of hypothalamic factors which may in turn influence the central and peripheral thermoregulatory processes. Administration of βE has been shown to alter the release of hypothalamic hormones.[38,39] Also, administration of hypothalamic thyrotropin hormone (TRH) caused hyperthermia in laboratory mice and desert rodents.[2,37] How endogenous opioids interface between the temperature sensors and the thermoregulatory effectors remains a mystery. Questions related to the effects of endorphins on metabolic, cardiovascular, respiratory, and behavioral functions have not yet been answered. Also, little effort has been directed to the central processing or metabolism of endorphins in animals acclimated to cold and/or hot temperatures. The only available report dealing with metabolism of βE in animals acclimated to heat and cold is summarized here in detail.

IV. CENTRAL PROCESSING AND/OR METABOLISM OF ENDORPHINS IN TEMPERATURE ACCLIMATED RODENTS

Davis et al.[22] studied central processing of βE in two wild desert rodents, *Peromyscus maniculatus* (white-footed deer mouse, *P. maniculatus,* P.m.) and *Peromyscus truei* (Pinon mouse, *P. truei,* P.t.) which ranged in weight between 20 and 30 g. Animals were trapped live from the Mohave desert in Nevada and were studied in comparison with Sprague Dawley rats (*Rattus rattus, R. rattus,* R.r.) weighing 100 to 200 g. All animals were housed individually in plastic cages in a room maintained at 28 ± 0.2°C and on a 12/12 light/dark cycle.

The two species of desert rodents were then randomly divided into three groups. The control group was kept at 28°C together with the white rats, whereas a second and third group of desert rodents were kept at 5 ± 0.2°C and 35 ± 0.2°C, respectively, for 5 weeks. At the end of the temperature acclimation period, all animals were sacrificed by cervical dislocation and the brain immediately removed for the in vitro study of βE processing as previously described.[13]

A. Studies at Thermoneutrality

Incubation of βE for 30 and 60 min with twice washed, whole brain, homogenates resulted in the production of several α- and γ-type endorphins in all three species studied. The rate of βE disappearance (half-life) at 5°, 28°, or 35°C was similar for both *Peromyscus truei* and *P. maniculatus* but much slower for the white rat (*Rattus rattus*) at 28°C. After a 60 min incubation only 1.5 to 3.0% of the βE remained unmetabolized for *P. truei* and *P. maniculatus* as compared to 23% for *R. rattus.* The data indicate that the turnover of βE was significantly slower in the white laboratory rat ($T_{1/2}$ = 27.7 min) than in either of the wild rodents, (P.t. = 9.8 min; P.m. = 11.7 min).

After 60 min of incubation with βE, both *P. truei* and *P. maniculatus* had twice as much α-E and γ-E formed as compared to the white rat. Recently, it was reported that a γ-endorphin generating enzyme (γ-EGE) is present centrally which may be responsible for the formation of γ-E from βE.[40] Des-tyrosine-γ-endorphin (DTγE; βE-(2-17)), which is formed by aminopeptidase cleavage at the Tyr-Gly bond of γ-E was found at a much lower concentration in the white rat than in the desert rodents. The production of another γ-E related peptide, des-enkephalin-γ-endorphin (DEγE; βE-(6-17)) was also higher in both desert rodents as compared to the white rat as shown in Figure 3. Therefore, both DTγE and DEγE which have both been shown to have putative behavioral affects in the facilitation of active avoidance behavior paradigm in rats,[6] are produced at much higher concentrations in twice washed, crude, whole brain homogenates of the wild, desert rodents vs. the white laboratory rat kept at 28°C.

B. Studies in Heat- and Cold-Acclimated Animals

Processing of βE by membrane-associated enzymes was also characterized in desert animal species acclimated to 5° and 35°C to determine the effect of heat and cold acclimation on

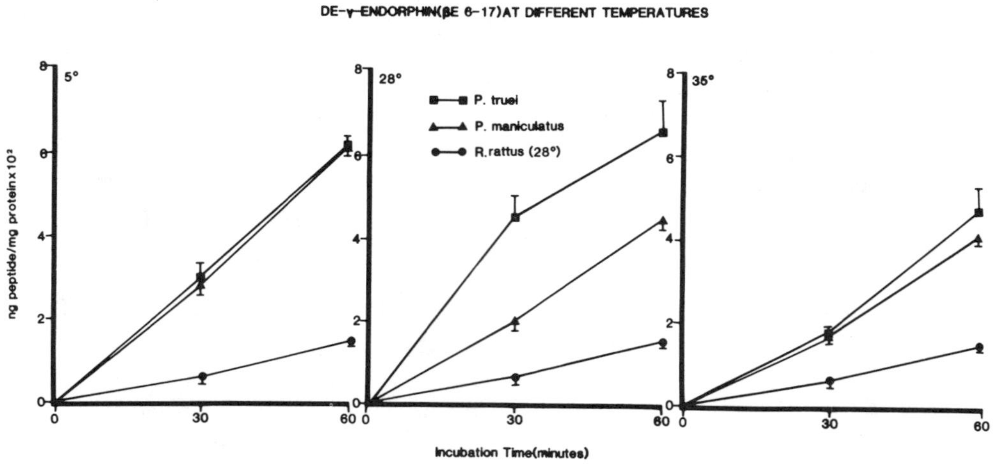

FIGURE 3. Formation of the peptide des-enkephalin-γ-endorphin (βE 6-17) from βE in three species of rodents acclimated to three environmental temperatures: 5°, 28°, and 35°C.[22]

Table 1
EFFECT OF TEMPERATURE ACCLIMATION ON PERCENT β-E (1-31) REMAINING UNCHANGED AND β-E (1-31) HALF-LIFE IN WHOLE BRAIN HOMOGENATES FROM TWO SPECIES OF DESERT RODENTS (P. t. AND P. m.) AND THE WHITE RAT (R. r.)

		Incubation time (min)		
Acclimation temp. (°C)	**Species**	**30**	**60**	**$T_{1/2}$ (β-E)**
5	P. t.	22.50 ± 6.8	5.90 ± 3.4	14.71
	P. m.	25.33 ± 3.8	4.70 ± 1.7	13.61
28	P. t.	11.90 ± 3.1	1.40 ± 0.7	9.75
	P. m.	11.50 ± 4.6	2.80 ± 1.9	11.64
	R.r.	46.0 ± 8.0	23.0 ± 2.1	27.73
35	P. t.	29.50 ± 4.5	8.60 ± 2.9	16.97
	P. m.	19.00 ± 2.3	3.10 ± 1.6	11.98

Note: P. t. = *Peromyscus truei*, P. m. = *Peromyscus maniculatus*, and R. r = *Rattus rattus*. Mean ± S.D.

From Davis, T. P. et al., *Comp. Biochem. Physiol.*, 48C, 105, 1986.

central βE turnover. The amount of βE remaining (percent of control) in the supernatant after a 60 min incubation with crude whole brain homogenates for both desert species acclimated to 5°, 28°, and 35°C is shown in Table 1. The amount of βE remaining in the supernatant from the 5° and 35°C acclimated animals was greater than that at the thermoneutral zone (28°C). There was a significant ($p < 0.05$) decrease in turnover of βE at either 5°C (P.t. = 14.7 min; P.m. = 13.6 min) or 35°C (P.t. = 17.0 min; P.m. = 12.0 min) in both species when compared to 28°C. This finding suggests that in wild rodents there may be an increase in the available pool of nonmetabolized βE for binding to the opioid receptor. Since βE is known to have analgesic properties, the more βE available to bind to the opioid receptor may be a beneficial adaptive response and help explain the decreased

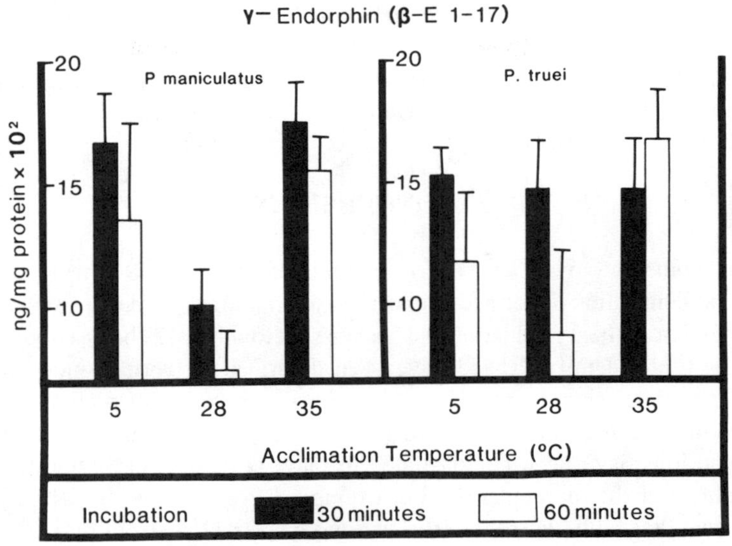

FIGURE 4. Formation of βE 1-17 (γ-endorphin) from βE after incubation of brain homogenates for 30 and 60 min in two desert rodents acclimated to various environmental temperatures.[14]

physical activity noted in temperature acclimated animals. At 5°C, animals curl to conserve heat, and at 35°C they spread their body to increase surface area for greater heat dissipation. Therefore, maintaining a higher available pool of βE may be a beneficial behavioral mechanism for heat conservation and/or dissipation.

Since heat and cold acclimation had similar effects on βE turnover, this suggests that changes in βE half-life are not specific to a given thermal stress and may be triggered by either a hot or cold temperature stress. This type of nonspecificity has been shown in previous studies on foot-shock stress in which plasma levels of βE increased, but hypothalamic and pituitary levels remained unchanged.[41]

Is there a possible temperature or species induced enzymatic alteration in temperature acclimated animals? The work of Davis et al.[22] showed that temperature acclimation to 5° and 35°C increased the potential accumulation of γ-endorphin from βE incubated with twice-washed brain homogenates from desert animals as shown in Figure 4. Based on the proposed metabolic pathway of Burbach et al.,[11] the data on the rodents studied suggest that acclimation to thermal stress may have altered the activity of the γ-endorphin generating endopeptidase resulting in increased production of γ-endorphin. The observation that acclimation to 5° and 35°C also increased the accumulation of DTγE (βE-(2-17)) supports an additional alteration in the activity of the tyrosinase responsible for the cleavage of the tyrosine from γ-endorphin.

In summary, since these data were obtained on crude twice-washed whole brain homogenates, it is perhaps premature to use the term processing which is usually used to refer to the post-translational cleavage and modification of the precursor proteins to their natural products. Also the relevence of these in vitro data to the in vivo situation remains unclear. However, the few available comparative data suggest a shift in the processing of βE in animals acclimated to different temperatures and between rodents of different species. Whether these in vitro findings represent actual in vivo events remains open to speculation, but it is interesting that species differences are apparent in the processing (metabolism) of βE by twice-washed whole brain membrane-associated proteolytic enzymes. The authors[22] have stated that since the brains of desert rats are very small it was not possible to study processing only in the hypothalamus which is the anatomical center of temperature regulation. A study of βE processing in the hypothalamus vs. the whole brain would provide an insight into the role α-, γ-, and β-endorphins play in controlling body temperature. Also, studies on administration of βE, α-E and γ-E on heat production and heat loss avenues in heat and cold acclimated desert rodents would aid in revealing the role of brain endorphins in mammalian thermoregulation.

V. CONCLUSIONS

Mammalian homeothermy is known to be regulated by the CNS where peripheral and central neuronal connections interface between the thermal receptors (sensors) and the thermoregulatory effectors (heat production and heat loss mechanisms). The essential components of such a system are identifiable and have been described by various models;[1] however, how the CNS translates signals from the sensors into appropriate instructional responses to the effectors remains a perplexing phenomenon. Several neurotransmitters, other brain peptides, and some ions have been demonstrated to play, at least in part, significant roles in the central control of thermoregulation. For example, several studies reported that opiate-like peptides can alter body temperature in various species.[4,5] Also, in one unique study,[22] the authors demonstrated a shift in central processing and/or metabolism of βE in temperature-acclimated rodents leading to accumulation of γ-type endorphins. On the other hand, questions such as: Do endorphins alter the feedback signals from the sensors? Are endorphins involved in altering neuronal transmission at the central thermostat level? and Is the role of endorphins on thermoregulation associated with its effects on mobilization of hypothalamic hormones, which in turn alter body temperature? remain open to debate and further investigations. Also, the crucial question of whether endorphins directly influence heat production and heat loss mechanisms has yet to be addressed by researchers.

REFERENCES

1. **Bligh, J.,** Temperature regulation, in *Stress Physiology in Livestock,* Vol. 1, Yousef, M. K., Ed., CRC Press, Boca Raton, Fla., 1985, 75.
2. **Yousef, M. K.,** Responses of small animals to heat stress and exercise, in *Environmental Physiology: Aging, Heat and Altitude,* Horvath, S. M. and Yousef, M. K., Eds., Elsevier/North Holland, New York, 1981, 91.
3. **Schonbaum, E. and Lomax, P.,** *The Pharmacology of Thermoregulation,* S. Karger, Basel, 1973.
4. **Brown, M.,** Thermoregulation, in *Brain Peptides,* Krieger, D. T., Brownstein, M. J., and Martin, J. B., Eds., John Wiley & Sons, New York, 1983, 301.
5. **Clark, W. G.,** Influence of opioids on central thermoregulatory mechanisms, *Pharm. Biochem. Behav.,* 10, 609, 1979.
6. **Bohus, B.,** Neuropeptides in brain functions and dysfunctions, *Int.J. Mental Health,* 9, 6, 1981.
7. **Gubler, U., Seeburg, P., Hoffman, B.J., Gage, L. P., and Udenfriend, S.,** Molecular cloning establishes proenkephalin as a precursor enkephalin-containing peptides, *Nature (London),* 295, 206, 1982.
8. **Höllt, V., Tulunay Cankat, S., Wood, K., Loh, H. H., and Herz, A.,** Opioid peptides derived from proenkephalin A, but not from proenkephalin B are substantial analgesics after administration into brain of mice, *Eur. J. Pharmacol.,* 85, 355, 1982.
9. **Kilpatrick, D. L., Taniquchi, T., Jones, B. N., Stern, A. S., Shively, J. E., Hullihan, J., Kimura, S., Stein, S., and Udenfriend, S.,** A highly potent 3200-dalton adrenal opioid peptide that contains both a {Met} and {Leu} enkephalin sequence, *Proc. Natl. Acad. Sci. U.S.A.,* 78, 3265, 1982.
10. **O'Donohue, T. C.and Dorsa, D. M.,** The opiomelanotropinergic neuronal and endocrine systems, *Peptides,* 3, 353, 1982.
11. **Burbach, J. P. H., De Kloet, E. R., Schotman, P., and De Wied, D.,** Proteolytic conversion of β-endorphin by brain synaptic membranes — characterization of generated β-endorphin fragments and proposed metabolic pathway, *J. Biol. Chem.,* 256, 12463, 1981.
12. **Davis, T. P., Culling, A. J., Schoemaker, H., and Galligan, J. J.,** β-Endorphin and its metabolites stimulate motility of the dog small intestine, *J. Pharmacol. Exp. Ther.,* 227, 499, 1983.

13. **Davis, T. P., Schoemaker, H., and Culling-Berglund, A. J.,** Characterization of *in vitro* proteolytic processing of β-endorphin by reversed-phase HPLC, *Peptides,* 5, 1037, 1984.
14. **Holaday, J. W., Law, P. Y., Tseng, C. F., Loh, H. H., and Li, C. H.,** β-endorphin: pituitary and adrenal glands modulate its action, *Proc. Natl. Acad. Sci. U.S.A.,* 74, 4628, 1977.
15. **Van Ree, J. M., Verhoeven, W. M. A., De Wied, D., and Von Praag, H. M.,** The use of the synthetic peptides γ-type endorphins in mentally ill patients, *Ann. N. Y. Acad. Sci.,* 398, 478, 1982.
16. **Burks, T. F., Davis, T. P., and McDougal, J. N.,** Metabolism and thermopharmacology of opioid peptides in rat brain, in *Environment, Drugs and Thermoregulation,* Lomax, P., Schoenbaum, E., and Cox, B., S. Karger, Basel, 1983, 94.
17. **Höllt, V.,** Multiple endogenous opioid peptides, *Trends Neurol. Sci.,* 6, 24, 1983.
18. **Blasig, J., Bauerle, U., and Herz, A.,** Endorphin-induced hyperthermia: characterization of the exogenously and endogenously induced effects, *Naunyn-Schmiedeberg's Arch. Pharmacol.,* 309, 137, 1979.
19. **Holaday, J. W., Wei, E., Loh, H. H., and Li, C. H.,** Endorphins may function in heat adaptation, *Proc. Natl. Acad. Sci. U.S.A.,* 75, 2923, 1978a.
20. **Holaday, J. W., Loh, H. H., and Li, C. H.,** Unique behavioral effects of β-endorphin and their relationship to thermoregulation and hypothalamic function, *Life Sci.,* 22, 1525, 1978b.
21. **Thornhill, J. A., Cooper, K. E., and Veale, W. L.,** Core temperature changes following administration of naloxone and naltrexane to rats exposed to hot and cold temperatures. Evidence for the physiological role of endorphins in hot and cold acclimatization, *J. Pharm. Pharmacol.,* 32, 427, 1980.
22. **Davis, T. P., Han, A., and Yousef, M. K.,** Central metabolism of β-endorphin in different species of temperature acclimated rodents, *Comp. Biochem. Physiol.,* 48C, 105, 1986.
23. **Krueger, H., Eddy, N. B., and Sumwalt, M.,** The Pharmacology of the Opium Alkaloids, Part 1, Public Health Reports, Suppl. 165, U.S. Government Printing Office, Washington, D.C., 1941.
24. **Chodera, A.,** Influence of Marsilid on the temperature response in rats after morphine, *Arch. Int. Pharmacodyn. Ther.,* 144, 362, 1963.
25. **Oka, T., Nozaki, M., and Hosoya, E.,** Effects of ρ-chlorophenylalanine and cholinergic antagonists on body temperature changes induced by administration of morphine to non-tolerant and morphine tolerant rats, *J. Pharmacol. Exp. Ther.,* 180, 136, 1972.
26. **Lotti, V. J.,** Body temperature responses to morphine, in *The Pharmacology of Thermoregulation,* Schonbaum, E. and Lomax, P., Eds., S. Karger, Basel, 1973, 382.
27. **Cox, B., Ary, M., Chesarek, W., and Lomax, P.,** Morphine hyperthermia in the rat; an action on central thermostats, *Eur. J. Pharmacol.,* 36, 33, 1976.
28. **Herrmann, J. B.,** The pyretic action on rats of small doses of morphine, *J. Pharmacol. Exp. Ther.,* 76, 309, 1942.
29. **Lotti, V. J., Lomax, P., and George, R.,** Temperature responses in the rat following intracerebral microinjection of morphine, *J. Pharmacol. Exp. Ther.,* 150, 135, 1965.
30. **Samanin, R., Kon, S., and Garattini, S.,** Abolition of the morphine effect on body temperature in midbrain raphe lesioned rats, *J. Pharm. Pharmacol.,* 24, 374, 1972.
31. **Rudy, T. A. and Yaksh, T. L.,** Hyperthermic effects of morphine: setpoint manipulation by a direct spinal action, *Br. J. Pharmacol.,* 61, 91, 1977.
32. **Clark, W. G. and Cumby, H. R.,** Hyperthermic responses to central and peripheral injections of morphine sulfate in the cat, *Br. J. Pharmacol.,* 63, 65, 1978.
33. **Wallenstein, M. C.,** Temperature response to morphine in paralyzed cats, *Eur. J. Pharmacol.,* 49, 331, 1978.
34. **Bloom, A. S. and Tseng, L. F.,** Effects of β-endorphin on body temperature in mice at different ambient temperatures, *Peptides,* 2, 293, 1981.
35. **Goldstein, A. and Lowery, P. J.,** Effect of the opiate antagonist naloxone on body temperature in rats, *Life Sci.,* 17, 927, 1975.
36. **Clark, W. G.,** Emetic and hyperthermic effects of centrally injected methionine-enkephalin in cats, *Proc. Soc. Exp. Biol. Med.,* 154, 540r, 1977.
37. **Huidobro-Toro, J. P. and Way, E. L.,** Studies on hyperthermic responses of β-endorphin in mice, *J. Pharmacol. Exp. Ther.,* 211, 50, 1979.
38. **Rivier, C., Vale, W., Ling, N., Brown, M., and Guillemin, R.,** Stimulation *in vivo* of the secretion of prolactin and growth hormone by β-endorphin, *Endocrinology,* 10, 238, 1978.
39. **Weitzman, R. E., Fisher, D. A., Minick, S., Long, N., and Guillemin, R.,** β-Endorphin stimulates secretion of arginine vasopressin *in vivo, Endocrinology,* 101, 1643, 1977.
40. **Burbach, J. P. H., Lebouille, J. L. M., and Wang, X.-Ch.,** Proteolytic conversion of neuropeptides into active fragments, in *Regulation of Transmitter Function: Basic and Clinical Aspects,* Vizi, E. S. and Magyar, K., Eds., Akademiai Kiado, Budapest, 1984, 237.
41. **Rossier, J., French, E. D., Rivier, D., Ling, N., Guillemin, R., and Bloom, F. E.,** Foot-shock induced stress increases β-endorphin levels in blood but not brain, *Nature (London),* 270, 618, 1977.

Chapter 16

ADAPTATION TO THE ENVIRONMENT: THE ROLE OF RED BLOOD CELLS

Naomi Meyerstein, Zipora Etzion, Dalia Mazor, and Reuven Yagil

TABLE OF CONTENTS

Abstract 132

I. Introduction 132

II. Experimental Design 132

III. The Challenge of Rehydration 133

IV. Shape Preservation and Osmotic Resistance 133

V. Possible Contribution of Hemoglobin 133

VI. Red Cell Membrane Proteins 135

VII. Comparison of Red Cells of the Camel with the Black Bedouin Goat 135

References 137

ABSTRACT

Camels and black Bedouin goats are known for their ability to tolerate long periods of dehydration and rapid rehydration. Man cannot survive prolonged dehydration or rapid rehydration because of plasma loss, hemoconcentration, and severe thermoregulation problems followed by hemodilution. The red blood cells of the camel have been found to have extreme osmotic resistance in hypertonic and hypotonic solutions. This extreme osmotic resistance persists during dehydration and rehydration. However, this amazing potential is not challenged by plasma osmolality. Similarly, the red cells of the black Bedouin goat, with their high osmotic fragility, are not challenged in vivo during rapid rehydration. Another possible contribution of the red cell to survival in dehydration could be resistance to high temperature. During dehydration, the camel's body temperature may rise to 41°C. This rise in body temperature reduces water loss, but may damage the cells; however, the camel's red cells tolerate well in vitro incubation in this temperature range, without affecting its osmotic resistance. The camel's hemoglobin is remarkably soluble, with unique resistance to alkali denaturation and to methemoglobin production. Its high affinity is maintained during dehydration, in accordance with the reduced metabolic rate. The camel's red cells are oval, non-nucleated cells, while all the other mammals have biconcave discs. The camel's red blood cells are rich in integral proteins and in intramembranous particles, and their spectrin is highly bound. They retain their oval shape in dehydration, but may double in volume when exposed to hypotonicity in vitro and become round on rapid rehydration in vivo. They also show extreme resistance to shape change by drugs. In summary, the camel's red blood cell has many unique features, but its contribution to survival in desert conditions is not yet clear.

I. INTRODUCTION

The camel, *Camelus dromedarius,* has amazing ability to withstand extreme desert conditions. It can survive long dehydration periods followed by rapid rehydration[1-3] as well as exposure to high ambient temperatures followed by cold nights. Several organ systems have been found to assist in the camel's adaptation to desert conditions; we would like to focus on the possible role of the camel's red blood cell (RBCs) in its unique adaptation to arid environment.

II. EXPERIMENTAL DESIGN

The camels were kept in open shade, exposed to the climate. They were fed a standard diet of 5 kg of wheat straw and 2 kg bovine concentrates per animal. When the animals were not in dehydration-rehydration experiments, they were given water *ad libitum*. The dehydration lasted 7 days, while the camels continued to eat, unaffected by dehydration. On the 7th morning, the animals were allowed to drink and usually did so rapidly and restored their body weight within several minutes.[4,5] No untoward effect was noticed and no hemolysis was detected during the rehydration period. Blood samples were taken 30 min after rehydration and then after 4 hr. The hematological findings (1974) were as follows.

Hematocrit during the summer was usually 28.5% ± 0.82, while during the winter it was 32% ± 1.02. During dehydration performed in the summer, the hematocrit averaged 25.6% ± 2.52, but the values were variable. A larger drop was noted in the hemoglobin level (21.9% decrease) and in the RBC count.[4] In certain dehydration-rehydration cycles these levels did not change or rose only slightly. An interesting correlation was found between ambient temperature and the hematological parameters.[6] When ambient daily temperature ranged between 33 and 38°C, dehydration caused 25% weight loss, the daily hemoglobin and hematocrit fluctuated greatly, and osmotic fragility of the cells increased during dehydration. The hematological fluctuations seemed to follow the changing ambient temperatures; when a similar experiment was conducted in milder temperature changes, body weight loss was only 11%, and the hematological fluctuations were less pronounced. Plasma osmolality never rose above 310 mOsm/kg during dehydration. Therefore, the heat stress affects water losses which then determine the changes in blood parameters.

III. THE CHALLENGE OF REHYDRATION

After 7 days of dehydration, the camels were allowed to drink water *ad libitum,* and usually regained their body loss. During this period plasma osmolality was reduced but did not decrease below 250 mOsm/kg in our samples. Water was rapidly leaving the GI system and entering the circulation, as shown by several studies.[7]

What could be the contribution of the camel's red blood cell to its survival during dehydration and rehydration?

IV. SHAPE PRESERVATION AND OSMOTIC RESISTANCE

The camel's red cells are oval, non-nucleated cells, in contrast to the discoid shape of other mammals' red cells. These oval cells have been shown to have osmotic stability in extremely hypotonic salt solutions.[8,9] Hemolysis starts at around 70 m*M* NaCl, reaches 50% at 47 m*M*, and maximum at 43 m*M*.[4] They also have extreme stability to hypertonicity, and maintain their shape in salt concentrations which are 20 times higher than that of normal plasma (Figure 1*). This osmotic stability exists during dehydration followed by rapid rehydration; however, during dehydration under severe climatic stress, osmotic fragility did increase.[4,5] However, this extreme osmotic potential does not seem to be challenged by plasma osmolality, whose minimum is 250 mOsm/kg to a maximum of 320 mOsm/kg during dehydration and rehydration cycles. The osmolality determinations during these periods were done daily during dehydration, and then 30 min and 4 hr after rehydration. It is possible that more remarkable hypotonicity exists during some time after rehydration. An interesting phenomenon is the appearance of round cells, 4 hr after rehydation. Forty percent of the cells were found to have equal axes. This observation was made in some but not all the dehydration and rehydration experiments.

Another interesting characteristic of the camel's red cell is its osmotic stability in different in vitro experiments. As during summer dehydration the animals' body temperature may rise above 41°C. We examined the cells' reaction to these temperatures. In vitro incubation at temperatures which may occur during dehydration have not affected the camel's cells, and they retained their osmotic stability (Figure 2).

V. POSSIBLE CONTRIBUTION OF HEMOGLOBIN

The hemoglobin of the camel has been studied, among other hemoglobins from other species, to learn about its structure and its possible relevance to the camel's ability to survive arid environments. Lin et al.[10] studied the structure and physicochemical properties of the camel's hemoglobin. They found that native camel hemoglobin contains 95% alkali-resistant hemoglobin with more positive charges than human hemoglobin. It has extreme solubility and resistance to high salt concentration. These two qualities may help during dehydration and ensure the hemoglobin solubility at its high cellular concentration — more than 45%. We have studied the camel's hemoglobin at birth and found that the hemoglobin of the newborn is alkali-resistant, like that of the adult camel. We also studied, by Hem-O-Scan studies, the oxyhemoglobin dissociation curve at different temperatures and physiological

* See glossy insert following page 148.

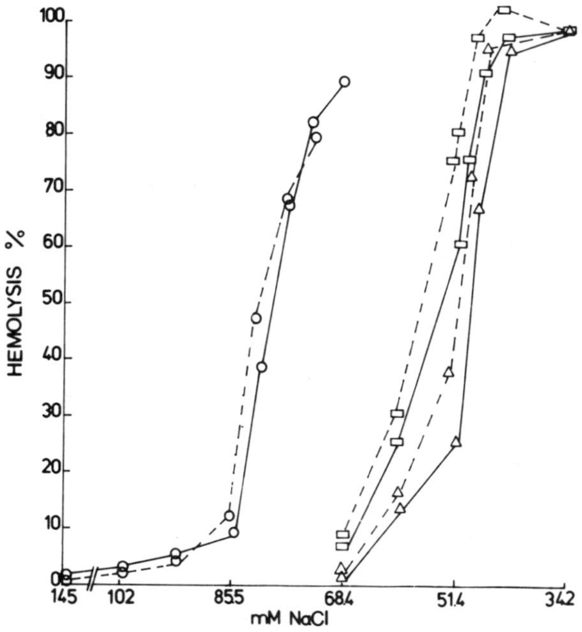

FIGURE 2. In vitro heating at 44°C of human and camel red blood cells.

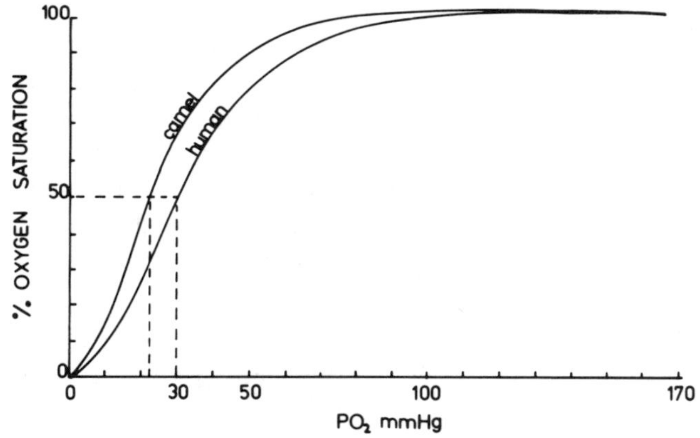

FIGURE 3. Oxyhemoglobin dissociation curves in red blood cells of camel and man, in normal hydration.

conditions. These experiments were performed on whole cells, at 37°C, the temperature at which human hemoglobin has P_{50} of 28.0 mmHg. The camel's dissociation curve is slightly shifted to the left, with P_{50} values which are similar to those of the other camelidae: P_{50} was 25 ± 2.2 mmHg at the control state, 25 ± 1.8 at dehydration, and 24 ± 1.5 after rehydration (Figure 3). There was no difference in oxygen potential release at those different physiological states. Thus, the camel retains its left shifted curve at dehydration. This may help in maintaining low metabolic rate in summer during dehydration.[11] When the curve was studied at 41°C, possible body temperature at dehydration, we found that the curve shifted to the right about 3 mmHg, as expected by increased temperature. Therefore, even at 41°C the camel's oxyhemoglobin dissociation curve does not shift to the right by more than 3 mmHg, and does not release oxygen abundantly. There is no necessity for this as cell metabolism is greatly decreased.

VI. RED CELL MEMBRANE PROTEINS

The camel's red cell retains its oval shape during dehydration,[4] and during cold storage.[12] It does change only after rehydration, when the cells become round.[4] It has also been shown that these cells are remarkably resistant to metabolic depletion, calcium loading, and heating to 60°, which induces disc-sphere transformation and fragmentation in human RBC.[13] A possible explanation for this could be the special arrangement of the membrane proteins, mainly spectrin and bands 3 and 4. Ralston[13] has shown that only after releasing spectrin from the ghosts by incubation with high concentrations of urea or other chemicals such as PCMB (*p*-chloromercuribenzoate, a special sulfhydryl reagent), do the cells turn from flat ellipses to small spheres.

The red cell lipids have been found to be quite similar in camels and humans.[14,15] However, the protein to lipid ratio is increased in the camel, with more proline and less glutamic acid. The membrane is rich in integral proteins and in intramembraneous particles, as demonstrated in scanning electron microscopy and freeze-etch studies, by Livne and Kuiper.[14] It has also been shown that these particles are larger and more densely distributed than in human membranes.

In summary, the secret of the camel's red cell membrane does not seem to be in a special component undemonstrated in other species; it seems that the unique stability of the cells to different external and internal factors lies in its special organization. It could be that small structural differences in bands 3 and 4, which have been found in camels,[13] tighten the cytoskeletal membrane (mainly the spectrin) and endow resistance to shape changes.

Another interesting aspect of the same resistance to shape change has been demonstrated by Smith et al.[16] They demonstrated that different amphipathic drugs, which induce sphere or stomatocyte transformation, have only minimal effect on the camel's red cells. Their conclusion is that structural rigidity of the cell membrane may alter the response, predicted by bilayer-couple hypothesis. This rigidity has also been demonstrated by the same group in deformability studies.[17] They have shown that llama red blood cells have reduced deformability, in ectocytometry studies, while suspended in dextran. However, when we studied filterability of whole blood and washed cells, taken in EDTA only (not in heparin), and suspended either in their own plasma, as whole blood or in phosphate-buffered saline, we have found that their filterability is even better than those of human blood.[20] Deformability decreased in dehydration and increased again during rehydration.

VII. COMPARISON OF RED CELLS OF THE CAMEL WITH THE BLACK BEDOUIN GOAT

The black Bedouin goat lives in the Sinai desert and survives prolonged periods of water deprivation.[18] Similar to the camel, the goat withstands 20 to 30% loss of body weight by dehydration, and consumes its water loss within minutes. Despite this similarity, their red cells are different and their mechanisms of survival in dehydration and rapid rehydration seem to be quite dissimilar. In contrast to the camel's low osmotic fragility, the black Bedouin goat has highly fragile cells.[19] If these cells had been exposed to a hypotonic environment, they would have hemolyzed and endangered the goat. However, as shown by Shkolnik et al.,[19] the rumen serves as a protective osmotic barrier during rapid rehydration, and the water is retained within the rumen for at least 5 hr after rehydration. Thus, the fragile red cell of the Bedouin goat is not exposed to hypotonicity during rapid rehydration.

As suggested by Shkolnik, the different red cells have different osmotic stabilities related to their taxonomic-phylogenetic grouping. As can be seen in Figure 4, the two desert animals compared here, the camel and the Bedouin goat, vary greatly in their osmotic stability. The camel has extreme stability, like the other camelidae, while the Bedouin goat has extreme

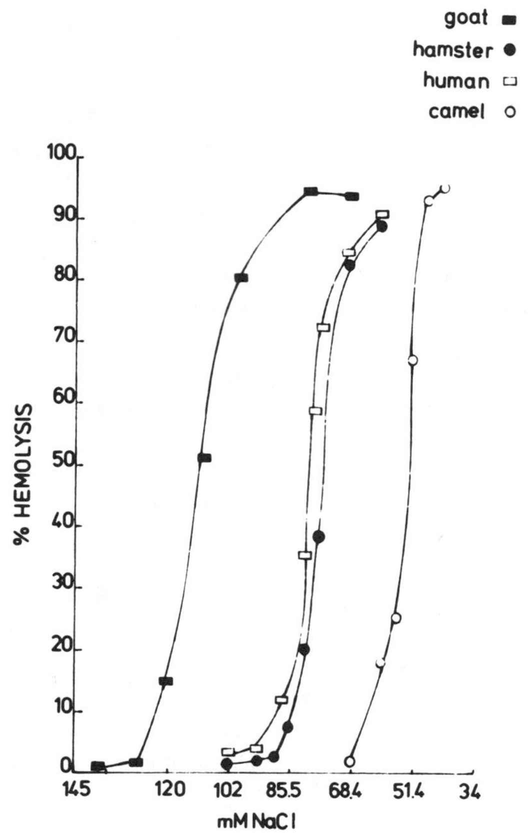

FIGURE 4. Osmotic fragility in camel, hamster, man, and Bedouin goat.

fragility, like other bovidae. Man and hamsters have red cells with intermediate qualities. It could be hypothesized that the harsh desert conditions allow animals with different behavioral and physiological adaptations to survive: the camel with its high resistance survives side by side with the goat, with the high sensitivity to hypotonicity, but with special arrangement to avoid hypotonicity.

A similar situation may exist in the case of the oxyhemoglobin dissociation curve and oxygen release. Camels have a left-shifted dissociation curve with low P_{50} values, like the other camelidae, living in different altitudes and water availability conditions; the black Bedouin goat most probably has P_{50} at values similar to those of other bovidae and man. Again, it seems reasonable to assume that the camel, whose interest is to produce less heat during dehydration in summer, can gain from a left-shifted curve. The goat can survive without this mechanism.

In conclusion, the camel has unique red cells with special potential for surviving heat exposure, acid base changes and osmotic stresses:

1. These cells have extreme osmotic stability in hypotonic media, which may occur during rapid rehydration and in hypertonic media, which may occur during severe hydration. In this aspect, it seems that the cell's potential markedly surpasses the physiological range. The cells are also resistant to heat.
2. These cells demonstrate shape conservation in different osmotic environments in vivo and in vitro which possibly maintains cellular function under these conditions.

3. The camel's hemoglobin is present in the red cell in large quantities: more than 45% of the cell volume is made of hemoglobin; this hemoglobin has extreme solubility and resistance to high salt concentration. The two qualities may ensure its solubility during dehydration. Its left shifted oxygen dissociation curve also may contribute to the animal's low metabolic rate in dehydration.

REFERENCES

1. **Schmidt-Nielsen, K.,** *Desert Animals,* Oxford University Press, London, 1964, 33.
2. **Macfarlane, W. V. and Siebert, D. D.,** Hydration and dehydration of desert camels, *Aust. J. Exp. Biol. Med. Sci.,* 45, 29, 1967.
3. **Yagil, R.,** Camels and Camel Milk, Food and Agriculture Organization, Monogr. FAO, 1982.
4. **Yagil, R., Sod-Moriah, U. A., and Meyerstein, N.,** Dehydration and camel blood. II. Shape, size and concentration of red blood cells, *Am. J. Physiol.,* 226(2), 301, 1974.
5. **Yagil, R., Sod-Moriah, U. A., and Meyerstein, N.,** Dehydration and camel blood. III. Osmotic fragility, specific gravity and osmolality, *Am. J. Physiol.,* 226(2), 305, 1974.
6. **Yagil, R., Sod-Moriah, U. A., and Meyerstein, N.,** The effects of environmental temperature and dehydration on camel blood, *Isr. J. Med. Sci.,* 12, 878, 1976.
7. **Etzion, Z., Meyerstein, N., and Yagil, R.,** Tritiated water metabolism during dehydration and rehydration in the camel, *J. Appl. Physiol. Resp. Environ. Exercise Physiol.,* 56, 217, 1984.
8. **Perk, K.,** The camel's erythrocyte, *Nature (London),* 200, 272, 1963.
9. **Ponder, E.,** *Hemolysis and Related Phenomena,* Grune & Stratton, New York, 1948, 346.
10. **Lin, Kuang-Tzu, D., Bhown Agit Singh, Chernoff, A. I.,** Studies on camel hemoglobin. I. Physico-chemical properties and some structural aspects of camel hemoglobin *(Camelus dromedarius), Biochim. Biophys. Acta,* 434, 110, 1976.
11. **Yagil, R., Etzion, Z., and Ganani, J.,** Camel thyroid metabolism: effect of season and dehydration, *J. Appl. Physiol.,* 45, 540, 1978.
12. **Meyerstein, N., Mazor, D., Etzion, Z., and Yagil, R.,** Permeability of the erythrocytes to glycerol and its acylated derivatives in the camel and dog, *Comp. Biochem. Physiol.,* 61A, 261, 1978.
13. **Ralston, G. B.,** Proteins of the camel erythrocyte membrane, *Biochim. Biophys. Acta,* 401, 83, 1975.
14. **Livne, A. and Kuiper, P. J. C.,** Unique properties of the camel erythrocyte membrane, *Biochim. Biophys. Acta,* 318, 41, 1973.
15. **Eitan, A., Aloni, B., and Livne, A.,** Unique properties of the camel erythrocyte membrane. II. Organization of membrane properties, *Biochim. Biophys. Acta,* 426, 647, 1976.
16. **Smith, J. S., Mohandas, N., and Shohet, S. B.,** Interaction of amphipathic drugs with erythrocytes from various species, *Am. J. Vet. Res.,* 43(6), 1041, 1982.
17. **Smith, J. E., Mohandas, N., Clark, M. R., Greenquist, A. C., and Shohet, S. B.,** Deformability and spectrin properties in three types of elongated red cells, *Am. J. Hematol.,* 8, 1, 1980.
18. **Shkolnik, A., Borut, A., and Choshniak, I.,** Water economy of the Bedouin goat, *Symp. Zool. Soc. London,* 31, 229, 1972.
19. **Choshniak, I. and Shkolnik, A.,** The rumen as a protective osmotic mechanism during rehydration in the black Bedouin goat, in *Osmotic and Volume Regulation,* Skadhauge, E. and Jorgensen, C. B., Eds., Alfred Bezon Symp. XI, Munksgaard, Copenhagen, 1978, 344.
20. **Etzion, Z.,** in preparation.

Chapter 17

INTERACTIONS BETWEEN CIRCULATION AND PLASMA FLUIDS DURING HEAT STRESS

Michal Horowitz and Shlomo Samueloff

TABLE OF CONTENTS

I. Introduction 140

II. Redistribution of Cardiac Output — A Thermoregulatory Reflex 140

III. Acid Base Balance and Tissue Oxygenation During Heat Stress 141

IV. Plasma Volume and Thermoregulation 144

References 148

I. INTRODUCTION

During exposure to extreme heat, the cardiovascular system plays a major role in thermal homeostasis. Heat load mobilizes cardiovascular mechanisms leading to increased heat dissipation. This is achieved by thermally induced reflexes resulting in a redistribution of cardiac output and accelerated heat transfer from the core to the periphery.

The cardiovascular system is involved with many homeostatic transporting functions. The transfer of body heat by circulating blood is linked with tissue oxygen supply, gas exchange, and acid base balance. It is therefore reasonable to assume that during heat stress the thermoregulatory activity of the cardiovascular system interferes with these functions. In the following discussion an attempt is made to delineate the interplay between cardiovascular thermoregulatory activity, plasma fluid shifts, tissue gas exchange, and acid base balance. We focus on the strategies by which the heat strained cardiovascular system manipulates these competitive parameters of homeostasis.

II. REDISTRIBUTION OF CARDIAC OUTPUT — A THERMOREGULATORY REFLEX

Subjection to heat load mobilizes the cardiovascular system to increase heat transfer from the core to the periphery. In the first place, this is achieved by increasing skin blood perfusion. In a heat stressed person, when thermoregulatory activity attains its maximal performance, a sixfold increase in skin blood flow was observed.[1] Since the capacity of blood volume and flow are limited, the demand for increased peripheral circulation is met by the cardiovascular system through an increase and/or redistribution of the cardiac output. The increased skin perfusion is concomitant with thermally induced splanchnic and renal vasoconstriction which facilitates blood flow and volume shift to the dilated skin vessels. It has been demonstrated that the mechanism of the shift is not related to the baroreceptor reflex and is not affected by a change in posture.[1]

The introduction of the microsphere technique has made it possible to obtain quantitative information on tissue blood flow of many organs simultaneously. Using this technique the distribution of blood flow from various organs has been measured in various species. Table 1 presents the data available.

Comparable data on rodents, both desert and nondesert dwellers, have been obtained recently in our laboratory. These data are presented in Figure 1. As in large mammals, heat stressed rodents exemplify splanchnic vasoconstriction with peripheral vasodilatation. This vasodilatation is most pronounced in the tail, ears, and ventral skin surfaces, particularly in the neck and chest areas. Unlike large mammals, however, almost no alteration in blood flow to renal vascular bed was observed in rodents.[5]

In desert rodents splanchnic blood flow is higher than in the laboratory rat, suggesting lower resistance in these vascular beds. During heat stress splanchnic vasoconstriction develops. However, from data obtained for anesthetized specimens this splanchnic vasoconstriction is less pronounced in the desert dweller. No other differences in organ blood perfusion were observed between desert and nondesert rodents.[6]

Cardiac output and its distribution prior and following heat stress was also measured in acclimated rodents.[5] In the laboratory rat acclimation did not affect the pattern of distribution of cardiac output to organs and tissues; however, due to a remarkable increase in cardiac output, blood perfusion both to peripheral and internal organs was elevated. In thermally dehydrated heat-acclimated rats splanchnic vasoconstriction is not significant. This may imply that the thermally induced splanchnic vasoconstriction is genetically acquired as an emergency mechanism in desert species. Attenuation of this response in the acclimated rat may be due to the increase in blood volume known to occur following heat acclimation. The better perfusion of internal organs may facilitate heat tolerance of the acclimated animals.

Table 1
SKIN AND SPLANCHNIC BLOOD FLOWS (% CARDIAC OUTPUT) IN THERMONEUTRAL AND MODERATE HEAT STRESS CONDITIONS IN MAMMALS, AS OBTAINED BY USING THE MICROSPHERES TECHNIQUE

	Thermoneutral			Moderate heat stress			
Species	**Skin**	**AVA**	**Splanchnic organs**	**Skin**	**AVA**	**Splanchnic organs**	**Ref.**
Sheep	12	2	38	12	9	19	2
Dog	1	1	15	1	5	10	3
Baboon	3	4.2	18	14	8.6	11.9	4

A significant feature of the "heat induced redistribution of cardiac output" is the shift of blood to peripheral arteriovenous anastomoses (AVA), allowing rapid increase in skin heat conductivity.[2,7] In sheep, during severe hyperthermia, 11% of the cardiac output is shifted to AVA.[2] Similar changes were measured for dogs,[3] and in rodents[6] the shift of blood flow to AVA can exceed 18%. Various studies have indicated that during heat stress vasodilation in AVA is controlled by the thermoregulatory integrating center in the anterior hypothalamus.[8]

With progression of heat exposure to severe hyperthermia several circulatory changes reverse their direction. Thus, skin blood perfusion returns to thermoneutral levels or even decreases.[2] In rodents, coincidently with decreased skin and AVA blood flow, an augmentation of splanchnic blood flow was observed. This reversal of circulatory changes during hyperthermia reflects the dominance of cardiovascular requirements over thermoregulation. Indeed, Horowitz and Nadel[9] have shown in both heat-stressed untreated and water deprived dogs a maintenance of cardiac filling pressure even while body temperature rises and plasma volume decreases.

The distribution of blood flow and the maintenance of blood pressure during heat exposure is related to the control of blood volume per body weight ratio as well. Adequate blood volume is a "must" for efficient thermoregulation. Heat-induced redistribution of cardiac output may therefore result in an alteration of plasma volume per body weight ratio. This problem of blood flow redistribution and plasma volume changes is discussed later in the chapter.

III. ACID BASE BALANCE AND TISSUE OXYGENATION DURING HEAT STRESS

Heat-stressed species have shown no impairment in oxygen transfer by the circulating blood. This had been found in the oxen,[10] goats,[11] and dogs.[12] However, during heat stress, the diminution of blood flow to certain organs may lead to tissue hypoxia, which together with heat-induced hyperventilation and excessive sweating pose a burden for maintenance of acid base balance.

The term acid base balance refers to the ratio of cation and anion concentrations in body fluids, and their activity is basically affected by changes in temperature. Carbon dioxide is the most abundant acid metabolite in the body and its effect on acid base balance is controlled by changes in respiration. Many other metabolites are nonvolatile organic acids and affect the standard bicarbonate levels in blood. Their concentration in blood depends on their turnover rate in the liver or their excretion by the kidney. Thus, deviation from normal acid/base ratio in body fluids can be compensated or regulated by respiratory and kidney mechanisms.

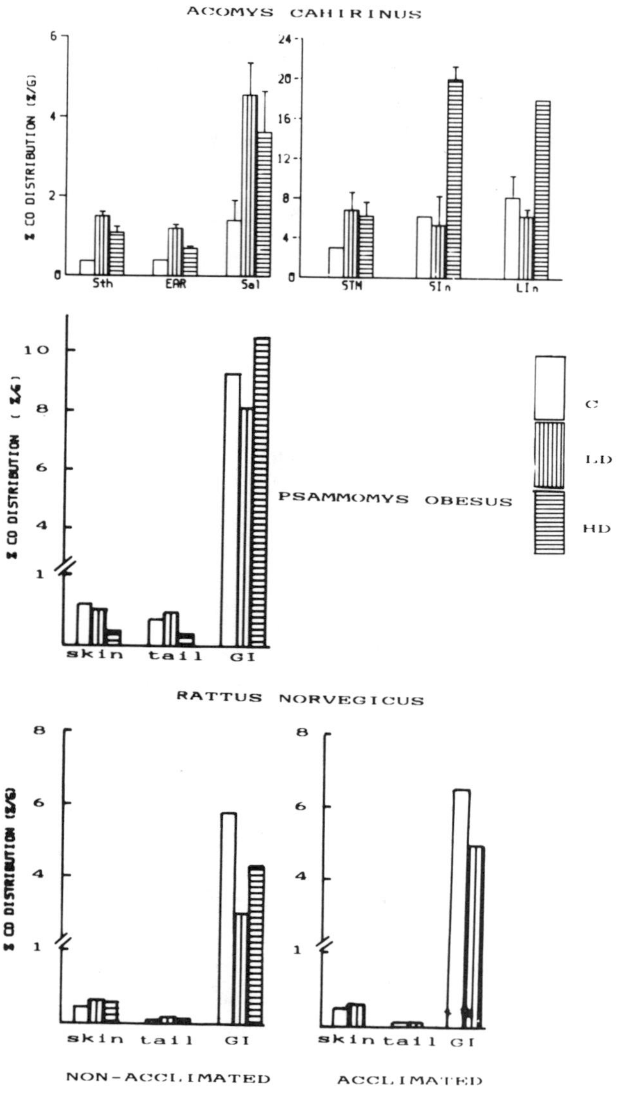

FIGURE 1. Cardiac output (CO) distribution to splanchnic and peripheral thermoregulatory areas in anesthetized controls and dehydrated rodent species. Data are expressed as % CO distribution per gram tissue. CO (mℓ/100 g body weight) for controls (C), low dehydration (LD), and high dehydration (HD), respectively were as follows: rats — 24.5, 21.6, 20.1; acclimated rats — 28.1, 28.0; *P. obesus* — 21.7, 26.8, 25.7. Sth, neck skin; Sal, salivary gland; STM, stomach; SIn, small intestine; LIn, large intestine; GI, gastrointestinal tract. Data for rats were adapted from Reference 5; data on *P. obesus* and *A. cahirinus* were adapted from Reference 35.

Figure 2 depicts acid base status in desert rodents and dogs during the transition from normal body temperatures to severe hyperthermia. During heat stress the sand rat (*Psammomys obesus*) maintains an elevated body temperature, and spreads saliva over the body surface for evaporating cooling, while the bedouin rabbits (*Oryctolagus cuniculus*) pant, and at very high temperatures pant and salivate. During heat stress dogs maintain body temperature at a normal level by panting. At normothermia average arterial blood pH, $PaCO_2$, and HCO_3 values in the nonanesthetized sand rat[13,14] are in the lower range of values reported

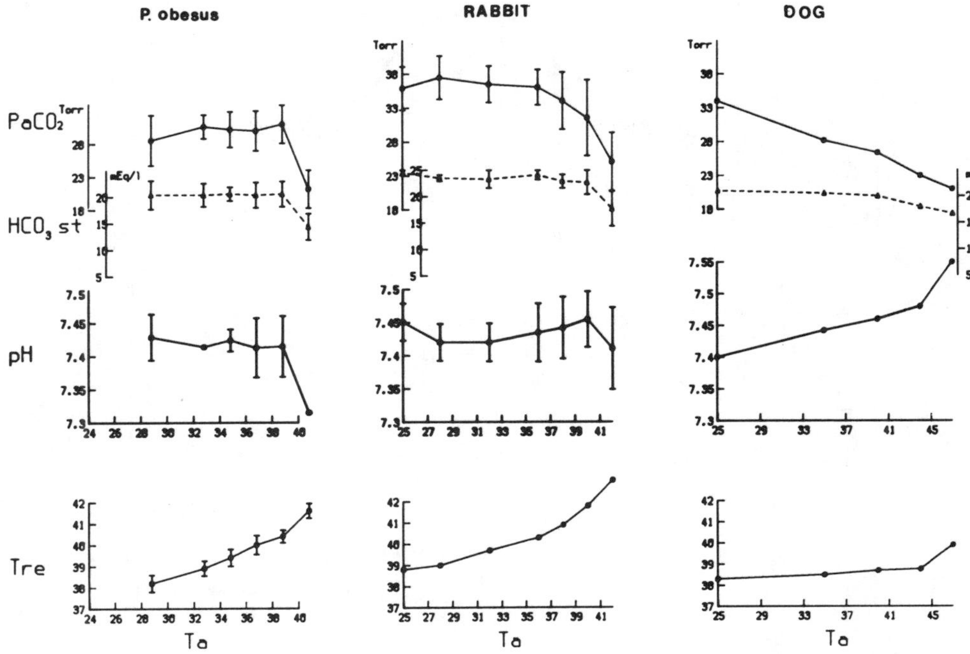

FIGURE 2. Rectal temperature, plasma pH, $PaCO_2$, and standard HCO_3 during the transition from normo- to hyperthermia in *P. obesus*, the bedouin rabbit, and the Sinai dog.[14,16,17]

for other mammals,[15] indicating a status of partially compensated metabolic acidosis. The similarly low values found in saluki and sinai dogs has been attributed to their diet.[16] At moderate hyperthermia, plasma pH level and standard bicarbonate values remain in the three species at normothermic levels. During severe hyperthermia, pH does change. In the sand rat, when the rectal temperature (T_{re}) exceeds 40°C, and in the rabbit at a T_{re} of 42°C, metabolic acidosis, as indicated from standard HCO_3 values, prevails.[14,17] In contrast, in the panting dog respiratory alkalosis develops gradually. Standard plasma HCO_3 in this species slightly decreases, indicating partial compensation by metabolic acidosis. This metabolic acidosis, however, is masked by respiratory alkalosis.[16] Similar changes in acid base balance, due to increased alveolar ventilation with progression of hyperthermia, has been observed in sheep and other panting species as well.[10-12] During heat exhaustion or at heat stroke in these species metabolic acidosis also develops.

Chronic exposure of human subjects to high ambient temperature during the summer leads to a shift of the plasma acid base level to the acid side. This observation was made in a 1-year-long study on two populations living in an arid area and exposed to two significantly different levels of environmental heat. During the summer months lowering of plasma alkaline reserve occurred, being more pronounced in subjects working in harsher climatic conditions. Thus, in humans, long-term exposure to environmental heat shifts metabolic acid base ratio to the acid side (Figure 3).[18]

Metabolic acidosis due to heat stress and hyperthermia is easier to reconcile. Current knowledge supports the idea that this metabolic acidosis is due to accumulation of lactic acid which might be a measure of cellular hypoxia. Metabolic acidosis due to increased lactate concentration, combined with high arterial PO_2 is a most common observation during hyperthermia. Such findings may suggest that lactate originates locally. Unfortunately, the available blood parameters do not indicate exactly where tissue hypoxia develops. From thermoregulatory considerations we can hypothesize some pathways for lactic acid accumulation as demonstrated in Figure 4. We assume that in sedentary species the major source

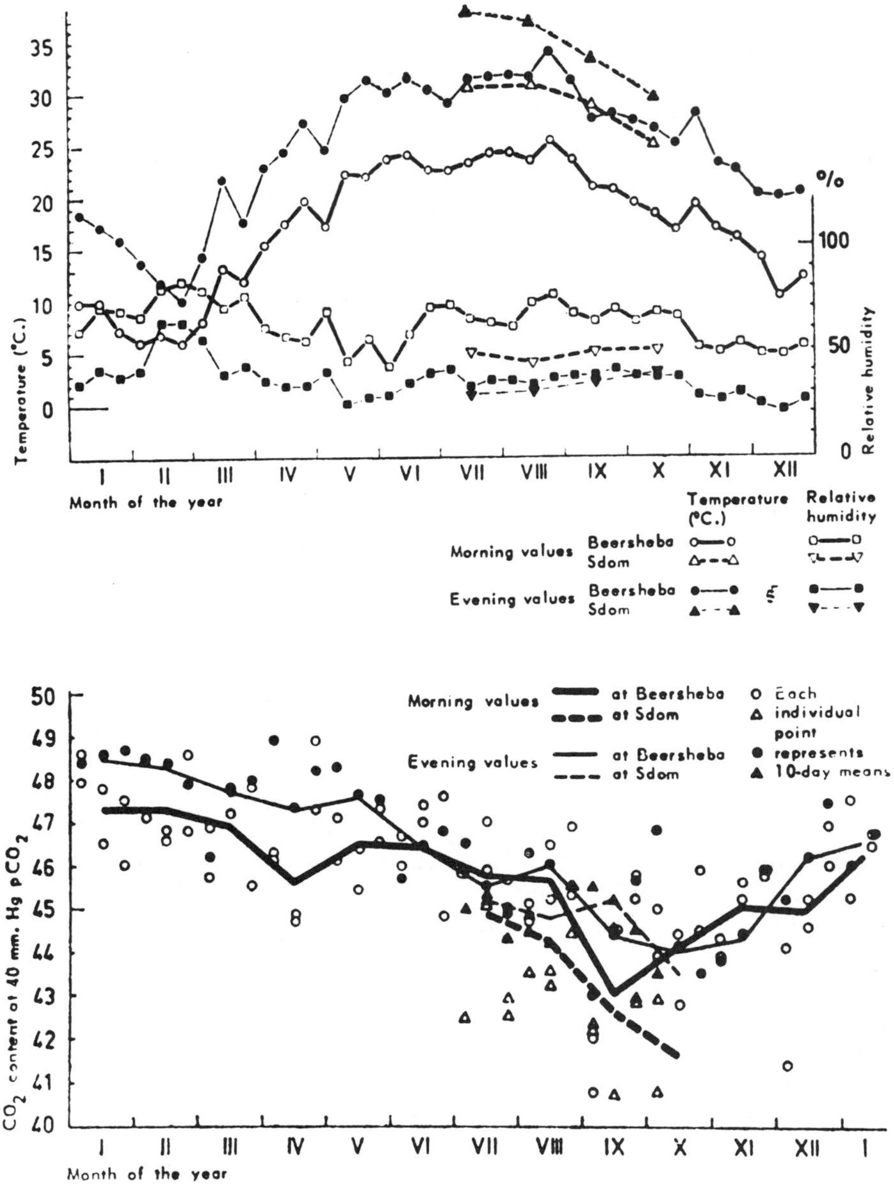

FIGURE 3. (Top) Dry bulb temperature and relative humidity data during the experimental period at the site of blood sampling. (Bottom) CO_2 combining power (alkaline reserve) of blood samples from human subjects in Beer-Sheva and Sodom year-round.[18]

of lactic acid is the splanchnic area where thermally induced reduction in blood circulation brings about an impairment of lactic acid turnover in the liver and in a reduction in oxygen supply to tissues and organs perfused by the splanchnic circulation. The increased metabolic demands by the hyperthermic tissues (Van Hoff effect) combined with the reduced oxygen supply are met by a shift of the metabolism to anaerobic pathway and the production of lactic acid.

IV. PLASMA VOLUME AND THERMOREGULATION

Circulating blood is the major avenue for heat conduction from the core to the periphery.

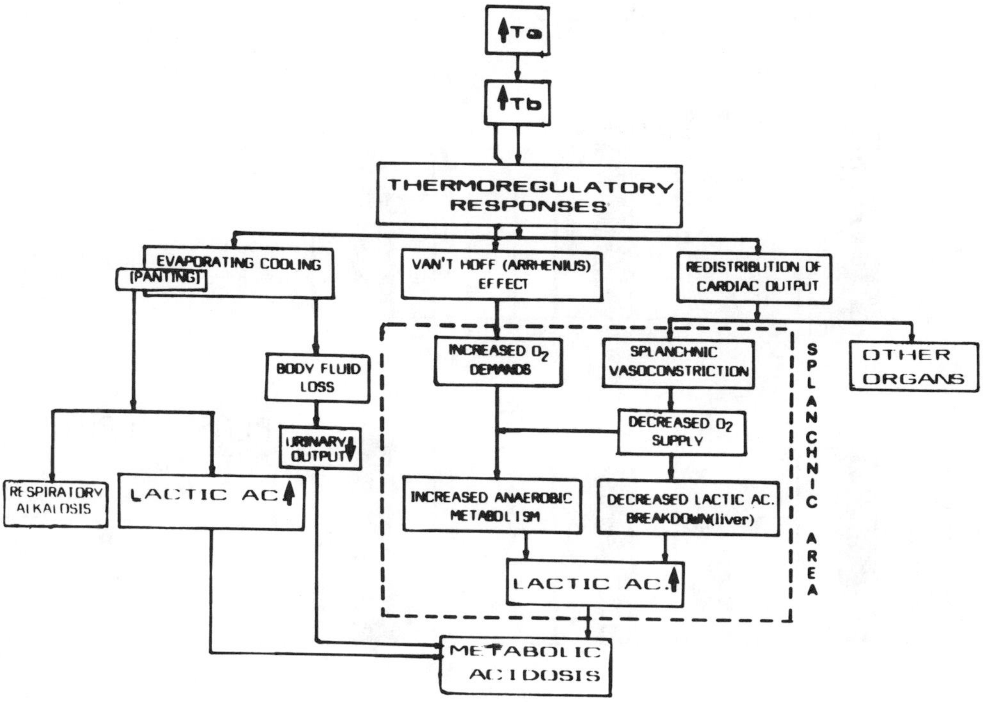

FIGURE 4. Possible pathways for metabolic acidosis during heat stress (a hypothesis).

Plasma volume loss during thermal stress results in a failure of thermoregulation and in an explosive rise of body temperature. The increase in blood volume during prolonged exposure to heat contributes to maintenance of blood pressure at a normal level at the time of peripheral thermoregulatory vasodilation. In humans, it has been repeatedly demonstrated[19-21] that loss of plasma water reduces the ability to control body temperature. Thermoregulatory failure, concomitant with thermal dehydration during desert hiking, was shown by Adolph et al.[19] to be due to a greater reduction in plasma volume than would be expected relative to total body water loss. Conversely, in the camel, which withstands remarkably well long periods of thermal dehydration, the plasma compartment contributes less than its proportional size to total body fluid loss.

The extensive studies of Schmidt-Nielsen[22] on the camel introduced the term plasma volume conserver, and it was assumed that this is a feature of desert species only. However, monitoring of plasma volume of both desert and nondesert species during prolonged exposure to heat stress has indicated that both species exhibit similar patterns of plasma volume changes: (1) an initial phase of plasma volume expansion,[9,23] (2) a period during which plasma volume per body weight is maintained, and (3) a breaking point at which plasma volume decreases out of proportion to total body water loss.[24,25] However, it has been demonstrated that desert dwellers experience a longer period during which plasma volume is maintained at its normal level.

The ability to maintain plasma volume depends on the conservation of plasma proteins, which provides the water retaining force of the plasma compartment. This is exemplified during thermal dehydration in Figure 5, in which the relations between plasma volume and total plasma protein mass are demonstrated. Plasma volume conservation during low dehydration (LD) coincides with maintenance of plasma protein mass, whereas failure in plasma conservation at high dehydration (HD) is concomitant with plasma protein loss.

Plasma protein mass depends on a dynamic equilibrium between transcapillary protein

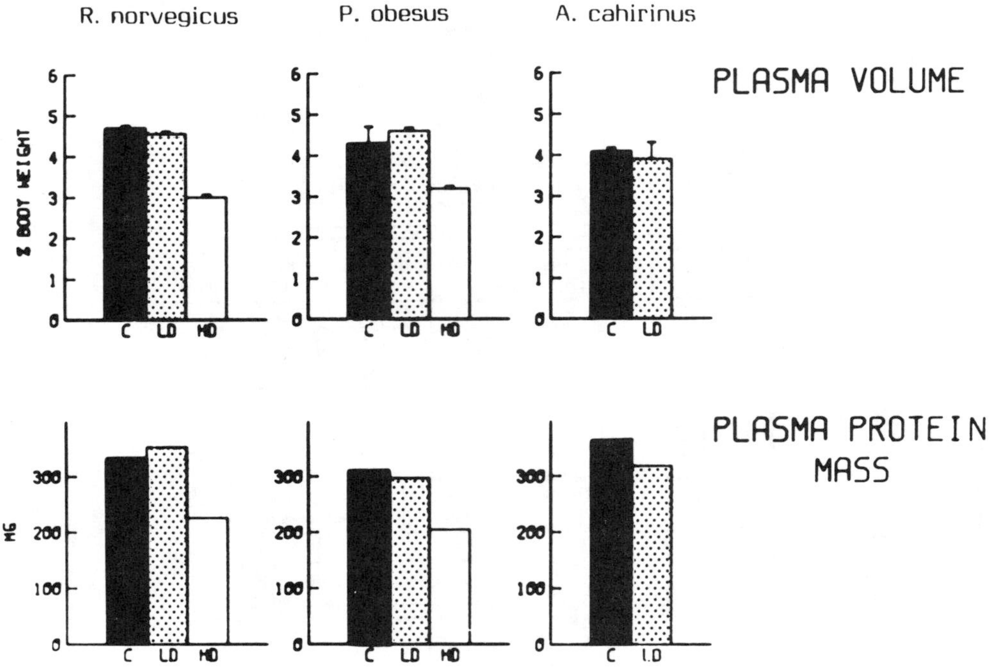

FIGURE 5. Plasma volume and total plasma protein mass in controls and dehydrated rodent species. C, control; LD, low dehydration; HD, high dehydration.[24,25,27]

loss, lymphatic return, and protein synthesis and breakdown. Unfortunately, no data are available on the changes in lymphatic return during thermal dehydration. However, we do have data on plasma protein synthesis and transcapillary efflux in both desert and nondesert species.

During thermal dehydration in the phase of plasma conservation albumin synthesis varies in the examined species. In the laboratory rat, which is a nondesert species, albumin synthesis increases by about 130%. In contrast, in the sand rat, a diurnal desert dweller, albumin synthesis decreases.[26] In the nocturnal desert species, the spiny mouse, albumin synthesis is elevated but not as much as in the rat.[27] Data are presented in Figure 6. While albumin synthesis varies in the three species examined, under thermal dehydration all exhibit a decrease in transcapillary protein efflux.[24,25,28] In the sand rat albumin efflux almost ceases; in the spiny mouse albumin efflux was reduced by 45%. In the laboratory rat the fall in albumin efflux was the least pronounced, being only 20%.

During severe dehydration plasma conservation ability fails. At this phase transcapillary protein flux increases in all species. In the rat albumin synthesis continues to be high.[27] No data are available on albumin synthesis in other species. In conclusion, the results obtained for the laboratory rat, for the nocturnal desert rodent (the spiny mouse), and for the diurnal desert rodent (the sand rat) suggest that change in transcapillary protein flux is the primary and the dominant mechanism for plasma water conservation. In the sand rat and possibly in other desert species as well, this mechanism is very powerful.[24] In the laboratory rat, the capacity of this mechanism is limited and the rat recruits a metabolic pathway of protein synthesis; however, this second mechanism is inadequate. The rat cannot maintain plasma water for prolonged periods of thermal dehydration.[25,26]

How then is plasma protein flux regulated? The vascular system comprises many capillary vascular beds, varying widely in their permeability characteristic. While the splanchnic area with its fenestrated and discontinued capillaries is very permeable, skin and muscle capillaries are poorly permeable. The arteriovenous anastomoses, which are widely distributed in the

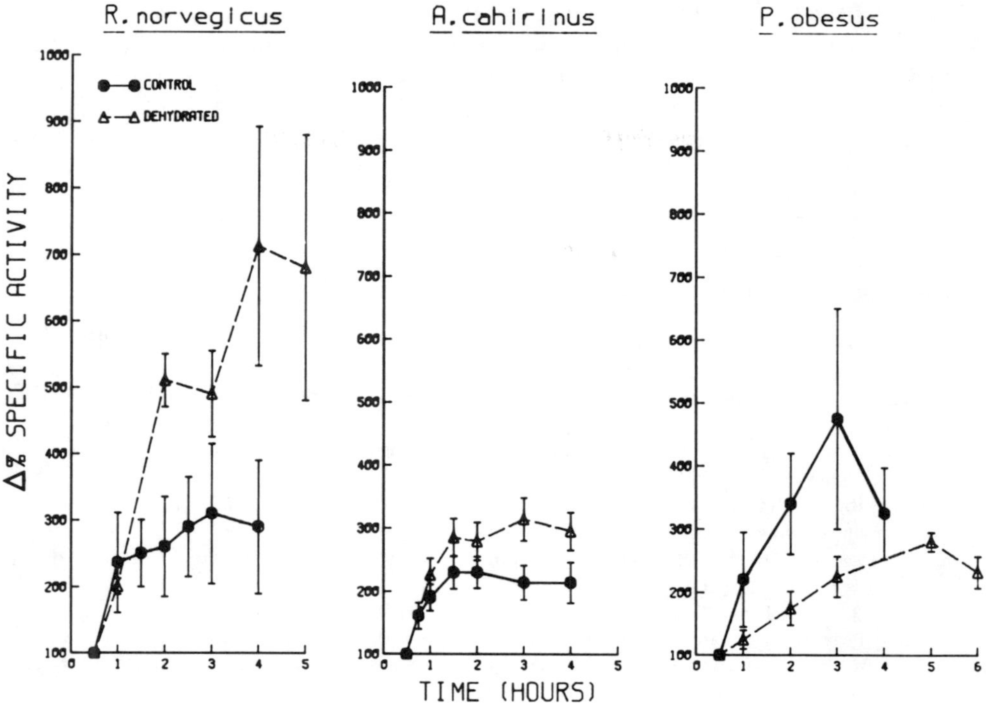

FIGURE 6. Plasma albumin synthesis in controls and thermally dehydrated (low dehydration) rodent species. Albumin synthesis is expressed as the increase (%) in ^{3}H L-leucine incorporated into plasma albumin.[26,27]

skin, are not permeable at all.[29,30] Alterations in distribution of cardiac output and shift of blood flow from the permeable splanchnic area to the poorly permeable skin capillaries or to the nonpermeable skin AVA can significantly affect transcapillary protein flux, plasma protein mass, and fluid shifts.

The preceding discussion on cardiac output distribution indicates that in rodents at moderate heat stress splanchnic vasoconstriction is concomitant with peripheral thermoregulatory vasodilation, whereas at severe heat stress and dehydration peripheral vasoconstriction and splanchnic vasodilatation occurs. These two phases of heat stress and dehydration coincide with the phases of plasma protein and fluid shifts, conservation, and loss. Since the capacity of the splanchnic circulation is about 20% of the total blood volume,[31] we may assume that during severe heat stress seepage of proteins from this vascular bed accounts for the high protein efflux from the circulation. Therefore, any changes in splanchnic perfusion may significantly affect plasma protein conservation and loss. This assumption is supported by a recent observation that phenoxybenzanine, a nonspecific α-blocker, when administered to heat-stressed rats, inhibits splanchnic vasoconstriction and elevates albumin efflux.[35] The opening of AVA in the skin at this stage of thermoregulation facilitates further protein conservation. In both the laboratory rat and the sand rat about 18% of the cardiac output is distributed through these channels. Splanchnic vasoconstriction coincident with peripheral vasodilation and the opening of skin AVA are all thermoregulatory reflexes. One can then suggest that during heat stress, plasma volume conservation and reflex thermoregulatory vascular reactions are coupled.

It seems that in heat stroke, the failure of thermoregulation is preceded by splanchnic vasodilation and closure of AVA which apparently leads to enhanced protein and plasma fluid loss. This assumption is supported by the findings of portal dilatation and minute intestine hemorrhages in dogs and humans suffering from heat stroke.[32,33] In the rat heat stroke model, the disappearance of endothelial lining in the liver vasculure was observed.[34]

One can assume from all these findings that the splanchnic circulation plays a major role in plasma volume conservation during the period of efficient thermoregulation, as well as in the development of heat stroke syndrome.

REFERENCES

1. **Rowell, L. B.,** Human cardiovascular adjustments to exercise and thermal stress, *Physiol. Rev.,* 54, 75, 1974.
2. **Hales, J. R. S.,** Effect of exposure to hot environments on regional distribution of blood flow and on cardiorespiratory function in sheep, *Pflugers Arch.,* 344, 133, 1973.
3. **Hales, J. R. S. and Dampney, R. A. L.,** The redistribution of cardiac output in the dog during heat stress, *J. Therm. Biol.,* 1, 29, 1975.
4. **Hales, J. R. S., Rowell, L. B., and King, R. B.,** Regional distribution of blood flow in awake, heat stressed baboons, *Am. J. Physiol.,* 237, H705, 1979.
5. **Horowitz, M., Hauzi Bar-Ilan, D., and Samueloff, S.,** Redistribution of cardiac output in anesthetized thermally dehydrated rats, *Comp. Biochem. Physiol.,* 81A, 103, 1985.
6. **Horowitz, M., Adler, J. H., and Samueloff, S.,** Redistribution of cardiac output of rodents exposed to thermal stress and dehydration, in preparation.
7. **Hales, J. R. S., Fawcett, A. A., Bennett, J. W., and Needham, A. D.,** Thermal control of blood flow through capillaries and arteriovenous anastomoses in skin of sheep, *Pflugers Arch.,* 378, 55, 1978.
8. **Iriki, M., Riedel, W., and Simon, E.,** Regional differentiation of sympathetic activity during hypothalamic heating and cooling in anaesthetized rabbits, *Pflugers Arch.,* 328, 320, 1971.
9. **Horowitz, M. and Nadel, E. R.,** Effect of plasma volume on thermoregulation in the dog, *Pflugers Arch.,* 400, 211, 1984.
10. **Hales, J. R. S., Findlay, J. D., and Mabon, R. M.,** Tissue hypoxia in oxen exposed to severe heat, *Resp. Physiol.,* 3, 43, 1967.
11. **Feistkorn, G., Nagel, A., and Jessen, C.,** Circulation and acid base balance in exercising goat at different body temperatures, *J. Appl. Physiol. Resp. Environ. Exercise Physiol.,* 57, 1655, 1984.
12. **Magazanik, A., Shapiro, Y., and Shibolet, S.,** Dynamic changes in acid base balance during heat stroke in dogs, *Pflugers Arch.,* 388, 1291, 1980.
13. **Bar Ilan, A., Marder, J., and Samueloff, S.,** Blood acid base status, whole blood and whole body values in sand rat (*P. obesus*) exposed to hypercapnia, *Comp. Biochem. Physiol.,* 81A, 571, 1985.
14. **Marder, J., Porat, I., Raber, P., and Adler, J. H.,** Acid balance and body temperature regulation of heat stressed *Psammomys obesus* (Gerbilinae): the effect of bicarbonate loss via saliva spreading, *Physiol. Zool.,* 56, 389, 1983.
15. **Altman, D. L. and Dittmer, D. S.,** *Biological Handbook: Respiration and Circulation,* Fed. Am. Soc. Exp. Biol., Bethesda, Md., 1971, 221.
16. **Krausz, J., Marder, J., and Eylath, U.,** Physiological responses of dogs on exposure to hot arid conditions, *Pflugers Arch.,* 370, 287, 1977.
17. **Marder, J., Sharir, R., and Lahman, E.,** Acid base balance of Bedouin rabbits exposed to high ambient temperatures, in preparation.
18. **Samueloff, S., Magnes, J., Lehman, M., and Vider, E.,** Diurnal and seasonal metabolic changes in acid-base balance of blood from human subjects living in a hot climate, in *Proceedings of the Lucknow Symposium on Environmental Physiology and Psychology in Arid Conditions,* United Nations Education, Scientific, and Cultural Organization, Liege, Belgium, 1964, 81.
19. **Adolph, E. F., et al.,** in *Physiology of Men in the Desert,* Interscience, New York, 1948, chap. 10.
20. **Fortney, S. M., Wenger, C. B., Bove, J. R., and Nadel, E. R.,** Effect of blood volume on forearm venous and cardiac stroke volume during exercise, *J. Appl. Physiol.,* 55, 884, 1983.
21. **Nielsen, B.,** The effect of dehydration on circulation and temperature regulation during exercise, *J. Therm. Biol.,* 9, 107, 1984.
22. **Schmidt-Nielsen, K.,** The camel, in *Desert Animals,* Clarendon Press, Oxford, 1964, chap. 3.
23. **Horowitz, M.,** Rapid plasma fluid expansion at the onset of heat stress, in *Abstr. Regional Congr. Int. Union Physiol. Sci.,* Jerusalem, 1984.
24. **Horowitz, M., Samueloff, S., and Adler, J. H.,** Acute dehydration: body water distribution in acclimated and non-acclimated *P. obesus, J. Appl. Physiol.,* 44, 585, 1978.
25. **Horowitz, M. and Samueloff, S.,** Plasma water shifts during thermal dehydration, *J. Appl. Physiol.,* 47, 738, 1979.

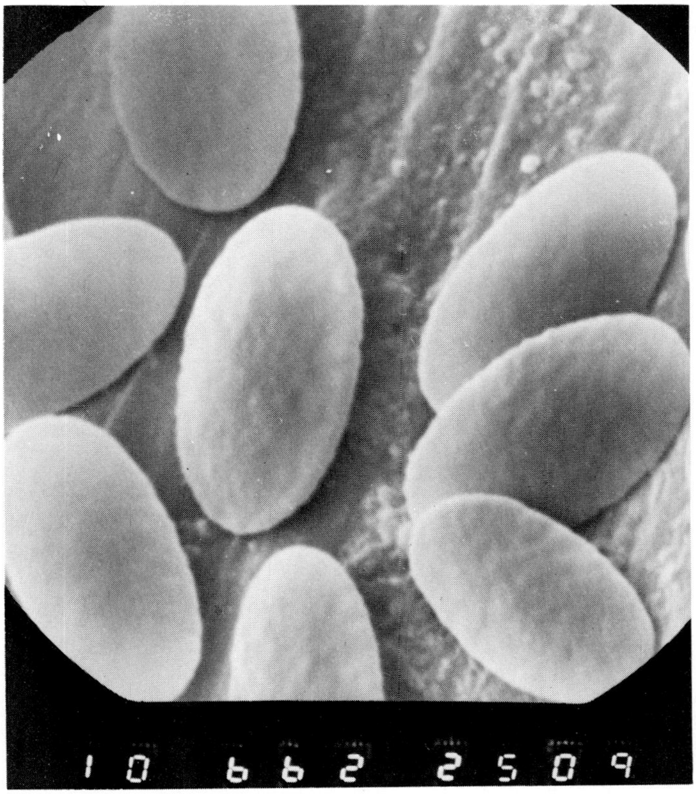

FIGURE 1. Camel's red blood cells after in vitro exposure to 20% NaCl. Determination by Hem-O-Scan in whole cells, at 37°C. Similar results were found in dehydration and rehydration.

26. **Horowitz, M. and Adler, J. H.,** Plasma volume regulation during heat stress: albumin synthesis vs. capillary permeability. A comparison between desert and non-desert species, *Comp. Biochem. Physiol.*, 75A, 105, 1983.
27. **Horowitz, M. and Borut, A.,** Blood volume regulation in dehydrated rodents: plasma proteins turnover and sedimentation coefficients, *Comp. Biochem. Physiol.*, 51A, 827, 1975.
28. **Borut, A., Horowitz, M., and Castel, M.,** Blood volume regulation in the spiny mouse. Capillary permeability changes due to dehydration, in *Comparative Physiol. Desert Anim.*, Academic Press, New York, 1972, 175.
29. **Rhodin, J. A. G.,** Vesicle and/or continuous channels, in *Cardiovascular Physiology: Microcirculation and Capillary Exchange*, Vol. 7, Kovach, A. G. B., Hamar, J., and Szabo, L., Eds., Pergamon Press, Elmsford, N. Y., 1980, 125.
30. **Daniels, P. M. and Prichard, M. M. L.,** Arterio-venous anastomoses in the external ear, *Q. J. Exp. Physiol.*, 41, 107, 1956.
31. **Bradley, S. E.,** The hepatic circulation, in *Handbook of Physiology: Circulation, Vol. 3*, Hamilton, W. F. and Dow, P., Eds., American Physiological Society, Washington, D.C., 1963, 1387.
32. **Kue, M. C., Bershon, I., Seftel, H., and Kent, G.,** Liver damage in heat stroke, *Am. J. Med.*, 49, 192, 1970.
33. **Daily, W. M. and Harrison, T. P.,** A study of the mechanism and treatment of experimental pyrexia, *Am. J. Med. Sci.*, 215, 42, 1948.
34. **Bowers, W. D., Hubbard, R. W., Leav, I., Daum, R., Conlon, M., Hamlet, M. P., Mager, M., and Brandt, P.,** Alterations of rat liver subsequent to heat overload, *Arch. Pathol. Lab. Med.*, 102, 154, 1978.
35. **Horowitz, M. and Givol, A.,** unpublished data.

Chapter 18

BLOOD FLOW PARTITIONING IN RESPIRATORY HEAT DISSIPATION: ITS RELEVANCE FOR WHOLE BODY AND BRAIN COOLING

Klaus Pleschka

TABLE OF CONTENTS

Abstract 152

I. Introduction 152

II. Methods 152

III. Results and Discussion 153
- A. Organization of Thermally Induced Blood Flow Control 153
- B. Cooling Effects on Brain vs. Whole Body of Cranial Heat Dissipation 154

IV. Conclusions 155

References 157

ABSTRACT

Blood flow partitioning to the respiratory mucosal surfaces in respiratory evaporative heat dissipation displays highly differential control. In panting animals with the mouth closed, enhancement of blood flow is confined to the nasal mucosa, while in animals panting with the mouth open, blood flow to the tongue is additionally increased in close correlation with the demands for heat dissipation. Two modes of neural blood flow control have been disclosed in dogs: adrenergic control of blood flow to nasal and tongue mucosa, and nonadrenergic control of tongue arteriovenous anastomoses. Heat dissipation mainly from cephalic surfaces implies preferential brain cooling superimposed on whole body cooling due to shunting of the returning cooled venous blood to intracranial veins. Apart from its potential local protective effect, this phenomenon points to the importance of extracephalic deep body thermosensors in the control of heat defense. This is most ostensible in birds, which lack significant hypothalamic thermoreception, but may exhibit significant degrees of selective brain cooling.

I. INTRODUCTION

In furred or feathered animals respiratory evaporative heat loss represents the most efficient and direct route for dissipating body heat. The increase in mucosal blood flow of the upper respiratory pathways provides enhanced heat transfer from the core to these surfaces whose glandular wetting and rapid ventilation accounts for the dissipation of the heat to the environment. The specific linkage between ventilatory and vasomotor control has long been recognized, but the underlying nervous respiratory and autonomic control mechanisms have mostly been investigated by dealing separately with one or the other system. While respiratory control in heat stress has been analyzed with regard to the interaction of chemoreceptor, thermoreceptor, and proprioceptor inputs,[1-6] the analysis of thermoregulatory adjustments of surface blood flow has established the principles of differential control of regional blood flow with respect to both the adrenergic and nonadrenergic autonomic cardiovascular innervation.[7-10] This chapter focuses on the interrelationship between these mechanisms of thermoregulatory blood flow adjustments in the surfaces of the upper respiratory pathway and respiratory activity in heat defense. Special attention will be paid to the involvement of neurally mediated and local influences in the fine control of blood flow in the capillaries, the nutrient channels of the evaporative tissues, and the high-volume, low-resistance shunts provided by the arteriovenous anastomoses (AVA). These interrelationships have been studied most thoroughly in the dog, a very heat-tolerant carnivore. Comparative data are available from various herbivores and several studies have been made on avian species with special regard to the relevance of cranial evaporation for whole body and selective brain cooling.

II. METHODS

The techniques employed in the studies on heat exchange and vascular readjustments in the respiratory pathways aimed at the evaluation of ventilatory as well as local vascular and general circulatory parameters. With respect to surface ventilation, respiratory frequency and, in part of the experiments, tidal volume, were recorded and respiratory evaporative heat loss (REHL) determined from water evaporation. Concerning the cardiovascular parameters, continuous recording of arterial pressure and of local arterial flows by pressure transducers and electromagnetic flow probes, respectively, were employed, while cardiac output and tissue blood flow partitioning were assessed by the radioactive microspheres technique permitting up to six measurements with different tracers in an experiment. Stimulation techniques comprised whole body heating as well as local stimulation of sensors in

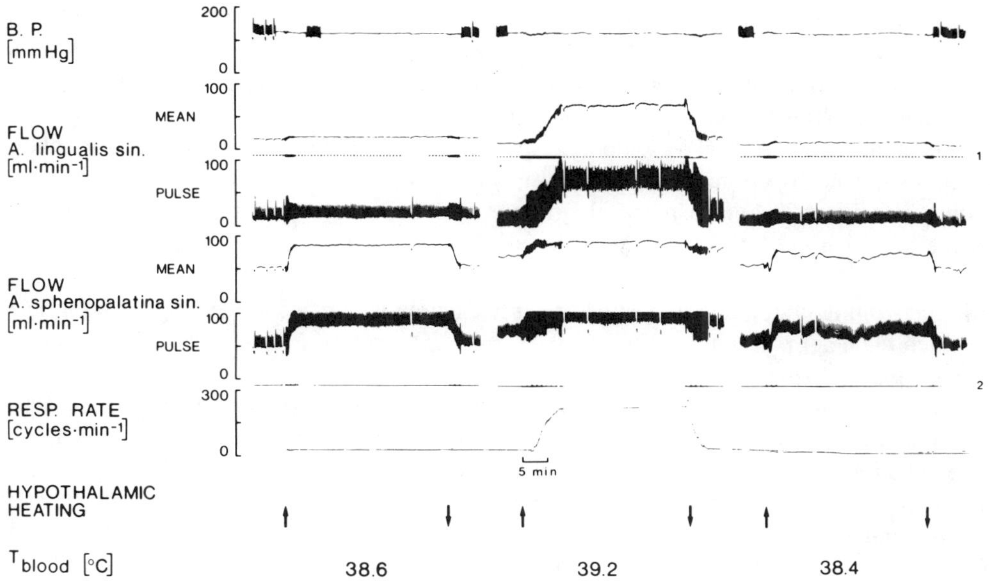

FIGURE 1. The effect of hypothalamic heating on blood pressure (B.P.), lingual (Flow A. lingualis sin.), sphenopalatine blood flow (Flow A. sphenopalatina sin.), and on respiratory rate at different blood temperatures in an anesthetized, spontaneously breathing dog. Marker 1 indicates 1 sec; marker 2, 1-min time intervals.[11]

the hypothalamus and spinal cord. The functions of autonomic innervation in controlling tissue blood flow were analyzed in denervation experiments and/or by pharmacological blockade of adrenergic, cholinergic/muscarinic, and ganglionic transmission. Acute experiments as well as surgical procedures in the preparation of chronic experiments were performed in inhalation anesthesia.

III. RESULTS AND DISCUSSION

A. Organization of Thermally Induced Blood Flow Control

Simultaneous measurements of blood flow in the sphenopalatine artery supplying the nasal evaporative tissues and in the lingual artery revealed differential vasomotor adjustments in dogs under combined external and hypothalamic heat stimulation (Figure 1). Blood flow to the nasal surfaces but not to the tongue increased upon heat stimulation, as long as the panting threshold was not reached. However, when the stimulus was strong enough to elicit panting, lingual blood flow was additionally enhanced. In each vascular region the underlying mechanism was a decrease in local vascular resistance.[11]

Analysis of the thermally induced vascular responses with regard to blood flow partitioning showed that the blood flow increase in the tongue was essentially confined to the opening of AVA. While this compartment received only 20.6% of the flow at rest, it contributed 69.5% to total blood flow during full panting with a rise of absolute blood flow in the lingual arteries from 20.4 to 146.9 mℓ/min/100 g.[9] In contrast, the heat-induced increase in nasal blood flow[11] was mainly confined to the mucosal capillary bed, in which flow was shown to rise from 19.3 mℓ/min/100 g at rest to 60.8 mℓ/min/100 g at rapid shallow panting and 114.5 mℓ/min/100 g at slower deeper panting.[12] The role of nasal AVA in thermoregulatory adjustments of nasal flow remains to be elucidated.

Local cooling of the canine tongue has been shown to enhance lingual blood flow by selectively reducing the tone in AVA smooth muscles.[13] This mechanism persists after efferent and sensory denervation and, thus, has to be ascribed to temperature effects on either the AVA smooth muscle tone directly or on the postganglionic neurons located in the tongue.[14] In effect, a positive feedback mechanism is established by cold-induced local vasodilatation, as it causes further blood flow enhancement when the tongue becomes exposed to ambient air temperature by open-mouth panting.

Interestingly, the lingual vasomotor response was found to be insignificant in panting sheep, even when open-mouth second phase panting was induced.[9] The reason may be seen in the differences in lingual mucosal structure of a carnivore and a herbivore, and in the degree to which the tongue may be exposed to unsaturated air in a hunting and a grazing animal.

In the panting dog, a major fraction of cardiac output is directed to the tongue and nose[12] of which the latter contributes 75% and the former 25% to total REHL of the conscious dog during moderate sustained running exercise.[9]

Concerning the neural control of thermally induced blood flow adjustments to the nose and tongue, it could be ascertained in accordance with previous suggestions that nasal vasodilatation in the dog was mediated exclusively by the decrease in α-adrenergic vasoconstrictor tone.[9] With regard to tongue blood flow in the dog, denervation experiments and electrostimulation of the chordalingual and glossopharyngeal nerves in connection with pharmacological blockade have presented evidence for a noncholinergic parasympathetic contribution to AVA blood flow control. The release of a hitherto unidentified transmitter seems to diminish the high intrinsic tone of the AVA smooth muscle cells.[9] This vasodilator innervation is especially involved in thermoregulatory adjustments of blood flow, as it can be activated by selective heat stimulation of specific deep body thermosensors like the hypothalamus and spinal cord.[15] Micro-electrostimulation of specific sites in the dog's brain stem which seem to represent a specific central vasodilator pathway has also been shown to induce nonadrenergic, noncholinergic AVA vasodilatation in the dog's tongue.[9]

B. Cooling Effects on Brain vs. Whole Body of Cranial Heat Dissipation

The arterial and venous vessels conducting blood to and from the exterior and interior of the skull are in close contact and sometimes form complex retia. In connection with prevailing heat dissipation from cranial surfaces, this vascular arrangement permits heat exchange between the arterial and venous blood.[16] The resulting preferential cooling of the brain is assumed to be of protective value in conditions of thermal stress.[17] In mammals with well-developed carotid retia, for instance Thomson's gazelle, the brain to trunk core temperature gradient was shown to increase from 0.4°C at rest to 2.7°C after a 7 min run at 40 km/hr.[18] Similar degrees of temperature dissociation have been observed in birds, due to the heat exchange over the ophthalmic retia.[19-21] From these and other findings it has been concluded that countercurrent brain cooling is extremely important in preventing excessive brain hyperthermia when animals have to cope with high body temperatures resulting from heat storage during exercise. However, it has also been recognized that this idea cannot be generalized, considering the slight dissociation between brain and core temperature in several heat-tolerant species. While differences in the degree of preferential brain cooling have been associated with the different strategies of sprinting and endurance running,[17] animals like goats with little sprinting capability but a well-developed brain cooling mechanism[22] would not fit in this concept, nor would long-distance flyers with effective brain cooling.[21]

Concerning the protective relevance of brain cooling in an endurance runner, the dog, interruption of venous return for cooled blood from the facial heat dissipating surfaces via the intracranial venous sinuses was shown to exert negligible influence on the primarily small temperature gradient between brain and trunk core, during work performance.[23] On the other hand, exercising goats were shown to exhibit temperature gradients of up to 1.5°C, but brain hyperthermia became relevant as a limiting factor in exercise performance only at temperatures above 42°C.[24] A special problem is posed by the observation that brain cooling may be most pronounced in, or even restricted to, the basal brain sections.[16,23] In hyperthermic rabbits the highest core temperatures were observed in the cerebello-medullary region,[25] which is notably susceptible to hyperthermia.[26]

The fascinating hypothesis of the protective value of preferential brain cooling has been greatly strengthened by those concepts of thermoregulation,[27] which attributed predominance in sensing deep body temperature to the hypothalamus. It was, however, recognized that attributing thermosensory control exclusively to the hypothalamus would disrupt thermal homeostasis in heat-exposed animals with effective brain cooling mechanisms. Thus, extrapolation of the idea of selective brain cooling to the extent that thermoregulation is essentially confined to the brain, with the body core following in open-loop fashion,[29] seems to be not fully tenable for theoretical reasons and is also challenged by the demonstration of significant contributions by extrahypothalamic thermosensors to the activation of respiratory heat defense in mammals.[30] Studies in the goat with its effective brain cooling system have shed light on the quantitative thermosensory contributions to its control by applying the technique of thermal isolation of the head against the trunk in chronic, conscious preparations. It was shown that at conditions of substantial brain hyperthermia the hypothalamic contribution to the stimulation of panting became, indeed, negligible in comparison to that of trunk core temperature.[31]

The notion that extrahypothalamic thermal inputs contribute to the control of heat dissipation underlying preferential brain cooling does not invalidate the importance of carotid heat exchange as a protective measure against brain hyperthermia. However, it raises the question to what extent heat dissipation from the body core in general, and from the brain in particular, may be independently controlled. As far as panting is concerned, the above theoretical considerations as well as experimental evidence seem to rule out selective control of brain cooling by the predominance of the hypothalamic thermal input. However, this input might exert specific influences on venous return via either intra- or extracranial pathways by corresponding changes in vasomotor innervation and, thus might regulate the degree to which the brain is preferentially cooled. This type of control has, in fact, been demonstrated both in mammals[32] and birds,[33] inasmuch as it effected protection of the brain against hypothermia in cold ambient conditions, possibly by directing the venous toward the extracranial pathway.

With special respect to the question of control of brain cooling in the heat by local venomotor adjustments, studies in birds seemed promising in providing a conclusive answer. In the avian class the hypothalamic thermosensory contributions to the control of respiratory heat loss are generally weak, but preferential brain cooling is well developed in many species. The question has been pursued by observing the appearance of brain cooling, of peripheral vasodilatation and of panting, in heat-stressed conscious ducks in which REHL was continuously monitored.[34] The animals were exposed to a supramaximal external heat load, while their core temperature was manipulated by heat extraction from the body with an intestinal thermode. Brain cooling was indicated by the degree of dissociation between hypothalamic and arterial blood temperature. Observation of the peripheral vasomotor state by monitoring web-skin temperature clearly showed that there was a close temporal relationship between the onset of general vasodilatation and of brain cooling, with brain cooling becoming relevant before, but being further enhanced by, thermal panting (Figure 2). According to these findings control of brain cooling is, indeed, established by vasomotor adjustments. However, the available evidence suggests that at least in birds, brain cooling is regulated within the scope of general control of convective heat transfer to the body surface.

IV. CONCLUSIONS

Water evaporation at the respiratory surfaces provides an effective avenue for heat dissipation in which autonomic control of circulatory heat transfer and of surface ventilation

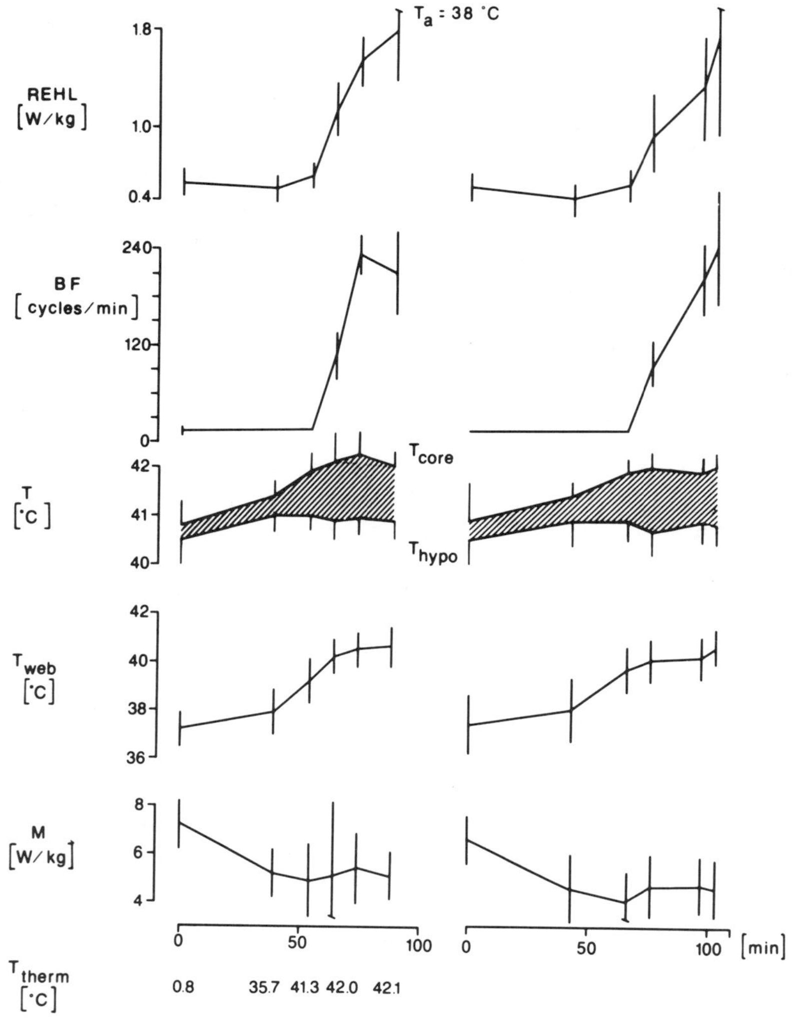

FIGURE 2. Average relationships between core temperature and various thermoregulatory parameters as a function of time in temperature loaded, conscious ducks. (REHL: respiratory evaporative heat loss; BF: breathing frequency; T_a: ambient temperature; T_{core}: core temperature; T_{hypo}: hypothalamic temperature; T_{web}: web temperature; Th_{therm}: thermode temperature; M: metabolic rate). (Left) during continuous reduction of intestinal heat extraction; (right) after stopping heat extraction at time zero. Average values (dots) and standard deviations (vertical bars) of 8 experiments. Significant differences (2 $p < 0.05$) between core and hypothalamic temperatures are indicated by asterisks.[34]

represent closely coordinated functions of the thermal input from the core and skin. While thermal inputs from the core originating in both hypothalamic and extrahypothalamic thermal sensors are relevant in mammals, birds rely mainly on extrahypothalamic inputs. In the dog, heat-induced blood flow to the nasal respiratory surfaces is directed to the capillary bed; the activity of its α-adrenergic innervation decreases in a continuous fashion with increasing thermal drive. Increase of flow to the tongue in the dog is closely correlated in time and intensity with the appearance of thermal panting. AVA perfusion represents the most significant contribution and is under nonadrenergic, noncholinergic parasympathetic active vasodilator control, with a hitherto unknown transmitter involved. Neurally induced AVA dilation is subject to positive feedback activation, due to the vasodilator effect of decrease in local tongue temperature as it occurs with the onset of open-mouth panting.

Due to the close anatomical relationship and special rete-like structures, prevailing heat dissipation from cranial surfaces permits preferential brain cooling by arteriovenous heat exchange. The degrees of brain cooling attained in various species under heat stress are highly variable, and so far, do not permit a consistent functional explanation for the observed differences. The available evidence suggests that the capacity of preferential brain cooling is determined by the anatomical preconditions for arteriovenous heat exchange, within which the degree of cooling depends on the general state of peripheral vasodilatation and of respiratory heat dissipation. Selective control of venous return to the heat exchanging arteriovenous sections may exist but has been demonstrated so far only as a protective mechanism against brain hypothermia in conditions of external cold stress.

REFERENCES

1. **Albers, C.,** Der Mechanismus des Wärmehechelns beim Hund. IV. Die Wechselwirkung zwischen Blutgasregulation und Temperaturregulation, *Pflugers Arch.*, 274, 184, 1961.
2. **Hales, J. R. S.,** Physiological responses to heat, in *MTP International Review of Science,* Physiology Ser. 1, Vol. 7, Robertshaw, D., Ed., Butterworths, London, 1974, 107.
3. **Iscoe, S., Young, R. B., and Jennings, D. B.,** Control of respiratory pattern in conscious dog: effects of heat and CO_2, *J. Appl. Physiol.*, 54, 623, 1983.
4. **Pleschka, K.,** Der Einflu β der Temperatur auf die elektrische Aktivität des Nervus phrenicus, Untersuchungen am aufgeschnittenen Regelkreis. II. Hyperthermie, *Pflugers Arch.*, 308, 357, 1969.
5. **Schoener, E. P. and Frankel, H. M.,** Effect of hyperthermia and $PaCO_2$ on the slowly adapting pulmonary stretch receptor, *Am. J. Physiol.*, 222, 68, 1972.
6. **See, W. R.,** Interactions between chemical and thermal drives to respiration during heat stress, in *Thermal Physiology,* Hales, J. R. S., Ed., Raven Press, New York, 1984, 353.
7. **Gregor, M., Jänig, W., and Riedel, W.,** Response pattern of cutaneous postganglionic neurones to the hindlimb on spinal cord heating and cooling in the cat, *Pflugers Arch.*, 363, 135, 1976.
8. **Iriki, M. and Simon, E.,** Regional differentiation of sympathetic efferents, in *Integrative Control Functions of the Brain,* Vol. 1, Ito, M., Tsukahara, N., Kubota, K., and Yagi, K., Eds., Elsevier/North-Holland, Amsterdam, 1978, 221.
9. **Pleschka, K.,** Control of tongue blood flow in regulation of heat loss in mammals, in *Reviews of Physiology, Biochemistry and Pharmacology,* Vol. 100, Springer-Verlag, Berlin, 1984, 75.
10. **Rowell, L. B.,** Cardiovascular adjustments to thermal stress, in *Handbook of Physiology, The Cardiovascular System. Peripheral Circulation and Organ Blood Flow,* Shepherd, J. T. and Abboud, F. M., Eds., Sect. 2, Vol. 3, Am. Physiol. Soc., Bethesda, Md., 1983.
11. **Pleschka, K., Kühn, P., and Nagai, M.,** Differential vasomotor adjustments in the evaporative tissues of the tongue and nose in the dog under heat load, *Pflugers Arch.*, 382, 255, 1979.
12. **Hales, J. R. S. and Dampney, R. A. L.,** The redistribution of cardiac output in the dog during heat stress, *J. Therm. Biol.*, 1, 29, 1975.
13. **Krönert, H., Wurster, R. D., Pierau, Fr.-K., and Pleschka, K.,** Vasodilatatory response of arteriovenous anastomoses to local cold stimuli in the dog's tongue, *Pflugers Arch.*, 388, 17, 1980.
14. **Pleschka, K., Diebold, K., Hardt, R., and Meyer, J.-U.,** Responsiveness of microcirculation and local cold vasodilatation to capsaicin in the intact and chronically denervated canine tongue, *Acta Physiol. Hung.*, 1986, in press.
15. **Roth, R.,** Thermoregulatorische Antworten von Zungendurchblutung und Atmung bei Reizung spinaler und zentraler Temperatursensoren am narkotisierten Hund, Inaugural Dissertation, Giessen, 1978.
16. **Baker, M. A.,** Brain cooling in endotherms in heat and exercise, *Ann. Rev. Physiol.*, 44, 85, 1982.
17. **Taylor, R. C.,** Exercise and thermoregulation, in *MTP International Review of Science,* Physiology Ser. 1, Vol. 7, Robertshaw, D., Ed., Butterworths, London, 1974, 163.
18. **Taylor, R. C. and Lyman, C. P.,** Heat storage in running antelopes: independence of brain and body temperatures, *Am. J. Physiol.*, 222, 114, 1972.
19. **Bernstein, M. H., Curtis, M. B., and Hudson, D. M.,** Independence of brain and body temperatures in flying American kestrels, *Falco sparverius, Am. J. Physiol.*, 237, R58, 1979.
20. **Kilgore, D. L., Boggs, D. F., and Birchard, G. F.,** Role of the rete mirabile ophthalmicum in maintaining the body-to-brain temperature difference in pigeons, *Am. J. Physiol.*, 129, 119, 1979.
21. **Pinshow, B., Bernstein, M. H., Lopez, G. E., and Kleinhans, S.,** Regulation of brain temperature in pigeon: effects of corneal convection, *Am. J. Physiol.*, 242, R77, 1982.

22. **Jessen, C. and Pongratz, H.,** Air humidity and carotid rete function in thermoregulation of the goat, *J. Physiol. (London),* 292, 469, 1979.
23. **Meyer, J.-U., Hales, J. R. S., and Pleschka, K.,** Respiratory evaporative heat loss in the exercising dog with and without interruption of nasal venous blood drainage to the brain, in *Thermal Physiology,* Hales, J. R. S., Ed., Raven Press, New York, 1984, 419.
24. **Caputa, M., Feistkorn, G., and Jessen, C.,** High brain temperature as a limit to exercise in goats, *Pflugers Arch.,* Suppl. 403, 188, 1985.
25. **Klein, W. and Riedel, W.,** Long-term recording of core temperature with chronically implanted silicon diodes, *Pflugers Arch.,* 403, 55, 1985.
26. **Khogali, M.,** Heat stroke: an overview, in *Heat Stroke and Temperature Regulation,* Khogali, M. and Hales, J. R. S., Eds., Academic Press, New York, 1983, 1.
27. **Benzinger, T. H.,** Heat regulation, homeostasis of central temperature in man, *Physiol. Rev.,* 49, 671, 1969.
28. **Young, B., Bligh, J., and Louw, G.,** Effect of thermal tachypnoe and of its mechanical or pharmacological inhibition on hypothalamic temperature in the sheep, *J. Therm. Biol.,* 1, 195, 1976.
29. **Cabanac, M. and Caputa, M.,** Open loop increase in the trunk temperature produced by face cooling in working humans, *J. Physiol. (London),* 289, 163, 1979.
30. **Mercer, J. B. and Simon, E.,** A comparison between total body thermosensitivity and local thermosensitivity in mammals and birds, *Pflugers Arch.,* 400, 228, 1984.
31. **Jessen, C. and Feistkorn, G.,** Some characteristics of core temperature signals in the conscious goat, *Am. J. Physiol.,* 247, R456, 1984.
32. **Mercer, J. B., Johnsen, H. K., Blix, A. S., and Hovedt, R.,** Central control of expired air temperature and other thermoregulatory effectors in reindeer, *Am. J. Physiol.,* 248, R679, 1985.
33. **Schmidt, I. and Simon, E.,** Temperature changes of the hypothalamus and body core in ducks feeding in cold water, *Pflugers Arch.,* 378, 227, 1979.
34. **Pleschka, K., Geisthövel, E., and Simon, E.,** Dissociation of brain and core temperature in the heat loaded, conscious pekin duck, in *Westerländer Gespräche,* Mainzer Akademie der Wissenschaften, F.R.G., 1986.

Chapter 19

THE EFFECTS OF TEMPERATURE AND PCO_2 ON AVIAN BLOOD O_2 AFFINITY: IMPLICATIONS FOR EXTRAPULMONARY O_2 SUPPLY TO THE BRAIN AND FOR LIFE AT HIGH ALTITUDE

Berry Pinshow, Marvin H. Bernstein, and Zeev Arad

TABLE OF CONTENTS

Abstract 160

I. Introduction 160

II. Materials and Methods 161
A. Preparation and Maintenance of Experimental Animals 161
B. Measurement of P_{50} 161
C. Statistical Analysis 162
D. Model Development 162

III. Results 163

IV. Discussion 164

V. Conclusions 170

Acknowledgments 170

References 171

ABSTRACT

Evaporation from the surfaces of the nasal and oral cavities and from the eyes in birds contributes to cerebral temperature regulation. A portion of the blood cooled in tissues close to these surfaces returns to the heart via paired ophthalmic retia (OR), along which countercurrent heat exchange takes place with arterial blood flowing anteriorly toward the brain. We used pigeons (*Columba livia*) to examine whether characteristics of blood reaching the cooling surfaces and OR, and whether conditions prevailing at these sites, favor O_2 and CO_2 exchange as well as heat exchange. We also measured effects of temperature on O_2 and CO_2 tensions (PO_2, PCO_2) and pH on blood of three additional avian species. Results indicate that shifts in blood O_2 affinity associated with changes in temperature and PCO_2 could augment bird brain O_2 supply by eliciting an exchange of O_2 and CO_2 between air and blood at the cooling surfaces and between venous and arterial blood in the retia. At high altitude the proposed mechanism might be of particular importance. We calculated that at 7000 m above sea level both O_2 tension and saturation in blood flowing to the brain from the retia could be double that in systemic arterial blood.

I. INTRODUCTION

Birds have a bilateral pair of countercurrent heat exchangers in their heads — the ophthalmic retia.[1-4] The physiological role of these retia is apparently involved in brain temperature regulation,[2-9] their function being analogous to that of the carotid rete found in many mammal species.[10]

The model developed to explain the role of the retia is schematically illustrated in Figure 1. The retia are situated behind the eyes with arterial blood reaching them via branches of the external ophthalmic arteries which themselves branch from the internal carotids.[3,4,6,11,12] Arterial blood is supplied to the brain via several routes, some flowing there directly and some coursing through the retia.[1,13-15] Arterial blood from the carotids also flows to the mucosa in the nasal and buccal cavities[12] and to the eyes.[1,12,16] The arterial blood that reaches these structures is cooled by evaporation of water from their surfaces. A portion of the cooled blood drains to the venous sides of the ophthalmic retia which consist of beds of intertwined arteries and veins. Here, it gains heat from blood flowing countercurrent to it in the arterial sides of the retia. The cooled arterial blood then flows to the brain and takes up heat from cerebral tissue.

The surface areas of the moist, richly vascularized buccal and nasal mucosa are increased by turbinates, folds, and papillae.[12] PO_2 and PCO_2 of ambient air in contact with these membranes are, respectively, always higher and lower than that of the capillary blood flowing in them, even at high altitude.[17] These facts led Bernstein et al.[18] to suggest that this brain cooling system may also have a respiratory function, i.e., O_2 and CO_2 exchange may take place between blood perfusing the evaporating surfaces and the atmosphere, and in the retia, bringing about an enhancement of the brain's O_2 supply.

We describe here a physiological model for how the brain's O_2 supply might be affected. We focused on the changes in the affinity of the blood for O_2 that would result from changes in blood temperature and PCO_2 occurring at the exposed nasal, oral, and ocular surfaces, and in the retia. To test the model, we measured the effects of temperature, PCO_2, and pH on O_2 afffinity in pigeon (*Columba livia*) blood in vitro. We assumed that shifts in the O_2 dissociation curve (ODC) would be reflected by changes in the P_{50}, the PO_2 at which half the hemoglobin in the blood is saturated with O_2. Thus, we estimated the positions of the pigeon ODC under various conditions, and calculated blood gas tensions and O_2 saturation during cephalic gas exchange. We examined the function of the proposed mechanism under normoxic conditions and under conditions of hypobaric hypoxia such as those that might be encountered during flight at high altitude.

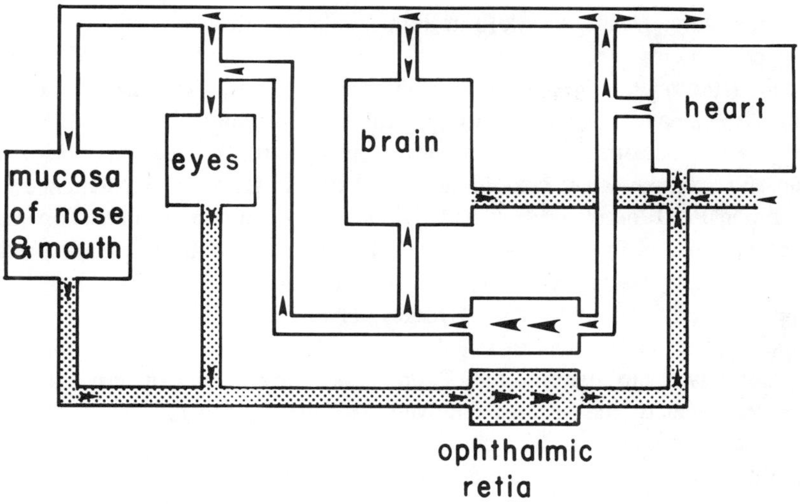

FIGURE 1. Simplified schematic diagram of major blood flow paths in a bird head following Midtgard.[4] Arteries are unshaded and veins dotted. Arrows show direction of flow. Arterial blood flows to the brain either directly or via the ophthalmic retia. Arterial blood flowing through the retia flows either to the brain or to the ocular region. A portion of the venous return from the moist anterior cephalic surfaces courses through the rete, cooling arterial blood by countercurrent heat exchange. For further explanation, see text.

Furthermore, to establish the generality of the effects of temperature on oxyhemoglobin dissociation in avian blood, we measured P_{50} with changes in blood temperature in three other avian species all known to possess ophthalmic retia: white-necked ravens, *Corvus cryptoleucus,*[3] mallards, *Anas platyrhynchos,*[4] and domestic fowl *Gallus domesticus.*[4]

II. MATERIALS AND METHODS

A. Preparation and Maintenance of Experimental Animals

Domestic pigeons (mean body mass 340 g) were purchased from a commercial animal dealer, A 40 cm cannula of polyethylene tubing (PE 10) was chronically implanted in a brachial artery of each bird while it was locally anesthetized (Carbocaine, Breon Laboratories). Cannulae were filled with heparinized avian saline, then sealed with an epoxy-filled section of a 23-gauge syringe needle. Cannulated birds were maintained in a climate controlled room $T_a = 23.0 \pm 0.5°C$, $40 \pm 5\%$ RH, 12L:12D) for at least 24 hr prior to their use in, and between experiments. Between experiments they were offered commercial pigeon chow (Purina) and tap water *ad libitum.*

At the beginning of an experiment, each bird was weighed, blindfolded, and lightly restrained in the dark. Each cannula was then attached to a syringe of heparinized saline. We waited 1 hr for birds to calm before sampling, and to allow for any lactic acid resulting from the stress of handling to be removed. To confirm this, anaerobic blood samples were obtained and PO_2, PCO_2, and pH were measured. After the 1-hr period, values were always within the range previously observed in resting pigeons.[19]

B. Measurement of P_{50}

PO_2 at half saturation (P_{50}) was measured in six pigeons by the mixing method following Scheid and Meyer.[20] Blood was tonometered at combinations of three temperatures (36°, 40°, and 44°C) and three CO_2 tensions (9, 18, and 33 torr). These values were chosen to cover the physiological range used in the model below. Duplicate blood samples were taken at each temperature. Deadspace fluid in the cannula was discarded, then 0.3 mℓ of blood was collected in a clean, heparinized, 1-mℓ tuberculin syringe. One half of the sample was tonometered (Radiometer BMS2 Mk2 Blood Microsystem) for 9 min in a gas mixture containing 25% O_2 and a proportion of CO_2 calculated to maintain a blood PCO_2 of 9, 18, or 33 torr at each measurement temperature. Concurrently, the other half was tonometered against an anoxic gas mixture containing N_2 and CO_2 in proportions calculated to result in the same blood PCO_2 as in the first half. Blood pH was not controlled. Tonometry gases were supplied either from bottles of certified mixed gases (Scientific Gas Products) or by a precision gas mixing pump (Wösthoff, model M301/a-F).

Two heparinized, gas-tight, glass syringes (Hamilton, 725LT) were flushed with the equilibration gases and aliquots of equal volume (100 μℓ) of the two tonometered blood samples were drawn into them through 23-gauge, stainless steel syringe needles. Any dead-space gas was ejected, the needles removed, and the syringe nozzles connected using a female-female Luer connector. The connector was made from a pair of Teflon Luer syringe caps (Hamilton, 16801). The closed end of each cap was ground down, the outer surfaces were etched (Tetra-etch), and the pair were aligned and glued end-to-end with epoxy resin (Duro Quick Mix). Thus, when the syringe nozzles were inserted in each end of the connector they abutted and the connection was gas tight. By pushing the plungers of the syringes back and forth ten times, complete mixing of the blood samples was obtained. No hemolysis was observed in centrifuged samples. After mixing, the syringe with the mixed sample was connected to an 18-gauge Luer stub and its plunger depressed until a few drops of blood dripped out. The remainder of the sample was then injected into a gas analyzer (Radiometer, BMS3 MK2 Blood Microsystem) and PO_2, PCO_2, and pH were measured. The whole procedure, from when tonometered blood was drawn into the syringes until injection into the gas analyzer, took 2.5 min or less, a short enough time to assure that no significant changes in gas tensions would be caused by erythrocyte metabolism.[21]

The gas analyzer and pH electrode were calibrated with standard gases (Radiometer, LG202 and LG302) and pH standards (Radiometer, S1500 and S1510) immediately prior to and immediately after each measurement, and corrections for drift were made.

To confirm that the results of the above-described static measurements could be used in our calculations for a model of the dynamic events taking place at the cephalic evaporative surfaces and in the retia, we mimicked the temperature changes that we assume take place. Duplicate samples of blood from three birds were tonometered at 36°C with either oxygenated or anoxic gases having a PCO_2 of 33 torr. These were anaerobically rewarmed to 42°C, then PO_2, PCO_2, and pH were measured. A second set of samples from the same three birds was tonometered at 42°C, cooled and measured at 36°C.

C. Statistical Analysis

Regression and other statistical analyses were done following Zar.[22] We chose $p < 0.01$ as the minimal acceptable level of significance.

D. Model Development

As we were unable to measure complete ODC we used the ODC for pigeon blood published by Hirsowitz et al.[23] to develop our model.[24] We chose to use these data because the P_{50} was almost identical to that we calculated from our data and because the original data are presented in full in the paper. We transformed the data of Hirsowitz et al.[23] for percent O_2 saturation (SO_2) and PO_2 to $\log(SO_2/(100 - SO_2))$ and $\log PO_2$ and computed a second order polynomial regression relating $\log PO_2$ to $\log(SO_2/(100 - SO_2))$. We then changed the constant of the equation, equivalent to $\log P_{50}$, in accordance with our measurements of the effects of temperature and PCO_2, thereby shifting the dissociation curve. We thus computed several dissociation curves for each scenario discussed below.

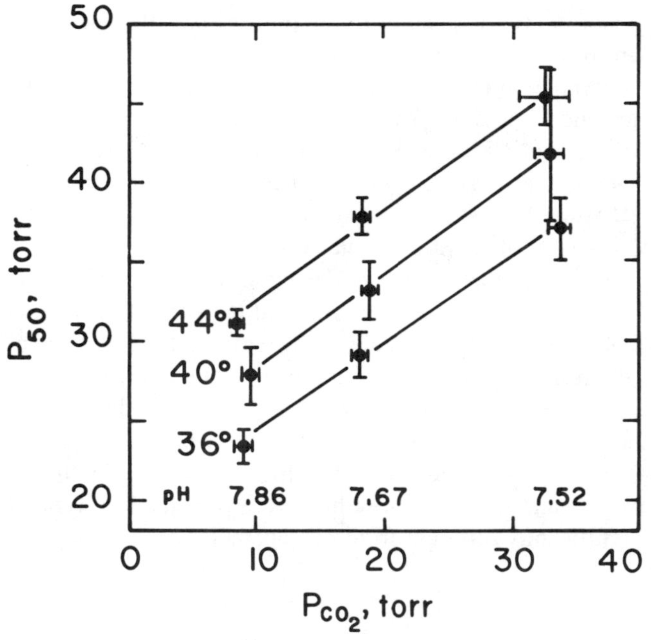

FIGURE 2. Relation of PO_2 at half saturation (P_{50}, torr) to temperature (°C), CO_2 tension (PCO_2, torr), and pH in pigeon blood. Measurements were made on duplicate samples from 6 birds at 9 combinations of temperature and PCO_2. Points represent means, vertical and horizontal bars represent span ± SD. Solid lines represent least-squares linear regression equations computed from all data for each temperature. At each combination of PCO_2 and temperature pH did not vary more than 0.01 units from the means which are shown below the curves. A multiple regression equation relating P_{50} to temperature, PCO_2, and pH was calculated for the combined data used in preparing this figure (Equation 1).

We assumed that the shape of the ODC of pigeon is not significantly affected by changes in temperature, PCO_2, or pH, an assumption recently substantiated by Maginniss et al.[43] Thus, the regression coefficients in the equation remained constant. We also ignored the direct effects of temperature on PO_2 and PCO_2, thereby making the model conservative. The Haldane effect is small in pigeon blood at 41°C[17] and is likely to be so at other temperatures as well and has therefore also been neglected.

To quantify the general effect of temperature on P_{50} in avian blood we used the above-described tonometry technique to measure the changes in P_{50} that occur with temperature in six white-necked ravens, six mallards, and six domestic fowl. These measurements were made at the same 3 temperatures used for pigeon blood, however PCO_2 was 33 torr for all measurements. pH was not controlled.

III. RESULTS

The relation of P_{50} to PCO_2, temperature, and pH in pigeon blood is illustrated in Figure 2. We used step-wise, least-squares multiple linear regression to relate these variables and found that pH had no significant effect on its own, being itself dependent on temperature and PCO_2. The relationship among P_{50}, temperature, and PCO_2 is described by the equation:

$$P_{50} = 1.049\ T + 0.573\ PCO_2 - 19.444$$

$$N = 54, \quad R^2 = 0.89, \quad F_{2,51} = 215.25, \quad p > 0.0001 \qquad (1)$$

Where T is temperature in °C, P_{50} and PCO_2 are in torr, N is the number of measurements, R^2 is the coefficient of multiple determination, F is the F statistic, and p is the probability that the regression correlation is not significant.

When blood was tonometered at 36°C and the temperature then changed anaerobically to 42°C, mean P_{50}, PCO_2, and pH were 49.2, 43.6, and 7.420 torr, respectively. When blood was tonometered at 42°C and the temperature then changed anaerobically to 36°C, mean P_{50}, PCO_2, and pH were 37.0 and 25.7 torr, and 7.565, respectively. The values for P_{50} were within 1 and 4 torr of the values calculated from Equation 1, using the corresponding values for PCO_2 and temperature. We consider these differences small enough to validate our use of Equation 1 to describe the P_{50} changes at the sites of cephalic heat exchange.

Our measured Bohr and Astrup factors did not differ from those reported by others.[23,25,26,29] The Bohr effect ($d\log P_{50}/dpH$) was −0.53 at 36°C, −0.46 at 40°C, and −0.50 at 44°C, the overall value being −0.48. The Astrup effect ($d\log PCO_2/dpH$) was −1.48 at 36°C, −1.38 at 40°C, and −1.82 at 44°C, the overall mean value being −1.53 for all temperatures.

Least-squares linear regression equations relating P_{50} and temperature for pigeon, white necked raven, mallard, and domestic fowl blood are presented in Table 1. The slopes of the lines are not significantly different from one another.

IV. DISCUSSION

The P_{50} values we measured for pigeon blood (Figure 2) are somewhat higher than those reported for pigeon blood in the literature. Lutz[25] summarized the available data measured at 41°C and pH 7.5. Three measurements were made at a PCO_2 of 35 torr, and corresponding P_{50} values were 29.5,[26] 31.6,[25] and 38[27] torr. However, at a PCO_2 of 29 torr, P_{50} was reported to be 39.2 torr by Hirsowitz et al.[23] This is not significantly different from the value calculated for these conditions by Equation 1.

Lutz[25] reports much variability in P_{50} values within all of the species he compared, and suggested that the differences may be accounted for by differences in measurement techniques, by intraspecific hemoglobin variability, by functional hemoglobin variability caused by hormonal status and physical fitness, by the presence of multiple hemoglobins, and by the effects of CO_2 and organic phosphates. Thus, although our measured values are higher than most of those previously reported, we used them in the presentation of the scenarios which follow. Using these values affects to a small degree the magnitude of the estimates for each step, but does not change the concept or validity of the model.

As in other vertebrates,[28] blood O_2 affinity in all four avian species examined in the present study and in geese[30] increased with decreasing temperature. According to Hirsowitz et al.,[23] the difference in P_{50} for pigeon blood between 41 and 37°C is 8.65 torr, corresponding to 2.16 torr/°C at pH 7.5 and a PCO_2 of 29 torr. We found that P_{50} for pigeon blood changes by 1.07 torr/°C. The discrepancy between the data of Hirsowitz et al. and our own may be explained by the above factors suggested by Lutz.[25] To maintain consistency, we used our own values in the following model.

The information on the effects of temperature and PCO_2 on pigeon blood O_2 affinity allows us to examine the hypothesis of Bernstein et al.[18] that the brain cooling system in birds also serves to supplement O_2 in cerebral arterial blood. Using the ODC for pigeons from Hirsowitz et al.,[23] shifted according to $P^{21,50}$ values calculated by Equation 1, we constructed the following scenarios describing the changes that might take place at the mucosal surfaces and in the retia. Many scenarios are possible, however, we have chosen to present five that are relevant to the hypothesis. Although the events described would occur simultaneously, they are presented stepwise for clarity. Calculations for the first four scenarios were made for normoxic sea level conditions.

Scenario I: Here, we have assumed the simplest hypothetical set of events: the surfaces

Table 1
LEAST-SQUARES LINEAR REGRESSION EQUATIONS RELATING P_{50} TO TEMPERATURE (T) IN THE BLOOD OF 4 AVIAN SPECIES

Species	N	Regression equation $y = b + ax$	r	S_x	S_y	S_b	S_{yx}	SS_x	RSS	Rdf	F
Pigeon	30	$P_{50} = -2.212 + 1.090\ T$	0.735	8.276	18.17	0.190	7.600	240	243.23	28	32.805
Mallard	30	$P_{50} = -11.545 + 1.482\ T$	0.794	8.276	28.86	0.215	8.605	240	309.44	28	47.278
Chicken	30	$P_{50} = 12.342 + 1.091\ T$	0.516	8.276	36.98	0.342	13.720	240	786.57	28	10.174
White-necked raven	30	$P_{50} = 0.867 + 1.089\ T$	0.862	8.276	12.98	0.119	4.784	240	98.13	28	81.241

Note: N: number of observations; r: product moment correlation coefficient; S_x, S_y, S_b: standard deviation of subscripted value; S_{yx}: standard error of the estimate; SS_x: sum of squares of x; RSS: residual sum of squares; Rdf: residual degrees of freedom; F: F statistic for the linear term. The statistical parameters are presented with more than 2 significant figures after the decimal point to allow comparison with other linear regression equations. Measurements were made on 6 birds of each species at 36, 38, 40, 42, and 44°C. PCO_2 was maintained at 33 torr for all measurements while pH was uncontrolled. All regressions are significant ($p < 0.011$), but none of the slopes differ significantly from one another.

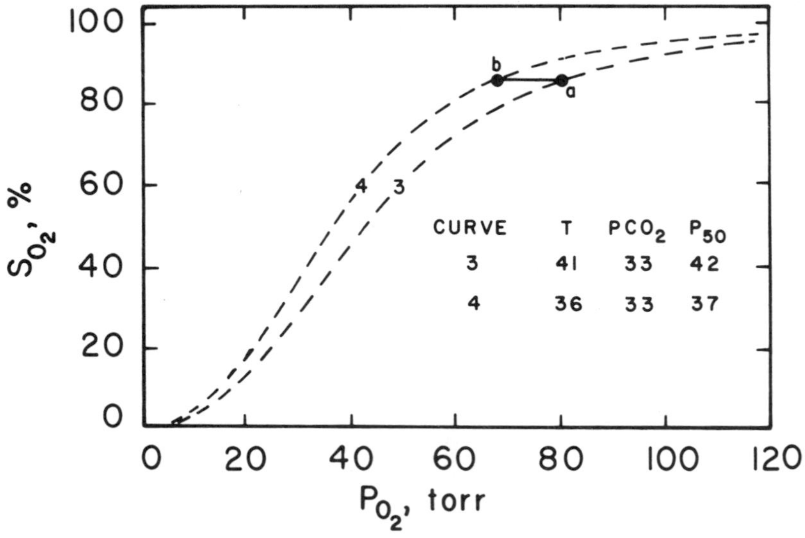

FIGURE 3. Relation between blood oxyhemoglobin saturation (SO_2, %) and blood O_2 tension (PO_2, torr) illustrating scenario I in text, in which it is assumed that the moist cephalic mucosa and ocular surfaces and the ophthalmic retia are sites of heat exchange only. Curves 3 and 4 correspond to P_{50} values listed, as calculated from respective combinations of temperature (T, °C) and CO_2 tension (PCO_2, torr) by Equation 1. Lettered points on curves are explained in text.

of the eyes, the mucosal surfaces of the nasal and oral cavities, and the retia are sties of heat exchange only. Gas exchange occurs neither between air and blood at the eyes or mucosa, nor between blood and mucosal tissue, nor between arterial and venous blood in the retia. In Figure 3, curve 3 applies to systemic arterial blood arriving at the mucosal surfaces and at the retia at body core temperature, assumed to be 41°C. We have also assumed that after being cooled, mucosal blood returns to the retia at 36°C, and curve 4 is the leftward-shifted ODC for blood at this temperature.

On curve 3, the arterial blood is assumed to have a PO_2 (PaO_2) of 80 torr and a saturation (SaO_2) of 87% (based on data of Weinstein et al.[17]). These values are represented by point *a*. The leftward shift to curve 4 moves point *a* to point *b*, and the cooled venous blood returning to the retia thus has a reduced PO_2. During countercurrent heat exchange along the length of the retia, the venous blood rewarms while retial arterial blood is cooled; if exchange is complete, as is likely,[4] the ODC for arterial blood becomes curve 4. Thus, arterial blood flowing from the retia to the brain would be expected to have a PO_2 reduced to point *b*, 70 torr, posing a potential disadvantage to brain oxygenation.

Scenario II: The next set of events differs from the preceding one only by the assumption that gas is exchanged between arterial blood and perfused mucosal tissues. It is still assumed that gas exchange does not occur between air and cephalic blood, nor between arterial and venous blood in the retia; the mucosal surfaces and the retia remain sites of heat transfer only. This is the situation implicit in discussions of the thermoregulatory function of the retia in the literature.[2-10,31-35]

Arterial blood is again assumed to arrive at the evaporative surfaces at 41°C, and is again represented by curve 3 in Figure 4. It cools to 36°C, eliciting a shift to curve 4. As previously stated, PaO_2 moves from point *a* to point *b*, but O_2 is now unloaded to the tissue. We have assumed that this reduces SaO_2 to 60% (point *c*). The blood also gains CO_2 from mucosal tissue, and we assume that this raises venous PCO_2 ($PvCO_2$) to 38 torr, which is within the range previously reported for mixed $PvCO_2$ in pigeons.[19] The change in $PvCO_2$ brings about

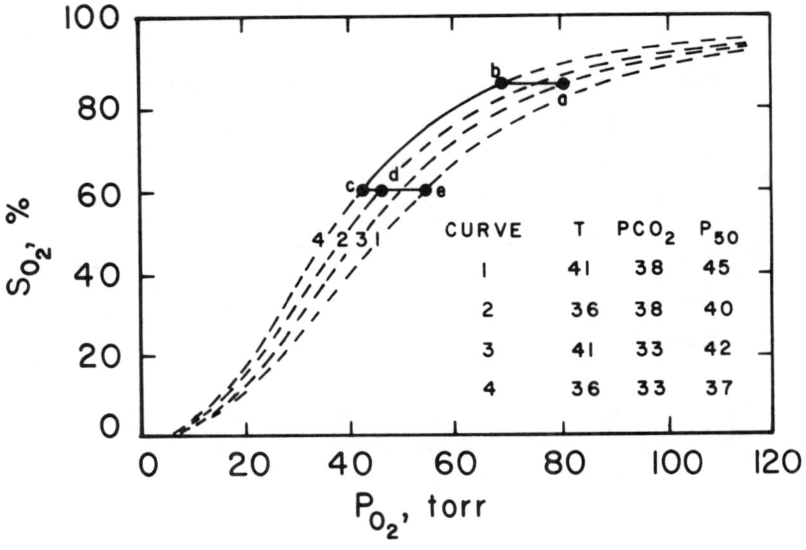

FIGURE 4. Relation between blood oxyhemoglobin saturation (SO_2, %) and blood O_2 tension (PO_2, torr) illustrating scenario II in text. In this scenario it is assumed that gas exchange occurs between arterial blood and perfused cephalic mucosal tissue, but not between mucosal blood and air, nor between retial arteries and veins, both being sites of heat transfer. Moist cephalic mucosal and ocular surfaces and the ophthalmic retia are the sites of heat transfer only. Combinations of temperature (T, °C) and CO_2 tension (PCO_2, torr) used for calculation of each curve by Equation 1 are listed as are P_{50} values (torr). Lettered points on curves are explained in text.

a shift in the ODC to curve 2, such that the PO_2 of blood returning to the retia is at point *d*. In the retia it rewarms, shifting the ODC to curve 1 and PO_2 to point *e*, 52 torr. Meanwhile, systemic arterial blood enters the retia at point *a* (87 torr), creating a PO_2 difference between points *a* and *e* of 35 torr. However, since it is assumed that no retial gas exchange occurs, arterial blood leaves the retia at point *b*, having only cooled several degrees, so that blood flowing from the retia to the brain will have a PO_2 reduced to 70 torr, as in scenario I. It is inherent, therefore, in the currently accepted model of brain cooling that cerebral PaO_2 will be reduced in proportion to the degree to which arterial cooling takes place in the retia.

Scenario III: It is difficult to envision an O_2 gradient between retial arteries and veins that would not result in O_2 transfer. This scenario, therefore, is the same as scenario II, except that countercurrent gas exchange is now additionally assumed to occur in the retia. Arterial blood arriving at the mucosa at 41°C (curve 3, Figure 5) cools and gains CO_2 from the tissues, the ODC shifting to curve 2 and PaO_2 moving from point *a* to point *b*. At the same time, O_2 is taken up by the mucosal tissues, reducing PaO_2 and SaO_2 to point *c*. When this blood arrives at the retia, it is rewarmed but CO_2 is also given up to the arterial blood flowing countercurrent to it. The ODC thus shifts back to curve 3, rather than to curve 1 as in the previous figure, and PvO_2 reaches 49 torr, point *d*. Arterial blood, having entered the rete at point *a*, cools, but also takes up CO_2 from the venous blood, moving to point *b* on curve 2. This results in a PaO_2 of 76 rather than 87 torr, and an arteriovenous PO_2 difference in the rete of 27 rather than 35 torr. If retial exchange is complete, venous blood will follow curve 3 to point *e*, and arterial blood will follow curve 2 to point *f*, corresponding to a PO_2 of 49 torr and SaO_2 of 64%. The reduction of SO_2 by retial gas exchange compounds the disadvantage of reduced PaO_2 in scenarios I and II, by concomitantly reducing brain O_2 delivery as well as the gradient for capillary-tissue O_2 diffusion.

Scenario IV: In this scenario our assumptions are based on the hypothesis of Bernstein

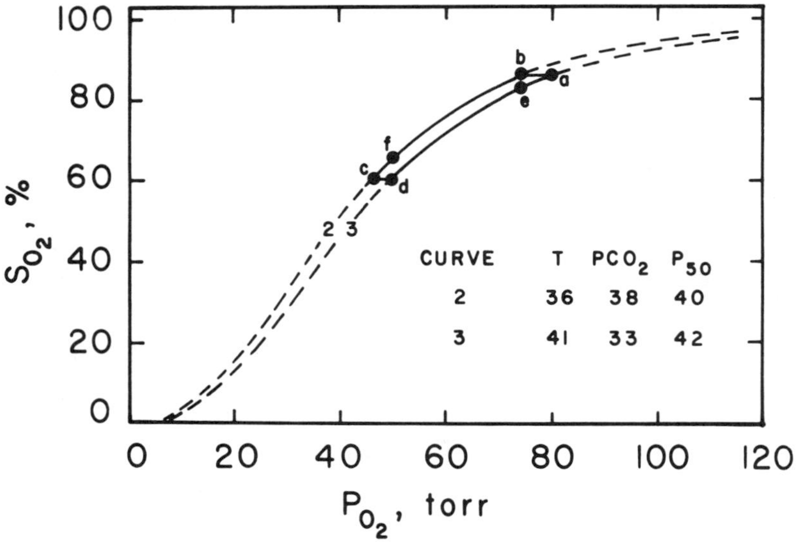

FIGURE 5. Relation between blood oxyhemoglobin saturation (SO_2, %) and blood O_2 tension (PO_2, torr) illustrating scenario III in text. The assumptions made in this scenario are the same as those made for scenario II (see Figure 4). However, in addition, it is assumed that arterial and venous blood in the ophthalmic retia engage in countercurrent gas exchange. Combinations of temperature (T, °C) and CO_2 tension (PCO_2, torr) used for calculation of each curve by Equation 1 are listed as are P_{50} values (torr). Lettered points on curves are explained in text.

et al.[18] that blood perfusing the evaporative surfaces exchanges gases with the atmosphere (Figure 6). Because of the steep PO_2 and PCO_2 differences that exist between the mucosal capillary beds and the atmosphere, and the large contact surface areas, it is further assumed that PCO_2 falls below and PO_2 rises above arterial levels, and that the amount of O_2 consumed by the mucosal tissues is negligible compared to the amount taken up by the blood from ambient air. In addition, it is assumed that arterial and venous blood in the retia engage in countercurrent gas exchange.

As in the previous scenario, arterial blood reaches the evaporative mucosal surfaces at point *a* and moves through point *b* to *c* as it cools and gives up CO_2 to the atmosphere. In contrast with the respiratory tract, the mucosa and eye surfaces possess no deadspace CO_2 to attenuate the PCO_2 gradient for diffusion. We have therefore assumed that in releasing CO_2 to the atmosphere the blood would undergo a reduction in PCO_2 by slightly less than half, since the CO_2 difference extends from 33 torr (arterial blood) to 0 torr (ambient air). Thus, the blood would have a PCO_2 of about 18 torr, moving the ODC to curve 6 and the PO_2 to point *c*.

With mucosal blood at point *c*, the PO_2 exchange difference from the atmosphere to the blood would be from 160 to 54 torr. We therefore assumed that mucosal blood reaches a saturation of 95% on curve 6, corresponding to a PO_2 of 73 torr (point *d*). On arrival at the rete the venous blood rewarms, moving to point *e* (curve 5). Simultaneously it gains CO_2 by countercurrent exchange with the arterial blood. If exchange is complete, the $PvCO_2$ will rise to 33 torr, shifting the ODC to curve 3 and raising PvO_2 to 108 torr (point *f*). Meanwhile, arterial blood reaching the rete at point *a* cools and gives up CO_2 to retial venous blood, reaching point *c* with a PO_2 of 54 torr. Thus, within the rete, the PO_2 gradient extends from 108 to 54 torr. For complete retial exchange, venous blood would move down curve 3 to 54 torr (point *g*), while arterial blood would move up curve 6 to 108 torr (point *h*).

The conclusions from this scenario are (1) that the combination of heat and gas exchange

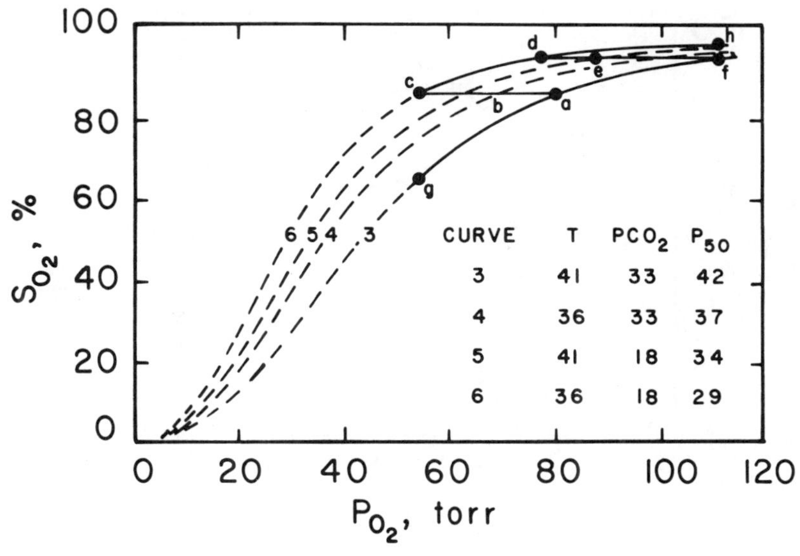

FIGURE 6. Relation between blood oxyhemoglobin saturation (SO_2, %) and blood O_2 tension (PO_2, torr) illustrating scenario IV in text. Here, in addition to the assumptions of scenario III (see Figure 5), it is assumed that both heat and gas exchange take place between blood and air at the surfaces of the moist cephalic mucosa and eyes. Combinations of temperature (T, °C) and CO_2 tension (PCO_2, torr) used for calculation of each curve by Equation 1 are listed as are P_{50} values (torr). Lettered points on curves are explained in text.

at the evaporative mucosal surfaces and in the retia could elevate the PO_2 and the SO_2 in arterial blood flowing from the retia to the brain, and (2) that the levels attained could be well above those ordinarily observed in the systemic arterial supply (i.e., 80 torr, 87%). At a maximum, in the present example, PO_2 could increase by 28 torr and SaO_2 could approach 100%. Indeed, these calculated values are very close to those measured in preliminary experiments by Bernstein et al.[18] Thus, these circumstances would comprise a significant advantage in enhancing brain O_2 delivery and diffusion.

Scenario V: A corollary to scenario IV is shown in Figure 7 for hypobaric hypoxia corresonding to an altitude of 7000 m above sea level, an altitude well tolerated by pigeons under various experimental conditions.[17] It is here that the proposed mechanism may be of great advantage.

At 7000 m above sea level, atmospheric PO_2, is 65 torr, (P_B = 308 torr[36]). At rest, pigeons had a mean body temperature of 39.5°C, a mean PaO_2 of 26 torr, and a mean $PaCO_2$ of 14 torr.[17] Arterial blood should therefore be at point *a* (curve 7, Figure 7), as it enters the mucosal tissue, and will move through *b* to *c* as it cools and releases CO_2. As atmospheric O_2 is taken up by the blood, PO_2 is assumed to increase along curve 10 to about 40 torr (point *d*), reducing the PO_2 difference by slightly less than half. This would raise SO_2 to 85%. In the rete the venous blood rewarms and gains CO_2 from arterial blood, shifting the ODC to curve 7. The retial venous blood will thus move through point *e*, arriving at point *f* with a PO_2 of 54 torr. Arterial blood entering the rete at point *a* will cool and give up CO_2 to the venous blood, its ODC shifting to curve 10 with a PaO_2 of 19 torr (point *c*). The resulting arteriovenous PO_2 difference will thus be 35 torr. If gas exchange is complete in the rete, the venous blood will move down curve 7 to point *g*, while PaO_2 will rise along curve 10 to 54 torr (point *h*), corresponding to 95% saturation. This represents a doubling of both PO_2 and SO_2 in the arterial blood flowing to the brain. The advantage, compared to an SO_2 of 40% and a PO_2 of 26 torr in systemic arterial blood, would be sustained O_2 delivery with little or no need for increase in cerebral blood flow even during flight at high altitude.

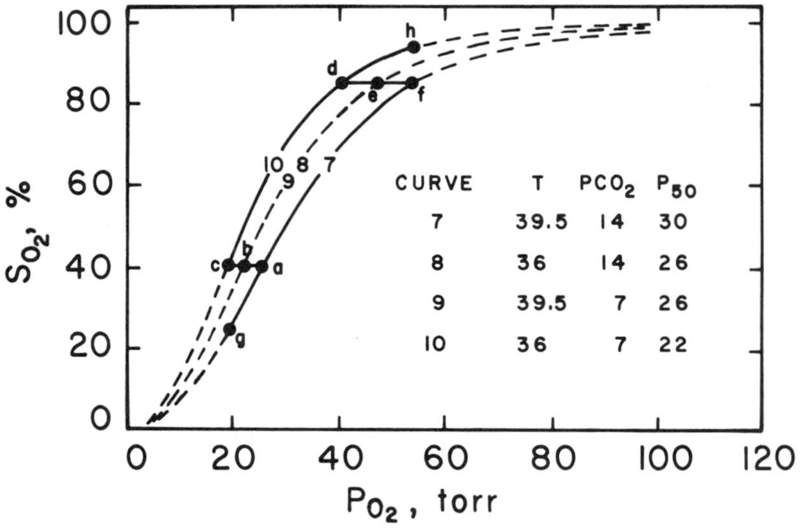

FIGURE 7. Relation between blood oxyhemoglobin saturation (SO_2, %) and blood O_2 tension (PO_2 torr) illustrating scenario V in text. The assumptions made in this scenario are the same as those made for scenario IV (see Figure 6); however, calculations were made for ambient conditions of hypobaric hypoxia at a simulated altitude of 7000 m above sea level. Combinations of temperature (T, °C) and CO_2 tension (PCO_2, torr) used for calculation of each curve by Equation 1 are listed as are P_{50} values (torr). Lettered points on curves are explained in text.

V. CONCLUSIONS

In birds, where some degree of brain cooling is unavoidable even at rest and cooling increases under heat stress or during exercise,[10] there exists the possibility that the suggested mechanism might be advantageous or even necessary, if only to offset the decrease in PO_2 that might be caused by cooling as described in scenario I. Further, when tissue O_2 supply is taxed, such as during exercise or the hypoxia of high altitude, the hypothesized mechanism might be obligatory to maintain adequate brain O_2 supply, perhaps reducing the need for augmented cerebral blood flow.[37]

The adaptive value of the proposed mechanism is clear, and the following argument may shed some light on its possible evolutionary development. In the late 19th century Williston[38] proposed the "cursorial" theory for the evolution of avian flight. Nopsca[39,40] added details to Williston's idea that flying birds evolved from terrestrial predators during the Jurassic era and recently credence was lent to the theory through paleontological[41] and physical[42] analysis. If flying birds did indeed evolve from cursorial predators, it seems logical that they might have evolved a mechanism for cooling their brains, as did many cursorial mammals, e.g., Fissipeds and Artiodactyls. These mammals are either predators or prey that might need to store heat during physical exertion associated with chasing prey or fleeing a predator while maintaining the brain cooler than the body. If a brain cooling mechanism that could also function to augment the brain's O_2 supply were present with the evolution of flight, birds would have been eminently preadapted for life and flight at high altitudes.

ACKNOWLEDGMENTS

We thank A. Allan Degen and Burt Kotler for helpful comments during manuscript preparation. This study was supported by U.S. National Science Foundation grant DCB-8402659.

REFERENCES

1. **Richards, S. A.,** Anatomy of the arteries of the head in the domestic fowl, *J. Zool. (London),* 152, 221, 1967.
2. **Kilgore, D. L., Bernstein, M. H., and Schmidt-Nielsen, K.,** Brain temperature in a large bird, the rhea, *Am. J. Physiol.,* 225, 739, 1973.
3. **Kilgore, D. L., Bernstein, M. H., and Hudson, D. M.,** Brain temperatures in birds, *J. Comp. Physiol. B,* 110, 209, 1976.
4. **Midtgard, U.,** Scaling of the brain and the eye cooling system in birds: a morphometric analysis of the *rete ophthalmicum, J. Exp. Zool.,* 225, 197, 1983.
5. **Bech, C. and Midtgard, U.,** Brain temperature and the *rete mirabile ophthalmicum* in the zebra finch *(Poephila guttata), J. Comp. Physiol. B,* 145, 89, 1981.
6. **Kilgore, D. L., Boggs, D. F., and Birchard, G. F.,** Role of the *rete mirabile ophthalmicum* in maintaining the body-to-brain temperature difference in pigeons, *J. Comp. Physiol. B,* 129, 119, 1979.
7. **Bernstein, M. H., Curtis, M. B., and Hudson, D. M.,** Independence of brain and body temperatures in flying American kestrels, *Falco sparverius, Am. J. Physiol.,* 237, R58, 1979.
8. **Bernstein, M. H., Sandoval, I., Curtis, M. B., and Hudson, D. M.,** Brain temperature in pigeons: effects of anterior respiratory bypass, *J. Comp. Physiol. B,* 129, 115, 1979.
9. **Kilgore, D. L., Birchard, G. F., and Boggs, D. F.,** Brain temperatures in running quail, *J. Appl. Physiol.,* 50, 1277, 1981.
10. **Baker, M. A.,** Brain cooling in endotherms in heat and exercise, *Ann. Rev. Physiol.,* 44, 85, 1982.
11. **Frost, P. G. H., Siegfried, W. R., and Greenwood, P. J.,** Arterio-venous heat exchange systems in the jackass penguin, *Spheniscus demersus, J. Zool. (London),* 175, 231, 1975.
12. **Midtgard, U.,** The blood vessels and the occurrence of arteriovenous anastomoses in cephalic heat loss of mallards, *Anas platyrhynchos* (Aves), *Zoomorphology,* 104, 323, 1984.
13. **Fedde, M. R. and Guffy, M. M.,** Routes of blood supply to the head of the Pekin duck, *Poultry Sci.,* 60, 1656, 1981.
14. **Kaku, K.,** On the vascular supply of the brain in the domestic fowl, *Fukuoka Acta Med.,* 50, 4293, 1959.
15. **Vitums, A., Shin-Ichi, M., and Farner, D. S.,** Arterial blood supply to the brain of the white-crowned sparrow *Zonotrichia leucophrys gambelii, Anat. Anz. Bd.* S116, 309, 1965.
16. **Wingstrand, K. G. and Munk, O.,** The pecten oculi of the pigeon with particular regard to its function, *Biol. Skrifter,* 14, 1, 1965.
17. **Weinstein, Y., Bernstein, M. H., Bickler, P. E., Gonzales, D. V., Samaniego, F. C., and Escobedo, M. A.,** Blood respiratory properties in pigeons at high altitudes: effects of acclimation, *Am. J. Physiol.,* 249, R765, 1985.
18. **Bernstein, M. H., Duran, H. L., and Pinshow, B.,** Extrapulmonary gas exchange enhances brain oxygen in pigeons, *Science,* 226, 564, 1984.
19. **Lutz, P. L. and Schmidt-Nielsen, K.,** Effect of simulated altitude on blood gas transport in the pigeon, *Resp. Physiol.,* 30, 383, 1977.
20. **Scheid, P. and Meyer, M.,** Mixing technique for study of oxygen-hemoglobin equilibrium: a critical evaluation, *J. Appl. Physiol.,* 45, 818, 1978.
21. **Scheid, P. and Kawashiro, T.,** Metabolic changes in avian blood and their effects on determination of blood gases and pH, *Resp. Physiol.,* 23, 291, 1975.
22. **Zar, J. H.,** *Biostatistical Analysis,* Prentice-Hall, Englewood Cliffs, N.J., 1984, 1.
23. **Hirsowitz, L. A., Fell, K., and Torrance, J. D.,** Oxygen affinity of avian blood, *Resp. Physiol.,* 31, 51, 1977.
24. **Pinshow, B., Bernstein, M. H., and Arad, Z.,** Effects of temperature and PCO_2 on O_2 affinity of pigeon blood: implications for brain O_2 supply, *Am. J. Physiol.,* 249, R758, 1985.
25. **Lutz, P. L.,** On the oxygen affinity of bird blood, *Am. Zool.,* 20, 187, 1980.
26. **Lutz, P. L., Longmuir, I. S., Tuttle, J. V., and Schmidt-Nielsen, K.,** Dissociation curve of bird blood and effect of red cell oxygen consumption, *Resp. Physiol.,* 17, 269, 1973.
27. **Baumann, F. H. and Baumann, R.,** A comparative study of the respiratory properties of bird blood, *Resp. Physiol.,* 31, 333, 1977.
28. **Wood, S. C. and Lenfant, C.,** Oxygen transport and oxygen delivery, in *Evolution of Respiratory Processes, a Comparative Approach,* Wood, S. C. and Lenfant, C., Eds., Marcel Dekker, New York, 1979, 193.
29. **Pionetti, J.-M. and Bouverot, P.,** Effects of acclimation to altitude on oxygen affinity and organic phosphate concentrations in pigeon blood, *Life Sci.,* 20, 1207, 1977.
30. **Danzer, L. A. and Cohn, J. E.,** The dissociation curve for goose blood, *Resp. Physiol.,* 3, 302, 1967.
31. **Crowe, T. M. and Withers, P. C.,** Brain temperature regulation in helmeted guineafowl, *S. Afr. J. Sci.,* 75, 362, 1979.
32. **Richards, S. A.,** Brain temperature and the cerebral circulation in the chicken, *Brain Res.,* 23, 265, 1970.

33. **Schmidt, I. and Simon, E.,** Temperature changes of the hypothalamus and body core in ducks feeding in cold water, *Pfluegers Arch.*, 378, 227, 1979.
34. **Scott, N. R., Johnson, A. T., and Van Tienhoven, A.,** Measurement of Hypothalamic temperature and heart rate of poultry, *Trans. Am. Soc. Agric. Eng.*, 13, 342, 1970.
35. **Scott, N. R. and Van Tienhoven, A.,** Simultaneous measurement of hypothalamic and body temperatures and heart rate of poultry, *Trans. Am. Soc. Agric. Eng.*, 14, 1027, 1971.
36. **List, R. J.,** *Smithsonian Meteorological Tables,* The Smithsonian Institution, Washington, D.C., 1971, 1.
37. **Grubb, B., Colacino, J. M., and Schmidt-Nielsen, K.,** Cerebral blood flow in birds; effect of hypoxia, *Am. J. Physiol.*, 234, H230, 1978.
38. **Williston, S. W.,** Are birds derived from dinosaurs?, *Kansas City Rev. Sci.*, 3, 457, 1879.
39. **Nopsca, F.,** Ideas on the origin of flight, *Proc. Zool. Soc. London,* p. 223, 1907.
40. **Nopsca, F.,** The ancestry of birds, *Nature (London),* 242, 136, 1923.
41. **Ostrom, J. H.,** Bird flight: how did it begin, *Am. Sci.*, 67, 46, 1979.
42. **Caple, R., Balda, R. B., and Willis, W. R.,** The physics of leaping animals and the evolution of pre-flight, *Am. Nat.*, 121, 455, 1983.
43. **Maginniss, L., Bernstein, M. H., and Pinshow, B.,** unpublished data.

Chapter 20

THE DESERT CAMEL — A REVIEW

Reuven Yagil and Zipora Etzion

The one-humped desert camel is superbly adapted to its environment. Its method of browsing, covering tens of kilometers a day, is compatible to an area where vegetation is sparse. The plants which are often thorny and have a high salt content are well digested by the camel and are preferred over other more succulent vegetation. The camel therefore has a much higher salt content of its alimentary tract than other animals. Absorption of the salts, with accompanying water is hormonally controlled and is important for the camel's survival. The kidneys are able to excrete the large salt load. Water and urea which are reabsorbed from the kidneys under the influence of ADH are recycled to the rumen, allowing for continued digestion of food even when the camel is severely dehydrated. The urea is also a source of protein via bacterial synthesis and degradation. In the dehydrated camel thyroid metabolism is depressed, conserving respiratory water losses by depressing oxygen consumption; insulin levels are lower, leading to hyperglycemia which with the hygroscopic nature of sugar adds to water retention in the bloodstream; body temperatures fluctuate greatly according to changes in environmental temperatures, reducing water losses for body cooling if strict homeothermia were to become necessary. Another important adaptive mechanism is the ability to rehydrate rapidly following losses of over 25% of body weight. Within 30 min of drinking a voluminous diluted urine is excreted; red blood cells swell and change from ovalocytes to spherocytes, conforming the rapid influx of water into the bloodstream. The exceptional osmotic stability of the red blood cells allows for the rapid absorption of water; ADH levels decline while aldosterone levels increase in order to return to a normal homeostasis.

Primitive pastoral management is the cause of bad reproductive performance. Coralling camels and controlled breeding allows for annual births, not once every 2 or 3 years; perinatal deaths are minimal and with PMS prepuberal camels have been brought into a fertile estrous and calvings did not present any problems. It is pertinent that the areas where the camel thrives, the severely drought-stricken areas of the world, are the areas where millions of people die each year from starvation. Many solutions are being sought for the endemic famine and the camel is now being considered a nutritious and reliable source of food because of its ability to survive, reproduce, and produce when water and food are scarce.

The desert-living camel (*Camelus dromedarius*) is an end-product of the adaptation of an animal to its environment. Other members of the camel family, which originated in North America when the land masses were still joined,[1] have adapted to the physiological stresses of heights, i.e., in the Andes mountains: llamas, alpaccas, vicunas, and guanacos; and to cold and aridity, i.e., in the Gobi desert in Asia: the two-humped bactrian.

The desert-living camel, the dromedary, has adapted morphologically, behaviorally, and physiologically to the harsh desert environment. The camel has had to overcome the combined effects of heat, lack of drinking water, and sparse vegetation. The vegetation in an arid area is sparse because of minimal rainfall. The annual plants, more luscious vegetation, appear only after rainfall. The hardy perennials are well adapted having deep penetrating roots and roots that spread to the sides, searching for water. The vegetation is therefore, spread thinly over an area producing the typical arid landscape. The hardy perennial plants have also undergone morphological adaptation. Their leaves are often curled and small to prevent transpiration losses. The leaves even change into thorns. The vegetation survives by absorbing salts with the accompanying water. These changes in grasses, shrubs, and trees make the vegetation not only sparse, but also not tasty for most animals. The high salt content of

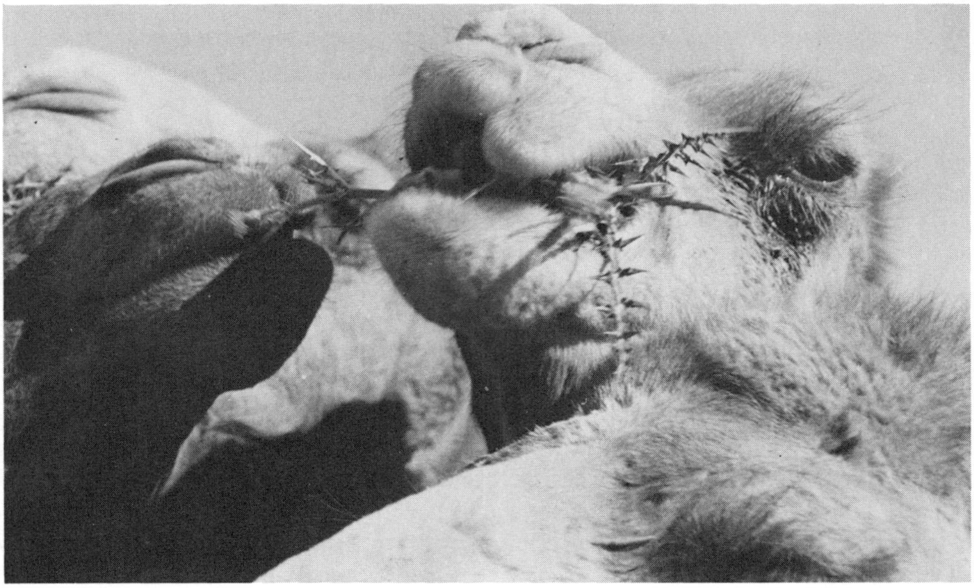

FIGURE 1. Camel eating branch with small leaves and large thorns.

desert vegetation is aggravated by the drinking water being brackish; the little drinking water that exists becomes highly salty due to the high degree of evaporation that occurs in areas with intense solar radiation.

Because of the sparse, widely spread out vegetation in an arid area, the camel is a browser. It takes a bite from one plant and then a bite from another, continually moving. It browses from the ground and then from the trees, often covering distances of up to 50 km/day in its normal search for food. Its long legs, long neck, and series of valves in arteries and veins allow the camel to easily cover these long distances and to rapidly move its head from the heights of trees to the ground, and vice versa, without problems of blood pressure fluctuations or blood flow complications.[2] The camel has no problems browsing from thorny branches or even eating the thorns themselves (Figure 1).

The anatomical and behavioral peculiarities of the camel are complemented by physiological mechanisms which are adapted to the high salt content of the fodder and drinking water. The high-salt vegetation is actually preferred, even over the more succulent pastures that are grazed by the true ruminants — cows, sheep, and goats. The preference for a salty diet ensures that the contents of the stomach and the intestine are rich in electrolytes.[3] It is the hormonal control of the absorption of the salts and water which enable the camel to withstand extended and repeated periods of drought,[4] which perennially confront mammals in arid zones. The camel's kidneys are able to easily excrete the absorbed salts in a concentrated urine even when the animals are severely dehydrated.[5]

There are two hormones which are responsible for the salt and water metabolism, aldosterone and ADH (vasopressin). The aldosterone[6] and apparently ADH as well,[7] cause absorption of salts and water from the mammalian alimentary canal. The two hormones act in conjunction with, and potentiate, each other. They act in water and salt reabsorption in the kidneys as well. Release of the two hormones in the dehydrated animal occurs through stimulation of osmoreceptors and baroreceptors, directly affecting specific nuclei in the hypothalamus. ADH and ACTH are released from the pituitary gland, the latter hormone leading to the release of aldosterone from the adrenal cortex. The salt and water content of the blood is vital for maintaining normal blood pressure.[8] Vasoconstriction is a phenomenon

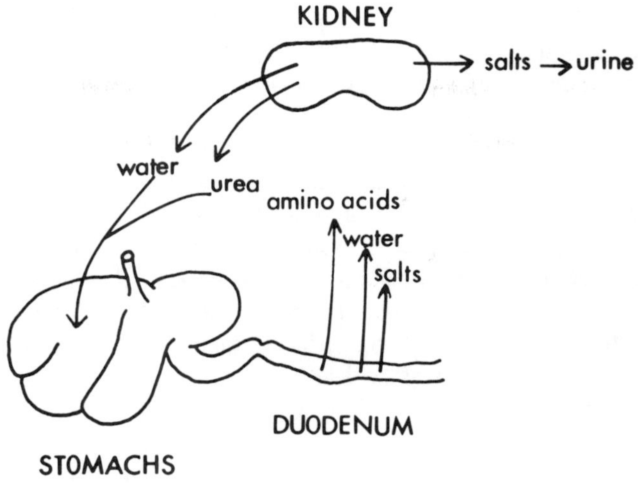

FIGURE 2. Recycling of urea and water to the stomachs from the kidneys.

for the maintenance of blood pressure. The vasoconstrictor and antidiuretic activities of the neurohypophysial hormone, even though they elicit two completely different and distinct phenomena are common to the one hormone. Instead of referring to the hormone by two names, ADH or vasopressin, a more suitable name for this hormone would be WGH (water governing hormone).[2]

For the severely dehydrated camel, in conjunction with the hormonally controlled uptake of alimentary salt and water, the effect of ADH on the kidneys is also of vital importance. Under the influence of this hormone water and urea are reabsorbed and recycled to the blood and then to the rumen.[9] The urea is utilized by the rumen flora for producing new generations of bacteria. The acid in the fourth, the true stomach destroys the bacteria, providing protein for degradation and absorption of amino acids in the intestines. The amino acids are utilized and eventually broken down to form urea which is recycled back to the rumen. The continual absorption and recycling of urea and water guarantees normal gastrointestinal function in the dehydrated camel (Figure 2). In this way camels were dehydrated for 54 days before the appetite declined.[10] Salt is lost from the body by renal excretion, even though aldosterone secretion is high.[4] The reason for this is that because a relative hypothyroidism exists in the dehydrated camel,[11] the nephron becomes less reactive to aldosterone.[12] The loss of salt, which is common for desert animals[2] is compensated for by the salty fodder and brackish drinking water.

The incongruity of increased plasma sodium[5] with decreased or unchanged osmolality and hematocrit[13] in the dehydrated camel can be explained by the above data, i.e., water and salt are absorbed from the gut, and while salt is excreted by the kidneys, water is reabsorbed. Urea takes water with it to the blood as does glucose that is present in higher concentrations in the dehydrated camel.[14]

Because of relatively large losses of plasma water by most mammals, dehydration leads to increased metabolism. In the dehydrated camel the thyroid metabolism, i.e., cellular metabolism in total, declines,[11] which reduces respiratory water losses as the respiratory rate declines,[15] and reduces the production of metabolic heat. Other small desert mammals also reduce their metabolism when they are exposed to heat but when dehydrated the metabolism increases,[16] which can be fatal. The reduced cellular metabolism leads to decreased insulin secretion, resulting in hyperglycemia,[14] which aids in water retention in the blood.

One of the most important mechanisms that the dehydrated camel has is an independence from a strict homeothermia,[17] and there are fluctuations of approximately 6°C in body temperature from early morning to late afternoon. This means that in the early morning, when the air temperatures are low, the body temperature is low; as the air temperatures rise, so do the body temperatures. Therefore, the difference between the outer air temperature and body temperature remains relatively the same. The uptake of heat by the body is, therefore, lessened. The camels utilize anatomical and behavioral features to potentiate the body temperature mechanism.[2] The large body of the camel heats up much slower than it would if it was a small animal. The camels squat in the direction of the sun, often huddling together, in order to present as small a surface area as possible directly exposed to the sun. The thick and hardened keratin pads under the chest and on all four "knees", are the only areas of the body that touch the underlying surface. The rest of the body is slightly elevated above the ground. As the ground was cool to begin with and remains in the shade of the animal's body heat is radiated to the cooler surface. In addition, convection around the animal has a cooling effect.

The ability to withstand water restriction for weeks on end and still remain active, a feat of which no other animal is capable, enabled man to traverse the harsh deserts of Australia and the Middle East, when horses died after 1 or 2 days. A less dramatic, but just as important mechanism for a dehydrated animal, is the ability to rapidly rehydrate. There are animals which rapidly replenish their water losses, such as dogs[18] and Bedouin goats[19] but as the imbibed water does not rapidly enter their bloodstream, these animals cannot be considered as being rehydrated. The goat, and most probably the dog, retain water in their alimentary tracts in order to prevent hemolysis. The camel red blood cells are virtually unaffected by hypotonic solutions,[13] therefore enjoying a rapid uptake of water into their bloodstream.[20] This explains why it takes well over 24 hr for the renal function of the Bedouin goat to return to normal, while the camel's renal function returns to normal within 30 min of drinking.[21] After rapid drinking the ADH and aldosterone levels, which were elevated by dehydration, rapidly decrease.[4] A few hours later the aldosterone concentrations start rising again and are drastically elevated 24 hr after drinking. The aldosterone now governs intestinal absorption and renal reabsorption of salt to return the body to a normal homeostatis.

The recycling of water, as discussed above, is very important for the lactating camel in drought areas. Milk secretion is a water-depleting phenomenon. It must be remembered that water makes up normally about 85% of the milk composition. In the dehydrated camel the water content of the milk is increased to above 90%,[22] which is important for the survival of their young. This fact explains why nomads traversing a desert take a milch camel with them, for the water in the milk as much as for the nutritional value. The secretion of water into the milk is a similar mechanism to the secretion of water into sweat, the two glands, milk and sweat, being ontogenetically very similar. As ADH is responsible for the secretion of a diluted sweat[23] and aldosterone causes a decline in salt content, it can be assumed that these hormones are the main causes of the secretion of the diluted milk (Figure 3). This has been confirmed by research on heat-stressed laboratory animals where it was ably demonstrated that both ADH and aldosterone led to the secretion of diluted milk.[24] The salt and water metabolism in the lactating camel is potentiated by the two hormones closely associated with lactation, prolactin and oxytocin. Prolactin acts on the intestines in a manner similar to that of aldosterone,[25] while oxytocin acts in a manner similar to ADH.[20] Therefore, for milk production, water and salt are absorbed from the alimentary canal and reabsorbed from the kidneys, and then the water is secreted into the milk (Figure 3).

The volume of milk secreted by a good milch camel can reach 40 ℓ/day.[27,28] The milk volume is unaffected by dehydration,[29] therefore, camel milk can be a vital source of water and nutrition for humans in severely affected drought areas.[30] Less than 2 kg of camel milk a day suffices to supply the entire protein needs of an adult person.[2] The milk is rich in

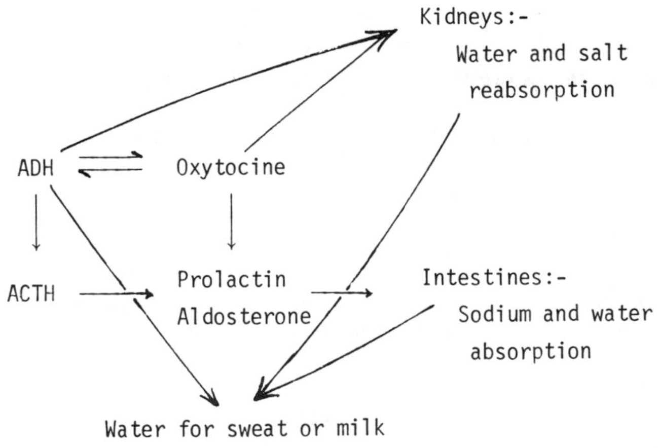

FIGURE 3. Hormonal control of water secretion into the milk.

vitamins, especially vitamin C, which is a valued commodity in an area where no other source is available. Another valuable property of camel milk is that it does not sour rapidly; whereas human milk sours within 24 hr, cow milk which is stirred fairly often sours within 3 weeks, and camel milk does not have a decline in pH even after 3 months. After 2 years of storage in a refrigerator the milk still retains its liquid form and, although it smells like a strong yogurt, is still edible. Camel's milk is far more acid than that of women or cows, most probably due to the high concentrations of ascorbic acid (vitamin C) and fatty acids.

Why then is the camel not utilized as a major source of food in drought areas? The main reason is that as the camel is considered a primitive animal, its herder is also considered primitive.[2] Another reason is that to date camel breeding is not economical. Both reasons, however, are steeped in the ancient nomadic husbandry practices, which do not lend themselves to improving, or even receiving the maximal benefits which can be derived from the camel. The long daily marches in search of food, away from the human centers, can be annulled by corralling the animals. This action has no negative effects on the camels and has many positive aspects. Corralled camels require far less water and food,[2] both important factors in drought-stricken areas. The camel's preference for salt allows for the introduction and propogation of hardy halophytes, which contain high concentrations of protein besides the salts and water, and therefore, guarantee ample fodder even in times of drought. Corralling the animals will greatly improve management, reproduction, and hence the production of animal protein for human nutrition.

The poor reproductive performance of the camel is partly due to pastoral management practices and partly due to inherent factors. A calf once every 2 to 3 years is not a physiological phenomenon but rather is caused by the need for milk by the owners. The females give birth in the winter and are kept close to the tent for their milk while the males are away grazing. The herd only unites in the summer when the males and females are not fertile.[2] Corralled camels produce calves once a year. Perinatal deaths are almost nonexistent in corralled camels because management and control of the partus and following days is simple. A major negative factor in the camel's fertility can also be overcome. Instead of a first calf being born when the female is 5 to 6 years of age, use of PMS injections into prepuberal camels (1.5 to 2 years of age) causes a normal reproductive cycle. There was a successful mating, gestation, and partus. As the she-camel is not a spontaneous ovulator, a surge of progesterone, as determined by radioimmunoassay, is a useful technique for pregnancy diagnosis. It is quite evident that with minimal intervention and with no great demands on the camel breeders the reproduction capability of the camel can be vastly improved.

Further research into the reproductive, nutrition, and lactation physiology of the camel will elevate this animal from a pure physiological curiosity to a useful animal for human nutrition in the very areas where this animal thrives, i.e, drought areas.

REFERENCES

1. **Epstein, H.,** *The Origin of the Domestic Animals of Africa,* Vol. 2, Africana Publishing, New York, 1971.
2. **Yagil, R.,** *The Desert Camel: Comparative Physiology. Comparative Animal Nutrition,* Vol. 5, S. Karger, Basel, 1985.
3. **Maloiy, G. M. O. and Clements, E. T.,** Colonic absorption and secretion of electrolytes as seen in five species of East African herbivorous mammals, *Comp. Biochem. Physiol.,* 67A, 21, 1980.
4. **Yagil, R. and Etzion, Z.,** Anti-diuretic hormone and aldosterone in the dehydrated and rehydrated camel, *Comp. Biochem. Physiol.,* 63A, 275, 1979.
5. **Yagil, R. and Berlyne, G. M.,** Glomerular filtration rate and urine concentration in the camel in dehydration, *Renal Physiol.,* 1, 104, 1978.
6. **Efstratopoulus, A. D., Peart, W. S., and Wilson, G. A.,** The effect of aldosterone on colonic potential difference and renal excretion in normal man, *Clin. Sci. Mol. Med.,* 46, 489, 1974.
7. **Robertson, G. L.,** Abnormalities of thirst regulation, *Kidney Int.,* 25, 460, 1984.
8. **Burnier, M., Biollaz, J., Brunner, D. B., and Brunner, H. R.,** Blood pressure maintenance in awake dehydrated rats: renin, vasopressin, and sympathetic activity, *Am. J. Physiol. Heart Circ. Physiol.,* 245, H203, 1983.
9. **Farid, M. F. A., Shawket, S. M., and Abdel-Rahman, M. H. A.,** Observations on the nutrition of camels and sheep under stress, in *Camels,* IFS Intl. Symp., Sudan, 1979, 126.
10. **Hassan, Y. M.,** A note on the effect of dehydration on a camel, *Sudan J. Vet. Anim. Husb.,* 12, 111, 1971.
11. **Yagil, R., Etzion, Z., and Ganani, J.,** Camel thyroid metabolism: effect of season and dehydration, *J. Appl. Physiol.,* 45, 540, 1978.
12. **Fregly, M. J. and Taylor, R. E.,** Effect of hypothyroidism on water and sodium exchange in rats, in *Thirst: Proc. 1st Int. Symp. Regul. Body Water,* Pergamon Press, Oxford, 1964, 139.
13. **Yagil, R., Sod-Moriah, U. A., and Meyerstein, N.,** Dehydration and camel blood. II and III. The effect of chronic dehydration and rapid rehydration on the shape, size and concentration of the camel red blood cell. Osmotic fragility, specific gravity, and osmolality, *Am. J. Physiol.,* 226, 301, 1974.
14. **Yagil, R. and Berlyne, G. M.,** Glucose loading and dehydration in the camel, *J. Appl. Physiol. Resp. Environ. Exercise Physiol.,* 42, 680, 1977.
15. **Schmidt-Nielsen, K., Crawford, E. C., Newsome, A. E., and Rawson, K. S.,** The metabolic rate of camels, *Fed. Proc.,* 22, 176, 1963.
16. **Yousef, M. K., Chu, D. T., and Haghani, Z.,** Intestinal transport and thyroid function in heat-acclimated desert rodents, in *Thermal Physiology,* Hales, J. R. S., Ed., Raven Press, New York, 1984, 491.
17. **Schmidt-Nielsen, K.,** *Desert Animals: Physiological Problems of Heat and Water,* Clarendon Press, Oxford, 1964.
18. **Adolph, E. F.,** Termination of drinking: satiation, *Fed. Proc.,* 41, 2533, 1982.
19. **Shkolnik, A., Maltz, E., and Chosniak, I.,** The role of the ruminant's digestive tract as a water reservoir, in *Digestive Physiology and Metabolism in Ruminants,* Ruckebusch, Y. and Thivend, P., Eds., Medical Technology Press, Lancaster, England, 1980, 731.
20. **Etzion, Z., Meyerstein, N., and Yagil, R.,** Tritiated water metabolism during dehydration and rehydration in the camel, *J. Appl. Physiol. Resp. Environ. Exercise Physiol.,* 56, 217, 1984.
21. **Etzion, Z., Berlyne, G. M., and Yagil, R.,** The effect of rapid rehydration on renal function in the camel, submitted for publication.
22. **Yagil, R. and Etzion, Z.,** The effect of drought conditions on the quality of camel's milk, *J. Dairy Res.,* 47, 159, 1980.
23. **Ingram, D. L. and Mount, L. E.,** *Man and Animals in Hot Environments,* Springer-Verlag, New York, 1975.
24. **Etzion, Z. and Yagil, R.,** Effect of exogenous ADH and aldosterone on milk in heat-stressed animals, *Comp. Biochem. Physiol.,* 69A, 129, 1981.
25. **Mainoya, J. R.,** Colon absorption of water and NaCl in the rat during lactation and the possible involvement of prolactin, *Experientia,* 37, 1083, 1981.
26. **Lawrence, R. A.,** *Breast Feeding: A Guide for the Medical Profession,* C. V. Mosby, St. Louis, 1980.

27. **Knoess, K. H.,** Milk production in the dromedary, in IFS Intl. Symp. Camels, Sudan, 1979, 201.
28. **Evans, J. O.,** personal communication of visit to Pakistan.
29. **Yagil, R. and Etzion, Z.,** Milk yield of camels (*C. dromedarius*) in drought areas, *Comp. Biochem. Physiol.*, 67, 207, 1980a.
30. **Yagil, R.,** *The Desert Camel,* S. Karger, Basel, 1985.

Chapter 21

AN EXERCISE IN THE EVALUATION OF BODY FAT CONTENT AS ILLUSTRATED BY THE SAND RAT (*PSAMMOMYS OBESUS*)

Jonathan H. Adler

TABLE OF CONTENTS

I. Introduction 182

II. Materials and Methods 182

III. Results 183

IV. Discussion 183
  A. Water Content 183
  B. Fat Content 184

V. Dynamic Aspects of Body Fat Content 184

Acknowledgment 186

References 186

I. INTRODUCTION

Body fat content, its distribution, and reserve capacity raises a number of demanding questions. The standard approach expressing fat content as percentage of body mass (Mb) does not satisfy functional requirements. Desert animals exposed to heavy heat loads and extreme seasonal fluctuations in food supply characteristic to their environment present a strong argument for a functional approach. The proper evaluation of fat reserves is of importance in order to understand desert animal survival.

The fat sand rat, *Psammomys obesus,* occupies arid habitats characterized by limited seasonal rainfall interspersed by long dry periods.[7] The food supply available to this species fluctuates in relation to the rainfall. The sand rat can accumulate fat when food is available in winter and spring. The metabolic rate is reduced when environmental temperature increases.[3]

The combination of accumulated fat and reduced metabolic rate contributes toward the sand rat's survivial capacity during the hot, dry seasons. Thus, the body fat content of this species is of particular interest regarding its natural history. The aim of this article is to show that the evaluation of body fat content in relation to metabolic rate rather than body weight has functional significance. Phenomena characterizing the sand rat will be used to demonstrate this point.

II. MATERIALS AND METHODS

The sand rats employed in this study were raised in the animal house of the Hebrew University Medical School in Jerusalem. They were descendents of animals captured in the Dead Sea area in 1969.[1] This race of *Psammomys obesus* is regarded as belonging to the subspecies terrasanctae.[5,10] The animals were fed Amrod 935 lab animal pellets *ad libitum* (produced by Ambar Feed Mills, Hadera, Israel) together with salt bush (*Atriplex halimus*). Twenty-six animals, 13 of each sex, weighing from 135 to 250 g were divided into two groups. One group was maintained at room temperature, the other was acclimated to 34°C for 2 weeks. Fat content, lean body mass (LBM), and water content were determined in both groups. The animals were killed by bleeding from the aorta while anesthetized with nembutal (30 mg/kg). The blood was collected, and its volume was measured. Body water was determined by the difference in weight prior to killing and dry carcass weight corrected for the water content of the blood withdrawn. The carcasses were desiccated under vacuum at 60°C. Fat was extracted employing a Soxhlet apparatus and then weighed according to the method of the Association of Official Agricultural Chemists.[2] Fat content was also determined on the basis of percent body water.[17]

$$\%\ \text{Body fat} = 100 - \frac{\%\ \text{body}^{H_2O}}{0.732}$$

In the present work fat content is expressed as percentage Mb and is also related to the metabolic rate.

The concept of percentage of metabolic fat content (%MFC) is proposed in Equation 3. It is an approach based on Brody's[6] Equations 1 and 2 showing the relation of oxygen flow ($\dot{V}O_2$) to Mb.

$$\frac{\dot{V}O_2}{Mb} = 3.8 \times Mb^{-0.25} \qquad (1)$$

Table 1
BODY WEIGHT (MB), FAT AS %MB, %MFC, AND %EFC IN SAND RATS EXPOSED TO DIFFERENT TREATMENT

Treatment	Mb (kg)	Fat %Mb	Fat %MFC	Fat %EFC	N
Room temperature	0.202 ± 0.020	22.4 ± 2.96	15.2 ± 2.32	18.7 ± 2.59	14
Acclimated	0.187.8 ± 0.031	18.07 ± 4.65	12.1 ± 3.12	23.35 ± 7.1	12
Difference		4.33	3.1	4.8	
Significance		$p < 0.01$	$p < 0.01$	$p < 0.05$	

Note: Values are given as mean ± standard deviation. N = number of animals, %MFC = fat content calculated as % of $Mb^{0.75}$, %EFC = fat calculated as % of $Mm^{0.75}$ corrected for O_2 consumption.

$$\dot{V}O_2 = 3.8 \times Mb^{0.75} \quad (2)$$

$$\%\ MFC = \%\ Fat \times Mb^{0.25} \quad (3)$$

The percentage of fat content (%EFC) which represents the actual value of fat as an energy reservoir depends on the animal's O_2 requirements. Oxygen requirements as a function of Mb may deviate from the line described by Equations 1 and 2. We, therefore, suggest that the animal's fat content be related to its apparent weight rather than actual Mb. The apparent weight will be referred to as its metabolic mass (Mm).

The Mm is defined as the apparent weight of the animal according to its O_2 consumption derived from Equation 1.

$$\%\ EFC = \%\ Fat \times Mm^{0.25} \quad (4)$$

Student's *t* test was employed for comparing treatment groups.

III. RESULTS

Data on fat percentage of Mb, percentage of MFC, and percentage of EFC of the two different treatment groups are presented in Table 1. Heat-acclimated animals had significantly less fat when calculated as percentage Mb as percentage MFC ($p < 0.05$). When fat content was calculated as percentage EFC the acclimated animals had significantly more fat ($p < 0.05$). There was no statistically significant difference in Mb between the acclimated and control groups. Neither was there a statistically significant difference in LBM. The body weight of males was 210 ± 32 g and that of females was 178 ± 32 g. The difference was statistically significant ($p < 0.05$).

When percentage of body fat for all the 26 animals studied was calculated on the basis of percentage LBM and compared to the observed fat content as determined by extraction, the values obtained were 20.3 ± 4.8% and 20.0 ± 0.5%, respectively. The difference between the observed and the calculated percentage of body fat was insignificant.

IV. DISCUSSION

A. Water Content

It is shown here that the water content of the sand rat is similar to that found in other mammalian species. Water content of the LBM in the sand rat was found to be 72 ± 0.5%. This result falls within the range found by Sheng et al.,[21] who reported values of between 70 and 76%. The characteristic mammalian value is considered by Rathbun and Pace[18] to be 73.2%.

B. Fat Content

Heat-acclimated animals had a significantly lower percentage Mb fat content than those kept at room temperature. Horowitz et al.[11] previously reported that in acclimated dehydrated sand rats percentage of body fat was sigificantly lower than in nonacclimated controls. According to Rathbun and Pace[18] fat content for the rat, guinea pig, and dog ranged from 9 to 15% Mb. Gutzeit et al.[9] found fat content in the spiny mouse (*Acomys cahirinus*) to be 10 to 22% of Mb on standard diets and 29.4 to 54.0% on a high fat diet. Kekwick[13] gives values for adipose tissue content in human beings as 14% for males and 22% for females at 25 years of age. Higher values are given for older individuals. The values for fat content as percentage of Mb in the above species overlap those found in sand rats. Thus, comment on the particular obese appearance of the sand rat is in order. The sand rat has a prominent suprascapular hump of fat and pronounced aggregates of cervical and prefemoral fat. This pattern of distribution permits fat accumulation without increasing subcutaneous insulation. MacFarlane[16] has reported this type of fat distribution to be characteristic of desert ungulates.

V. DYNAMIC ASPECTS OF BODY FAT CONTENT

From an anatomical quantitative point of view, we can compare the fat content of a 200 g sand rat to a 400 kg steer, both with 20% fat, yet is this approach functionally valid?

If fat is regarded as an energy reservoir, its availability must be balanced against energy requirements. Considering energy requirements according to $\dot{V}O_2$ relative to size, it becomes apparent that energy requirements per unit (Mb) decrease as size increases.

Studying oxygen consumption of different species ranging in size from the shrew to the elephant, we must examine Equation 2. $Mb^{0.75}$ is regarded as the metabolic weight and relates body volume to surface area. These relationships have been discussed in detail by Blaxter,[4] Brody,[6] Kleiber,[14] and Schmidt-Nielsen.[19,20] Since O_2 requirements are proportional to $Mb^{0.75}$, larger animals will require less O_2 per unit weight. Thus, for a given percentage of body fat content, they will have a larger energy reserve than a smaller animal. Plotting %MFC = y, Mb = x, on a log scale as in Figure 1, it can be seen clearly that percentage MFC increases with Mb for any given fat percentage of Mb.

Using Equation 3, it can be shown that a 100 g rat with 10% Mb fat will have 5.62% MFC. In order that a hog weighing 100 kg be provided with 5.62% MFC 1.78% Mb fat will suffice. The same hog with 10% Mb fat will have 31.6% MFC. In order to have a 100 g rat with 31.62% MFC, 56.23% Mb fat will be required. While a hog with 10% Mb fat will be fashionably slim, a rat with as much as 56% Mb fat will be incongruous.

If we are to remain faithful to the need to relate fat content to metabolic requirements when comparing species, in addition to variations in weight, it must be borne in mind that all species do not exactly fit the slope described by Equation 2. Some may appear above or below the line. In some species oxygen requirements vary with environmental changes. Ben Porat et al.[3] showed that for sand rats kept at room temperature (25°C) $\dot{V}O_2$/g/hr = 0.82, and for acclimated animals $\dot{V}O_2$/g/hr = 0.52 in the thermoneutral zone. Frenkel and Kraicer[8] showed that for the sand rat in its thermoneutral zone $\dot{V}O_2$/g/hr = 0.51 mℓ, and the albino rat at normal room temperature requires close to 1 mℓ O_2/g/hr. How are we to compare the fat content of different species or different individuals of the same species under different physiological conditions? In order to relate fat content to body weight as a function of metabolic requirements for different groups of rodents on an equal basis, the following suggestion is offered. Weigh the animals according to $\dot{V}O_2$/g/hr rather than Mb, using Equation 1. If $\dot{V}O_2$/Mb is known, the apparent Mb can be derived.

Let us regard this derived value as the Mm of the animal. The body fat content expressed

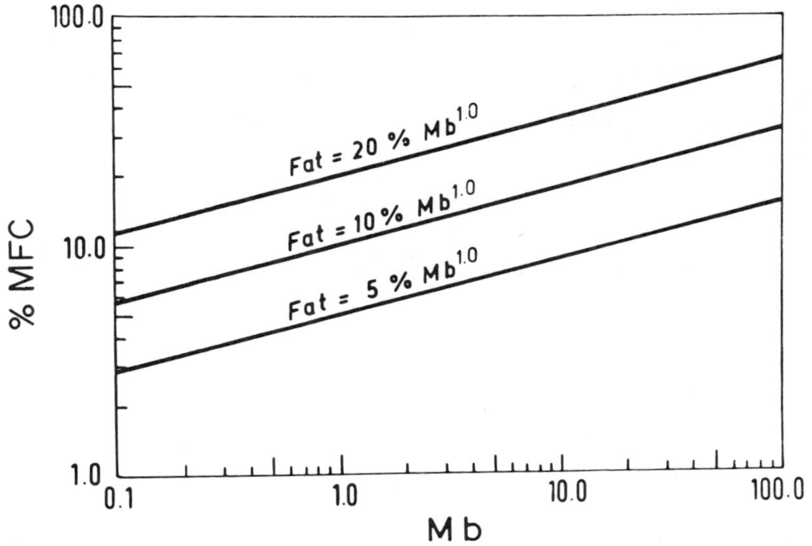

FIGURE 1. Body fat expressed as a function of metabolic rate. Log 1 MFC (metabolic fat content − total body fat calculated as % of body mass to the power 0.75) plotted against log Mb (body mass).

as $\%Mm^{0.75}$ is the effective fat content (%EFC). Thus, to answer the question of how fat an animal is in relation to others, the reply can be based on percentage of Mb fat, if we are interested in anatomical morphometric relationships. For functional comparisons it is more meaningful to relate to the animal's metabolic requirements. This can be done by relating to percentage MFC showing that for a given percentage Mb fat, the larger animal will be fatter if we think of fat in terms of energy storage.

Fat content can also be fitted to the concept of isokinetic behavior as described by Kleiber.[15] If we calculate the fat as $\%Mm^{0.75}$ when deviations in $\dot{V}O_2$/g/hr from the line described by the equation $\dot{V}O_2 = 3.8 \times Mb^{0.75}$ occur, we can fit different patterns into one isokinetic series. Isokinetic behaving animals are those that have rates of intermediary metabolic transfer proportional to metabolic weight $Mb^{0.75}$. Therefore, their turnover is described by the following equation of Kleiber[15]:

$$\text{Turnover rate} = \frac{\text{transfer rate}}{\text{pool content}} = \frac{Mb^{0.75}}{Mb^{1.0}} = k \cdot Mb^{-0.25}$$

On the basis of fat as percentage of Mb, a 200 g rat with 15% fat does not differ from a sand rat with the same dimensions. If we relate body fat to $Mb^{0.75}$ of the animals and determine the percentage MFC, animals with the same dimensions of weight and percentage of body fat retain their similarity. Larger animals with the same percentage of Mb fat will have a larger percentage MFC (Figure 1).

On the basis of percentage EFC, in the case of the 200 g sand rat at room temperature utilizing 0.82 mℓ/O_2/g/hr Mm = 461 g and for an acclimated sand rat utilizing 0.52 mℓ/O_2/g/hr Mm = 2852 g. Thus, 15% fat of Mb in terms of percentage EFC will be 10.03 for the albino rat, 12.35 for the sand rat at room temperature, and 19.49 for the acclimated sand rat. In the case of the 200 g albino rat in which $\dot{V}O_2$/g/hr is close to 1% MFC = %EFC since it fits the line $\dot{V}O_2 = 3.8 \times Mb^{0.75}$.

For the acclimated sand rats in Table 1, percentage of fat is lower than for the room temperature control when calculated as percentage of Mb or as percentage of MFC, but when calculated as percentage EFC the acclimated animal is fatter. Thus, while acclimation and heat treatment may reduce body fat content it does not necessarily reduce the effective fat stores. The elevation of percentage EFC is an interesting feature of desert adaptation synchronizing seasonal reduction of metabolic rate with an alternating fluctuating seasonal capacity to replenish depot fat.

ACKNOWLEDGMENTS

The work was supported by a grant from the Israel Commisson for Basic Research.

REFERENCES

1. **Adler, J. H., Roderig, Ch., and Gutman, A.,** Breeding sand rats (*Psammomys obesus*) with a diabetic predisposition for laboratory investigation, *Rufuah Vet.*, 33, 1, 1976.
2. Association of Official Agricultural Chemists, *Official Methods of Analysis*, AOAC, Washington, D.C., 1973, 356.
3. **Ben Porat, G., Adler, J. H., and Samueloff, S.,** On the thermoregulation in *Psammomys obesus, Meriones crassus* and *Meriones tristrami, Isr. J. Med. Sci.*, 12, 897, 1976.
4. **Blaxter, L. K.,** *The Energy Metabolism of Ruminants*, Hutchinson Scientific & Technical, London, 1967, 88.
5. **Bodenheimer, F. S.,** *Animal Life in Palestine*, L. Mayer, Jerusalem, 1935, 98.
6. **Brody, S.,** *Bioenergetics and Growth*, with special reference to the efficiency complex in domestic animals, Reinhold, New York, 1945, 359.
7. **Daly, M. and Daly, S.,** On the feeding ecology of *Psammomys obesus* (Rodentia, Gerbillidae) in the Wadi Saoura Algeria, *Mammalia*, 37, 548, 1973.
8. **Frenkel, G. and Kraicer, P. F.,** Metabolic pattern of sand rats (*Psammomys obesus*) and rats during fasting, *Life Sci.*, 1(5), 209, 1972.
9. **Gutzeit, A., Renold, A. E., Cerasi, E., and Shafrir, E.,** Effect of diet-induced obesity on glucose and insulin tolerance of a rodent with a low insulin response, *(Acomys cahirinus), Diabetes*, 28(8), 777, 1979.
10. **Harrison, D. L.,** in *The Mammals of Arabia*, Vol. 3, *Lagomorpha, Rodentia*, Ernest Benn, London, 1972, 597.
11. **Horowitz, M., Samueloff, S., and Adler, J. H.,** Acute dehydration: body water distribution in acclimated and non-acclimated *Psammomys obesus, J. Appl. Physiol. Res. Environ. Exercise Physiol.*, 44, 585, 1978.
12. **Jeanrenaud, B.,** Hyperinsulinemia in obesity syndromes: its metabolic consequences and possible etiology, *Metabolism*, 27, 1881, 1978.
13. **Kekwick, A.,** in *Handbook of Physiology, Adipose Tissue*, Section 5, Amercian Physiological Society, Washington, D.C., 1965, 617.
14. **Kleiber, M.,** *The Fire of Life*, John Wiley & Sons, New York, 1961, 177.
15. **Kleiber, K. L.,** in *Energy Metabolism*, Academic Press, New York, 1965, 430.
16. **MacFarlane, W. V.,** Adaptation to environment, in *Handbook of Physiology*, Section 4, American Physiological Society, Washington, D.C., 1964, 509.
17. **Morales, M. F., Rathbun, E. N., Smith, R. E., and Pace, N.,** Studies on body composition, *J. Biol. Chem.*, 158, 677, 1945.
18. **Rathbun, E. and Pace, N.,** Studies on body composition, the determination of total body fat by means of the body specific gravity, *J. Biol. Chem.*, 158, 667, 1945.
19. **Schmidt-Nielsen, K.,** Energy metabolism body size and problems of scaling, *Fed. Proc.*, 29, 1524, 1970.
20. **Schmidt-Nielsen, K.,** in *Animal Physiology, Adaptation and Environment*, Cambridge University Press, London, 1975, 235.
21. **Sheng, H., Russel, P. A., and Huggins, A.,** A review of body composition studies with emphasis on total body water and fat, *Am. J. Clin. Nutr.*, 32, 630, 1979.

Chapter 22

PHYSIOLOGICAL LIMITATIONS TO DAIRY PRODUCTION IN THE SUBTROPICAL CLIMATE OF ISRAEL

A. Berman and D. Wolfenson

TABLE OF CONTENTS

Abstract 188

I. Introduction 188

II. The Path from Past to Present 188

III. The Present Problems 189

IV. Conclusions 193

References 193

ABSTRACT

The attainment of high dairy productivity in a hot climate is initially dependent upon the presence of a breed, the potential genetic productivity of which fits the availability of feeds and their quality, as well as upon the acquisition of proper veterinary care. It is only when these conditions are fulfilled that physiological functions become major factors limiting the rate of production.

In many respects the problems of feed intake and milk production in hot environments can be viewed as if they are part of a heat exchange system comprising animal and ambience. This simplified approach indicates that the solutions to the problems lie in increasing heat loss from the animals. It implies the use of shelter engineering to reduce ambient thermal load and of cooling the animals. The reproductive response to heat stress is not sufficiently clear to enable the formulation of a tentative approach.

I. INTRODUCTION

Dairy cattle productivity is determined by their growth, lactation, and reproduction. These determinants of productivity are the outward expression of a variety of tightly interlaced physiological functions. The maintenance of these functions within certain limits is a prerequisite for the expression of the genetic potential for productivity. It is only when limiting factors are kept at a minimum operating level that diary cattle may reach their maximal productivity.

The limiting factors may lie in the thermal environment, the quantity and quality of feed available to the animals, the extent to which their health is maintained by proper veterinary care, and not the least by the daily management to which they are subjected. It is the combination of all these factors that determines the biological performance of dairy cattle. No less important is the socioeconomic situation, which determines the extent to which environmental and genetic limitations can be reduced to attain high productivity.

The part played by the different factors in limiting productivity obviously changes with the characteristics of the environment as expressed in its climatic and nutritional features. It is the purpose of this chapter to depict the path followed by the development of dairy production in Israel, from about 60 years ago to the present, to refer to some of the production problems and to examine some aspects of the scientific dilemmas encountered when trying to reduce the factors limiting dairy cattle productivity.

II. THE PATH FROM PAST TO PRESENT

Dairy production in Israel is now above 9000 kg milk per cow per year, one of the highest in the world. Its development to the present state occurred over a period of close to 60 years. It was characterized by significant changes in attitudes to the nature of the factors limiting performance of dairy cattle in a subtropical climate. The initial concept was that breeds which evolved in a region carry physiological attributes that provide them with better adaptability to the local environment. Of the breeds endogenous to the region, the different strains of the Syrian breed were the closest to the dairy type. The milk production of these strains was low (300 to 1000 kg per cow per year), however, and efforts to increase it were not successful. The alternative approach of introducing temperate zone breeds met with harsh results, as the animals died of diseases which were thought at that time to be due to tropical degeneration. It took a number of years for veterinary care to reach the stage of knowledge required to prevent tick-transmitted diseases from being production-limiting factors.

To increase productivity, Holstein bulls were used for breeding the cows. Thereby crosses were obtained which were increasingly closer to the temperate zone breeds in their characteristics. Dairy production thus gradually increased.[1] During this period, the housing system changed, as loose housing was adopted instead of the closed-barn types introduced from Europe that were previously used. This change in the nature of the shelters considerably reduced the thermal load to which animals were exposed, to about 50% of the outdoor radiant heat load.[2] Also, increasing amounts of concentrates were used in the ration, which reduces the metabolic heat produced, and consequently improves dairy cow performance in hot weather.[3]

At this stage, which was attained soon after the end of World War II, the question of the adaptability of the crossbred animals to the local climate and their possible superiority over temperate zone breeds had to be examined. This question became critical, due to the large inflow of refugees from Europe into Israel, whose food requirements could not be met by the natural growth of the cattle population. The feasibility of importing temperate zone cattle to supply these food requirements was unknown. Their adaptability to the local climate became of crucial importance. By that time, the crossbred dairy cattle in Israel reached up to ten generations of crossing back to the Holstein breed.

A study carried out at that time[4] indicated that in the crossbred cattle the degree of relationship to the temperate zone breeds did not affect the thermoregulatory reactions of the animals; this was true for minimal and peak rectal temperatures as well as for their diurnal changes. It was also true for respiratory rates, sweating rates,[5] and hair coat characteristics such as hair fiber diameter, length, and weight per unit surface.[6] Neither were affected by the seasonal changes in these parameters of adaptability to the climate. All these comparisons were carried out at similar production levels. An effect of milk level production on rectal temperatures was evident, however, in that they gradually increased with rising milk yield. All these strongly indicated that resistance to heat stress is unlikely to be a characteristic of breeds enogenous to warm and hot climates, but it is probably due to their low productivity and lack of response to improved environments. The outcome of economic necessities and of the results of that study was the import of large numbers of cattle from the U.S. These formed the backbone of the present dairy industry.

III. THE PRESENT PROBLEMS

The present state is that practically all dairy cattle are artificially inseminated and progeny testing of the sires is the rule. Food is freely available to the animals in a ration that contains about 70% concentrate feeds. Therefore, neither feed quantity not its quality are likely to be the main factors limiting milk production and fertility. In these conditions, environmental factors play a marked role in limiting the productivity of dairy cattle. The variation between months of the year was shown to be the largest factor of variance for both milk production[7] and fertility[8] second only to differences between herds. The decrease in fertility in summer is mostly due to the adverse effect of the summer on the cows rather than on the potential fertility of the semen.[9] Thus, the problem is to define the factors responsible for this seasonal reduction in milk production and fertility.

The depression of both milk production and fertility occurs in mid-summer and extends into the late fall (Figures 1 and 2). This adds little support to the possibility that the depression of productivity is caused by the seasonal changes in photoperiod, although photoperiod was shown to affect both milk production and endocrine responses in dairy cattle at higher latitudes.[10] The direct effects of thermal stress also are unlikely to be solely responsible for the seasonal effects on productivity, as its depression extends into late fall, a time at which ambient temperatures are not likely to affect productivity. It is probable that this seasonal pattern is caused by an interaction of direct and indirect effects of heat stress on milk production and reproduction.

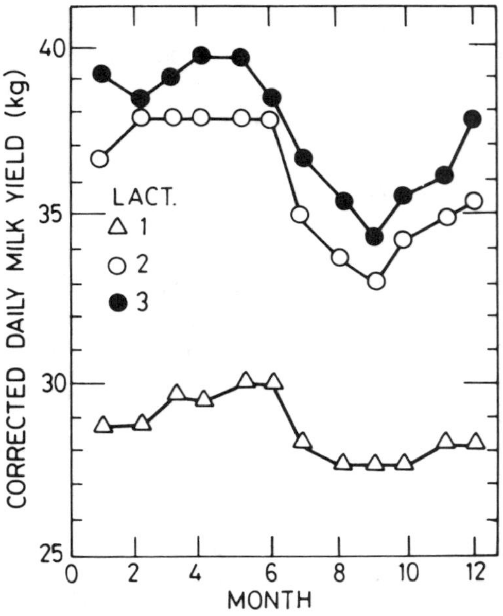

FIGURE 1. Monthly changes in milk production at the time of first insemination (about 75 days postpartum) in kibutzim in 1984. Yields corrected for herds and sires effects. Symbols: △ — first lactations, ○ — second lactations, ● — third and later lactations.

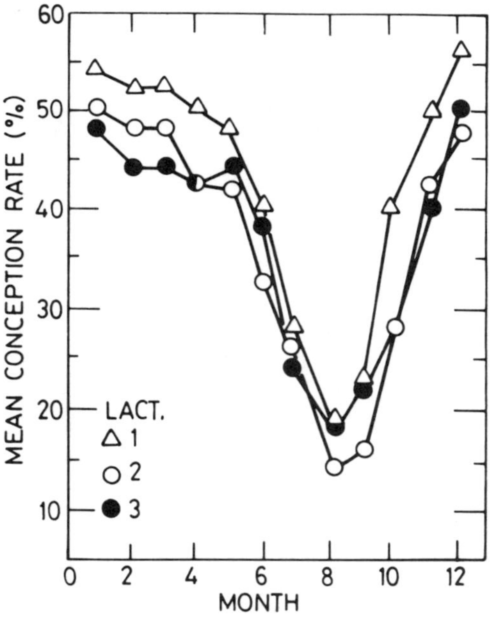

FIGURE 2. Monthly changes in conception rates from first inseminations at about 75 days postpartum in kibutzim in 1984. Data corrected for herds, sires, and inseminators effects. Symbols: △ — first lactations, ○ — second lactations, ● — third and later lactations.

A number of studies were carried out in the near natural conditions of the commercial herds to determine the direct effects of climate. These were assessed by the diurnal changes in thermal state of cows in different seasons. They indicated that at air temperatures of about 25°C, the combined radiant and convective heat loss are reduced to 50% of the values at 8°C, the animals becoming increasingly dependent upon evaporative heat loss to dissipate their metabolic heat production.[11] The latent heat equivalent of mean maximal evaporation rate of high producing cows was only about half the heat produced by a 30 kg milk-producing cow.[12] This entails that the evaporative capacity of the dairy animal might maintain normal body temperature at moderate ambient temperatures, but it is not sufficient for the high producing dairy cow. These studies indicated that in summer marked diurnal increase of about 1.2°C in rectal temperatures prevails in contrast to the only small changes occurring in the winter. It should be mentioned that even in the winter (10 to 20°C) body temperature stability is attained by activation of skin water loss at noon to the maximal levels reached in the summer.[12,13] It also indicated that ambient temperatures of 24 to 26°C seemingly are the upper limit at which high producing dairy cows maintain body temperature stability.[14]

The consequences of body temperature rises are first evident in their effect on feed intake and energy turnover. On calculating data of other studies[15,16] it was found that a 1°C increase in rectal temperature is associated with a reduction of about 3.0 kg TDN in feed intake. The reduction in feed intake is, however, only partly compensated by the increase in food digestibility associated with it.[17] Both the reduction in food intake and the increase in digestibility are probably related to the lower ruminal motor activity and increased retention time of digesta in the intestinal tract of ruminants.[18,19] As the change in ruminal activity upon exposure to heat takes about 1 hr to develop,[20] it is presumably related to the concomitant change in body temperature. Metabolic rate also is inversely related to rectal temperature changes within the day as well as between seasons; the seasonal increase in mean rectal temperature was associated with a 20% reduction in mean daily metabolic rate.[21]

An effect of milk production level on the rectal temperature of the high producing dairy cow was also observed.[14] That effect was to be expected in view of the heat increment of lactation. It is thus possible that the increased body temperature which occurs during peak lactation might play also a role in limiting appetite below the nutritional requirements at this period, especially so in the summer. It should be stressed, however, that a milk production depressing effect of higher than normal body temperatures was evident even when cows were force fed via a ruminal fistula the amount of food refused, so that their food intake equaled the amount eaten at comfort conditions.[22] These results strongly indicate that even when food quantity and quality are adequate and indoor fed so that they do not have to be sought in a sun-exposed pasture, body temperature probably is a major limiting factor for dairy cow productivity in warm climates.

In this context, another response of the dairy cow should be considered. A marked increase in water intake was reported in cows exposed for short periods to high ambient temperatures in climatic chambers; the increment in water intake was much beyond the increase in water requirements due to enhanced water losses.[23] This increase in water intake serves the purpose of reducing body temperature through the ingestion of a relatively cool mass of a high heat capacity. This increase in water intake is associated with marked increases in urine output, but the overall result is the onset of hemodilution, reflected in both lower hematocrit and plasma protein concentration.[17] These two studies were carried out on cows producing about 10 to 15 kg milk per day. Preliminary results of a study in progress carried out on high producing cows (35 to 40 kg milk per day) in normal management conditions[24] indicated that in cows stressed by summer heat a 20% increase in water intake vs. that in cooled cows (123 vs. 103 ℓ/day) was associated with a 10% reduction in hematocrit values, supporting the findings in the previously mentioned studies carried out in cows exposed to acute heat stress in climatic chambers. In the field study it was found that the milk produced by the heat-stressed cows was diluted similar to the changes in hematocrit. It is not clear whether the increased water output in milk represents but another avenue of excess water disposal, or an impairment of milk formation processes.

The effect of ambient temperature on fertility is by far a more complex one, due to the multifactorial nature of fertility, the interaction between direct and indirect effects, as well as the extended period required for the establishment of a lasting pregnancy. A large number of studies indicated marked sensitivity of fertility to ambient temperature. The following assessment of reproductive responses to heat stress relates specifically to animals exposed to the natural sequence of climate, to avoid the complications due to acute exposure to climatic chamber conditions, in which acclimation modifies the response of the animals.

It was shown that the decrease in fertility during chronic exposure to seasonally high ambient temperatures is due to the interruption of pregnancy in its early stages.[25] As progesterone is considered be a major determinant of pregnancy maintenance in its early stages, the effects of heat stress on its systemic levels were extensively studied.

The effects of heat stress on progesterone levels are evident in both seasonal changes and within a season between animals exposed to different intensities of heat stress. In cycling lactating animals exposed to the seasonal changes in climate, luteal phase progesterone levels were higher in summer than in winter in one study,[26] while the reverse was found in another study,[27] but no such seasonal difference was found in beef animals.[28]

In studies carried out in lactating cows exposed to the outdoor summer climate and in which heat stress intensity was varied by management means, progesterone levels increased with heat stress in the southern U.S.,[30] while the reverse was true in other studies in Israel[30,31] and in Guadeloupe,[32] however, in these cases fertility is markedly depressed in summer. One could assume that this difference in the effects of heat stress might be due to the difference in milk production of the animals, since in the U.S. studies milk yield of experimental animals was considerably lower than in the studies carried out in Israel (10 to 20 vs. 30 to 40 kg/day). This difference in response might be due to the effect of lactation per se on the progesterone response to heat stress. A comparison of lactating and dry nonpregnant cows[26] indicated a seasonal summer reduction in progesterone in dry nonpregnant cows in Arizona and the opposite response in lactating cows. However, in studies carried out in Israel and in Guadeloupe progesterone levels were lower during heat stress in both lactating[30-32] and dry pregnant cows.[24]

This apparent contradiction might be related to the times of bleeding the animals. A diurnal increase in progesterone levels was shown, which correlated with rectal temperature increases.[31] In the studies carried out in Israel and Guadeloupe, the animals were bled in the morning, while in the U.S studies they were bled close to noon, when body temperatures are close to maximal. As the intensity of the environmental heat stress was higher in the U.S. studies, it might be presumed that it induced an increase in progesterone levels. The origin of this increased progesterone might be extraluteal, probably from the adrenal cortex, resulting from incomplete adrenal cortical conversion of progesterone to cortisol, and this was reflected in the lower concurrent cortisol levels.[33] This was suggested on the basis of the negative relationship between cortisol and progesterone in heat-stressed heifers.[34] However, in lactating cows, cortisol and progesterone levels were highly correlated with each other and with rectal temperature.[31] No significant increase in progesterone levels was found in heat-stressed steers[35] and only a very small increase (of about 0.2 to 0.4 ng/mℓ) in dairy cows was found on the day of estrus.[31,36] These findings leave open the question of the origin of the increase in progesterone during heat stress.

It should be emphasized that in the aforementioned studies the changes in progesterone were on the order of 1 to 1.5 ng/mℓ. It might be questioned whether a reduction in progesterone of this magnitude is critical for the maintenance of pregnancy. If physiologically significant by itself, the effect of such a reduction in progesterone level should presumably be apparent also in normal conditions, in the absence of heat stress. The difference in progesterone levels after insemination between pregnant and nonpregnant or noninseminated animals would be an index of the significance of a 1 to 1.5 ng/mℓ difference in progesterone levels between heat-stressed and nonheat-stressed animals. Levels of progesterone in pregnant cows were higher than those of nonpregnant animals by about 1 ng/mℓ from day 7 to 12 after estrus; the difference increased to about 2 ng/mℓ on day 16 after estrus.[37,38] Conception rates were higher in animals with a higher progesterone level during the first 8 to 9 days after insemination.[39,40] Other studies reported no dependence of embryo presence or embryo normality upon progesterone levels.[31,41,42] It is possible that the variance in results depends upon the criteria used to screen nonpregnant cycles as normal cycles for comparison of their progesterone levels with those of the pregnant animals. At their best, these data do not allow negation of the possibility that the aforementioned climate-induced reductions in progesterone levels might affect maintenance of pregnancy. The meaning of the increases in progesterone on heat stress and their effect on early pregnancy maintenance is not clear. It is possible that the impairment of reproduction in cows exposed to heat stress is also due to alteration of other functions.

IV. CONCLUSIONS

At the onset of summer it is likely that the direct effects of heat predominate depressing fertility, food intake, and milk production. Evidence from herd feed intake data in Israel[43] indicates that high producing cows continue to produce normal amounts of milk in the summer, while their food consumption is depressed. An extended period of low feed intake during the summer probably creates a situation in which body stores are increasingly depleted. As a result, during the summer a nutritional stress probably forms in high producing dairy cows and increases in intensity, to reach its peak in the fall. This nutritional stress is superimposed over the thermal stress, which decreases in the fall. The combined effect of nutritional and thermal stresses is thus likely to be maximal at the end of summer. This might explain the fact that peak milk production, which is attained about 3 to 4 weeks after parturition, is lower in the fall than in early summer. These factors as a whole would tend to extend the duration of the effects of summer heat stress beyond the actual duration of the summer.

A variety of means is available and more are being developed to alleviate the stress of the heat. These are decisions which have to be evaluated for their usefulness in economic terms, since they have to be used in the agricultural system. In this context, research should aim to define the phases of the lactation and reproductive cycles which are more sensitive to the stress of heat. Alleviation of heat stress at these phases would be the more efficient economically.

REFERENCES

1. **Hirsch, S. and Schindler, H.,** The Syrian and the Dutch-Friesian cattle and their crosses in Israel, *Ktavim,* 7, 1, 1957 (in Hebrew).
2. **Rosen, J., Berman, A., and Volcani, R.,** The microclimate in an open shed in the Coastal Plain of Israel, *Isr. J. Agric. Res.,* 11, 211, 1961.
3. **Leighton, R. E. and Rupel, I. W.,** Effects of fiber content of the ration on milk productions and hot weather discomfort of producing dairy cows, *J. Dairy Sci.,* 39, 937, 1956.
4. **Berman, A.,** Thermoregulatory Reactions of Holstein-Syrian Crosses, Ph.D. thesis, Hebrew University, Jerusalem, 1958.
5. **Berman, A.,** Influence of some factors on the relative evaporation rate from the skin of cattle, *Nature (London),* 179, 1256, 1957.

6. **Berman, A. and Volcani, R.,** Seasonal and regional variations in coat characteristics of dairy cattle, *Aust. J. Agric. Res.,* 12, 528, 1961.
7. **Bar-Anan, R. and Genizi, A.,** The effects of lactation, pregnancy and calendar month on milk records, *Anim. Prod.,* 33, 281, 1981.
8. **Ron, M., Bar-Anan, R., and Wiggans, G. R.,** Factors affecting conception rate of Israeli Holstein cattle, *J. Dairy Sci.,* 67, 854, 1984.
9. **Amir, D., Bar-El, M., Kalay, D., and Schindler, H.,** The contribution of bulls and cows to the seasonal differences in the fertility of dairy cattle in Israel, *Anim. Reprod. Sci.,* 5, 93, 1982.
10. **Tucker, H. A., Petitclerc, D., and Zinn, S. A.,** The influence of photoperiod on body weight gain, body composition, nutrient intake and hormone secretion, *J. Anim. Sci.,* 59, 1610, 1984.
11. **Berman, A. and Meltzer, A.,** Critical temperature in lactating dairy cattle: a new approach to an old problem, *Int. J. Biometerol.,* 17, 167, 1973.
12. **Berman, A. and Morag, M.,** Nychthemeral patterns of thermoregulation in high producing cows in a hot-dry near natural climate, *Aust. J. Agric. Res.,* 22, 671, 1971.
13. **Berman, A.,** Thermoregulation in intensity lactating cows in near natural conditions, *J. Physiol. (London),* 215, 477, 1971.
14. **Berman, A., Folman, Y., Kaim, M., Herz, Z., Wolfenson, D., Arieli, A., and Gramber, Y.,** Upper critical temperatures and forced ventilation effects for high yielding dairy cows in a subtropical climate, *J. Dairy Sci.,* 68, 1488, 1985.
15. **Johnson, H. D., Ragsdale, A. C., Berry, I. C., and Shanklin, M. D.,** Effect of various temperature humidity combinations including influence of acclimation on feed and water intake of Holstein cattle, *Univ. Mo. Agric. Exp. Stn. Res. Bull.,* 846, 1963.
16. **Kibler, H. H.,** Thermal effects of various temperature-humidity combinations on Holstein cattle as measured by eight physiological variables, *Univ. Mo. Agric. Exp. Stn. Res. Bull.,* 862, 1964.
17. **McDowell, R. E., Moody, E. G., Van Soest, P. J., Lehmann, R. P., and Ford, G. L.,** Effect of heat stress on energy and water utilization of lactating cows, *J. Dairy Sci.,* 52, 188, 1969.
18. **Atterby, J. T. and Johnson, H. D.,** Effects of environmental temperature, controlled feeding and fasting on rumen motility, *J. Anim. Sci.,* 29, 734, 1969.
19. **Waren, W. P., Martz, F. A., Asay, K. H., Hildebrand, E. S., Payne, C. G., and Vogt, J. R.,** Digestibility and rate of passage by steers fed tall fescue, alfalfa and orchard hay in 18 and 32°C ambient temperatures, *J. Anim. Sci.,* 39, 93, 1974.
20. **Gonyou, H. W., Christopherson, R. J., and Young, B. A.,** Effects of cold exposure on some aspects of behaviour of feedlot cattle, *Appl. Anim. Ethol.,* 5, 1123, 1979.
21. **Berman, A.,** Nychthemeral and seasonal patterns of thermoregulation in cattle, *Aust. J. Agric. Res.,* 19, 181, 1968.
22. **Wayman, O., Johnson, H. D., Merilan, C. P., and Berry, I. L.,** Effect of ad libitum or forced feeding of two rations on lactating dairy cows exposed to temperature stress, *J. Dairy Sci.,* 45, 1472, 1962.
23. **Thompson, H. J., Worstell, D. M., and Brody, S.,** Influence of temperature, 50 to 105°F, on water consumption in dairy cattle, *Univ. Mo. Agric. Exp. Stn. Res. Bull.,* 436, 1949.
24. **Flamenbaum, I., Wolfenson, D., and Berman, A.,** unpublished results, 1985.
25. **Stott, G. H. and Williams, R. J.,** Causes of low breeding efficiency in dairy cattle associated with seasonal high ambient temperatures, *J. Dairy Sci.,* 45, 1369, 1962.
25a. **Collier, R. J., Doelger, S. G., Head, H. H., Thatcher, W. W., and Wilcox, C. J.,** Effects of heat stress during pregnancy on maternal hormone concentrations, calf birth weight and postpartum milk yield of dairy cows, *J. Anim. Sci.,* 54, 309, 1982.
26. **Wolff-Vaught, L., Monty, D. E., and Foote, W. C.,** Effect of summer heat stress on serum luteinizing hormone and progesterone values in Holstein-Friesian cows in Arizona, *Am. J. Vet. Res.,* 38, 1027, 1977.
27. **Rosenberg, M., Herz, Z., Davidson, M., and Folman, Y.,** Seasonal variations in plasma progesterone and conception in primiparous and multiparous dairy cows, *J. Reprod. Fertil.,* 51, 363, 1977.
28. **Rhodes, R. C., Randel, R. D., and Long, C. R.,** Corpus luteum in the bovine: in vivo and in vitro evidence for both a seasonal and breedtype effect, *J. Anim. Sci.,* 55, 159, 1982.
29. **Thatcher, W. W.,** Effects of season, climate and temperature on reproduction and lactation, *J. Dairy Sci.,* 57, 360, 1974.
30. **Rosenberg, M., Folman, Y., Herz, Z., Flamenbaum, I., Berman, A., and Kaim, M.,** Effect of climatic conditions on peripheral concentrations of LH, progesterone and oestradiol-17B in high milk yielding cows, *J. Reprod. Fertil.,* 66, 139, 1982.
31. **Erk, H.,** Physiological, Productive and Reproductive Responses to Heat Stress Relief in Dairy Cows, M. Sc. thesis, Hebrew University, Jerusalem, 1985.
32. **Gauthier, D.,** Technique permettant d'ameliorer la fertilite des femelles francaises frisonnes pie noire (FFPN) en climat tropical. Influence sur l'evolution de la progesterone plasmatique, *Reprod. Nutr. Dev.,* 23, 129, 1983.

33. **Abilay, T. A., Johnson, H. D., and Madan, M.,** Influence of environmental heat on peripheral plasma progesterone and cortisol during the bovine estrus cycle, *J. Dairy Sci.*, 58, 1836, 1975.
34. **Abilay, T. A., Johnson, H. D., and Seif, S.,** The effect of acute heat exposure on plasma cortisol and progesterone response of Zebu and Scotch Highland heifers, *Phillip. J. Vet. Anim. Sci.*, 1, 84, 1975.
35. **Abilay, T. A., Mitra, R., and Johnson, H. D.,** Plasma cortisol and total progestin levels in Holstein steers during acute exposure to high environmental temperature conditions, *J. Anim. Sci.*, 41, 113, 1975.
36. **Dunlap, S. E. and Vincent, C. K.,** Influence of postbreeding thermal stress on conception rate in dairy cattle, *J. Anim. Sci.*, 32, 1216, 1971.
37. **Lukaszewska, J. and Hansel, W.,** Corpus luteum maintenance during early pregnancy in the cow, *J. Reprod. Fertil.*, 59, 485, 1980.
38. **Fonseca, F. A., Britt, J. H., McDaniel, B. T., Wilk, J. C., and Rakes, A. H.,** Reproductive traits of Holsteins and Jerseys. Effects of age, milk yield, and clinical abnormalities on involution of cervix and uterus, ovulation, estrous cycles, detection of estrus, conception rate and days open, *J. Dairy Sci.*, 66, 1128, 1983.
39. **Remsen, L. G., Roussel, J. D., and Karihaloo, A. K.,** Pregnancy rates relating to plasma progesterone levels in recipient heifers at day of transfer, *Theriogenology*, 18, 365, 1982.
40. **Rosenberg, M., Kaim, M., and Folman, Y.,** Three treatments for estrus synchronization in dairy cows — a comparison of their effects on progesterone concentrations and fertility, *Proc. 10th Int. Congr. Anim. Reprod. Artificial Insemination*, 1984, 346.
41. **Maurer, R. R. and Echternkamp, S. E.,** Hormonal asynchrony and embryonic development, *Theriogenology*, 17, 11, 1982.
42. **Linares, T., Larsson, K., and Edqvist, L. E.,** Plasma progesterone levels from oestrus through day 7 after A.I. in heifers carrying embryos with normal or deviating morphology, *Theriogeneology*, 17, 125, 1982.
43. **Remer, Y.,** personal communication.

Chapter 23

DISPLACEMENT OF THERMAL NEUTRALITY IN THE ARTIFICIAL ACCLIMATED AND SEASONAL ACCLIMATIZED DOMESTIC FOWL

Amichai Arieli

TABLE OF CONTENTS

I. Introduction 198

II. Thermoneutral Zone 198

III. Acclimatization and Acclimation in the Domestic Fowl 198

References 202

I. INTRODUCTION

Homeothermic animals differ from one another in qualitative and quantitative characteristics of the thermoregulatory mechanisms. This variance stems from wide morphological and functional differences between animals. It is also due to the large diversity in their habitats.

II. THERMONEUTRAL ZONE

According to the mode of activation of heat loss and heat production mechanisms, the ambient temperature spectrum might be divided into three zones:[1]

1. The cold zone, in which heat loss mechanisms are activated minimally and heat production varies in accordance with thermostatic needs
2. The hot zone, in which evaporative heat loss is activated while heat production is moderately raised
3. The thermoneutral zone, in which heat production is minimal and constant, and sensible heat loss is activated according to needs

The thermoneutral zone is limited by two critical temperatures. The lower critical temperature (T_{cl}) is the ambient temperature at which heat production starts to rise due to cooling, and by the upper critical temperature (T_{cu}) above which heat production rises with increasing ambient temperature, and at which heat loss mechanisms (mainly evaporation) are activated vigorously. In the domestic fowl evaporation originates mainly in the respiratory tract.

A permanent change in the nature of the environment causes reactions which are aimed toward a long-run improvement in the ability of the animal to withstand the new environment. Thus, due to chronic changes in ambient temperature there are morphological modifications (e.g., changes in insulation), functional modifications (e.g., a transfer from shivering to a nonshivering thermogenic mechanism, NST), and regulatory modifications (a delay or an advance of the activation of thermoregulatory responses).[2]

According to the nature of the chronic exposure a distinction can be made between acclimatization and acclimation.[3] During acclimatization an animal is exposed to a complex of environmental changes, such as the transition from winter to summer, which is characterized by changes in air temperature, photoperiod, and availability of nutrients. In the acclimation process only one environmental variable is modified, for example, a change in air temperature in a controlled climatic chamber.

III. ACCLIMATIZATION AND ACCLIMATION IN THE DOMESTIC FOWL

The purpose of the present study is to compare the effects of seasonal acclimatization to that of artificial acclimation on displacement of thermal neutrality of the domestic fowl.

The experiment was carried out in mature light laying fowls, a crossbreed of White Leghorn and Rhode Island Red, with a mean body weight of 2 kg. The laying rate was 50% and the animals were fed *ad libitum* a standard commercial mixture. The effect of seasonal acclimatization was tested in fowls which were raised in an open shed in individual cages. Over a 4-year period the responses to climate in these animals were measured in different seasons in ten experimental periods. Mean daily temperature in the winter was 13°C, whereas the mean daily temperature in summer was 26°C. The amplitude of mean daily ambient temperature was 12°C. The lighting regime was 14 to 16 hr of light per day.

These animals were also artificially acclimated under food and light conditions that were similar to the shed conditions for a period of 1 to 2 months. Heat acclimation was performed

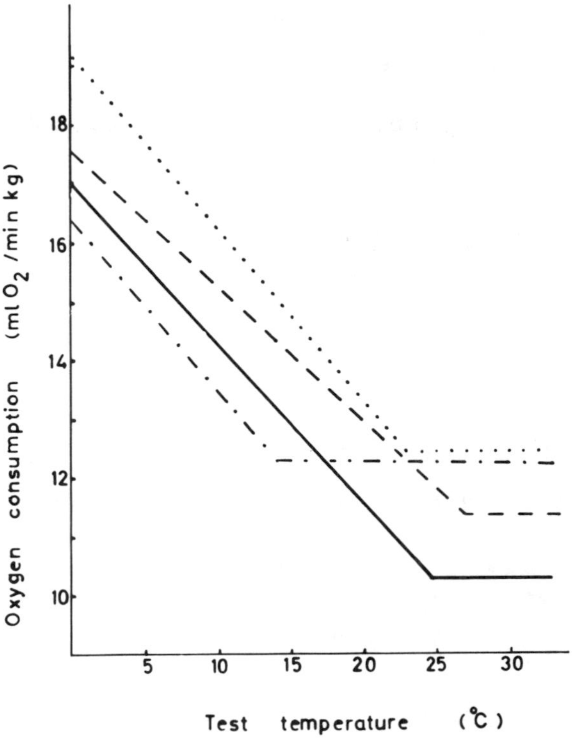

FIGURE 1. MMR and T_{cl} in acclimated and seasonal acclimatized domestic fowls. Data for the seasonal acclimatized animals were obtained from regression analyses of MMR and T_{cl} on adaptation temperatures.[4,5] Depicted are estimates for a typical summer (———, mean daily temperature 26°C) and winter (—•—•—•, 13°C) in Israel's coastal shore, and for 1 month cold (• • • •, 5°C) and heat (— — — —, 28°C) acclimated fowls.

by exposing winter fowls to 28°C, and cold acclimation was performed by exposing summer fowls to 5°C. Thermoregulatory indices, namely oxygen consumption, respiratory rate, and body temperature of these animals were measured in the laboratory under ambient temperatures ranging from 2° to 32°C. Details are presented elsewhere.[4,5]

A comparison between oxygen consumption of fowls acclimatized to winter or summer shows that acclimatization to summer is followed by a reduction of 20% ($p < 0.001$) in minimal metabolic rate (MMR) concomitantly with a rightward shift of 10°C ($p < 0.001$) in the lower critical temperature.

The possibility that the mean daily temperature, which deviates by ±6°C in a daily cycle, can serve as a reliable index of the acclimatization temperature was examined. Highly significant correlations ($p < 0.001$) were found between mean daily temperature and T_{cl} or MMR (data from ten different seasons). This suggests that mean daily temperature may serve as a genuine index of the acclimatization temperature despite its daily fluctuation or its seasonal variation. Regression analysis of these relationships indicated that an increase of 1°C in the acclimatization temperature brought about a decrease of 1.3% in MMR and to an increase of 0.85°C in T_{cl} (Figure 1).

On the other hand, cold acclimation for 1 month was followed by a similar 1% increase in MMR per 1°C decrease in acclimation temperature ($p < 0.01$), but no change in T_{cl} resulted. Heat acclimation was followed by a much smaller (0.5%) decrease of MMR per

Table 1
THE EFFECT OF DURATION OF ACCLIMATION TO COLD ON MMR AND T_{cl} IN DOMESTIC FOWLS

Acclimation period	MMR (mℓ O_2/min/kg)	T_{cl} (°C)
Control	11.3 + 0.5	17.6 + 1.3
1 month	13.0 + 0.6[a]	18.2 + 1.2
2 month	12.4 + 0.4	12.4 + 1.5[a]

Note: Data are means and S.E. (N = B).

[a] A significant difference (p <0.05) in comparison with control.

1°C increase in acclimation temperature, and T_{cl} was shifted rightward by a 0.87°C/1°C increase in acclimation temperature (p <0.01), similar to what occurred on seasonal acclimatization. Such changes in T_{cl} have considerable energetic implications. Therefore, it is noteworthy that summer and a 1-month period of heat acclimation have similar effects on the displacement of T_{cl}, while a 1-month period of cold acclimation differs from winter acclimation (Figure 1).

In heat-acclimated fowl, energy budget was the most economical, as these animals are always within the thermoneutral zone. In the naturally acclimated fowl, T_{cl} was always close to the mean daily ambient temperature. During most of the 24-hr cycle these animals are therefore exposed to thermoneutral conditions, and only during the coldest hours of the night would heat production be expected to increase by up to 15% above MMR. On the other hand, the 5°C acclimated fowl continuously dwells below T_{cl}. This is an expansive pleasure, as in order to maintain homeothermy metabolic rate has to increase by about 40% above MMR.

Two factors may contribute to a displacement of T_{cl}: changes in MMR and insulation. About 60% of the leftward shift of T_{cl} in the winter acclimatized fowl is explained by an increase in MMR, while the remaining 40% has to be explained by an improved insulation in the cold season. Likewise, in the heat-acclimated fowl, 65% of the displacement in T_{cl} is explained by decreased insulation and 35% are due to decreased metabolic rate.

In contrast, in the cold-acclimated fowl during 1 month of acclimation, the increase in MMR was not associated with a significant change in T_{cl}. This might be interpreted as a decrease in insulation. A rather unexpected decrease in insulation might originate in a sluggish development of heat conservation under constant cold conditions. As an increased blood supply is needed for the supply of nutrients to the skin cells, for growth of feather, the period of feather development might be associated with an increased heat loss.[6]

Such a possibility was tested by exposing these animals to a cold (5°C) environment for 2 months (Table 1). A decreased MMR and a leftward shift of T_{cl} (in comparison with a 1 month cold-acclimated fowl) are compatible with slower development of insulation under a constant cold.

Differences in efficiency of insulation might also be induced by a functional alteration, for instance, shift from shivering to nonshivering thermogenesis.[7] This might be related to the fact that shivering increases convective heat loss to the surroundings.

The possibility that changes in insulation by a chronic exposure to cold in the fowl might also be induced by a functional modification was investigated in this study. For this purpose the integrated electromyographic activity of leg muscles was measured concomitantly with oxygen consumption of summer and 2 month cold-acclimated fowls exposed to air temperatures ranging between 25° and 2°C. Details are presented elsewhere.[8] In both the cold acclimated fowls and summer controls, acute cold exposure induced an increased oxygen consumption which was linearly related ($p < 0.01$) to the increased EMG activity. Hence, it appears that in the domestic fowl shivering is the predominant means of thermogenesis regardless of the acclimation status. In other words, in this animal the displacement of T_{cl} is not influenced by a functional alteration of heat production mechanisms. Hence, increased insulation and metabolism account mainly for the falling T_{cl} under chronic cold.

It appears that there may exist several indices for T_{cu}.[9] In the present study the T_{cu} was estimated by the air temperature at which respiratory frequency increased above 60 respirations per minute and at which body temperature increased by 0.3°C above that at the T_{cl}.[5] An increase in acclimatization temperature by 1°C was associated with an increase in 0.27 in T_{cu} ($p < 0.01$).

In contrast, artificial acclimation to heat or cold (1 and 2 months) had no significant effect on T_{cu}. Hence, it appears that only limited changes in T_{cu} occur on acclimatization to summer as well as on heat acclimation. This may indicate that in the well-insulated domestic fowl changes in vasomotor activity are less important. It may also be that the present adaptation temperatures (26°C as a mean daily temperature in summer or 28°C as a constant heat) were not severe enough to induce sharp changes in evaporative heat loss. These temperatures, however, are typical of the local climate.

That the changes in T_{cu} were small as compared with that of T_{cl} may imply that the adaptive modifications which take place during acclimatization in the fowl are mainly insulative and metabolic. Such a conclusion is in line with the excellent insulation of these animals.

What is the potential of adaptation to heat conditions in the domestic fowl, a descendant of the jungle fowl? From combining the estimates of T_{cl} and T_{cu} (Figure 2) as functions of the acclimatization temperature, it is obvious that the thermoneutral zone is wider in winter than in summer. Extrapolation of these estimates demonstrates that the two critical temperatures would essentially coincide at an acclimatization temperature of 32°C, which actually means conditions of 26°C at night and 38°C at noon. Under such conditions the potentials of vasomotor and metabolic rate are apparently exhausted.

Hence, it is probably impossible for a producing fowl to maintain homeothermy in an acclimatization temperature above 32°C. It is noteworthy that by plotting T_{cu} and T_{cl} against constant acclimation temperature, the extrapolation lines coincide at 35°C. Thus 35° to 38°C might be regarded as the maximal tolerated temperature at which homeothermy and productivity can be maintained. In the present study egg production contributed to metabolic rate a strain that was equal to half the maintenance level. Higher laying rate would probably reduce the tolerated temperature. Ambient temperatures of 30° to 32°C are regarded as the upper limit for the laying fowl in commercial flocks.[10]

In this regard the fowl contrasts with man in which increased metabolic activity, through muscular exercise, for example, improves heat tolerance.[11] This difference probably underlines the importance of insulation in the energy balance of the fowl. The lack of ability to sweat and a diminished vasomotor activity also act to reduce potential of heat adaptation.

The excellent insulation is probably related also to lack of NST in the fowl as well as in other birds. Brown fat is recognized as an important source of NST. This tissue is absent in the whole class of birds.[12] Brown adipose tissue also probably has a role in the dietary regulatory mechanism for heat dissipation.[13] Such a mechanism obviously has a negative economical significance and is also a disadvantage under hot climate conditions. Whether such a dietary regulatory mechanism exists in the fowl and has influence on thermal neutrality must be investigated further.

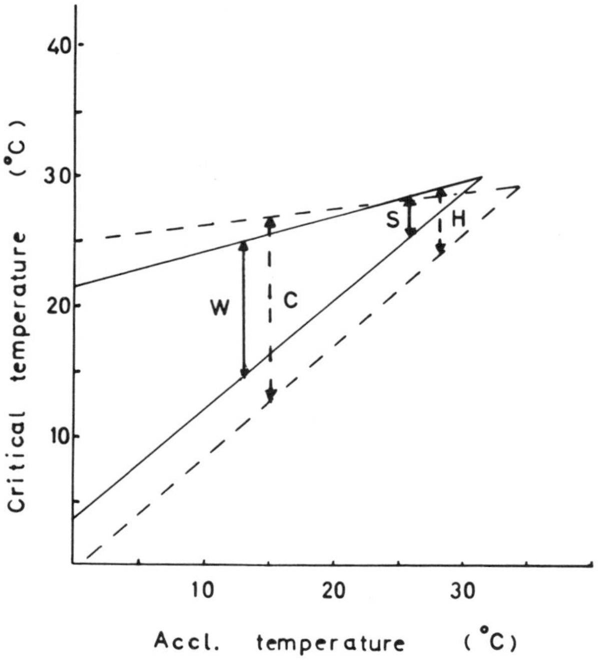

FIGURE 2. Potential of adaptation to heat in summer acclimatized and in heat acclimated fowls. Lines depict lower and upper critical temperatures as a function of the adaptation temperatures. Solid lines denote seasonal acclimatization (data from a 4-year survey), broken lines denote artificial acclimation to heat. Arrows indicate thermoneutral zone at the adaptation temperature: winter (W), summer (S); heat-acclimated fowls (H), and their winter controls (C).

REFERENCES

1. **Mount, L. E.,** *Adaptation to Thermal Environment,* Edward Arnold, London, 1979, 14.
2. **Hensel, H., Bruck, K., and Raths, R.,** Homeothermic organisms, in *Temperature and Life,* Precht, H., Christopherson, J., Hensel, H., and Larcher, W., Eds., Springer Verlag, Berlin, 1973, 503.
3. **Bligh, J.,** *Temperature Regulation in Mammals and Other Vertebrates,* North Holland, Amsterdam, 1963, 271.
4. **Arieli, A., Berman, A., and Meltzer, A.,** Seasonal acclimatization in the female domestic fowl, *Br. Poult. Sci.,* 20, 505, 1979.
5. **Arieli, A., Meltzer, A., and Berman, A.,** The thermoneutral temperature zone and seasonal acclimatization in the hen, *Br. Poult. Sci.,* 21, 471, 1980.
6. **Payne, R. B.,** Mechanism and control of molt, in *Avian Biology,* Vol. 2, Farner, D. S. and King, J. R., Eds., Academic Press, New York, 1972, 103.
7. **Heldmaier, G.,** Cold adaptation by short daily cold exposures in the young pig, *J. Appl. Physiol.,* 36, 163, 1974.
8. **Arieli, A., Berman, A., and Meltzer, A.,** Cold thermogenesis in the summer-acclimatized and cold-acclimated domestic fowl, *Comp. Biochem. Physiol.,* 63C, 7, 1979.
9. **Bligh, J. and Johnson, K. G.,** Glossary of terms for thermal physiology, *J. Appl. Physiol.,* 35, 941, 1973.
10. **Emmans, G. C.,** The effect of temperature on the performance of laying hens, in *Energy Requirements of Poultry,* Morris, T. R. and Freeman, B. M., Eds., British Poultry Sciences, Edinburgh, 1974, 79.
11. **Chaffee, R. R. J. and Roberts, J. C.,** Temperature acclimation in birds and mammals, *Annu. Rev. Physiol.,* 33, 155, 1971.

12. **Johnston, D. W.,** The absence of brown adipose tissue in birds, *Comp. Biochem. Physiol.,* 40A, 1107, 1971.
13. **Rothwell, N. J. and Stock, M. J.,** A role for brown adipose tissue in diet-induced thermogenesis, *Nature (London),* 281, 31, 1979.

Index

INDEX

A

Acceleration, 5
Acclimation, 14, 31, 198
  fowl, 198—202
Acclimatization, 14, 34, 37, 198
  degree of physiological changes in, 28
  fowl, 198—202
  heat, 59—66
Accommodation, 5
Acculturation, 5
Acid base balance, heat stress, 141—144
Acrophase, 5
Adaptation, 14
  heat, 60
  inactivity, 75—83
  system-theoretical background of, 18—20
  thermal loads, 17—25
Adaptive physiology, 3—9
Adiabatic process, 5
Aerobic fitness, 86, 92—95, 98
Aerobic power, see VO_2max
Afferent systems, 122
Aging, exercise-heat acclimation, 98—101
Alarm reactions, 5
Albumin, 146—147
Aldosterone, 173—174, 176
Allen's rule, 5
Alveolar gas, 46, 49
Ama, 44
Ambient factors, 12—13
Ambient sound, 5
Ambient temperature, 124, 143, 192, 198
Amplitude of sound, 5
Anemometry, 5
Anti-diuretic hormone, 173—176
Arctic clothing, 36
Arterial blood, 160, 166—169
Arterial blood pressure, 90
Arteriovenous anastomoses, 146—147, 152—154, 156
Artificial acclimation, 31, 61, 201
Artificial acclimatization, 30
Ascent blackout, 43—50
Ashkenazim, 29—33
Astrup effect, 164
ATA, 46
Atmosphere, ambient factors, 12—13
Attenuation, 5
Audio frequency change, 5
Audiogram, 5
Audiometry, 5
Australian aborigine, 28
Autophasing, 5
Autoregulation, 5
Autorhythmometry, 6
Avian blood O_2 affinity
  Astrup effect, 164
  Bohr effect, 164
  countercurrent gas exchange, 167
  countercurrent heat exchangers, 160, 166
  effects of temperature and PCO_2 on, 159—172

B

Baroreceptors, 174
Bedouin goats, red blood cells, 132, 135—137
Bedouins, 29—33
Bedrest, see Deconditioning; Inactivity
Bends, 6
Bergmann's rule, 6
Biological clocks, 6
Biological rhythms, 6
Biometeorology, 4
Biosphere, 6
Biotype, 6
Blood flow, 52, 55
  heat dissipation, 151—158
  heat stress, 141
Blood volume, 61, 140
  exercise conditioning, 76
  heat strain, 87
Body core temperature, 79
Body fat, 117, 181—186
  exercise-heat stress, 96
Body fluid deficit, 105
Body fluids, 60
Body heat content, 52
Body temperature, 18, 22, 30, 33, 41, 60, 114, 124, 191
  dehydration, 132
  endorphins, role of, 128
  exercise, 87
  ranges, 122
Bohr effect, 164
Brain cooling, 151—158, 160, 164, 170
Brain peptides, 122, 128
Breath-hold diving, 43—50
Brown fat, 38, 201

C

Camel, 145, 173—179
  red blood cells, 131—137
Candela, 6
Cardiac activity, 33
Cardiac output, 60, 140, 142, 147, 152, 154
  exercise, 87
  exercise-heat stress, 90
  redistribution of, 140—141
Cardiovascular fitness, 99
Cardiovascular strain, 99
Cardiovascular system, thermal homeostasis, 140
Catecholamines, 114

Cellular hypoxia, 143
Central blood volume, 81—82
  exercise-heat stress, 87
Central nervous system, 114, 122, 128
Central thermoadaptive modifications, 21
Chemical thermosuppression, 119
Chemoreceptor, 152
Chilblain, 6
Chronobiology, 6
Chronopathology, 6
Chronopharmacology, 6
Chronotoxicology, 6
Circulatory actions, hydration during exercise-heat stress, 85—90
Circulatory stress, 34
Climatic zones, 28
Cold
  adaptation to, 117—118
  fat loss with exercise in, 39—40
  gender-related differences, 40—41
  genetic adaptations to, 36
  metabolic consequence of exercise in, 35—42
  nonshivering thermogenesis, 36—38, 41
  physical conditioning, 40—41
  shivering, 36—37
  voluntary exercise, 36, 41
Cold acclimation
  fowl, 199—200
  opioid peptides, 125—128
Cold acclimatization, 37—38
Cold adaptation, 21
Cold dehydration, 40
Cold exposure, 13, 22
Cold-induced vasodilation, 6
Cold load, 18—19
Cold receptors, 21
Cold stress, 22, 40
Cold therapy for obesity, 40—41
Cold zone, 198
Conductive hearing loss, 6
Core-shell model, 52, 54, 56
Core temperature, 76
  aerobic fitness, 92
  exercise, 87—88
  exercise-heat stress, 90
  heat acclimation, 93
  hot-dry/hot-wet climates, 98
  inactivity, 82
  sweating rate, 89
Coriolis acceleration, 6
Coriolis force, 6
Corticosteroids, 118
Corticosterone, 117
Cortisol, 192
Countercurrent gas exchange, 167
Countercurrent heat exchangers, 160, 166
Cranial heat dissipation, 154—155
Cross-adaptation, 22, 40
Cutaneous blood flow, 86, 89
Cutaneous thermoreceptors, 21
Cutaneous vasodilation, exercise, 87

D

Dairy productivity, 187—195
Death, 104
Decibel, 6
Decompression, 45
Decompression sickness, 45
Deconditioning, thermoregulatory adaptations to, 75—83
Deep body temperatures, 97
Deep diving, 45
Definitions, 4—9, see also specific terms
Dehydration, 39, 89, 97, 108, 132, 135, 137, 145
  defined, 6
  hemoglobin, 133
  metabolism, 175
  milk volume, 176
  plasma volume, 145—146
Des-enkephalin-γ-endorphin, 125—126
Des-tyrosine-γ-endorphin, 125
Diapause, 6
Diving time, 48—49
Dogs, 141—143, 152
Doppler effect, 7
Dormancy, 7
Dry heat, gender considerations, 97

E

Eccrine sweat, 86
Eccrine sweat gland, 89
Ecology, 7
Ecophysiology, 4
Effective fat content, 183, 185—186
Efferent systems, 122
Electromyographic activity, 200
Endocrine systems, 114, 117, 122
Endogenous opioids, thermoregulation and, 124—125
Endogenous rhythms, 7
α-Endorphin, 122, 128
β-Endorphin, 122, 124, 128
γ-Endorphin, 122, 128
Endorphins, 122—123
  central processing, 125—128
  metabolism of, 125—128
  role of, 122
Environmental physiology, 4
Environmental stress
  coping with, 18
  human adaptability, 28
Epinephrine, 118
Ergonomics, 7
Eskimo, 28
Esophageal temperature, 80
Estrogen, 96
Euhydration, 86
Evaporative heat dissipation, 152
Exercise

cold, 35—42
total body sweat losses during, 81
water, 51—57
Exercise conditioning, 76
Exercise-heat acclimation
aerobic fitness, 92—95, 98
aging, effects of, 98—101
factors which alter human physiological responses during, 91—102
gender considerations, 96—98
physical training, 92—95
Exercise-heat stress
hydration during, 85—90
physiological effects, 87—90
water loss, 86
Exercise hyperemia, 57
Exercise tolerance, 81
Exogenous rhythms, 7

F

Fat insulation, changes during exercise in water, 51—57
Fat loss, exercise in cold, 39—40
Fat thickness, 54
Feed intake, 188, 191, 193
Fertility, 189, 192—193
Final rectal temperature, 93
Forearm blood flow, 29—34
Fowl
acclimation, 198—202
acclimatization, 198—202
thermal neutrality, 197—203
Free running rhythm, 7
Frostbite, 7
Functional adaptation, 14, 18

G

Gender considerations
exercise-heat acclimation, 96—98
exercise in the cold, 40—41
humid heat, 103—110
Genetic adaptations, cold, 36
Glucocorticoids, 114, 117
Glossary, 4—9
Goats, 141, see also Bedouin goats
Gold mines, heat acclimatization, 67—74
Growth, 188
Growth hormone, 114, 116, 118

H

Hamsters, 136
Heart rate, 29—30, 60—61, 63—64, 105—106
deconditioning, 80
exercise, 87
heat acclimation, 93
inactivity, 82
submaximal exercise, 78—79
Heat, adaptation to, 60, 118—119
Heat acclimation, 31, 59, 86, 140
fowl, 198—200
opioid peptides, 125—128
Heat acclimatization, 30, 59—66
gold mines, 67—74
Heat dissipation, 60, 63, 88, 140
blood flow, 151—158
peripheral adaptation, 92
Heat exhaustion, 68, 143
Heat flow, 52
Heat loss, 114, 119, 122, 128
Heat production, 60, 64, 122, 128, 198
dairy productivity, 191
hormonal control of, 113—120
Heat storage, 97
Heat strain, 87
Heat stress, 13, 24, 87, 106, 170
acid base balance, 141—144
dairy productivity, 192—193
gender considerations, 96—97
interactions between circulation and plasma fluids during, 139—149
tissue oxygenation, 141—144
Heat stress index, 7
Heat stroke, 68—70, 73, 104, 143, 147
Heat stroke syndrome, 148
Heat tolerance, 118, 140
exercise conditioning, 76
inactivity, 82
physiological differences, 92
Heat tolerance test (HTT), 68—69, 71, 73
Heat transfer, 140
Hematocrit, 77, 104—105, 108, 132—133, 175, 191
Hemoconcentration, 132
Hemoglobin, 77, 104—105, 108, 132, 137
contribution of, 133—134
variability, 164
Hemolysis, 132—133, 176
Homeothermy, 128, 201
hormonal control of, 113—120
variations, 122
Hormone control, 113—120
Hormones, 114
adaptation to thermal stress, 117—119
Hot-dry climates, 97—98
Hot-wet climates, 97—98
Hot zone, 198
Human adaptability, population studies on, 27—34
Humid heat
gender considerations, 96
sweat loss, 103—110
voluntary dehydration, 103—110
Hydration, exercise-heat stress, 85—90
Hydration level, 86, 89
Hydrocortisone, 114, 116
Hydrosphere, ambient factors, 12—13
Hyperbaric, 7

Hypercarbia, 44
Hyperglycemia, 173, 175
Hyper-heat-tolerance, 69
Hyperhydration, 86, 90
Hyperosmolality, 86, 89
Hyperthermia, 70—71, 122, 154—155
  endogenous opioids, 124
  heat stress, 141
  metabolic acidosis, 143
  morphine, 124
Hyperthyroid, 118
Hyperventilation, 46, 49, 141
  shallow-water diving, 44
Hypervolemia, 89
Hypobaric, 7
Hypocapnia, 44
Hypohydration, 86—90, 104, 107
Hypometabolism, 114, 117
Hypothalamo-pituitary-thyroid axis, 119
Hypothermia, 36, 122
  morphine, 124
Hypothyroid, 118
Hypotonicity, 136
Hypovolemia
  deconditioning, 76—77, 79, 82
  exercise-heat stress, 86, 89
Hypoxia, 44, 47, 49, 141, 160, 169
  deep dives, 45

I

Inactivity, thermoregulatory adaptations to, 75—83
Incomplete rehydration, 107
Infrasound, 7
Insulation, 36, 52, 200—201
  during exercise, 54—55
  at rest, 54—55
Insulin, 118
Involuntary dehydration, 104, 109
Ionizing radiation, 7

K

Kurds, 29—33

L

Lactation, 188
Lactic acid, 143—144
Lean body mass, 182
Leucine enkephalin, 124
Lingual blood flow, 153
Lithosphere, ambient factors, 12—13
Llama red blood cells, 135
Local sweating, 76
Lower critical temperature, 118, 198
Lumen, 7
Lux, 7

M

Mammalian thermoregulation, 122
Maximal aerobic power, see VO_2max
Maximal heart rate, 78
Menstrual cycle, 77, 96
MET, 55—56
Metabolic acidosis, 143, 145
Metabolic consequences, exercise in cold, 35—42
Metabolic fat content, 182, 185
Metabolic rate, 18, 21, 28, 30—31, 33, 52, 54, 64, 114, 200
  body fat, 182
  exercise-heat stress, 88
  heat acclimatization, 60
  hormonal mechanisms, 116—117
  inactivity, 82
Methionine-enkephalin, 124
Microclimate, 7
Microclimate acclimatization, 69
Milk composition, 176
Milk production, 188—189, 191, 193
Milk secretion, 176
Morphine, 122
  thermoregulation and, 124
Morphine-like substances, 122
Morphological adaptations, 18, 24
Morphological modifications, 198
Mountain sickness, 7
Mucosal blood flow, 152
Muscle, changes during exercise in water, 51—57

N

Naloxone, 122—124
Nasal mucosa, 152
Natural acclimatization, 30, 33—34, 61, 64
Nervous system, 122
Neuroendocrine system, 114, 117
Neurohypophysial hormone, 175
Neurotransmitters, 128
Nonshivering mechanisms, 114, 118
Nonshivering thermogenesis, 21—22, 198, 200—201
  exercise in cold, 36—38, 41
Noradrenaline, 21, 38, 118
Nystagmus, 7

O

Opioid peptides, 121—129
Oral contraceptives, 77
Organism-environment interactions, 14
Organismic stress, 13
Osmoreceptors, 174
Osmotic resistance, 133
Overacclimatization, 71—72
Oxen, 141

Oxygen consumption, 30, 46, 52, 115—116, 183—184
deconditioning, 81
inactivity, 82
Oxygen dissociation curve, 160
Oxygen saturation, 160
Oxyhemoglobin dissociation curves, 133—134, 136

P

Panting, 142—143, 152, 154, 156
Peak oxygen uptake, 81
Peripheral adaptation, heat dissipation, 92
Peripheral adaptive modifications, 20—21
Peripheral arteriovenous anastomoses, 141
Peripheral blood flow, 90
Peripheral circulation, 28, 33—34
heat strain, 87
heat stress, 140
Peripheral vasoconstriction, 147
Peripheral vasodilation, 140, 145, 147
Permanent threshold shift (PTS), 8
Phenoxybenzamine, 147
Phentolamine, 21
Photosensitivity, 8
Physical conditioning, 40—41
Physical deconditioning, 81, see also Deconditioning
Physical training, exercise-heat acclimation, 92—95
Physicochemical environment, 12—13
Pitch, 8
Plasma hypovolemia, see Hypovolemia
Plasma protein, 145—147
Plasma volume, 61, 63—64
deconditioning, 76—78, 82
exercise-heat stress, 86, 89—90
heat stress, 141
submaximal exercise, 81
thermoregulation and, 144—148
Pollutant, 8
Population studies on human adaptability, 27—34
Presbyacusis, 8
Proenkephalin A, 122
Proenkephalin B, 122
Progesterone, 96, 192—193
Progressive dehydration, 104, 107
Prolactin, 118
Proopiomelanocortin, 122—123
Proprioceptor, 152
Propylthiouracil, 118
Psychrometric chart, 8
Psychrometry, 8
Pure tone, 8

R

Random noise, 8
Rectal temperatures, 21, 24, 52, 105—106, 108
exercise-heat stress, 88
heat acclimatization, 60—63, 70
heat tolerance, 71
milk production, 191
Red blood cells, 131—137
Regulatory modifications, 198
Rehydration, 39, 132, 135—136
challenge of, 133
delay following water loss, 104
Releasing factors, 114
Renin-aldosterone, 86
Reproduction, 188
Resistance (to heat, cold, etc.), 8
Resonance, 8
Respiratory adaptation, 14
Respiratory alkalosis, 143
Respiratory evaporative heat loss, 152, 154—156
Respiratory heat loss, 36, 52
Respiratory pathways, 152
Resting heart rate, 31, 33
Resting metabolism, 29, 31—33
Risk assessment, 70
Rumen, 135, 173
Rumen flora, 175

S

Salivary flow rate, 24
Salt conservation, 60
Shallow-water blackout, 43—50
Shivering, 22—23, 124, 198, 200—201
exercise in cold, 36—37
Shivering mechanism, 36, 114
Shivering thermogenesis, 21—22
Shivering threshold, 37, 41
Skin blood flow, 76, 140—141
Skin insulation, 52—54
Skin temperature, 52, 60, 97, 105
exercise-heat acclimation, 94—95
Sodium chloride solution, 104—109
Sodium conservation, 60, 64
Sound, 8
Sound intensity, 8
Sound power, 8
Sound pressure, 8
Splanchnic blood flow, 141
Splanchnic vasoconstriction, 140, 147
Splanchnic vasodilation, 147
Strain, 8, 13, 61
Stress, 8, 13, 61
Stressful environment, 4, 11—15
Stressful thermal environments, 122
Stressors, 13
Stress physiology, 4
Stress/strain relationship, 13
Stroke volume, 87
Structural adaptation, 14
Subcutaneous fat, 52—54
Submaximal exercise, 78—81
Summer acclimation, 61

Superficial shell, 56—57
Sweat composition, 104
Sweating, 22—23, 60
  onset of, 60, 63
Sweating capability, 98
Sweat loss
  hot-dry/hot-wet climates, 98
  humid heat, 103—110
Sweat output, 86
Sweat rate, 60—62, 76, 88—89, 105—106, 108—109
  exercise-heat stress, 86, 89—90
  water depletion, 104
Sweat sensitivity, 60

T

Temporary threshold shift, 8
Thermal homeostasis, 36
  cardiovascular system, role of, 140
Thermal lability, 122
Thermal loads, adaptations to, 17—25
Thermal neutrality, 197—203
Thermal stresses, 4
  adaptation to, 117—119
  plasma volume, 145
Thermoafferent pathway, 22
Thermoafferent systems, 21
Thermogenetic reactions, 21
Thermography, 38
Thermoneutrality, 125
Thermoneutral zone, 198
Thermoreceptor, 152
Thermoregulation, 18, 33, 122—123
  endogenous opioids and, 124—125
  morphine and, 124
  opioids and, 124—125
  plasma volume and, 144—148
  shifting burden of, 70
Thermoregulatory adaptations, see Adaptation
Thermoregulatory failure, 145
Thermoregulatory mechanisms, 17—25, 53, 56, 198
Thermoregulatory reflex, 140—141
Thermoregulatory responses
  hydration during exercise-heat stress, 85—90
  impairment by bedrest, 82
Threshold deviations for effector mechanisms, 21—24
Thyroid gland, 119
Thyroid hormones, 118
Thyroid metabolism, 173, 175
Thyrotropin releasing hormone, 118
Thyroxine, 114, 116—118
Tissue blood flow, 140, 152—153
Tissue insulation, measurement of, 52—54
Tissue oxygenation, heat stress, 141—144
Tolerance, 8
Tolerance adaptation against heat, 24
Total body fluid loss, 145
Total body fluids, 81
Total body insulation, 52, 54—56
Total body sweat losses during exercise, 81
Total body sweat rate, 94
Total body water, 86
Total sweat rate, 80
Triiodothyronine, 114

U

Ultraviolet light, 8
Upper critical temperature, 118, 198
Urea, 173, 175

V

Van Hoff effect, 144
Vasoconstriction, 36, 55, 174—175
  inactivity, 82
Vasodilation, 56, 60
Ventilation, 36
Vertigo, 8
Vibration, 5, 9
Voluntary dehydration, 86
  humid heat, 103—110
Voluntary exercise, cold exposure, 36, 41
VO_2max, 81
  exercise-heat acclimation, 94, 96—97
  exercise-heat tolerance or acclimation, 93

W

Water
  drinking of, 103—110
  fat insulation changes during exercise in, 51—57
  muscle changes during exercise in, 51—57
Water depletion, 104
Water intake, 86, 191
Water loss, 86
Wet-bulb globe temperature (WBGT), 70—73
Whole body cooling, 151—158
Winter acclimation, 61

Y

Yemenites, 29—33